ARJUNA–ODYSSEUS

Bringing together the study of the Greek classics and Indology, *Arjuna–Odysseus* provides a comparative analysis of the shared heritage of the *Mahābhārata* and early Greek traditions presented in the texts of Homer and Hesiod.

Building on the ethnographic theories of Durkheim, Mauss, and Dumont, the volume explores the convergences and rapprochements between the *Mahābhārata* and the Greek texts. In exploring the networks of similarities between the two epic traditions, it also reformulates the theory of Georges Dumézil regarding Indo-European cultural comparativism. It includes a detailed comparison between journeys undertaken by the two epic heroes – Odysseus and Arjuna – and more generally, it ranges across the philosophical ideas of these cultures, and the epic traditions, metaphors, and archetypes that define the cultural ideology of ancient Greece and India.

This book will be useful to scholars and researchers of Indo-European comparativism, social and cultural anthropology, classical literature, Indology, cultural and post-colonial studies, philosophy and religion, as well as to those who love the Indian and Greek epics.

N. J. Allen is a social anthropologist and a retired Reader in the Social Anthropology of South Asia, University of Oxford, UK. His research interests are Himalayan studies, world-historical approach to kinship systems, sociology of Durkheim and more especially Mauss, and Indo-European cultural comparativism.

'This is a volume for the ages. N. J. Allen is the dean of British comparativists; and no one has perceived more clearly or argued more persuasively for the shared structures of Greek and Sanskrit epic, features commonly held by cause of common ancestry. These twenty-four chapters are jewels, every one, to be read and re-read: rejoice in their brilliance.'

– **Roger D. Woodard,** Andrew van Vranken Raymond, Professor of the Classics, University of Buffalo (The State University of New York)

'Every educated person knows that the languages of north India are related to those of Europe and that they all derive, in the distant past, from an Indo-European forebear spoken on the steppes of Russia. But how many realize that the key motifs and stories of the *Iliad* and *Odyssey* – so often heralded as the beginning of European literature, somehow springing fully formed from the brain of Homer – in fact go back likewise to those ancient beginnings and share that origin with South Asia's great epics, the *Ramayana* and the *Mahābhārata*? No one has pursued the comparisons that prove this common origin point with such tenacity and persistence as N. J. Allen. The publication of a collection of his essays on this theme, essays previously scattered in obscurity, is a major scholarly event and should mark the coming of age of Indo-European Cultural Comparativism.'

– **David N. Gellner,** Professor of Social Anthropology, University of Oxford

'N. J. Allen's *Arjuna–Odysseus* extends the foundational work of Georges Dumézil by supplying an anthropological dimension to Indo-European studies. Allen brings to bear his sensibility as an ethnographer of South Asia, his long-term engagement with Greek and Indic texts, and an expansive knowledge of anthropological theory and comparative ethnography built up over decades of teaching. The result is a feast of insightful case studies that advance a new understanding of Indo-European cultural ideology while making a major contribution to the study of epic poetry in ancient Greece and India.'

– **Charles Stewart,** Professor of Anthropology, University College London

ARJUNA–ODYSSEUS

Shared Heritage in Indian and Greek Epic

N. J. Allen

LONDON AND NEW YORK

First published 2020
by Routledge
2 Park Square, Milton Park, Abingdon, Oxon OX14 4RN

and by Routledge
52 Vanderbilt Avenue, New York, NY 10017

Routledge is an imprint of the Taylor & Francis Group, an informa business

© 2020 N. J. Allen

The right of N. J. Allen to be identified as author of this work has been asserted by him in accordance with sections 77 and 78 of the Copyright, Designs and Patents Act 1988.

All rights reserved. No part of this book may be reprinted or reproduced or utilised in any form or by any electronic, mechanical, or other means, now known or hereafter invented, including photocopying and recording, or in any information storage or retrieval system, without permission in writing from the publishers.

Trademark notice: Product or corporate names may be trademarks or registered trademarks, and are used only for identification and explanation without intent to infringe.

British Library Cataloguing-in-Publication Data
A catalogue record for this book is available from the British Library

Library of Congress Cataloging-in-Publication Data
Names: Allen, N. J., author.
Title: Arjuna-Odysseus : shared heritage in Indian and Greek epic / N. J. Allen.
Description: New York : Routledge, 2019. | Includes bibliographical references and index.
Identifiers: LCCN 2019028153 (print) | LCCN 2019028154 (ebook)
Subjects: LCSH: Arjuna (Hindu mythological character) | Odysseus, King of Ithaca (Mythological character) | Homer. Odyssey. | Mahābhārata.
Classification: LCC BL1138.4.A75 A45 2019 (print) | LCC BL1138.4.A75 (ebook) | DDC 883/.01—dc23
LC record available at https://lccn.loc.gov/2019028153
LC ebook record available at https://lccn.loc.gov/2019028154

ISBN: 978-0-367-26047-7 (hbk)
ISBN: 978-0-367-34830-4 (pbk)
ISBN: 978-0-429-29412-9 (ebk)

Typeset in Bembo
by Apex CoVantage, LLC

In memory of Norman Saunders, the head Classics teacher at Rugby School in the 1950s, who both introduced me to Homer and encouraged me to think that an academic career might be a possibility; also, to those narrators among the Thulung Rai of East Nepal who, around 1970, kindled in me an unforeseen love of mythology.

CONTENTS

FIGURES

TABLES

ACKNOWLEDGEMENTS

I thank first the Radhakrishnan Memorial Bequest Fund for a grant that enabled me to employ editorial assistance; without such help the book would not have materialized. I thank also the many seminar convenors and audiences, in the UK and abroad, whose questions have facilitated elaboration of my arguments. At Oxford, the Institute of Social Anthropology, and Wolfson College have provided very congenial and helpful academic environments, and I am grateful to the many holders of copyright who have permitted reuse of articles.

So many individuals have assisted in different contexts that a list can only be incomplete and unfair. However, I should like to mention Saroja Bhate at Pune, David Parkin, David Gellner, Roger Woodard, Ken Dowden, Françoise Létoublon, Pierre Sauzeau, Emily West, Krešimir Vuković, James Hegarty, and Felix Padel (my initial Editorial Assistant).

ABBREVIATIONS

Aen.	Vergil's *Aeneid*
Apd.	Apollodorus
Appx	Appendix
Bh. Gītā	*Bhagavad Gītā*
Ch.	Chapter
CE	Critical Edition of *Mahābhārata*
CSL	Clay Sanskrit Library
Gk	Greek
Hes.	Hesiod
Il.	*Iliad*
IE	Indo-European
Od.	*Odyssey*
JJC	Fund supporting the CSL
LIMC	Lexicon *iconographicum mythologiae classicae*
Mbh.	*Mahābhārata*
Pat.	Patañjali
PIE	proto-Indo-European
QS	Quintus Smyrnaeus
rappr.	Rapprochement
RV	*Rigveda* (*Ṛgveda*)
Sk	Sanskrit
Th.	Hesiod's *Theogony*
tr.	translation, translated
WD	Hesiod's *Works and Days*

SIGNS

~ as in A ~ B, 'A in relationship to B'; such relationships may include //.

// as in A // B, 'A parallels B', or as in A ~ B // C ~ D, 'the relationship of A to B parallels that of C to D'.

* (a) marks PIE forms reconstructed by linguists; (b) marks text relegated to footnotes by CE editors.

[...] Square brackets often indicate text that I have added to the original publication.

INTRODUCTION

As is well known, similarities between Sanskrit and Ancient Greek go back to a common origin in the family tree of Indo-European (IE) languages. But when attention is called to the similarities between the two epic traditions, the situation is less clear. Often similarities are simply ignored, but when they are recognized as more than sporadic coincidences, explanations are sometimes offered in terms of human psychology or 'universal folklore', or else in terms of borrowing (either by the East from the West or vice versa). Such explanations may seem plausible a priori, but the simpler explanation – and, we shall claim, the better one – is common origin and subsequent transmission along with the languages.

Defining the field of study

India–Greece comparison is not an isolated undertaking, but the field in which it lies is neither well-known nor well institutionalized; it does not even possess a really satisfactory name. I usually call the wider field Indo-European cultural comparison (or comparativism), implying a contrast with IE linguistic comparativism (aka IE philology); but in addition to being clumsy, my label might suggest, wrongly, that language is not part of culture. The field has sometimes been thought of as a speciality within 'comparative mythology', but its focus on a single well-documented and much studied language family means that in practice it is a different sort of undertaking. The difference has sometimes been recognized, as in the title of Littleton 1982, by talking of the 'new comparative mythology', but novelty wears off, and the implied separation of myth from other aspects of oral cultures (social structure, ritual, law . . .) is unhappy.

The definition and description of the language family belongs to IE philology, and the cultural comparativist can take for granted the framework provided by that well-established discipline (with its degree courses, journals, and conferences);

but a comparativist necessarily engages also with several other disciplines. For a start, anyone interested in comparing cultures is, consciously or not, practising anthropology, and no one interested in early India can ignore religious studies. The Arjuna in my title is the interlocutor of Kṛṣṇa (= Krishna) in the *Bhagavad Gītā* – a section of the *Mahābhārata* that is often treated as the most sacred text in all Hinduism. But, in addition, an IE comparativist needs to relate to the specialist philologies, here mostly classics and Indology but, in other contexts, Iranian, Germanic, or Celtic studies – to mention only the most obvious branches.

Part of the framework provided by the linguists is the IE family tree. To simplify a little, the tree starts with a reconstructed proto-language, which splits into branches, which in turn split into sub-branches, and so on. Such a schema shows which languages are closely related to each other: the taxon they belong to has a relatively recent common origin, shown as a 'node' or branching point in diagrams. Languages that are more remotely connected have the node that connects them further back in the tree. For our purposes, it is enough to say that Sanskrit and Avestan (the language of the early Zoroastrian texts) belong in the Indo-Iranian taxon, while Indo-Iranian languages belong together with Greek in a larger taxon whose connecting node lies further back. The common origin of Sanskrit and Latin lies even further back.[1]

Though it is not strictly necessary here, one would like to attach dates and geographic locations to the speakers of both the IE and the lower-order proto-languages. On this topic, comparativists have to rely heavily on archaeology. Opinions vary, but many think that proto-Indo-European (PIE) was spoken in the fifth or fourth millennium BC in southern Russia, north of the Black Sea (cf. Kortlandt 2018); some postulate an earlier 'primary' Indo-Hittite homeland south of the Caucasus. The common origin of Sanskrit and Greek can perhaps be dated to around 2500 BC. Archaeology is increasingly being supplemented by human genetics, but this development is of limited relevance to the questions posed here.

Notes on the history of the field

Most nineteenth-century scholars interested in India had received education in classics, and they quite often noted similarities between Sanskrit and Greek traditions. A thorough collection and evaluation of their comparisons might well uncover insights that ought to be acknowledged in a proper history of the field, but Indologists' and classicists' attitudes changed in the next century, and IE cultural comparison became deeply unfashionable. We shall come back shortly to the post-1938 work of Dumézil, which is often regarded as a re-foundation of the field.

Meanwhile, an important step was taken by another French scholar. Émile Durkheim (1859–1917) envisaged a distinct academic discipline that would study social phenomena, embracing what are now distinguished as sociology and social anthropology. To this end, he founded a substantial new journal (actually a yearbook) entitled *L'Année sociologique*, and he recruited his nephew Marcel Mauss to help him with the phenomena classified as religious. In preparation for this role, Mauss was sent to Paris to study Indology with Sylvain Lévi, the leading French specialist at the time. One outcome of this was that, in the *Année* for 1903, Durkheim and Mauss co-authored a lengthy paper on 'some primitive forms of classification'. Adopting a world-historical approach, they presented case studies of classifications from tribal societies in North America and Australia, before turning to the ancient literate cultures of China, India, and Greece – Greece being presented as ancestral to modern scientific thinking. In brief, they argued that in early societies the classification of members of society into units of social structure, for example clans, was projected onto the rest of the universe. Thus, a particular clan might be made to correspond to all sorts of thing: a particular biological species (a totem), a cardinal point, colour, season, and so on. Later, as in China, social structure became separated from the other correspondences, which themselves endured, often being used in divination. With the rise of scientific thinking, this sort of correspondence too became obsolete (cf. Allen 2000a: 39–60).

Early in life, Georges Dumézil (1898–1986) acquired an impressive knowledge of IE languages and began his comparative studies of the cultures, with works indebted to Frazer's *Golden Bough*. What he regarded as his significant work only began in 1938, with an insight that he attributed to attending the lectures of the sinologist Marcel Granet. Granet recognized his basic debt to the 1903 essay of Durkheim and Mauss, and although Dumézil never refers to that essay, his trifunctional theory of IE ideology can be viewed precisely as a 'primitive form of classification' (as is recognized by Desbordes 1981: 49 or Tiryakian 1981: 86). To simplify again, the IE speakers recognized a classification of their society into priests, warriors, and producers and projected this division of labour onto other aspects of their world view or ideology. The sociostructural categories specified the functions attributed to their membership – namely (respectively) magico-religious sovereignty, force, and fertility or fecundity. Since the triad was conceived hierarchically, Dumézil came to talk of the first, second, and third functions, and when the tripartition was recognized by an analyst in other aspects of the cosmos, the same terminology proved convenient. Thus, all sorts of entities could 'manifest' or 'represent' a particular function, provided that the entity in question was accompanied by manifestations of the other two functions. Around 1950, Dumézil realized (much as Durkheim and Mauss had realized regarding China) that the actual social structure need not always parallel the other correspondences.[2]

Dumézil's fundamental study of the *Mahābhārata* appeared in 1968, but after 1938 he said relatively little on Greece. Always controversial, his work has been subject to the ups and downs of fashion, and its diffusion has been limited for several reasons. He avoided formal supervision of students; the sheer mass of his publications and their multi-disciplinary erudition have deterred some would-be followers (let alone translators and publishers); and – most relevant here – problems intrinsic to his trifunctionalism have comforted both his explicit critics and those who simply prefer to ignore his findings.

In 1961, the Rees brothers published *Celtic Heritage*, which could have reshaped the field. It raised the idea of a devalued fourth function in IE ideology and even hinted at a fifth category relating to totality and centrality. Though well aware of the book, Dumézil was by now too wedded to trifunctionalism to develop the Reeses' ideas, but they were the initial stimulus that led to my pentadic theory of IE ideology.

As for the subsequent history, I confine myself to two comments, both illustrating the relative neglect of IE comparativism within *Mahābhārata* studies. Brockington (1998) conscientiously covers the approach (and summarizes my Ch. 2) in a dozen pages of his grand 525-page survey, but he does not exploit it, and Hiltebeitel, whose early work (e.g. 1976) contributed to it so usefully, later abandoned comparativism altogether.

Composition of this book

Over the last thirty years, I have published around sixty relevant articles – too many for a single volume – so I have had to be selective. Sanskrit tradition was usually the starting point, and in some articles it was treated by itself to develop or illustrate my pentadic theory. More often the papers were comparative, using material from Rome, Ireland, Scandinavia, Iran, or Nuristan,[3] but since the commonest comparanda were from Greece, this was the obvious focus for a book. However, it seemed useful to include two chapters (Chs 1, 15) whose thrust was primarily theoretical, and one unpublished paper (Ch. 24) previously presented only at seminars. For reasons of length, I have reluctantly omitted several of my published Sanskrit-Greek comparisons. After considering other possibilities, I have presented them in order of publication.

Apart from Chapter 11, the papers have not been substantially rewritten, but they have been retouched to correct typos, unclarities, inaccuracies (too many!), and other infelicities. Square brackets, which in the original sometimes contained glosses, have also been used here for addenda of various sorts (including cross-references), when I judged that such indications were worthwhile. The shift from article to book format has involved much standardization and consolidation of references, and the articles have been given new titles more appropriate to their new context. I have translated three articles that were previously available only in French (Chs 6, 9, 17), and include the English original of one published only in Italian (Ch. 15).

Since the later papers usually refer to several earlier ones, the collection into a single volume will facilitate following up particular points, but such convenience is only one of my purposes. The conclusions for which I argue are ones that many readers will not expect, and if I am to be persuasive, the sheer quantity of evidence is important; it is much easier to ignore a single article than a convergent set of twenty-four.

Objectives

The selected papers have hitherto been widely dispersed. The originals appeared in ten print journals, most often the *International Journal of Hindu Studies* (Chs 5, 11, 12), but also in two electronic journals (Chs 21, 22), five conference volumes

(Chs 8, 9, 13, 16, 18), and one collection (Ch. 2). Such dispersal in a sense mirrors the state of the field. Many scholars find it fascinating, and pursue it, either consistently or sporadically, from different points of view, often taking little notice of other writers. Some are straightforward Dumézilians, working within the trifunctional paradigm. A few, recognizing the limitations of that schema, work with an explicit four-function schema (Sauzeau and Sauzeau 2012), or they accept the three functions but explore manifestations of the IE heritage that lie outside them (De Martino 2015). The erudite Martin West rejects trifunctionalism, finding it neither illuminating nor useful (2007: 4); the less wide-ranging Fernando Wulff Alonso (2014) does likewise.[4] Similarly, Janda (2000), who uses IE etymologizing to tackle interesting questions about Greek ritual and pantheon, essentially uses neither Dumézil nor the *Mahābhārata* (one passing reference each!). One aim of the present book is to provide a reasonably consolidated argument for a particular view of the field, developed in light of this and other secondary literature.

This approach relates to a number of different fields. In one sense, it is merely an outgrowth of IE philology, a further step in the sequence leading from sound laws via comparative syntax to the comparative IE poetics exemplified by Watkins (1995). Whether it can ever achieve a 'scientific' status comparable to the various branches of linguistics is debatable, but I aspire to comparable rigour of argument. The ideal student would be as well equipped to handle IE philology as cultural materials – a competence that I cannot claim.

Another objective bears on Indology and classics – or, more precisely, on how these disciplines are envisaged. Typical presentations of Indian culture move quickly from the archaeology of the Indus Valley civilizations and the arrival of the Indo-Aryan speakers to the copious texts surviving from the Vedic period. They then present classical Hinduism, including the epics, as developing from the Vedas, perhaps with input from pre-Aryan Indian populations. As Dumézil sensed, this approach ignores the quantity of IE heritage that bypassed the Vedas and can be demonstrated only by comparison.

A comparable limitation applies to early Greece. After the Minoan and Mycenaean periods, standard accounts move to the archaic period, which includes Homer and Hesiod. Over the last few decades, input from Anatolia and Mesopotamia has been much discussed, but the possible influences from these areas have scarcely been weighed against the IE heritage that I hope to demonstrate.[5] The enormous literature on the Greek hexameter tradition (a term that covers also the 'Homeric Hymns' and the Epic Cycle) routinely ignores evidence such as is assembled here, but when account is taken of this evidence, a good deal can be said about the ancient oral heritage on which the Greek bards were building. Consequently, many long-debated questions take on new aspects. For instance, no writer on the Cycle should ignore the fact that the five-phase structure of the Trojan War parallels that of the Kurukṣetra War.

Though Indology and classics are the disciplines most directly addressed, the book should also interest historians and historiographers. Dumézil claimed that he was in fact a historian, justifying his claim succinctly but clearly; however, he thought (rightly) that historians in general would not accept him or his 'ultrahistory' (1973a: 10–12). Such rejection is in fact illogical: IE philology tells the history of IE languages, and Dumézil provides the basis for a history of IE ideology and literature.

After a career in anthropology, I could expatiate on links between that background and the present book, but having sketched my biography elsewhere (Allen 2003a), I shall here be brief. One basic link is provided by Durkheim and Mauss (1903), with their interest in world history of classification, starting from societies that lack writing. Though the present book is about texts, it takes for granted their development from oral traditions. These traditions prove to have been more sophisticated, elaborate, and enduring than one might expect; orality should not be underestimated.[6] The comparison between Indian and European cultures is a natural topic for a lecturer in the Social Anthropology of South Asia (see particularly Ch. 15), but the book also tries to contribute to the comparativism implicit in the very idea of anthropology.

Within anthropology, one should not overemphasize mythology and literature; narratives are only one aspect of the epic traditions, which also bear on politics, law, social structure, values, cosmology, ontology – indeed on most aspects of culture. The *Mahābhārata* emphasizes its own encyclopaedic range, and the place of Homer and Hesiod in Greek education is well known. The book inevitably leaves whole subjects unexplored. But if a choice has to be made among the ordinary categories of social phenomena, this is a book about religion and a contribution to religious studies.

The nineteenth century was already well aware that Greek Zeus (like Jupiter) was etymologically cognate with Vedic Dyaus, but their relationship goes well beyond the theonyms (esp. Chs 10, 11). Of the other Vedic gods, we shall meet particularly Indra, Agni, and Brahmā, not to mention the most prominent deities of classical Hinduism – Vishnu/Kṛṣṇa, Śiva, and Durgā. Religious doctrines and practices will also appear, notably yoga (Ch. 5) and sacrifice (Ch. 21). Since the *Mahābhārata* is a Hindu text, Hinduism is the Eastern religion that receives most attention, but I do not know whether it retains more Indo-European heritage than does Buddhism (cf. Chs 13, 18).

Criteria for evaluation

As the last section claimed, the book addresses various audiences who, in judging it, will inevitably bring to bear their own disciplinary backgrounds. To the single-region philologists, I have one plea. The book is above all a comparative undertaking and should be judged as such, not by the criteria applying within Indology or classics. I do not know the secondary literature in either field as well as is expected of a specialist. I do not pretend to, and I have avoided inflating the bibliography with entries promoting such a pretence. This does not imply disrespect for the specialisms but simply reflects a reasonable division of academic labour. My priority has been to promote IE cultural comparativism by arguing for the pervasiveness of the IE heritage in Indian and Greek material. If, in ranging so widely, I have committed oversimplifications, I hope specialists will object, rejecting or filling out the offending rapprochements – rather than simply ignoring them.[7]

To fellow IE comparativists, I have a different plea. In focusing on Indo-Greek comparison, I have often alluded to pentadic theory but have not tried to assemble here the full array of arguments that support it – many of which involve Rome or internal analyses of the *Mahābhārata*. The book contains only a selection of my papers, and those who seriously wish to evaluate the theory need to read more widely.

Those interested in methodology may wonder whether the notion of 'similarity' is sufficiently precise to bear the weight I give it. At present, I am content to leave the notion commonsensical and barely theorized, but two points merit note. First, a similarity is always in respect of something: entity A resembles entity B as regards such and such. But similarities are not necessarily exclusive or one-to-one relationships. A may resemble C, D . . . in other respects (providing one-to-many relationships), and B, C, D . . . may resemble P, Q, R . . . as well as A (many-to-many). Second, a single similarity between two narrative entities is difficult to interpret – one scarcely knows what to make of it. A comparison between two stories becomes far more interesting when it reveals both multiple similarities and, even more, similar relations between the similarities (e.g. homotaxial relations, i.e. similarities of sequence). These abstract comments will receive repeated illustration later.

A question that I ask myself is whether the sequence of selected publications over the three decades bears any particular significance. What can be said about how later papers relate to earlier ones? Are there any clear turning points? As regards theory, a break of sorts separates the four-functional position of 1987 from the basically pentadic schema used thereafter, and rather than expressing pentadic theory in terms of four functions (one of them split), I now sometimes talk of five 'supercategories' – but that is only a matter of analytical terminology. An early focus on the *Odyssey* is later supplemented by interest in the *Iliad* and other early Greek texts. But, although, even in the early 1990s, I was confident that a book needed to be written on Indo-Greek comparison, the topics chosen for particular chapters depended on more or less random factors, for instance the focus of conferences I wanted to attend. In the absence of any overall strategy, I followed where curiosity led, and later papers mainly complement or extend the argument of earlier ones.

Referencing, translations, and transcription

The Sanskrit *Mahābhārata* is an enormous work: the twenty-two separately bound volumes of the Critical Edition (CE) occupy just over three feet on my bookshelf; by itself, it could occupy a scholar for a lifetime. Compiled in Poona (1933–1966), the CE draws on numerous Sanskrit manuscripts in various scripts, and by comparing them attempts to reconstruct the earliest accessible form of the written epic (first half of first millennium AD?). Scholars differ on whether the reconstructed text is to be preferred to versions that are actually attested, notably the 'Vulgate' (late Cy 17), but the CE includes, in footnotes or appendices, most of what is to be found in attested versions.[8] Unless otherwise indicated, I follow the CE main text.

The *Mahābhārata* consists of eighteen books *(parvans)*, each divided into chapters *(adhyāyas)*. Most of it is written in stanzas (called shlokas or *anuṣṭubh*), consisting of four (rarely six) eight-syllable *pādas*. My full references take the form A, B, C – book and chapter always being separated by a comma; a shloka (C) is usually referred to as a whole, but individual *pādas* can be distinguished with lowercase a, b, c, d. In principle, the whole epic is also structured into 100 Minor Books *(upaparvans)*, which can sometimes usefully indicate narrative articulation. Meanings given for individual Sanskrit words are taken from the standard dictionary by Monier-Williams.

Dumézil's production was also enormous: the helpful catalogue by Coutau-Bégarie (1998) lists seventy-three books and 540 items. Some of the books (such as *Religion romaine archaïque* (originally 1966) and *Heur et malheur du Guerrier* (1969a), vary significantly between editions, but many others vary scarcely or not at all. For these others, the least confusing procedure is to cite the original publication, though the bibliography also indicates with a superscript the edition I have regularly used; translations are usually my own. In citing my own articles, I have previously wavered between the cover date as stated in the publication and the date when the text became available; but I here prefer the former.

A good introduction to the *Mahābhārata* is Smith (2009), which translates nearly 11% of the CE text and summarizes the rest, chapter by chapter. An old translation (1883–1896) covers the whole Vulgate and remains useful; though formerly attributed to its editor P.C. Roy, it is in fact by Ganguli. The Clay Sanskrit Library conveniently presents the transliterated Sanskrit of the Vulgate, with facing translation, but is not yet complete. The Chicago translation is of the CE and has been much used, but it too is incomplete – van Buitenen (1973–1981) translates Books 1–5 and 6,14–40 (which includes the *Bhagavad Gītā*), while Fitzgerald (2004) translates Books 11 and 12,1–167. These are the translations I have mostly used, but there are others.

Sanskrit words have usually been italicized and supplied with their diacritics, though a few common ones (like *varṇa*) have often been slightly anglicized. As an occasional aid to those readers whose Sanskrit may be rudimentary, I sometimes separate with a hyphen the components of compound words. Greek vocabulary has been transliterated, and Greek names follow Hornblower et al. (2012).

Envoi

In his reception speech to the Académie française, Dumézil (1979, extract in 1992: 311–312) discusses academic life as a game. He starts from the classification of games (by Roger Caillois) under the four headings *alea* (chance), *agōn* (competition), *mimicry* (the English word), and *helix* (games of 'excitement, dizziness, literally *tourbillon* – whirlwind or whirlpool'). All of these have their place within comparativism, including the 'dizziness or exhilaration *(vertige, ivresse)* of solutions that suddenly present themselves.' But, continues Dumézil, this field has additional features that justify proposing a fifth heading *(studium)*: the game (the *ludus scientiae*) never really finishes, and any apparent victory will be recast as scholarship progresses. I hope that some readers will experience and enjoy the *vertige* – comparable, I suppose, to the feeling John Keats records in his sonnet 'On first looking into Chapman's Homer':

> Then felt I like some watcher of the skies
> When a new planet swims into his ken.

Notes

1 The traditional tree diagram is not the only way to diagram or think about the relations between the IE languages, but it should not be dismissed (cf. Kozintsev 2018).
2 Dumézil (1968: 15) – a much-quoted passage.
3 The Nuristanis, formerly called Kafirs ('Infidels'), live in north-east Afghanistan and speak or spoke languages that form a subgroup within Indo-Iranian.
4 For my reviews of these two books, see Allen (2007e) and Allen (2015c).
5 In any case, though similarities between Greek and West Asian traditions can certainly be found, they do not necessarily prove influence. If the PIE culture was as elaborate and enduring as I suppose, other hypotheses need consideration.
6 This has been common, as is noted, for instance, by Dundes (1965: 217); one should not forget the astonishing achievements of pre-literate Indian grammarians such as Pāṇini.
7 Dumézil was already making similar pleas in 1941: 27–32.
8 Footnotes in the CE are marked by an asterisk; as in the appendixes, the text they contain is referred to by line numbers, not shloka numbers.

1

A STARTING POINT

Since my purpose is to argue for a development or expansion of Dumézil's theory, I have to begin with a statement of it. This has often been done before, but I try to do it in such a way as specifically to facilitate my own case.

Dumézil's theory[1]

The theory starts from the methods and findings of comparative linguistics. Comparison of the Indo-European (IE) languages shows similarities so numerous and so precise that the languages must go back to a common origin, a proto-language (or group of dialects) that was once spoken in a smallish area but which subsequently dispersed and differentiated. Presumably, the speakers shared other aspects of their culture, and in particular an 'ideology', a general view of the world and society; this would have spread and differentiated alongside the language, leaving equally little trace in the archaeological record. For evidence of it, one must look instead to the written sources (in general, the earlier ones), where it would manifest itself in a range of contexts: in institutions (particularly social structure, legal codes, the pantheon, ritual offices, acts and invocations) and in narratives (myth, legend, folklore). It is by comparative study of such material that Dumézil, since 1938, has been developing his theory, helped by a few others who can loosely be termed Dumézilians.[2]

According to this theory, the Indo-Europeans conceived of the world as dependent on the co-operation of three forces or principles or 'functions'. These abstract principles are not usually attested explicitly, as such; what we find is rather their manifestations. Thus, the analyst must devise his own labels for the abstractions. Since the functions are usually manifested in a particular order, which also commonly represents their rank, the labels Dumézil uses are the ordinals 'first, second, third'. For brevity and convenience, I shall usually use my own labels Fl, F2, F3.

The first function, Fl, pertains to the sacred, to religious and magical power, to the juridical and to sovereignty; F2 to physical force and war; F3 to fecundity, abundance, and prosperity with their conditions and consequences: peace, nourishment, health, sensual pleasure, beauty, large number. When it comes to applying the theory, the full definitions are important, but for mnemonic purposes, one can say that Fl is sacred power, F2 warrior force, F3 fecundity/prosperity. A function can be envisaged either as a *cluster* of ideas or as a *focal* idea surrounded by a penumbra of associations or connotations; but in either case it must be envisaged as one element within a three-element structure.

The theory can scarcely be presented intelligibly, let alone plausibly, without examples. 1 refer, *very* briefly, to three. Hindu tradition conceives of society as consisting ideally of four strata or components called *varṇas*. The first three, the 'twice-born', are in several senses a group set apart from the fourth. Within the triad, highest rank goes to the Brahmins, who are priests dealing directly with the sacred, therefore Fl; then come the warrior Kṣatriya – F2, then the humbler Vaiśya, the producers of wealth – F3. Or take the Greek story of the origins of the Trojan War. Three goddesses compete before Paris for the prize of beauty. Hera offers sovereignty – Fl; Athena offers victory in war – F2; Aphrodite offers the beautiful Helen – F3 (Dumézil 1968: 582). Or again, among the most ancient ritual officiants in Rome were the three *flamines maiores*: the first served Dius Fidius, who was very closely linked with the sovereign Jupiter – Fl; the second served the warlike Mars – F2; the third served the humbler Quirinus, who is linked with peace and with festivals for agricultural prosperity – F3 (Dumézil 1974: 163–172).

Though it is not Dumézil's habit, such examples can usefully be summarized in tabular form. In each row, one writes first the particular culture and context (institutional or narrative), then the representatives of each function in turn. The representatives will thus form three columns, each linked with one function (Table 1.1).

The two-dimensional display corresponds to Dumézil's two rules for trifunctional analysis (1977: 224, 1979: 77, 1982: 113). Looking horizontally, the terms in a *row* must be distinct, solidary, homogeneous, and exhaustive. Thus, the varṇas are non-overlapping, and mention of one implies the others. They are homogeneous *qua* categories of twice-born, and they and they alone make up the twice-born as a whole. Looking vertically, each entry in the *column* unambiguously relates

TABLE 1.1 Tabulation of results of three well-triangular known trifunctional analyses

Culture	*Context*	*F1*	*F2*	*F3*
Hinduism	theoretical social strata	Brahmins	Kṣatriya	Vaiśya
Greece	deities in episode of epic	Hera	Athena	Aphrodite
Rome	category of priest	fl. dialis	fl. dialis	fl. quirinalis

Note: Making the functions head columns rather than rows is not only convenient typographically but also conventional in that structuralists regularly show syntagmatic relations horizontally and paradigmatic ones vertically.

to the cluster of ideas defining the column's function; it need not relate to *all* the individual ideas in the cluster (especially in the case of F3), but it must be shown convincingly to belong in its own column and not in any of the others. Thus, the Vaiśya are not associated with sensual pleasure or beauty (as Aphrodite is), but their place in the F3 column is earned by their association with wealth, and there are no arguments for putting them in the Fl or F2 columns.

The simplest possible manifestations of the ideology have one representative per function, as in the examples cited so far, but a single function may have more than one representative: for instance, in a single context, F3 is sometimes represented by twins. Moreover, such multiple representation of a single function may be sporadic and apparently unsystematic, but it may also be so common and consistent as to justify recognition of a subordinate level of structure. The best-known example relates to Fl, which not uncommonly shows an internal binary split between a friendly aspect named after the Vedic god Mitra and an alien anxiety-provoking one named after his associate Varuṇa. Dumézil's theory is concerned with three *functions*, not with triplicity per se; and it can readily accommodate more than three entries per row and even the subdivision of columns.

I have introduced the theory as though the functions came first, the examples second, as if the columns had headings before they had contents. In fact, Dumézil *first* saw the analogy between the varṇas and the flamens (1938), and only subsequently, in light of other examples, abstracted the definitions of the functions. Similarly, the theory that the three functions together constituted *the* ideology was not an a priori postulate; it was a judgement formed as examples of manifestations accumulated and proved to be surprisingly pervasive. By pervasiveness I mean not so much the number of Indo-European societies in which manifestations can be recognized (this naturally depends on the date and character of the available sources) but rather the frequency of examples, the variety of types of context in which they occur, and the importance of the manifestations within the cultures. It seems that the ideology is most pervasive among the Celto-Italics and Indo-Iranians, that is, at the two geographical extremes of the IE world, which are thought to have been more conservative than the centre.

This macrohistorical point brings us to two broad issues that have not received sufficient attention: what is the relationship of the trifunctional ideology, on the one hand, to contemporary ideologies in the IE world, and on the other hand, to ideologies elsewhere?

IE macrohistory: from segmentary ideology to non-segmentary ideologies

The IE-speakers of today, dispersed over all the continents, call on various and competing ideologies including Christian, Islamic, Marxist, liberal, and mixed. Opinions would differ on how to set about analyzing them, but no one suggests that trifunctional analysis offers the key. One feels intuitively that modern ideologies are qualitatively different from the sort of thing that Dumézil envisages (indeed this may account for part of the hostility his theory has encountered). It is not merely that modern ideologies are consciously in competition, while the trifunctional ideology was presumably taken for granted. The main point is that modern ideologies do not consist of discrete clusters of ideas such as could form the headings for columns containing lists of their manifestations. Let us use the term 'segmentary' to distinguish ideologies that are susceptible to display in columns from non-segmentary ones that are not. A segmentary ideology is one that organizes the major ideas that it handles into a small number of sharply contrasting clusters.[3]

To stress the typological contrast is not to deny the historical continuity. The legacy of the old ideology may be detectable today in various forms, ranging from straightforward punctate manifestations in folkloristic contexts to diffuse attitudes. One thinks of the recent discovery of a trifunctional triad of saints in a festival still performed at Gubbio in Italy (Dumézil 1979: 123–143) and of the enduring importance of the varṇas in India. But these cannot be recent *inventions*. They are clearly survivals, creations of earlier times. In broad terms, the trifunctional ideology is ancient history, dead and gone, or at most transmuted beyond recognition.

From this point of view, the history of the Indo-Europeans consists in a transition from an early period, when the segmentary ideology was creative and pervasive, to the contemporary period, when it has, to all intents and purposes, given way to non-segmentary ideologies. However, the idea of the earlier period lacks precision. The problem is not only practical – the patchiness of the evidence from early times, the difficulty of reconstructing prehistory – but also conceptual. Continua are often difficult to handle, and an ideology can very easily be only partly alive. It might be alive for the masses, dead for the elite, or vice versa. It might be strong enough to effect adaptations, too weak to inspire genuine innovation. It might be alive in narrative, dead so far as institutions were concerned. And so on. I imagine that even the earliest of our sources date from periods when the ideology was no longer as alive as it had been when the proto-Indo-European (PIE)-speakers were beginning to disperse. However, it would be arbitrary to assume that *that* was the time when the segmentary ideology was at its strongest. The process of decline could well have begun earlier – one can say nothing about dates. Nevertheless, either the notion of a long-term global loss of segmentation from the ideology is incorrect or one is forced to hypothesize a period when the segmentariness was at its maximum. To conceptualize this period, it is helpful to construct an ideal type, a model society in which the trifunctional ideology was as alive and creative and pervasive as an ideology could be.

One could start by assembling from all over the IE world all the types of context in which manifestations have been discovered, and one could try to devise others, and for each type of context there would be row after row of manifestations. The members of the society would experience as obvious the unity of a function, the homogeneity of the entries in a column. The ideology would not only pattern the social structure, institutions, and narratives but also dominate speculation on the macrocosm and the microcosm and guide the interpretation of events and the assimilation or development of cultural innovations.

Such a model is intended simply as an aid for reflection. It is not necessary to imagine that it was ever realized in all its simplicity and consistency, or that the subsequent history of the ideology consisted of nothing but decline in segmentariness. Global recrudescences seem implausible, but one cannot exclude occasional bursts of creativity in particular types of context. Even so, the overall trend has to be decline, and to conceptualize such a process, we need a starting point.

IE and non-IE: segmentary ideologies viewed anthropologically

Dumézil sometimes presents his own comparative method as a transposition to a larger scale of the comparisons routinely undertaken on a smaller scale, for example by Hellenists who compare Dorians, Ionians, and so forth (Dumézil 1973: 11). But he is well aware (ibid: 21–22) that something should be gained by moving to a wider scale again, beyond the range of individual language families. This means abandoning the well-tested family-tree approach to comparison but opens up other sorts of questions. In particular, do we know of other societies possessing segmentary ideologies that are as systematic as the one we have attributed to our model society?

In fact we do, though they have usually been discussed in different analytical vocabulary, in terms not of 'ideologies' but of totemism, symbolic classification or (more recently) isomorphisms. Some of the clearest examples come from Australia, though similar phenomena are not uncommon in the tribal world. The *locus classicus* remains the 1903 essay by Durkheim and Mauss on primitive classification. This rich paper, often misunderstood [Allen 2000a: Ch. 2], would certainly be important in any exploration of the intellectual roots of Dumézil. He himself has often attributed the genesis of his theory to the influence of Mauss and, above all, Granet (e.g. in Dumézil 1981a: 21), and it would be easy to show Granet's debt to the paper by Mauss and his uncle.[4]

After their introduction, Durkheim and Mauss start off by collecting reports from aboriginal Australia to the effect that all the members of the social world (the tribe) and all the contents of the natural world (animate or not) are parcelled out into a small number of discrete classes. Thus, a single class will contain not only humans of a certain category but also particular species of plant and animal ('totems') and sometimes meteorological phenomena, heavenly bodies, 'elements' such as fire, and so on. How similar is such a *classification* to the *ideology* of our model society? The small fixed number of classes corresponds to the small fixed number of columns, but one can perhaps recognize two main differences.

First, the Australian material appears to put more emphasis than Dumézil does on the totalities structured by the classification. We shall return to this issue.

Second, the Australian classifications, as reported before 1903, primarily concern the concrete and visible rather than spiritual forces or principles. It is not clear what abstractions, if any, give coherence to the classes and provide a rationale for the allocation to them of particular contents; in other words, there is no obvious equivalent for the functions that define and label the columns in the IE case.[5]

For our purpose, it is not necessary to pursue these differences by recourse to further sources, old or new. The point is that they do not suffice to make the term 'ideology' inappropriate to the ethnographic material (nor, conversely, to make 'classification' inappropriate to the philological material). The Australian classifications, at least sometimes, structure myth and ritual as well as society and the cosmos, and they are segmentary and pervasive in very much the same way as the model ideology is.

A fourth function?

Our model society is useful for a second purpose. In trying to make the ideology as pervasive as possible, our approach was to maximize the number of rows. This is in line with the overall thrust of Dumézilian work, which has concentrated on recognizing new manifestations. But the diagram has two dimensions: we could make it pervade more of the culture if we added a column. In a sense, Dumézil himself does this when he sometimes recognizes representatives of the totality per se. For instance (Dumézil 1974: 575–576), the Roman *rex sacrificolus* is closely linked with the flamens and might be placed in a sparsely filled column together with a few comparable figures.[6] But what I have in mind is rather a quite separate column for a fourth function.

As before, let me give a definition before examples. F4 pertains to what is other, beyond, or outside. This focal idea may connote psychological remoteness, social disqualification (as of strangers and slaves), enmity to the gods (as of demons), and forces alien to order, harmony, and continuity (such as chaos, strife, and death), but it may also connote what is beyond understanding, the uncanny, mysterious, otherworldly, and paradoxical. I emphasize the potential for ambiguity and paradox, for the manifestations of F4, though often devalued and associated with negative affect, will sometimes be just the reverse.

To some, this definition will sound familiar. In fact, a fourth function was first proposed by Alwyn and Brinley Rees (1961: 112–139); the book is often cited, but this particular proposal has not been followed up. All I have done is systematize the Reeses' concept and elaborate it a little in light of what I take to be further manifestations. The proposal will stand or fall by its success in application to the details of particular cases. However, to present these in any satisfactory way is a long job, and I deliberately concentrate here on preliminary and more theoretical questions.

One such question is whether there are general or a priori grounds for suspecting the existence of a fourth function. The question has two aspects: quantitatively, is there any reason to think that segmentary ideologies would be more likely to have four classes or columns than three? And qualitatively, is the cluster of ideas covered by the proposed new function the sort of thing one might expect to find within an ideology?

An argument from social structure

The only approach I can see to the quantitative issue is to consider what is characteristic of tribal social structures. Dumézil himself has recently been very guarded about the historical realities of IE social structure. His method tells us about ideas, not behavioural fact, and the triadic division of labour (priests, warriors, and producers) may have been only an ideal (Dumézil 1968: 15), or it may have applied only to part of society, to certain 'specialized' clans or families (Dumézil 1958: 18). As to the origins of the ideology, he has little to say, the implication being that speculation on something so unknowable is a waste of time.[7] However, Dumézil's method is calqued on that of comparative philology, and for the anthropologist, using other methods, such agnosticism is not compulsory.

So far, we have used Durkheim and Mauss primarily as a convenient source for showing that in possessing a segmentary ideology the early Indo-Europeans resembled some other tribal populations. However, the authors' main concern was not the existence of such tribal ideologies but their origin. Their argument was that the classification of the non-human world was a projection onto it of the structure of society itself. There is one strong argument in favour of this view.[8] Tribal social structures are typically segmentary, in just that sense of 'segmentary' that we have been using of ideologies. That is, they classify the total population of the society into a small number of sharply bounded categories, such that the categorization of each individual for important purposes is unambiguous. Whatever the ultimate reasons, and whatever the rules governing recruitment to the categories, and whatever the accompanying ideology, this is empirically the case. In contrast, the natural world does not present itself to us, and there is no reason why it should have presented itself to early tribals, as segmented into classes each containing plants, animals, stars, and so forth. That the structure of society should have been projected onto nature is comprehensible, the reverse is not. To propose that the two sorts of structure were invented simultaneously would be unhelpful; it would merely increase the mystery surrounding these matters rather than decreasing it.[9]

If this line of thought is correct, the origins of the IE ideology are to be looked for in tribal social structures. Ignoring for a moment the unclarity of the notion of 'origin', we can now ask whether, in light of the widest possible comparison, tribal social structures are more likely to be triadic or quadripartite. But the question can perhaps be made more precise. Social structures in general, and tribal ones in particular, are usually based on kinship, on rules of marriage and recruitment (cf. Allen 1986). There are three major types of segmentary social structure:

1. In a structure based on *sections* (such as are common in Australia), the individual is recruited to an exogamous section, to which neither of his parents belong.
2. In a structure based on unilineal descent groups (or more briefly *clans*), the individual is recruited to the exogamous descent group that contains one of his parents but not the other.
3. In a structure based on *endogamous groups* (e.g. castes) the individual is recruited to the group that contains both parents. (Classes, the units of social structure most familiar to ourselves, are statistically defined units, not segmentary ones.)

The question we are posing can therefore either be left as a general one concerning all segmentary structures or it can be refined so as to apply to the type of social structure that one considers most relevant to the proto-Indo-Europeans. I would suggest that either approach makes a quadripartite structure more likely than a tripartite one.

Let us briefly consider each type. Recalling the varṇas, Dumézilians may be tempted to think of early IE society in terms of endogamous strata, but of the three types, this is probably the one least relevant to questions about origins. Endogamous groups (in practice ranked) are characteristic of early literate societies such as supply our written sources, but they are much less characteristic of preliterate, tribal societies. So it may well be irrelevant to ask whether (as I suspect) four-stratum societies are not in practice more common than three-stratum ones. As for section-based structures, it is very hard to imagine them in the absence of a particular type of kinship terminology, recognizable by the presence of 'prescriptive' equations between cognates and affines. Comparison of surviving IE languages does not point to such equations, and one must conclude that if such a social structure ever existed among the ancestors of the Indo-Europeans, it was at a period so remote as to be inaccessible to the methods of philology. However, section systems are regularly quadripartite in character, and as we shall see, their relevance cannot be so easily dismissed.

In the ethnographic record as a whole, by far the commonest form of tribal segmentation is into clans, and it seems certain that the Indo-Europeans had them. It would therefore seem reasonable to envisage their segmentary ideology developing as the projection of a clan-based social structure. The question we are asking could then be rephrased: are three-clan or four-clan societies more frequent? Unfortunately, I do not know the answer to this empirical question, but my impression is that four-clan societies are far more common. If so, the argument does not demand that the proto-Indo-Europeans themselves should have had four clans; it could have been their ancestors. Given that the ideology remained detectable for millennia after the dispersal, it might very well have survived for as many or more millennia before that time. The ideology cannot have originated later than the dispersal, but we have no means of saying how much earlier it may have originated.

There is perhaps one further step we can take. So far, we have been envisaging a segmentary ideology deriving from a clan-based social structure but surviving the transformation that changed the maximal unit of social structure from exogamous clan to endogamous stratum. If a segmentary ideology has such powers of endurance, why assume that it originated with clans? It could have survived an even earlier transformation that gave rise to clans. I feel obliged to raise the question, which may seem excessively speculative, because I have put forward an argument (Allen 1986) to the effect that the first human social structures were quadripartite and based on sections (or similar units). According to this theory, clan structures would ultimately derive from these earlier structures (in which unilineality was not fundamental). The Durkheim–Mauss hypothesis suggests that these primal societies ('tetradic' ones, I called them) would have had isomorphic quadripartite ideologies, and one has to envisage the possibility that this is the ultimate origin of the quadrifunctional ideology.

In view of the many uncertainties and the vast but incalculable stretches of time that are involved, it would be ridiculous to put much weight on the quantitative argument. How could one possibly prove that the ancestors of the proto-Indo-Europeans did not go through a period when they lacked a segmentary ideology or even a segmentary social structure? One can only work in probabilities. But let us summarize. Unless Dumézil is basically wrong, the proto-Indo-Europeans had a segmentary ideology. Segmentary ideologies are most easily understood as the projections of segmentary social structures. Quadripartite segmentation seems empirically more common than tripartite, and is also (on one theory) the oldest form of human social structure. Therefore, even before one examines the IE material, a quadripartite ideology is more likely than a tripartite one. Of course, it is theoretically possible to envisage a quadripartite ideology being totally recast into a tripartite mould, but a priori such a hypothesis is neither neat nor economical.[10]

Intrinsic plausibility of F4, and lack of 'closure' of F1–3

The qualitative question, simpler perhaps, turns on what one expects of an ideology. Dumézil does not spend much time on definitions of the term, but I have collected about a dozen remarks bearing on his use of it. Thus, he writes (1985: 312):

> By analogy with the words 'theology' and 'mythology', which mean respectively the articulated system of deities, and the more or less coherent and finite set of myths, I mean by 'ideology' the inventory of directing ideas that dominate the thinking and behaviour of a society.

Elsewhere he talks of realizing (towards 1950) that the trifunctional ideology, where one finds it, may only be, and perhaps always have been, 'an ideal, and at the same time a means of analysing and interpreting the forces which ensure the course of the world and the life of men' (Dumézil 1968: 15).

Since I cannot be categorical, perhaps my reaction to the second quotation is best put in the form of questions. Would one not expect ideologies to give a place to what stands outside or beyond the forces that ensure continuity? What about the forces of chaos and destruction that *threaten* the course of the world and ensure the *death* of men? Are they not perhaps even more fundamental than the others, and can they really reasonably be accommodated *within* them? Is it justified to equate ideology and ideal? My feeling, which is not limited to segmentary ideologies, is that descriptions of world views in general give so much space to what is outside, anomalous, and alien, that a theory which has a specific place for the Other is a priori more plausible than one which does not. (I prefer to leave this as an impression derived from ethnography rather than trying to call on Jungian psychology, which for its own reasons might also favour a fourth function relating to the shadowy and repressed.)

Not only is an outsider function intrinsically plausible, but nothing in Dumézil's general theory works against it. When it comes to the analysis of particular manifestations, there will sometimes be frank disagreement between a three- and a four-functional interpretation, but on most issues, quadrifunctional theory complements and subsumes Dumézilian theory rather than contesting it. The notion of a fourth function presupposes the three others, and Dumézil's concept of ideology leaves room for expansion. He is perfectly clear that the three functions do not exhaust the ideological heritage from PIE times: 'However important, even central, the ideology of the three functions may be, it is far from constituting all the shared IE heritage that comparative analysis can glimpse or reconstruct' (Dumézil 1958: 89). Dumézil sometimes expresses irritation at the overemphasis on the trifunctional aspect of his oeuvre (1981a: 34), and he lists four other types of representation that he has worked on (1968: 305): the mythology of beginnings, of fires, of seasons, of eschatology [endings]. Presumably this extra-functional heritage lies outside the 'inventory' of dominant *idées directrices*. One certainly cannot leap to the conclusion that all of this ideological material can be subsumed within a unitary scheme containing a fourth function, but there is no a priori reason why at least some of it should not be.

The notion of completeness or closure is in fact a point of weakness in trifunctional theory. One of its rules of method, cited earlier, is that the terms in a row should be exhaustive, that is, they should add up to a totality. But nothing prevents a three-element totality being set within a four-element one. We have noted that, compared with Australian classifications, trifunctional ones put relatively little emphasis on totalities. If the three functions are only a subordinate ideological grouping within a larger one, perhaps this is not surprising.

Might the same idea be taken one step further? Might the four functions themselves be a subordinate grouping within an even larger whole constructed by adding a fifth function? I can see nothing to recommend this logical possibility. The argument from social structure is against it, and I have found no empirical evidence in favour. Indeed, I hope to show elsewhere that there are senses in which F4 as it were completes a closed cycle, Fl-2-3-4-1 . . . such that one might almost prefer to call it F Nought, F0. To envisage an ideology of this sort, one with clusters of ideas adding up to a well-defined totality, is not of course to envisage a society that had no other ideas, no extrafunctional representations. To take just one important topic, no doubt all societies have views on gender, but it is not clear that this aspect of ideology is subsumed by the functions.[11]

Neglect of F4

Trifunctional theory will soon reach its fiftieth anniversary, and the idea of a fourth function has passed its twenty-fifth. This very neglect might give rise to scepticism: surely the idea would have been taken up sooner if there were really anything in it? A full explanation for the neglect would have to take account of many factors: the intellectual history of individuals, the difficulties in coming to grips with the field, the sort of people attracted to it, the sociology of academic disciplines and the opposition which the trifunctional theory itself has had to face. But four points are worth making here.

1 The very term 'function' may have been an obstacle. If a function is defined as a principle – a fundamental idea or cluster of ideas which together with two (or three) others makes up an ideology – then there is no problem in envisaging a function pertaining to what is other, outside, and beyond. But the ordinary use of the word is less abstract and less specialized. One thinks first perhaps of the function of an object (a tool, or a pillar) or, especially in sociology, of the function of an occupation or profession. Dumézil himself has wondered if the term was well chosen (1968: 15–16). Priests, warriors, and producers obviously perform functions for society, but, except perhaps in ritual, the social function of the outsider is less obvious.

2 It is not only with regard to social roles that F4 is more abstract than the others. Its very definition is abstract, 'empty', without obvious visual associations. In fact, F4 is not self-sufficient but relational; something can only be other, outside, or beyond relative to a conceptual starting point. It would not be surprising therefore if the internal coherence of the column of F4 representatives turned out to be less easy to appreciate than that of the other three columns. Typically, F2 representatives, whether humans, gods, symbolic objects, events, or whatever, are the easiest to recognize as such because they relate simply to physical force or war. At the other extreme, the full definition of F3 is quite complex, and its representatives form such a heterogeneous category that the concept has sometimes been dismissed by Dumézil's opponents as a 'rag-bag' (Dumézil 1981a: 37, 1982: 50). The quality of 'F4-ness' may be at least as difficult to pin down as 'F3-ness', but, if so, one is probably making a mistake in trying to pin it down in that way, that is, in trying to find an absolute quiddity in what is more a matter of relations. The point could be properly discussed only in light of numerous examples, but it may help account for the neglect of F4.

3 Turning from columns to rows, one may again find the F4 representative least easy to recognize. According to Dumézil's rules of method, the representatives of the three functions must be homogeneous; one must argue for a 'classificatory intention' (Dumézil 1980: 224).[12] To be other, outside, or beyond is to be in some sense heterogeneous, so by definition a representative of F4 is likely to stand somewhat apart from the Fl–3 representatives. This certainly does not dispense the quadrifunctional analyst from the requirement to demonstrate classificatory intention. As we shall see from examples, a candidate for F4 interpretation will tend to be in some sense heterogeneous, but it must be homogeneous in another and more embracing sense. One could talk of a limited or qualified or relative heterogeneity. But any sort of heterogeneity will tend to disguise the adherence of the F4 element to the same structure as its companions.

4 No doubt by far the most important reason for the neglect of F4 is the very large number of entirely satisfying trifunctional analyses. A certain proportion of them can be revised in light of quadrifunctional theory, but the proportion is probably small. However, for several good reasons, this is not an argument against a fourth function. On the contrary, it is what one would expect, given the relative heterogeneity of the function.

Synchronically, the apartness of F4 might in some contexts simply make it irrelevant; in others, its alienness, positively or negatively valued, might make it tabooed, either as too transcendent to mention or too abominable. Diachronically, if for either or both of these reasons there were at any time fewer contexts in which it was represented, then in the course of the macrohistorical decline or transmutation of the IE segmentary ideology, one would expect the F4 column to be the most vulnerable to blurring and dissolution.

Even if there were no contexts in which F4 was originally tabooed or irrelevant, it would probably still be the first to become unrecognizable. Since F1–3 form a substructure that is not only simpler and more concrete but also more homogeneous, solidary, and close-knit than the total structure of Fl–4, they are a priori more likely to survive as a structure. It might be objected that by the same argument since F4 by itself is simpler and presumably internally more homogeneous than the triadic grouping, it ought to survive even better. Perhaps so, but in the absence of Fl–3 elements there would be no means of recognizing an F4 element. Just as within trifunctional theory, an element can in general be allotted to a function only when it is closely associated with elements belonging to the other two functions, so, at least for the moment, it must be a strict rule of quadrifunctional analysis not to recognize an element as F4 unless it is accompanied by elements allotted to Fl–3; otherwise, the way is open for endless inconclusive arguments. This does not imply that F4 is or ever was less important than the other functions; I leave open the question whether or not there was a time when the Fl–3 component of the ideology was alive and creative while F4 had fossilized. My point is simply that, given the definition of the fourth function and the macrohistory of the segmentary ideology, one would expect manifestations of the total structure to be less frequent than manifestations of Fl–3.

Examples

At long last, we can turn to a few manifestations of the fourth function. The following accounts are presented far too briefly to constitute analyses. Their purpose is rather to illustrate the implications of the previous theoretical arguments.

1 Ever since Vedic times, Hindu tradition has emphasized the totality of the four varṇas, that is, the twice-born *plus* the Śūdra or serfs, whose duty is simply to serve the others. The reason Dumézilians give for ignoring the fourth varṇa is that originally the Śūdra, or rather their ancestors or predecessors, were not

IE-speakers. But even if this is so, it clearly does not stop them being representatives of a function within the IE ideology. They qualify as F4 equally well whether the predecessors were outsiders, outsiders who were enslaved and became insiders, or insiders who were ritually beyond the pale. Whatever their past, the Śūdra are homogeneous qua varṇa, heterogeneous qua once-born. The fact that the first reference to Śūdra is in a late book of the Rigveda proves nothing; the earlier hymns are silent on so much, and in any case, one can interpret the Dāsa or Dasyu as forerunners of the Śūdra. Nor does the rest of the comparative material bearing on the Indo-Iranian speakers contain anything I can find that is incompatible with my interpretation.

2 The story of the origin of the Trojan War contains not only the three rival goddesses quarrelling at the marriage feast of Peleus and Thetis but also, from earliest times it seems, the judge who chooses between them. When appointing a judge, one normally looks for an outsider, and Paris is an outsider as human, as not present at the feast, and as Trojan; for although the Trojans speak Greek and worship Greek gods, they are outsiders from a Greek point of view. Moreover, a mortal appointed to judge between immortals is a figure of paradox, which by itself would justify construing Paris as F4. If there is a difficulty, it is that compared with the goddesses, he might be thought *too* heterogeneous, too little part of a single structure. While I do not accept this, it hardly matters, for some versions of the myth do involve a fourth goddess closely related to the action. The golden apple, the prize for the fairest, is thrown among the guests by Eris, Goddess of Strife. Excluded from the guest list (for obvious reasons), Eris qualifies perfectly as F4.

3 Dumézil's very first trifunctional paper, 'La préhistoire des flamines majeurs' (1938), notes that this triad is part of an ancient hierarchical pentad, the *ordo sacerdotum* (Festus, s.v.). Listed before the three flamens and closely associated with the first (the *dialis*) comes the *rex sacrificolus* and after them comes the *pontifex*. Let us move swiftly past the rex, whom Dumézil interprets as representing the synthesis of Fl–3, and focus on the pontifex. It would take us too far afield to follow up the comparison Dumézil makes between the pontifex and the Vedic *adhvaryu* (in my view, unpersuasively). Compared with the flamens, the pontifex is heterogeneous (a) by virtue of his name, (b) because he is not associated with an individual deity, and (c) because his job is to oversee religious observance in general. He is also a figure of paradox: at a feast, the rex reclined at the top, the pontifex at the bottom, but it was the pontifex, 'judge and arbiter of matters divine and human', who nominated the rex; the rex may have been *maximus* and *potentissimus* (Festus), but it was the title of pontifex that was appropriated by the emperors. Finally, he alone is closely associated with death. According to Livy (1.20.7), Numa, the second king and mythical founder of the office, entrusted the pontifex with overseeing not only the rituals for the gods above *(caelestes caerimonias)*, but also funeral rituals and the propitiation of the dead *(iusta funebria placandosque manes)*. For all these reasons, the pontifex is to be seen as F4.

4 For good measure I conclude, no less briefly, with one case not referred to previously. The standard Roman annalistic tradition recognizes seven kings, starting from Romulus, the founder of the city, and ending with the foundation of the Republic. Dumézil convincingly interprets the first four trifunctionally: Romulus and Numa represent Fl (the Varuṇa and Mitra aspects)[13]; Tullus represents F2, and Ancus F3 (Dumézil 1968: 269ff.; Poucet 1985: 171–179). There he stops. The careers of Servius (Dumézil 1969a: 103ff, Dumézil 1973: 116–124) and Tarquin the Proud (Dumézil 1985a: 105ff.) are analyzed as historicized myth but without being closely related to the 'unitary, coherent, structured' narrative of the previous reigns. However, the Tarquins, elder and younger, were outsiders, essentially Etruscans, and between them came Servius, who was semi-divine and a slave – a paradox indeed. Some would no doubt argue that the gap between the first four and the last three is the gap between mythical kings and more or less historical ones and would call on archaeology for support. But is it not in fact the gap between Fl–3 and three representatives of F4?[14]

Notes

1 First published in 1987 as 'The Ideology of the Indo-Europeans: Dumézil's theory and the idea of a fourth function'.

2 Results from the first two decades were summarized in Dumézil (1958). The secondary literature is considerable, for example Dumézil (1981a) or, in English, Littleton (1982). Specialists in particular branches of IE culture have attacked Dumézil's views on their own fields, but I know of no sustained or well-informed attempt to attack the theory as a whole.

3 [Instead of 'segmentary' I have sometimes preferred 'partitional' [Allen 1991]. Farmer et al. (2000) use 'correlative', putting the emphasis on the linkage between 'rows' rather than on the division of a totality.]

4 Though the 1903 paper is not cited, its influence is probably detectable in the breakthrough article of 1938 (reprinted as Dumézil 1969b: 164): 'Il est rare, chez les demi-civilisés, que la classification d'une catégorie de concepts ne soit pas solidaire d'autres classifications'.

5 Maddock (1973: 103–104) suggests, like Durkheim and Mauss (1903: 16–17), that in one particular case, the dark–light opposition is used as a classificatory principle, but that it is combined with wet–dry. He recognizes that the problem is under-researched but doubts whether such classifications ever achieve complete coherence.

6 [At this early date, I did not see that the priestly rex belongs in a *well-filled* column of representatives of F4+.]

7 Talking to an interviewer six months before his death, Dumézil (1986: 19) says that he imagines the ideology forming in the context of a tripartite social organization, but continues: 'Je dis cela aujourd'hui, je risquerai peut-être autre chose dans peu de temps. Mon travail n'est pas là : il est dans la comparaison de choses *historiquement,* textuellement attestées'.

8 *Pace* the English editor (Needham 1963: xxiv–vi), who apparently thinks the Durkheim–Mauss position is groundless.

9 Cf. Maddock (1973: 128–129) who, without using the concept of segmentariness, concludes that the Aboriginal world order is modelled after the human social order, suggesting that 'it could not very well be derived from anywhere else'.

10 [For an attempt to link pentadic theory to a fivefold model of social structure, see Allen (2012b).]

11 [Over the next few years, I changed my mind about a fivefold ideological whole. For an attempt to tackle gender, see, now, Allen (2018) – I think that within the proto-ideology, feminine gender was sufficiently devaluing to allow construal under F4−. As such, Dumézil's 'trivalent' or 'omnivalent' goddesses (e.g. Dumézil (1992): 150) can sometimes be paired with 'transcendental' male representatives of F4+.]

12 For instance, an IE story which happens to mention a priest, a sword, and a god of wealth is not *ipso facto* trifunctional. However, if a hero on a journey meets with these three heterogeneous entities one after another, and with nothing else, then they become a homogeneous sequence of encounters, and one could argue for a classificatory intention and a trifunctional interpretation.

13 [No! Romulus represents F4+, not an aspect of F1. Dumézil almost glimpsed this (Dumézil 1958: 13–14 = Dumézil 1992: 89–90) when he mentioned Romulus the unifier *(le rassembleur)*, whose name was 'reserved to cover the final synthesis' (of the 'original' components of Roman society).]

14 Shortly after his breakthrough, Dumézil seems to have come close to the notion of F4: the Śūdra, '*en marge ou au-dessous*' relative to the twice-born, are aligned not only with the craftsmen of Ireland and Gaul, who are '*en marge*' relative to the Druids, warrior aristocracy, and herdsmen, but also with the pontifices, who are '*au-dessous*' the flamens (Dumézil 1939: 10). But he soon came to see such apparent parallels as independent developments (Dumézil 1985a: 192–210). For a good discussion of 'the passage from the triad to the tetrad' from the orthodox Dumézilian position, see also Dubuisson (1985).

2

FIVE RELATIONSHIPS

Semigrand open crocodile music hath jaws

– *James Joyce* Ulysses *('Sirens')*

The main body of the paper consists of straightforward comparison: I try to demonstrate that a certain stretch of the *Odyssey* and a certain stretch of the *Mahābhārata* tell two versions of the same story.[1] Towards this end, I argue that this story goes back to proto-Indo-European (PIE) times and is related to PIE matrimonial law (or custom, if one prefers that word in a non-literate context). As for introduction, I take for granted some general knowledge of the Greek epic,[2] but (in the hope of widening my audience) say a little about the Indian. Similarly, I take for granted the framework of Indo-European (IE) comparative linguistics but comment briefly on the comparative study of other aspects of IE culture.

Like the Greek (and this may or may not be coincidence), the Sanskrit tradition has preserved two epics, the *Rāmāyaṇa* and the *Mahābhārata (Mbh.)*. The most obvious feature of the *Mahābhārata* (which includes a miniature version of the *Rāmāyaṇa*) is its length – around eight times the *Iliad* and *Odyssey* put together. But it is not as intractable as this figure may suggest. For many purposes one can ignore the frame narratives (which tell how the story was first told), the embedded independent narratives, and the long didactic passages of Hindu philosophy (including the *Bhagavad Gītā*). This leaves the main narrative, whose essential unity and coherence are nowadays widely recognized by scholars.[3] Apart from their well-structured narratives, the Sanskrit epics also have in common with the Greek that they enjoyed immense cultural and educational prestige. They too were carried overseas (notably to Indonesia) and provided the materials for a great deal of later creative work in poetry, drama, and the plastic arts (not to mention television). Moreover, both epic traditions were related to cultic activity.

In both cases, the earlier history is uncertain and controversial. Homer seems to have been first committed to writing around 700 BCE, the *Mahābhārata* perhaps three to five centuries later, though the process in India may have continued into the first few centuries CE. However, both traditions were certainly oral before they were written (indeed to some extent oral transmission in Indian vernacular languages continues in the present day), and it is the history during the oral phase that interests us here.

I suppose most scholars envisage the Greek epic as taking shape from Mycenaean times onward (perhaps incorporating influences from the Middle East, as has been argued for instance by West 1988b: 169 ff.), and similarly, most Indologists probably envisage the Sanskrit epics as originating in India.[4] However, there is no a priori necessity to think in such local terms. Since the Greek and Sanskrit languages go back to proto-Indo-European, the Greek and Sanskrit epics could go back to a PIE oral epic. For some decades, the philologists have been reconstructing phrases and meters of an *indogermanische Dichtersprache*, a PIE poetic language (e.g. Schmitt 1968), and it is not inconceivable that comparative study of the epics should enable one similarly to reconstruct the narrative themes in the poets' repertoire.

A sceptic might argue that such a prospect is unrealistic. Morphology and lexicon change relatively slowly, and this is what makes it feasible for linguists to grasp the common language lying behind Greek and Sanskrit. Are not narratives a different matter altogether? For one thing, people make them up. For another, even if they are handed on over the generations, they would change at such a rate that even if a proto-epic did exist, we should have no hope of reconstructing it.

In light of the work of Georges Dumézil, such a priori pessimism is unjustified. In his massive comparativist undertaking, he has demonstrated that many aspects of culture, including some narratives, were in fact transmitted to different areas of Eurasia along with the IE languages and remain recognizable as having this history. One cannot hope to give in a couple of paragraphs a satisfactory introduction to an oeuvre whose place in intellectual history will one day, I think, come to be seen as standing at least on a par with that of Lévi-Strauss.[5] I limit myself to four points.

First, one major reason for the relative neglect of Dumézil's work lies in the sociology of knowledge. The work does not conform to current disciplinary boundaries. For most anthropologists, it lies on the other side of a boundary with philology. But Dumézil is not an IE philologist in the ordinary sense, since although he knew and used the relevant languages, his main innovatory contribution lies not in linguistics but in cultural history. Yet if he is an ancient historian, it is not in the normal sense of a specialist in some well-recognized discipline such as Celtic, Germanic, classical, or Indo-Iranian studies: he is essentially a comparativist, drawing on all of them. There are thus very few academics whose *business* it is to come to grips with his oeuvre, or teach it – and it is large.

Second, another reason for the widespread neglect, even hostility towards him, is no doubt that the ideology that he reconstructs for the PIE speakers, and of which he finds so many traces in the surviving materials, is of a type which, though anthropologically entirely plausible, is unfamiliar to the modern West. He describes it as based on three 'functions' – perhaps better thought of as three pigeon-holes. Each pigeon-hole is clearly characterized, and given any context or totality, the ideology will tend to organize or classify it into elements that are distributed neatly into the three holes. I shall return later to the functions (which I actually believe to have been four in number, one of them commonly subdivided). But I make one point here: since the general trend within the IE world has been *from* pigeon-holing ideologies *to* non-pigeon-holing ones, cultural materials which manifest the functional pattern are likely to be more conservative than those which do not – other things being equal [Ch. 1].

Third, Dumézil in effect reconstructs not only the abstract ideological framework of the PIE speakers but also aspects of certain domains in which the ideology manifested itself – social division of labour, law, ritual, theology, and (what interests us most here) narrative, both mythic and epic. When I say he 'reconstructs', I simplify. In practice, just as many comparative linguists are cheerfully agnostic about the phonetics of the starred forms they find it convenient to use, so Dumézil puts little emphasis on trying to imagine life in the PIE homeland.[6] What he does is take for granted that a PIE culture once existed – somewhere, sometime – and use this uncontentious assumption to explore the similarities between surviving cultural products in different parts of the IE-speaking world. The interest lies in the comparison, and the 'reconstruction' is left implicit. I shall mostly follow his example in this.

Fourth, the greater part of Dumézil's IE work relates the western and eastern extremities of the IE world. Celtic, Italic, and Germanic materials are confronted with Indo-Iranian ones, Rome and India providing the favourite comparisons. Greece in general, and Homer in particular, seemed to him to have diverged too far from the PIE cultural heritage to provide much material for the comparativist. However, as will become clear, this is not altogether the case.

So much for my main source of inspiration and guide to method. To summarize: I shall compare two stretches of narrative, emphasizing their similarity. I shall then argue that the similarity is due to a common PIE origin, and I try to strengthen the argument by exploring the relationship with the IE functions.

The wider picture

Before beginning, I must contextualize the relevant section of the *Mahābhārata*. Of the work's eighteen books, the first five lead up to the great eighteen-day battle, which starts with the *Gītā* in Book 6. Book 12 onward is aftermath. The battle is between the Kauravas, the 'Baddies', and the Pāṇḍavas, a set of five brothers. The central one, third in birth order, is Arjuna, son of Indra King of the Gods. Shortly before the great battle, the five Pāṇḍavas undergo a twelve- or thirteen-year banishment (Books 3–4), but this is not the first reference to the theme of exile. Two earlier exiles or quasi-exiles occur in Book 1. At the end of the first, Arjuna wins the hand of Draupadī, and the five brothers collectively marry her. Soon afterwards, Arjuna infringes the rule they have established by interrupting his eldest brother while the latter is alone with Draupadī and off he goes into exile again, this time without his brothers. I shall mention all three exiles, but it is Arjuna's that is our main Indian text. It is not very long – some ten pages in the translation by van Buitenen (1973: 400–411).

I can now start the comparison proper.[7] Arjuna's exile is presented as a pilgrimage around the holy bathing places of India: the four cardinal points are visited in order, moving clockwise. But the hero's ritual bathing is far less salient than his successive encounters with females, (in essence) one per quarter. Among Homeric heroes, only Odysseus makes a journey bringing him in contact with a series of women, and my project is to relate the two journeys. More precisely, I shall try to demonstrate homologies between particular females as shown in Table 2.1. But before coming to the details, I look at the two narrative structures as wholes.

Consider first some of the differences (incidentally, it is harder to be exhaustive, or even systematic, in the treatment of differences than in that of similarities). Arjuna, one of five brothers, is only just married and has little warrior experience; Odysseus, brotherless, has a teenage son and is a seasoned warrior. Arjuna, though not a king, incarnates a god; Odysseus is a king, but wholly human. Arjuna travels by land, though he visits sacred waters; Odysseus voyages, visiting land now and then. Arjuna goes where he wants; Odysseus is at the mercy of the supernaturals and the elements. For Arjuna, the journey is ostensibly a fixed-term penalty for an offence, but it could well have been enjoyable (it is never the reverse); for Odysseus, the journey involves much uncertainty and explicit suffering. Arjuna's journey is schematic in that it conforms to the schema of centre and cardinal points; Odysseus' is not. Arjuna sets off from 'home'; at the point where Homer takes up the story, Odysseus has already been journeying from Troy for two years. Finally, as regards narrative technique, Arjuna's journey unrolls straightforwardly from start to finish; Homer tells the story by means of inserted retrospective narratives, so that the two episodes that actually happen first are only recounted in the course of episode IV.

TABLE 2.1 Correspondences between females in the two narratives

	Mahābhārata		*Odyssey*	
	Draupadī	(C: Indraprastha)	Penelope	(Ithaca)
I	Ulūpī	(N: Ganges Gate)	Circe	(Aeaea)
II	Citrāṅgadā	(E: Maṇipura)	Sirens etc.	('Straits')
III	Vargā etc.	(S: Southern Ocean)	Calypso	(Ogygia)
IV	Subhadrā	(W: Dvārakā)	Nausicaa	(Scheria)
	Draupadī	(C: Indraprastha)	Penelope	(Ithaca)

Note: The locations of the females are shown in brackets. The hero leaves his main wife (in the top row), encounters females I–IV during the four episodes of his journey, and returns to his main wife. Correspondences are shown horizontally except in rows II and III: Citrāṅgadā corresponds to Calypso, Vargā plus friends to the Sirens plus Scylla and Charybdis.

On the other hand, there are some global similarities:

1 Both heroes are central to their respective epics, and neither journey could be excised without serious alteration in the overall plot (it is Subhadrā who ultimately ensures the continuity of the Pāṇḍava line).
2 Both heroes are married before their respective journeys and return to this primary wife afterwards.
3 If the Greek sea monsters are treated as a single narrative unit (a step in the argument that I shall justify later), and if Vargā is regarded as subsuming her four companions, then in the course of his journey, each hero has four encounters or liaisons with females other than his primary wife.[8] The four encounters constitute the foci of the four episodes into which the journey can be divided.
4 Of the hero's four encounters, in both cases, three are with humans or with anthropomorphic supernaturals while one is with water monsters (if the Sirens can be included under this heading). The former are either frankly sexual liaisons or (as in the case of Nausicaa) rich in hints of sexuality, while the encounters with water monsters are asexual relationships.
5 Both heroes start off in company, but their companions suffer attrition, and by episode III or IV, both are alone.

Detailed comparisons

I come now to details. But first I must emphasize one rule of method. Whenever attention is drawn to such and such a shared motif in episode *x*, then that motif occurs *in no other episode of either journey*. For each episode, I shall summarize the *Mahābhārata* but assume knowledge of Homer.[9]

Episode I is much shorter in India and contains no equivalent for Odysseus' solo hunting expedition, for the companions turned to pigs, for the protective drug revealed by Hermes, for Elpenor with his broken neck, or for the dialogues with the dead in Hades. Nonetheless, there are enough similarities to make my case.[10]

I. Ulūpī (1,206)

> Arjuna has set out with his Brahmin friends and settled at the Gate of the Ganges. The priests light ritual fires and offer flowers on both banks of the river, so that the area becomes surpassingly beautiful. Arjuna bathes in the Ganges and makes an offering to his grandfathers. As he is about to emerge and perform a fire rite, Ulūpī, daughter of the King of the Snakes, pulls him under the water. Arjuna finds a fire in the palace and performs the rite there. He then asks Ulūpī who she is and why she has brought him to this lovely land. She explains that, on seeing him enter the water, she has fallen hopelessly in love. She overcomes Arjuna's scruples by arguing that in giving himself to her he will save her from dying of love, and hence will be observing *dharma*, the highest law. Persuaded by this argument, he does as she wishes, but leaves the palace next morning with the rising sun.

6 Both stories include a visit to an underworld.[11] The Snake-King's palace is itself underneath the waters; Odysseus crosses the Ocean to Hades.
7 Both underworld visits involve a fiery ritual directed to the dead – Odysseus' two friends flay and burn sacrificial sheep.
8 Both females are ostensibly at risk of their lives, Ulūpī from amorous passion, Circe when Odysseus threatens her with his sword.
9 Both Ulūpī and Circe take the sexual initiative.
10 In neither case is the offer immediately welcomed; both females must overcome the hero's scruples by means of words (respectively, ethical argument and oath).
11 Both females possess magical powers over the human body. Ulūpī, as will be seen later, possesses a magic stone that she uses to resuscitate Arjuna when he has been (to all appearances) 'killed' by Babhruvāhana; Circe can turn Odysseus' companions to swine and back again by the use of drugs.
12 Both females show a supernatural knowledge of the past. Ulūpī already knows the reasons for Arjuna's exile; Circe knows the woes and wrongs suffered by the wanderers.

These seven points will have to suffice, and I pass on to Sanskrit episode II, which corresponds to Greek episode III. A major difference concerns the girl's father: Calypso's father, Atlas, plays no role in the action.

II. Citrāṅgadā (1,207)

> Arjuna travels onward, visiting various mountains, fords [*tīrthas*], and hermitages. In the course of this journey he makes donations of many thousands of cows, as well as giving dwellings to Brahmins. At the gates of the kingdom of Kaliṅga the Brahmins turn back, and the hero continues with only very few companions. Coming to Maṇipura (aka Maṇalūra), he happens to catch sight of the princess walking in the city, and desires her. The king agrees to the union on condition that the son born of it shall remain with him. Arjuna accepts, and stays for a longish period.

13 In both traditions this episode is sketchy relative to the others – events in Maṇipura are covered in fewer than ten shlokas.
14 Both episodes open with references to large numbers of cattle, which are disposed of in an act having religious significance. Arjuna makes his massive pious donation; Odysseus fails to prevent his companions impiously killing the cattle of the Sun.
15 Shortly afterwards, in both cases, the size of the party is abruptly reduced. The turning back of the Brahmins corresponds to the drowning of Odysseus' impious crew.
16 In both cases, this liaison is much longer than the first one. Arjuna spent one night with Ulūpī, three months or years (the point is debated) with Citrāṅgadā; Odysseus spent one year with Circe (plus 24 hours after the visit to Hades), seven years with Calypso.

17 Now, for the first time, non-Homeric Greek epic becomes important. Homer says nothing of any offspring from Odysseus' liaisons with Circe or Calypso, let alone of course from his encounter with Nausicaa. However, according to later sources (see Frazer 1921: 301–305), he had a son Telegonus, by either Circe or Calypso. Much later on in the story, subsequent to the destruction of the suitors, Telegonus comes to Ithaca and kills his father with the spine of a stingray. Similarly, Arjuna has a son called Babhruvāhana by Citrāṅgadā. Much later on, subsequent to the Great War, Arjuna revisits the eastern quarter (CE 14,78–80, [tr. Ganguli IV Book 14: 150–157]), and Babhruvāhana kills his father with a snake-like poisonous arrow. Parricide is not a commonplace event, and the two sons must be cognate. In view of the other reasons for linking Calypso and Citrāṅgadā, one can be pretty certain that the obscure Cyclic poet Eugammon of Cyrene was preserving the PIE tradition when he gave Calypso, rather than Circe, as the parricide's mother.[12]

III. Vargā (1,208–209)

In episode III, as already implied, a multiplicity of Greek monsters corresponds to a single type of Indian monster. The other main difference is that the Greek hero *escapes from* the monsters, the Indian *redeems* them.

> Arjuna approaches some bathing places in the South. Five of them were formerly favoured by religious ascetics but are now occupied by large crocodiles which drag away visitors. Ignoring the warnings given by some ascetics, Arjuna visits one of the sacred *tīrthas*, and bathes in it. He is promptly seized by its crocodile, but he succeeds in pulling the reptile onto land, whereupon it turns into a beautiful female. She is Vargā, a nymph who used to roam the forest with her four girl-friends. Once, on a journey, the quintet had encountered a handsome Brahmin practising his austerities. The girls sang and danced to seduce him, but after sternly resisting their temptations, he finally cursed them to spend a century as crocodiles. Responding to their pleas for mercy, he foretold their rescue. Another sage told them where to spend the period of their punishment, knowing that Arjuna would rescue them in due course. Indeed, having already rescued Vargā, the hero now performs the same service for her four friends.

18 Both heroes receive warnings of the dangers awaiting them in certain waters but are undeterred: Circe's warnings about the monsters correspond to those given by the ascetics.

19 In both cases, the water monsters are somehow multiple. The *six* heads of Scylla correspond to the *five*-member group of crocodiles.[13]

20 Both stories link the theme of female water monsters to that of seductive female singers, and in both cases, the second theme in some sense precedes. In India, the singers are the same beings as the crocodiles, but in an earlier phase

of their lives. In Greece, the Sirens are separate beings from the more obviously monstrous Scylla and Charybdis, but they are encountered just before them in the course of the journey. The unity of the quasi-Sirens and monsters in the Sanskrit is part of the justification for treating the Greek equivalents as a single narrative element (the relationship with functions providing a further argument).

21 The duality of Scylla and Charybdis parallels the two phases in Arjuna's dealings with Vargā. First, Vargā grabs the hero, as Scylla grabs Odysseus' six friends, then Arjuna pulls Vargā onto land, as Odysseus grabs the fig-tree over Charybdis.

22 To revert to post-Homeric sources (see, e.g. Grimal 1982), in both traditions, the females have been metamorphosed into monsters as a punishment. Moreover, both types of Siren figure undergo a second transformation as a result of the hero's visit. Vargā and friends change back into nymphs, the Greek Sirens die (Apd. *Epit.* 7.19), perhaps by suicide.

IV. Subhadrā (1,210–213)

Episode IV is particularly complex, in both traditions. The major difference is that Arjuna actually marries Subhadrā, while in Homer, Odysseus does not even sleep with Nausicaa. In addition, Subhadrā's brother Kṛṣṇa plays a fundamental role in the whole *Mahābhārata* and elsewhere, while the most obvious homologue in the Greek is a very minor character. I shall indicate later how at least the first of these discrepancies can be resolved.

> Following a return visit to Maṇipura, Arjuna tours the bathing places in the west until Kṛṣṇa comes to meet him at Prabhāsa. They go together to Mount Raivataka where Kṛṣṇa has arranged entertainment – decorations and food, actors and dancers. After enjoying them, Arjuna goes to his bed, and while he is telling his friend about his journey, he falls asleep. The next day they go in a golden chariot to Dvārakā, where Arjuna is welcomed by crowds. A few days later the local people hold a large festival on the same mountain. Again the mountain has been embellished, and there is music, dance and song. A number of those attending the festival are named, some of them being drunk.
>
> Kṛṣṇa and Arjuna are strolling through the confusion when the latter sees Subhadrā in the midst of her friends. He is smitten by the god of love. Recognizing this, Kṛṣṇa explains that the girl is his sister. Arjuna asks his advice. Of the two modes of marriage appropriate for a warrior, Kṛṣṇa points out the risks attached to 'marriage by concourse' *(svayaṃvara)*, which leaves the choice ultimately up to the woman, and recommends marriage by capture.
>
> After they have returned to the city, Arjuna, well armed, sets off in a golden chariot yoked with Kṛṣṇa's two horses, pretending to be going hunting. Subhadrā has been attending the festival. Having paid homage to

the mountain and its deities, she has finished her ritual circumambulation and is setting off for Dvārakā. Arjuna abducts her by force and sets off for Indraprastha. Her armed escort raises the alarm. At the court-house the magistrate sounds the war-drum, and the warriors assemble en masse. Drunk, and angered by the abduction, they prepare to pursue Arjuna. Balarāma blames his half-brother for the guest's behaviour. Kṛṣṇa again discusses the modes of marriage, presents Arjuna's action as entirely right and proper, welcomes the union and proposes a diplomatic approach to the abductor. Arjuna is induced to turn back and hold a wedding at Dvārakā, before completing his exile and returning home.

23 In both stories, the hero's hosts come from elsewhere. The Phaeacians migrated from Hypereia under Alcinous' father because they were being plundered by the Cyclops. The people of Dvārakā migrated from Mathurā during Kṛṣṇa's lifetime because they were being attacked by a more powerful king (2,13.35–50).

24 Both kingdoms eventually suffer what a modern might term a natural catastrophe. The sea-faring Phaeacians have their ports blocked with a mountain by Poseidon, while in Book 16, Dvārakā sinks beneath the ocean.

25 In both traditions this fourth episode unrolls in a multiplicity of locations, initially rural, later largely urban. The Scherian seashore corresponds to Prabhāsa and Mount Raivataka, the city of the Phaeacians to Dvārakā.

26 At a more detailed level of topography, both heroes start beside water (Prabhāsa is a *tīrtha*) and move uphill. Odysseus climbs a slope *(klitus)* to his thicket, Arjuna ascends Raivataka.

27 Both heroes on their 'hills' are woken by a noise: Arjuna by songs, music, and praises, Odysseus by the shout of the maidens when their ball falls into the river.

28 Both stories describe pleasures enjoyed in the countryside. Arjuna enjoys watching singers and dancers on the decorated mountain; Nausicaa sings and plays ball with her maidens.

29 Both heroes tell their stories just before falling asleep. Arjuna nods off while narrating to Kṛṣṇa; Odysseus narrates the last part of his journey during his first night in Scheria before sleeping on the porch.

30 Both stories involve wheeled vehicles. Arjuna rides in, and later borrows, Kṛṣṇa's splendid horse-drawn chariot; Nausicaa borrows her father's mule cart.

31 When encountering his female, each hero is assimilated to a hunter. When setting off to abduct, Arjuna pretends he is going hunting. Odysseus emerging from a thicket is compared, in a typical Homeric simile, to a lion going hunting among cattle, sheep, or deer.

32 Both heroes are, or claim to be, amazed by the sight of the female. (The point may seem banal, but I recall my rule of method: not one of the other encounters inspires similar amazement in the hero.)

33 Both traditions here describe at least two crowd scenes, large gatherings of the citizens or of particular categories of citizens.

34 At one of these gatherings, both epics include lists of names of males who, as individuals, play a minimal or even totally unspecified role in events. Although I cannot find any etymological links between the thirteen empty names of warriors who attend the Raivataka festival, and the eleven 'empty' names of the noble youths at the Phaeacian games, it is the presence of the lists that is striking.

35 Both heroes encounter from the local youths an initial hostility which is later resolved. The details are particularly complicated, and I merely note that the vilification of Arjuna by Balarāma (who is pacified by Kṛṣṇa) corresponds to the insult of Euryalus, for which Alcinous makes him apologize.

36 In both cases, the female's brother is on particularly friendly terms with the hero. Nausicaa's brother Laodamas, an exquisite dancer, corresponds to Subhadrā's brother Kṛṣṇa, also a notable dancer (in later Hindu tradition). Laodamas, as I have said, is a minor figure while Kṛṣṇa's role in Hinduism is comparable to Christ's within Christianity; so the comparison is intriguing.

37 At the end of episode IV both heroes receive magnificent gifts, Arjuna as dowry accompanying Subhadrā, Odysseus simply on the initiative of Alcinous.

38 On their return home, both heroes encounter from their original wives an initial distrust or reserve.

Complication

The thirty-eight points of similarity are a selection from about twice as many, some of which relate to quite small details in the language of the two texts. But I hope they suffice to show that the similarities between the two traditions cannot be ascribed to accident or to vague resemblances between societies 'at a similar stage of development'. The strongest argument against such dismissals is the distribution of the similarities. These are not isolated clichés of the epic genre scattered at random across the story, but details situated precisely within the narrative structure specified by Table 2.1 and characterized by the global resemblances 1–5.

However, the analysis cannot stop at this point. The relationship between the two epics is more complex than the comparison between the two journeys indicates. It is true that the end of Odysseus' wanderings corresponds to the second of the three exiles in the *Mahābhārata*, but it seems that the start of the voyage corresponds to some extent to the first exile and that the end has superimposed on it certain features from the third exile (Book 3). I concentrate on the end, doing little more than hint at comparisons which need to be explored in much greater depth.[14]

Urvaśī (3,38–40, 163–164)

During the Pāṇḍavas' great twelve-year exile, Arjuna goes off by himself to the north. He undertakes increasingly severe religious austerities, ultimately subsisting for a month on wind alone. He is taken to Heaven, where he sees a nymph called Urvaśī. He studies dancing and singing with the Gandharva Citrasena,

> who becomes his friend. [Now comes a passage rejected from the main text of the CE.] Urvaśī receives from Indra a divine messenger who tells her to prepare for love-making with Arjuna. She goes to visit him at night. But Arjuna's attitude is one of embarrassed reverence, not love, since the nymph is a distant forebear of his. She departs angrily.

The comparisons are with Odysseus' involuntary austerities resulting from storm and sea; the blissful, quasi-heavenly land of Scheria; Nausicaa being told by Athena to prepare for her wedding; Odysseus' sense of *sebas* (reverence), when he accosts her. Citrasena parallels Nausicaa's friendly brother, Laodamas the dancer.

One major discrepancy between the Greek and Sanskrit episode IV was the lack of sexual relations between the Greek hero and heroine, but this is precisely paralleled by Arjuna's unconsummated encounter with Urvaśī. One can reasonably say that Nausicaa, the nubile female of the fourth encounter, corresponds structurally to Subhadrā, but corresponds in much of her content to Urvaśī. The other major discrepancy was the relative insignificance of Laodamas as compared with Kṛṣṇa. This too has a parallel – in the relative insignificance of Citrasena.

Four-functional interpretation

What is to be made of the historical relationship between the Greek and Indian narratives? If Homer was written down half a millennium earlier, was the story perhaps carried to India, maybe by Alexander's troops, or later, or even earlier? One objection to this, out of many, is the order of events in the narrative. By the fourth century at any rate, the Homeric texts were no doubt well on their way to being standardized, and it would be surprising, to say the least, if the Indian bards had managed to rework the narrative so as to eliminate all traces of Homer's sophisticated embedded narrative technique. But I have an additional and more interesting line of argument.

Let us return to Dumézil and his functions, bearing in mind that the presence of a functional pattern in narratives is probably an index of conservatism. I assume that Dumézil is essentially right in recognizing within the IE ideological inheritance three clusters of ideas: F1 pertaining to religion and the sacred, F2 to physical force and war, F3 to fecundity, wealth, and associated ideas. I have argued elsewhere that Dumézil's view of the ideology needs to be expanded (Allen 1991, 1996). The three classical functions are as it were 'framed' by a fourth function pertaining to what is other, outside, or beyond. Frequently, one finds two contrasting representatives of the fourth function. One of them is positively valued and often in some sense transcendent, while the other is negatively valued and may be associated with death, destruction, demons, and the like. I refer to such elements as F4+ and F4−, respectively. So are the five major relationships that structure the journey narrative a manifestation of this pattern?

A good deal of the work needed to answer this question has already been carried out by Dumézil, in a study (1979) that starts off with a comparison between

Sanskritic and Roman matrimonial law. The best-known Indian text to discuss the topic is the *Manusmṛti* or Code of Manu (again dating from around the turn of the eras). Manu (3.20–34) actually presents a list of *eight* types of marriage but, as Dumézil notes, the first four are very similar, and the list can readily be reduced to five major types, three of which are clearly related to his functions. Using a single label for the first (conflated) type (cf. Trautmann 1981: 288 ff.), I introduce English labels and order the list in the simplest way. These then are the types on which Dumézil focuses attention:

gift of a bride *(kanyādāna)*	F1
marriage by capture *(rākṣasa)*	F2
purchase of a bride *(āsura)*	F3

Very briefly, the gift of a bride is assimilated to an offering to the gods and is specially recommended for priests; marriage by capture involves the use of physical force and is recommended for warriors; purchase of a bride connotes haggling with the bride's father over the price *(śulka)*, and in comparison to the others is somewhat dishonourable and most appropriate for merchants. These modes relate respectively to the realms of religion, force, and wealth, and each has a related form in Rome, which reinforces the argument that the classification is proto-Indo-European.

Manu lists two other major modes, marriage by mutual choice *(gāndharva)* and the *paiśāca* mode. The latter occurs when a man unites in secret with a woman who is asleep, drunk, or mad – that is, (my gloss) not in her normal state. But marriage by mutual choice is closely related to a ninth type, *svayaṃvara*, or marriage by concourse, which is not mentioned by Manu but is common in the epics. This type occurs when a princess makes her choice from a group of suitor princes who have assembled for the purpose, and who may participate in a competition. In a slightly aberrant listing, the *Mahābhārata* (1,96.7 ff.) rates it as the best of the modes. Conversely, the law codes generally agree that the *paiśāca* mode is the worst; indeed they often treat it last, and sometimes (Āpastamba, Vasiṣṭha) omit it altogether. So these two modes are both to some extent excluded and heterogeneous and thereby qualify as F4; one is valued, the other the converse. Dumézil's analysis can therefore be supplemented as follows.

marriage by concourse *(svayaṃvara)*	F4+[15]
paiśāca union	F4–

The question can now be rephrased (I conflate two issues that are theoretically distinct and start with the *Mahābhārata*). Do Arjuna's five relationships conform either to the five modes of marriage or to the functions?

The marriage with Draupadī is by concourse (F4+). Being polyandrous, it is in any case heterogeneous and wholly outside the norm. But although it is a scandal, it is one for which the text offers religious justifications of several sorts, and it is certainly presented as correct for the Pāṇḍavas.

The encounter with Vargā and friends is not even sexual, let alone a marriage, and the females are not asleep, drunk, or mad. But, qua monsters, they are certainly heterogeneous relative to the others, and they are *not their real selves*. One should also note the symmetry. The F4+ relationship with Draupadī involves five males and one female, the F4− encounter involves five females and one male; all the other liaisons are one-to-one. Thus, in spite of the absence of sexual union, the encounter can reasonably be aligned with the F4− *paiśāca* union. Perhaps sexuality was present in earlier versions of the story (maybe even pre-PIE ones).

As for the one-to-one unions, that with Subhadrā is explicitly a marriage by capture (F2). The Sanskrit does not identify the remaining two liaisons with an explicit mode of marriage. However, that with Citrāṅgadā involves Arjuna taking the initiative, submitting to the bride's father's demands, and conceding to him a *śulka* ('price'). The term, used nowhere else in the story, is precisely the one used in Nārada's definition of the F3 marriage by purchase. The union with Ulūpī resembles marriage by gift in that the initiative comes from the bride's side, and the text specifically refers to gifts, using the root *dā- (pradānam).*[16] Moreover, the whole episode is pervaded by references to religion and ritual.

The results of the analysis can be summarized as in Figure 2.1.

The argument has been that the Greek relationships correspond one-for-one with the Sanskrit, but they do not relate directly to the cardinal points. The next question is whether they relate directly either to the functions or to the modes of marriage.

In some post-Homeric sources the marriage of Odysseus and Penelope somewhat resembles a marriage by concourse (Pausanias 3.12.1), and it is closely associated with the gathering of the princes of Greece to woo Helen (e.g. Apd. *Bibl.* 3.10.8). To a certain extent it therefore conforms to the type which in India would be F4+ (no doubt too, Odysseus stringing the bow amidst the suitors is participating in an event of a similar type [see Ch. 17]). The various monsters might be thought sufficiently heterogeneous relative to the other females to suggest F4−, though the gap between the Sirens and Circe is perhaps not really very great. As for the other episodes, none of them, as they stand, relate unambiguously either to functions or to modes. At most one can find odd hints: in Circe's case, as in Ulūpī's, the sexual initiative comes from the bride's side.

Let us sum up the implications of what has been said about functions. The PIE speakers tended to organize all sorts of domains and contexts into clear-cut structures such that the elements involved were distributed into a number of ideological

	F1	
F2	F4+	F3
	F4−	

FIGURE 2.1 Relationship between the cardinal points at which females live (cf. Table 2.1) and Arjuna's modes of union with them

pigeon-holes, technically called functions. Dumézil says that there were three functions, the first of which was sometimes split (into Mitra and Varuṇa aspects, roughly speaking into close and distant). I say that there were four functions, and that the fourth was very often split into positively valued and negatively valued. We both draw on a great deal more evidence than is even alluded to here.

In the particular case of matrimonial law, the trifunctionalist attributes to PIE culture the recognition of three modes of marriage, each related to a function; the implication is that in increasing the number of types, the Indians innovated. The quadrifunctionalist looks at the matter the other way round. The PIE speakers would have recognized five modes, and in retaining them, the Indians were conservative; if they innovated, it was only in increasing the number from five to eight. In either case, PIE culture related some marriage types to functions. The present chapter shows that the PIE corpus of narratives included one (myth, epic, legend – it hardly matters here) in which a hero contracted five types of union or relationship. If the proto-narrative resembled the *Odyssey*, the relationships were not clearly related to functions, and India innovated in making the link. But I have already accepted Dumézil's argument that, in 'legal' contexts at any rate, the PIE speakers did relate marriage types to functions, and if so, it is much more likely that the proto-narrative also made the connection – unlike the *Odyssey*, but like the *Mahābhārata*. In other words, in this respect too, the Indian epic is far more likely to be the conservative one. This helps to support the earlier conclusion that the narrative similarities are not due to influences from Greece on India. Incidentally, it also shows that Dumézil was right in thinking that Homer had moved a long way from his IE heritage; if there was a mistake, it was in underestimating the amount of heritage that remains recognizable.[17]

Concluding discussion

In conclusion, I note a few areas that invite further work:

1. At the most general anthropological level, this chapter relates to the conceptualization of marriage outside as well as inside the IE world, a topic that is sometimes approached simplistically in terms of bride-price versus dowry.
2. This chapter presents another manifestation of the four-functional ideology, together with an example of how easily manifestations of F4 can be overlooked [cf. Ch. 1].[18] There are certainly many more.
3. The association between functions and cardinal points might repay further attention (cf. Allen 1991: 148–150).
4. As regards India, it ought to be possible to relate what has been said earlier about Kṛṣṇa to the rise of Vaishnavism. Would it be possible to argue that Kṛṣṇa not only corresponds to Laodamas and Citrasena but also has, so to speak, expanded his role so as to take on much of the narrative and conceptual material which in the *Odyssey* is distributed among other characters? In a general sense, Kṛṣṇa is to Arjuna as Athena is to Odysseus.

5 Coming to narrower problems, the comparison casts a little light on the composition of the epics, that is, on what used to be called 'the Homeric question' and on its Indian equivalent. Significant parts of both narratives go back to PIE times, and it is certain that some material contained in 'post-Homeric' sources, as well as some relegated material in the Pune CE, belong in this archaic category (comparisons 17 and 22; Urvaśī episode). At least in one case (comparison 31), a 'Homeric' simile seems to be equally old [see Ch. 3].

6 Finally, and obviously, how extensive is the relationship between Greek and Indian epic outside the passages we have been considering? It cannot be coincidence that fairly soon after the Urvaśī episode Arjuna finds himself in disguise at the court of King Virāṭa, while fairly soon after the Nausicaa episode Odysseus finds himself in disguise in his own palace.

Notes

1 First published in 1996 as 'The hero's five relationships: a proto-Indo-European story'.

2 See, for example Camps (1980), or for the *Odyssey*, Griffin (1987).

3 Recent bibliographies in Katz (1989) and Sharma (1991). The major specialists have been Biardeau (Biardeau 1985–6 provides a convenient summary and introduction to the epic), and Hiltebeitel (e.g. 1976, 1988). My own approach derives more from the systematic comparativism of Dumézil (1968).

4 Thus, van Buitenen writes: 'That the main story of *The Mahābhārata* was a conscious composition is, to me, undeniable, and one poet, or a small group of them, must have been responsible for it . . . When was this old lay first composed? Certainly after the very early Vedic period' (1973: xxiv).

5 The best overview is Dumézil (1987); see also Allen (1993b). [I did not then know of Dumézil (1992), which I recommend – despite its introduction of irritating slips in the writing of Greek.]

6 Thus, he seldom draws on archaeology. For that discipline, see Renfrew (1987), whose attack on Dumézil in Chapter 10 is vitiated by serious misunderstandings (cf. Allen 1993b: 127–128), and Mallory (1989), who is broadly pro-Dumézil.

7 This chapter derives from a much longer study, which is still in progress – hence the somewhat compressed style. [The longer study was never completed as such; this book is the nearest approach!]

8 Encounters, liaisons, relationships – none of the terms apply perfectly to all and only the major hero-female interactions in both stories. 'Relationship' is the most abstract term and has the advantage of including the interaction of hero and first wife, which is more than an encounter. However, the term is too inclusive to be ideal: thus, Odysseus has a relationship with Arete, but this is not one of the five alluded to in the chapter's title and is not included in Table 2.1.

9 The main Homeric passages are as follows: for Circe 10.133–12.36; for Calypso 5.55–268, 7.244–266 and (cattle of the Sun) 12.127–141, 260–425; for the monsters 12.37–126, 153–259, 426 to end; for Nausicaa 5.441–end of 8, 11.333–376, 13.1–187.

10 For each of the four encounters, I give the number(s) of the *adhyāya* (= chapter) in the CE, which is the text translated by van Buitenen.

11 I continue the numbering of similarities where I left off earlier.

12 [Starting from the well-recognized Circe–Calypso similarities, Emily West (2014) shows convincingly that Circe parallels not only Ulūpī but also Bhīma's partner Hiḍimbā, whose story comes in the Pāṇḍavas' first exile (1,139–143).]

13 [For a better comparison, see Ch. 6.]

14 Details of the Urvaśī episode are given in Appx I.6 of the CE (= vol. 4: 1047–53), [tr. Ganguli (1993) I: Book 3: 99–104].

15 Dumézil thinks marriage by concourse developed in the context of chivalry as a public and orderly variant of the more intimate mutual choice mode, and he construes both as F2. As I hope to argue elsewhere, the relationship should be reversed. The mutual choice mode is probably a privatized and democratized variant of the F4+ concourse mode. The point need not be argued here since none of Arjuna's unions is by mutual choice – *pace* Katz (1989: 62), who interprets the Ulūpī union in that way.

16 Since the text presents Arjuna, not the bride's side, as making the gifts, the union does not clearly exemplify the F1 mode, but it relates to the F1 complex of ideas.

17 During the 1980s, Dumézil did in fact propose a number of Homeric analyses, notably a convincing trifunctional analysis of the modes of action used by and against Circe (1982: 166 ff.).

18 Dumézil rightly ascribes the inclusion of the *paiśāca* mode in the Indian codes to the pandits' desire for completeness in their enumerations (1979: 33), though he does not wholly appreciate the force of his remark. Here is a further example of the understandable tendency to overlook the heterogeneous F4 and its representatives. The *Mahābhārata* is widely available in India in the form of comic strips, and 'Arjuna's 12-year exile' is covered in Pai (1989). The 'text' covers all four encounters (quite accurately), but the accompanying map (p. 11) omits the visit to the Southern Ocean (presumably because of the vagueness of the localization).

3

HOMER'S SIMILE

Origin of a simile

The prehistory of the Homeric epics is a topic of perennial fascination.[1] Whenever they reached written form (around 650 BC according to West 1995), all would agree that these works built on an earlier Greek tradition of oral epic expressed in a specialized poetic language. But Indian epic too developed from earlier oral traditions (which in their case cannot have reached written form until at least the fourth century BC), and one wonders what can be learned from a comparative approach to the two traditions. Comparison is possible in many ways and at many levels of generality, but the present chapter is quite narrowly focused. I am concerned, not with Homer or Vyāsa (the mythic sage supposed to have composed the *Mahābhārata*), but with two small portions of the texts ascribed to them. At the heart of this chapter is a four-line simile in the *Odyssey* (5.394–397) and a six-shloka passage from the main narrative in Book 3 of the *Mahābhārata* (39.25–30).[2]

When these two 'focal' passages are compared in isolation, the differences between them are so numerous and the similarities so abstract that one could reasonably regard the passages as unrelated. However, if one looks at the contexts or narrative settings within which these brief passages occur, the picture changes: the similarities are so numerous and various that some explanation is needed. Direct influence of one epic on the other is implausible, and the best explanation is that both stretches of narrative derive from a common origin, which I call the proto-narrative. But if the contexts are related in this way, it becomes far more likely that the focal passages are related similarly. The question then arises whether the focal section of the proto-narrative was a simile or part of the main story. If it was the latter, as I argue, we can learn something about the genesis of one Homeric simile. This is my main aim.

Settings

Where and when the proto-narrative was told is an interesting question, and I suspect that it was where and when the proto-Indo-European (PIE) language was spoken. However, since that issue is separate from the task of demonstrating the existence of the proto-narrative and the presence in it of the ancestor of the focal passages, I need say no more. I start with a brief introduction to the focal passages and their context.

Book 5 of the *Odyssey* narrates Odysseus' journey from Calypso's island of Ogygia to Scheria. The sea passage starts easily but then turns into an ordeal. The hero's raft is wrecked in a storm sent by Poseidon, and it is only after further hardship that he succeeds in landing. However, between the storm and the landing, the ordeal temporarily intermits: Poseidon departs, the sea becomes calm, the shore is close, and the hero feels optimistic. This is where the simile comes: Odysseus, relieved at the sight of land, is compared to children whose father begins to recover after a long, wasting illness.

Book 3 of the *Mahābhārata* narrates the twelve-year exile of the five Pāṇḍava brothers and their shared wife, Draupadī. After many dreary months of exile, Arjuna (the third brother by order of birth but in many ways the central character of the epic) leaves his family and undertakes a journey to Heaven to meet his divine progenitor Indra, King of the Gods. Going north to the Himalayas, he performs austerities in honour of Śiva.[3] The god descends in the guise of a tribal hunter and defeats the hero in hand-to-hand conflict. After reconciliation with Śiva and dealings with certain other gods, Arjuna is carried up to Heaven in Indra's chariot.

The focal passage comes between Arjuna's austerities and his fight with Śiva – in other words, between the two halves of an ordeal. It links the two halves by introducing a group of seers *(ṛṣis)*, who are so worried by Arjuna's austerities (which will give him awesome supernatural powers) that they go to Śiva and express their anxiety. The god reassures them, and they disperse happily. Their happiness, I shall argue, is cognate with that of the children in the Homeric simile.

Starting point

How might one arrive at such a comparison? The search for similarities between epics in different Indo-European (IE) languages, and particularly between the 'oldest' such epics (i.e. the first to be written down), is so obviously a reasonable undertaking that it needs no justification. The problem is how to go about looking for similarities. A priori, they might exist at any level from the tiniest motifs to massive underlying structures, and it is far from obvious what needs comparing with what.

One starting point might be the comparisons undertaken by others. However, although sporadic resemblances have often been noted, systematic comparisons between the two narratives are fewer than might be expected. Dumézil, the dominant figure in IE cultural comparativism, wrote his classic analysis of the *Mahābhārata* (Dumézil 1968 part I) essentially without drawing on the Greek material, and when he did compare Greek and Indian epic traditions (1971 part I), it was with reference to the essentially extra-Homeric figure of Heracles.[4] In spite of the archaisms of the Greek language, he saw Homer as too creative and too innovative to provide much scope for the comparativist (1968: 580–581), and I have not found in his work any reaction to the comparison by Germain (1954: Ch. 1) between the scenes in which Odysseus and Arjuna respectively overcome rival suitors in an archery competition. However, the search for rapprochements continues. For instance, Dubuisson (1991) shows that comparison between Helen of Troy and Sītā in the *Rāmāyaṇa* needs to be pursued, and Jamison (1994) convincingly compares one feature of the abductions of Helen and Draupadī. Baldick (1994), although in my view overambitious, methodologically unsatisfactory, and over-reliant on an untenable adaptation of Dumézil's functional schema, has the merit of at least suggesting the scale and importance of the questions that await detailed investigation.

The present chapter in fact takes off from my earlier one [Ch. 2], summarized in Allen (1993a), which compared two series of females: those that Odysseus encounters in the second half of his return journey from Troy, and those that Arjuna encounters (towards the end of Book 1) when, ostensibly as a penance, he visits the four quarters of India. The comparisons were as follows: Circe ~ Ulūpī (both of them magicians); Sirens, Scylla, and Charybdis ~ Vargā and her four friends (singing temptresses transformed into crocodiles); Calypso ~ Citrāṅgadā (both relatively colourless); Nausicaa ~ Subhadrā; and finally Penelope ~ Draupadī (the heroes' main wives). The rapprochement between Nausicaa and Subhadrā was based on fifteen points of similarity between their respective episodes, and yet the two women also differ profoundly: Subhadrā marries Arjuna, Nausicaa does not marry Odysseus. Nausicaa's amorous desires are encouraged by Athena, and her father proposes the match, but Odysseus avoids any marital or sexual entanglement.

Should one simply say that on this particular point the two epics have diverged? That would be a mistake. One needs to read on from Book 1 to the next passage in which Arjuna leaves his wife and co-husbands, goes on a journey, and encounters a female. This occurs early in Book 3, during his visit to Heaven, where the female in question is the beautiful nymph Urvaśī. Indra suggests a love affair and the nymph is enthusiastic, but the hero avoids entanglement. Thus, Urvaśī resembles Nausicaa in one of the most salient respects in which Subhadrā differs from her.

Given that two rapprochements are in play (Nausicaa ~ Subhadrā and Nausicaa ~ Urvaśī), one immediately asks whether the proto-narrative contained a single female, as in the Greek, or two females, as in the Sanskrit. The Indian females are not only entirely distinct but also well integrated in their respective episodes, and do not look like doublets. Thus, it is easier to envisage Nausicaa as a conflation of two proto-narrative figures than to envisage Subhadrā and Urvaśī as having split between them features deriving from a unitary proto-Nausicaa.

Whatever one thinks about this diachronic issue, the Nausicaa ~ Urvaśī rapprochement suggests a new direction in which to pursue the comparison. Working backwards in the story from the encounter of maiden and hero, one wonders about

TABLE 3.1 Two journeys by Arjuna compared with one journey by Odysseus

	Mbh. 1	*Od.*	*Mbh. 3*
nubile female	Subhadrā	Nausicaa	Urvaśī
her home	Dvārakā	Scheria	Heaven
hero's journey	from Maṇipura	from Ogygia	from forest

the comparability of the journeys that bring the two of them together. Table 3.1 may clarify the matter.

Whereas Arjuna's Book 1 journey from Maṇipura to Dvārakā is devoid of adventure, the journeys containing the focal passages – Ogygia to Scheria, Kāmyaka forest to Heaven – both feature ordeals. Thus a comparison *might* prove rewarding. For my present purpose, namely to elucidate the ailing father simile, it is not necessary to compare the journeys in full, though I hope to do so elsewhere [cf. Ch. 5]. Moreover, since Nausicaa parallels Subhadrā as well as Urvaśī, the Ogygia–Scheria journey to some extent parallels Arjuna's Book 1 journey as well as his Book 3 journey, but since the former contains no equivalent to the focal passages, it is of no further relevance here.

As has already been hinted, the argument falls into two halves. Part I looks at the two journeys as wholes, in terms of the traveller, the episodic structure, a few selected details, and the narratology. Part II compares the focal passages. Figure 3.1 relates to the overall structure of both journey stories but does not attempt to show the relative amounts of text devoted to each episode in each epic. The central stretch 3 represents the focal passages, while 2 and 4 represent the two halves of the ordeal.

§1. The context

The hero

Apart from being central figures in their respective epics, Odysseus and Arjuna have in common the adventure that I took as my starting point: having left their main wives in one place, they have encounters with females in four different areas before returning to the original wife. In addition [Chs 2, 4], towards the end of their lives, they both fight a duel with one of their sons (not the most salient one) and are associated or identified with a horse. Thus, the two journeys we are about to compare are undertaken by heroes whose lives run in parallel at other times.

hero's journey	—	======	≡≡≡≡≡≡	======	—
phases of journey	1	2	3	4	5

FIGURE 3.1 Overall structure of the Sanskrit and Greek journeys

Structure of the journey

Phase 1

For both heroes, the journey starts easily and agreeably (as we shall see), and it is only when the physical distance has largely been traversed that the ordeal begins. As already noted, the ordeal falls into two parts, separated by the Intermission (3) containing the focal passages.

Phase 2

In Part I, the storm progressively destroys Odysseus' raft, and Arjuna's austerities become progressively more severe. Odysseus sees his raft reduced to an unnavigable hulk, then to a single plank, and finally finds himself swimming naked, buoyed up only by Ino's *krēdemnon* (her veil, mantilla, or shawl – 5.373). Arjuna settles down in his Himalayan glade and month by month increases the severity of his dietary regimen and his ascetic or yogic exercises. In month four he lives 'on wind alone' (i.e. undertakes a total fast), standing on tiptoe with arms raised (39.23).

Phase 4

In Part II of the ordeal Odysseus is first thrown against a rough rock and then dragged off it, losing some of his skin in the process and almost drowning. He must still swim on, until he finds the river mouth where he can land. Here he collapses, prostrate and scarcely breathing. As for Arjuna, the hunter (Śiva in disguise) picks a quarrel with him over a wild boar that they both shoot simultaneously, and the duel proceeds from arrows to stones, then to punching and wrestling, until the hero is reduced to an unconscious heap.

From one point of view, Odysseus' ordeal continues as he staggers uphill to pass the night in a heap of leaves and ends only the next afternoon when Nausicaa provides him with food and clothing. However, his sufferings on land can be envisaged as a separate episode from those at sea, and for present purposes, we need not go beyond the landing.

Phase 5

The happy end to his ordeal at sea occurs when Odysseus prays to the unnamed river god, who responds by facilitating his landing (451–453). For Arjuna, the end to his ordeal comes when he is granted a vision of Śiva in his divine form and, after praying to him, receives forgiveness, praise, a supernatural weapon, and instantaneous recovery from the bodily harm he has sustained.

The global comparison can be summed up as in Table 3.2, which suggests titles for the episodes in the hypothetical proto-narrative. The titles will also be used to refer ['tradition-neutrally'] to the corresponding stretches of the attested narratives.

TABLE 3.2 Global comparison between the two journeys

Phase	*Odyssey*	*Mahābhārata*	*Proto-narrative*
1	Seventeen days on raft	yogic journey	Easy Transit
2	the storm	Arjuna's austerities	Ordeal I
3	calm, and simile	seers visit Śiva	Intermission
4	difficult landing	duel with Śiva	Ordeal II
5	helped by River God	helped by Śiva	Happy Ending

The similarities between the two journeys must of course be weighed against the considerable differences. The two heroes themselves contrast in many ways [Ch. 2], and their purposes too are quite different, at least on the surface. Odysseus has for a long time been pining to return to his home in Ithaca, while Arjuna is obeying the instructions of his elder brother Yudhiṣṭhira and seeking divine weapons from Indra (38.13). This is with a view to the ultimate defeat of the Pāṇḍavas' enemies and a return to the royal capital, but it is only in this indirect and very long-term sense that he is setting off on a homeward journey. In fact, whereas Odysseus is returning to his beloved Penelope, Arjuna is leaving his beloved Draupadī in the forest.

During the Easy Transit, Odysseus traverses the ocean more or less naturalistically, steering his well-provisioned raft before the gentle breeze that Calypso provides, while Arjuna speeds overland like the wind itself – his 'Indra-yoga' makes him as fast as thought (38.27). Moreover, the ordeal has a different meaning in the two cases. Although he has been warned by Calypso of the woes in store for him (207), Odysseus is presented as the involuntary victim of Poseidon's anger (occasioned by the blinding of Polyphemus eight years previously). In contrast, Arjuna's austerities are more or less voluntary: though they are oriented to Śiva, they are not inflicted by the god, nor are they a penance. Arjuna addresses himself to Śiva because of the instructions he is given, not only by Yudhiṣṭhira, but also by Indra himself who, disguised as a Brahmin ascetic, meets his son in the Himalayas and encourages him (38.43, 163.13).

Odysseus grasping the inanimate rock against which the wave has flung him is not very like Arjuna seizing the hunter god at the climax of their duel, and Athena's help during Ordeal II has no parallel in the Sanskrit. Odysseus prays to the river god before he collapses on the shore, while Arjuna collapses before he prays to Śiva. Śiva is relevant right from the start of Ordeal I through to the Happy Ending, while Poseidon departs at the end of Ordeal I (381), and nothing obvious connects him with the rock or with the river god, let alone with the ailing father simile. At most, one can reflect that the difficulties of the landing accord with the god's parting words (379), that is, with his hope that the suffering *(kakotês)* still in store for Odysseus will not seem trivial.

In view of all these differences (and more could be added), a sceptic would still have a case for doubting that the two journeys are cognate. I now try to counter such doubts by a closer look at episode A.

The Easy Transit

1 As Odysseus realizes when Calypso first tells him about his voyage, his course lies across a great and fearful stretch of sea that is never crossed by ships (5.175–176), let alone by rafts. As he travels northwards, Arjuna penetrates a ghastly thorny forest, which is inhabited by wild animals and by more or less supernatural beings, but avoided by ordinary humanity (*mānuṣa-varjitam* 39.13–14). So both heroes are travelling unfrequented routes.

2 While Odysseus steers, sleep does not fall upon his eyelids (271) – apparently for the whole period of seventeen days. Arjuna reaches the mountains in a single day but presses on day and night without fatigue (*divā-rātram atandritaḥ* 38.28–29). So both heroes show unusual resistance to exhaustion.

3 Following the instructions of Calypso, Odysseus navigates by keeping his eye on certain stars (272–277), while Arjuna sets off 'sighing and looking upwards' (*ūrdhvam udīkṣya* 38.17) – for no obvious reason. Thus, both heroes gaze at the sky.

4 In the Greek, the end of the Easy Transit is marked by two references to mountains: on the eighteenth day, Odysseus sees the shadowy mountains of Scheria (279), and it is from the mountains of the Solymi [in Lycia?] that Poseidon sees the hero. Arjuna's Easy Transit ends in the Himalayas, and a number of mountains are named (Gandhamādana, Himālaya, Bhṛgu's Peak, Cold Mountain). Moreover, in his prayer to Śiva, Arjuna claims that the great mountain on which he has been stationed is one that the god particularly cherishes (*dayitam* 40.48). Thus, both heroes head for mountains, and both gods are linked with mountains.

5 My final point comes from just before Ordeal I. When Poseidon catches sight of the raft, he gathers the clouds, agitates the sea with his trident, and rouses the winds: 'and darkness *(nux)* rushes down from heaven' (294). When Arjuna enters the forest at the foot of the mountains, heaven resounds with conches and drums. A rain of flowers falls to earth, and a multitude of clouds, spread across the sky, veils the whole area (*chādayām āsa sarvataḥ* 39.14–15). In the Sanskrit, the meteorological phenomena have no obvious narrative function beyond underlining the cosmic significance of the occasion, and the text goes on to emphasize the physical beauty of the mountain glade where Arjuna settles down to his austerities. The Himalayas are of course often wreathed in clouds, but a naturalistic reading does not accord with the drums and rain of flowers, and the clouds and darkness probably constitute a significant similarity.

These five points, though individually tiny, cumulatively add weight to the rapprochement between the two journeys.[5] They are also of interest for their bearing on the question of whether the journey in the proto-narrative was over land or sea – points 3 and 5 *might* be taken to imply the latter. However, I leave that issue open and turn to a rapprochement of a very different character.

The double narration

In Homer, the journey from Ogygia to Scheria is essentially told twice over. So far, reference has been made solely to the third-person account in Book 5, but when Odysseus reaches the palace of Alcinous, the story is told a second time, more briefly and in the first person (7.267–286). The Book 5 version, told as it were directly by Homer, occupies about 200 lines, the Book 7 version, expressed in the words of Odysseus, only about twenty.[6]

Similarly, in the Sanskrit, I have mostly referred to the main account of the journey, as given in Chapters 38–41 and expressed in the third person. But when Arjuna re-joins his wife and brothers and recounts his adventures during his five-year absence, he covers the story a second time, and naturally in the first person. This second telling is shorter than the first, being confined within the single Chapter 163. In terms of shlokas, one might calculate the relative lengths as 128:45.

There are certain complications. The Sanskrit third-person narrative does not purport to relate to Vyāsa in the way the Greek is often taken to relate to Homer: it purports to be told in the first instance by Vaiśaṃpāyana, one of Vyāsa's pupils. More importantly, within the third-person narrative, the Easy Transit is covered twice. Before the ordeal begins, Vaiśaṃpāyana's interlocutor Janamejaya interrupts the narrator to ask for a really full version, and the story starts again (although it actually covers the Easy Transit *less* fully than before). Furthermore, all three accounts differ in detail. However, none of this detracts from the rapprochement: both epics narrate this particular journey at least twice, and the ordering and relative length of the third- and first-person versions are similar.

Apart from the general relationship between the two heroes, the argument for a proto-narrative lying behind the two journeys is thus based on the concordance between three separate types of comparison: the global structure of each story, the details of its opening section, and the way in which it is told.

§2. The focal passages

When Poseidon departs, Athena (intervening on earth for the first time since Odysseus left Troy) calms most of the storm winds, with a view to easing her protégé's arrival in Scheria. However, he continues to be tossed about on the waves for another forty-eight hours, and it is only the third day that brings a windless calm. At this point, he is raised by a wave and sees the land.

> It was like the sudden joy of children when they see their father out of danger; the father has suffered from some disease, has been in torment, has wasted away month after month, victim of some detested power; but then the gods rescue him from distress, and so there is sudden joy; such joy came upon Odysseus now with the sight of land and trees . . . .
>
> *(tr. Shewring)*

In the four lines of the simile proper the reader fleetingly meets four agents or types of agent, two human and two supernatural: (A) the father with the wasting disease, (B) the children (or sons) who move from anxiety to joy, (C) the detested power or hateful spirit *(stugeros daimōn)* who afflicts the father, and (D) the gods *(theoi)* who release him.

It is plausible to imagine, and to imagine Homer's audience imagining, that the children, once they were aware of their father's condition, and perhaps the father himself, tried by prayer or ritual to influence the spirit, the gods, or both (I am not sure whether the difference is significant).

Outside the simile, but within the Intermission, three other agents are relevant: (E) Odysseus, the ship-wrecked mariner who glimpses safety, (F) Poseidon, the god who has afflicted Odysseus and whose waves continue to buffet him even when the god has departed, and (G) Athena, the goddess who begins to help the hero on Poseidon's departure.

The surprising feature of the passage is that Odysseus is compared, not with the ailing father, but with the children. Both parties presumably rejoice at the action of the gods – indeed the *aspasion* of line 397 could allude to the joyful relief of father or children or both, and it would certainly be more logical to compare the lone Odysseus to the lone father (both of them have been suffering physically) rather than to the sons, a collectivity who have only been suffering mentally and, furthermore, wholly or partly on behalf of a third party. Moreover, if the comparison were between Odysseus and the father, the aptness of the simile would be enhanced in that the affliction of the father by the spirit would correspond to the affliction of Odysseus by Poseidon, and the action of the gods would correspond to the assistance provided by Athena. However, the fact remains that it is the joyful relief of the children, implied by the *aspasios* of line 394, that is compared with that of Odysseus. Naturally, the simile, and its relationship to other similes, have come in for their share of commentary from Eustathius and Alexander Pope down to Moulton (1977: 128–130) and Heubeck (1992: 339), but comparison with the Sanskrit introduces so much new material to work on that I doubt if much would be gained by summarizing previous scholarship.

I take up the Sanskrit immediately after the account of the austerities (39.20–24).

> (Shloka 25:) Then all the great seers went to the god who wields the Pināka [a particular bow or spear used by Śiva]. They prostrated themselves before the dark-throated Lord and sought his grace. As a group they informed him of the activity of Phalguna [Arjuna]: 'This mighty Pārtha [Arjuna] has taken up his position on the heights of the Himālayas, and is standing in awesome, almost impossible self-mortification, sending smoke in all directions.[7] O Lord of the Gods, we none of us know what he intends. He is causing us intense anxiety. It would be best if he were stopped.'

The Great Lord said:

> (28:) 'Go quickly, cheerfully and unfatigued to the place from which you came. I know the intention that is fixed in his mind. It is not any desire for Heaven, or for sovereignty, or for long life. I shall accomplish all that he desires this very day.'

Vaiśaṃpāyana said:

> (30:) When the truth-telling seers heard the words of Śiva, they went back with joyful hearts, each to his own ashram.

In the Indian context, the anxiety of the seers is entirely natural, for it commonly happens that ill-intentioned beings perform prodigious feats of austerity and thereby extort from the gods boons that endanger the orderly running of the cosmos. An example is provided by two mutually cooperative demons in 1,201–204. I summarize:

> Deciding to conquer the universe, the brothers Sunda and Upasunda go to the Vindhya Mountains and practise awesome austerities. They live on wind, stand on their toes with arms raised, and heat the mountains so that they belch smoke. The gods fail to distract them, and finally Brahmā, though refusing them immortality, grants them what is almost the equivalent, namely invulnerability to all save each other. They soon conquer the entire universe except for Brahmā's Heaven, slaughtering brahmins and seers, and putting an end to Vedic practices. They are eventually induced to kill each other, and Indra's rule is restored.

There are several comparable demons, such as Rāvaṇa (whose power is based on a thousand years of austerities), Hiraṇyakaśipu, and his descendant Bali. Thus one understands both the potential threat inherent in Arjuna's behaviour and the importance attached to knowing his objective.

The Greek and Sanskrit passages have already been compared as constituting part of the Intermission (the break between two episodes in the ordeal), but in addition the focal passages present a change of scene and a change of personnel. The simile removes us momentarily from the seas off Scheria to an unspecified place on land where a sick man is lying. The Sanskrit passage removes us momentarily from the mountain where Arjuna has settled to the unspecified location where the seers find Śiva. The god tends to live on Mount Kailāsa (also in the Himālayas), but wherever the meeting takes place, Śiva has to fly down (*niṣpapāta* 40.3) in order to fight Arjuna. As regards personnel, the simile introduced no less than four new agents, whereas in the Sanskrit equivalent, the only new participants are the seers. However, the two sets of agents can be matched as follows (A, B, etc., refer back to the previous list of participants in the Greek).

A Arjuna, the hero-ascetic whose unprecedented austerities occasion the seers' anxiety. The normal effect of such austerities is naturally to cause bodily wasting (Shee 1984: 289–292). In this case, in the first-person text (163.16), Arjuna says, 'My vigour *(prāṇa)* did not decline – it was like a miracle.' This can perhaps be regarded as a naturalistic retouch intended to make more plausible Arjuna's good showing in his combat with Śiva, but in any case, the four-month fast can be compared with the slow languishing of the ailing father. The asceticism gives supernatural power, the illness does not, but both involve long-drawn-out bodily stress.

B The seers. The seers start out in mental anguish (*saṃtāpayati naḥ* 39.27) but are told to be cheerful (*samhṛṣṭā* 28), and do indeed disperse in a mood of joy (*prahṛṣṭā-manaso* 30). Their change of mood precisely parallels that of the children, though the Greek leaves the initial unhappiness implicit in the situation and in the double use of *aspasios* 'gladly welcomed, glad'.

One big difference between children and seers lies in their relationship to agent A. The Seers are not Arjuna's children (he has in fact had sons by Draupadī and by three of the females he met during his Penance). On the other hand, Arjuna and seers are linked. As Śiva tells him, in a previous body (*pūrva-dehe* 41.1) he was Nara, companion of Nārāyaṇa; and, as is often stated (e.g. 1,210.5), these were both seers. So Arjuna, though not father to the seers, is in a sense their senior colleague.

C Śiva. The god has not so far afflicted Arjuna, but he is the final cause of the first part of the hero's ordeal and could be described as afflicting him in the second part, even though both we (the readers) and the seers know that all will end well. Śiva's role is in fact ambiguous, for although he will ultimately help Arjuna, in his hunter guise he appears to be a deadly enemy. This hostile and destructive aspect of the Indian god parallels the hateful demon who afflicted the Greek father.

D Śiva again, but this time in his friendly aspect, the aspect implied by the name I use (*śiva* 'auspicious, gracious, kindly'). This is the aspect that he shows to the seers during the interview when he gives them reassurance and a promise, and which he shows to Arjuna after the duel, when he fulfils the promise. I suggested earlier that the happy outcome in the simile could well have followed prayer addressed by the children to the gods. If so, the prayer would correspond to the seers' address to Śiva.

Since the Sanskrit passage is not a miniature scenario segregated within a simile but part of the main story, the distinction between the four roles discussed so far and the remaining three is much less sharp than in the Greek.

E Arjuna again, but whereas in A, Arjuna was seen through the eyes of the fearful seers as someone located elsewhere and potentially dangerous, he is here seen through his own eyes or those of the audience, for both of whom he is present on this earth, familiar and unthreatening. In the Greek, the gap between A and E was that between the ailing father in the simile and Odysseus in the main story, but here it is more subtle. It is between Arjuna seen from Mount Kailāsa (or wherever Śiva is) and Arjuna seen from the perspective of humanity.

F Śiva again, as in C and D, but considered in the wider context of the epic (cf. Scheuer 1982) and beyond it. I do not attempt to discuss the general question of the relationship between Śiva and Poseidon, the two trident-wielders.

G Indra. During his journey, each hero has not only a divine opponent, real or apparent, but also a divine helper, who intervenes once before the Intermission: if Śiva corresponds to Poseidon, it is Indra who here corresponds to Athena. The situation is slightly different from F, since whereas a Poseidon ~ Śiva rapprochement seems to be a promising hypothesis to explore in a number of contexts, this would hardly apply to Athena ~ Indra.[8] However, the latter rapprochement, though doubtless only of limited scope, is not altogether bizarre, for Athena is daughter of Zeus King of the Gods, while Indra is himself King of the Gods. Moreover, in the particular context of the two journeys, there is a sense in which Athena and Zeus taken together correspond to Indra: the return of Odysseus via Scheria is initially decreed by Zeus on the prompting of Athena (start of Book 5), while the journey of Arjuna to Heaven is initially planned and announced by Indra (1,225.9–12).

If we concentrate on the focal passages themselves, the essence of the comparison can be expressed as in Figure 3.2:

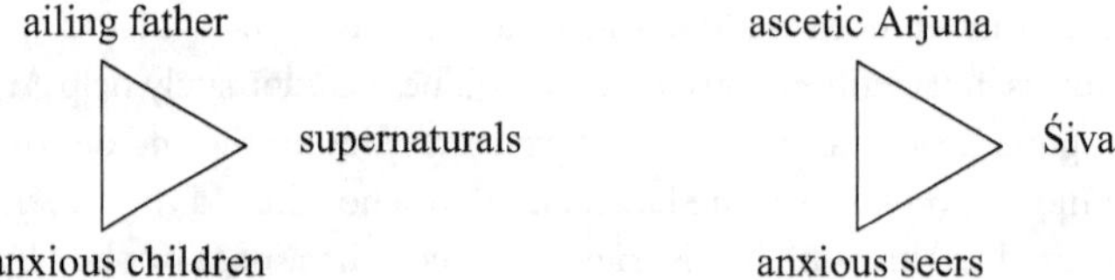

FIGURE 3.2 Triangular relations between major agents in Homer's simile and in the *Mahābhārata* story

Note: The schema omits the protagonists' helpers.

Naturally, considerable differences separate the Greek simile and the Sanskrit story. For instance, as regards the father and Arjuna, to waste from illness and to undertake austerities are only remotely similar: *tapas* is not a *kakotēs*. Similarly, the children rejoice at a cure, or the start of it, while the seers rejoice on receiving information and a promise, well before its fulfilment. Finally, the Greek supernaturals, split into the hateful spirit and the unspecified plural *theoi*, contrast with the unitary named figure of Śiva. Nevertheless, taken together with the similar contexts, the similarities between the focal passages justify postulating a proto-narrative.

Concluding discussion

While it is of course impossible to reconstruct proto-narratives in detail, one can reasonably propose schemata of a certain degree of abstraction: *something* must have existed corresponding to the triangular structure. I suggest three elements as follows:

1 A man who, voluntarily or not, underwent prolonged physical stress, probably involving loss of body weight.
2 A collectivity, of unspecified number and lacking individual names, who were at first worried by the condition of the man but ended up relieved and happy.
3 One or more supernaturals who were implicated in the man's condition but intervened to bring it to an end, thus causing the happiness.

No doubt too, the episode involving these figures was set apart from the main story of the journey, if only in that its location was different from that of the hero's adventures.

But was the episode located within a simile or was it not? Unless further evidence can be adduced (e.g. from wider Greco-Sanskrit comparison, or from other IE traditions), one can work only in probabilities. Moreover, comparative mythologists must beware of repeating the error of those early nineteenth-century comparative linguists who tried to derive non-Indic languages directly from Sanskrit rather than from proto-Indo-European (cf. Dubuisson 1993: 115–120): even if contexts occur where the Sanskrit does seem remarkably conservative, it too will have departed from the proto-narrative in some respects. Nevertheless, I suppose that the focal passage with its triangular structure was originally located in the main story.

One line of argument for this relies on generalities. An epic cannot exist without a main story, but it can exist without lengthy similes, however aesthetically valuable they may be; indeed, such similes seem to be a stylistic feature more typical of Homer and epics influenced by him than of epics in general. Thus, the chances are that they were not characteristic of the proto-narrative but developed within the Greek tradition.

A stronger line of argument depends on the details of the passages. As we noted, the relationship between the simile and the main plot is awkward: Odysseus, whose ordeal is apparently relenting, is compared, not to the sick man who is in the same situation, but to the children, who are in a different one. If the proto-narrative had a simile, either it made the same comparison, in which case the awkwardness has survived for many centuries (which seems implausible), or it made a different and more logical one, in which case the change is inexplicable. If the proto-narrative was more like the Sanskrit, no such problems arise. The Sanskrit story makes excellent sense, and its general form could well be old. I thus envisage the original main plot as including an episode in which the hero underwent an ordeal and aroused in a collectivity anxiety that was relieved by supernatural intervention.

If so, the development of the Greek tradition was roughly as follows. The main plot of the proto-narrative was more elaborate than in Homer, and in particular it distinguished between two females encountered by the hero: with the first (who came last in a series of four consecutive encounters with females) the hero had sexual relations, while with the second he avoided them. A distinction was also made between the two journeys which brought together hero and female. In conflating both the two females and the two journeys, the Greek has tended to simplify the main story line, even if – arguably – the reduction in number of characters and events is counterbalanced by greater complexity in detail and motivation. Much the same can be said of its treatment of the focal passage: it has simplified the main story by extracting the anxious collectivity and relegating them to the simile, so that the main story can concentrate on the hero, his ordeal, and the relevant deities. However, the simplification is counterbalanced by complications of a new kind. Thus, one effect of introducing the simile has been to multiply the number of distinct agents and entities, so that the ailing father becomes distinct from the hero, new supernaturals are involved, and the wasting disease with its cure becomes distinct from the ordeal with its triumphant ending.

This account makes it clear why the simile should focus on the joy of the children rather than of the father. It is because the simile was not originally devised to illustrate the joy of Odysseus but rather represents in compressed and encapsulated form what was originally part of the main story. In that story, the change from anxiety to joy was experienced not by the hero, who was probably elsewhere, but by an anonymous collectivity, and in constructing the simile, Greek tradition has retained the old locus for the emotion.

Notes

1 First published in 1996 as 'Homer's simile, Vyasa's story'.
2 Unless otherwise indicated, all citations are from CE Book 3. The translation by van Buitenen (1975) includes a general introduction.
3 Here and elsewhere I use the name Śiva to cover the variety of theonyms applied to the god.
4 Preciado-Solis (1984), without reference to Dumézil, compares Heracles and Kṛṣṇa, but makes less use of the epic than of the 'later' Purāṇas. Guttal (1994) treats both epics as the products of individual poets, ignoring the traditions to which they belong. See also the thesis of Vielle [published in 1996].
5 And conversely, the global rapprochements support the tiny ones – the circularity is not vicious.
6 I ignore the very brief reference to the journey in Odysseus' first speech to Nausicaa (6.170–172), his subsequent reference to the Book 7 account (12.450–453), and the *oratio obliqua* summary of his travels addressed to Penelope [23.338].
7 *Tapas*, 'austerity, self-mortification', is from the root *tap-* 'heat'. The unprecedented severity of Arjuna's *tapas* is emphasized again in 78.20.
8 One might rather expect Athena ~ Durgā [as in Ch. 8].

4

HERO AND HORSE

Why is a culture the way it is?[1] Because that is how far it has evolved along some worldwide scale(s); because of such and such outside influences or local inventions; because it works; because that is how the human mind has here expressed itself; because it benefits those with power. All the standard 'isms' can help in answering the general question, but they are not exhaustive: there is another approach, seldom aligned with the others, but of long standing, and sometimes of use when others are not.

If one asks why a *language* is the way it is, everyone knows that the answer lies partly in the prehistoric proto-language from which it derives. One cannot automatically transpose from language to culture, but the two have often been transmitted alongside each other, and were so all the more, I suppose, when the world had fewer people in it and more space around them. So, one can often ask of a cultural feature whether it goes back to a reconstructable feature of the proto-culture associated with the proto-language. We all know this in a shadowy way, and do not need a Dumézil to remind us; but the scope and limits of 'language-family based cultural comparativism' still need exploration.

The Greek material

The cultural feature examined here comes from classical Greece. It is widely known that there is more to the story of Odysseus than we learn in Homer. When the hero visits Hades, Tiresias prophesies that his adventures will continue after his return to Ithaca, and accounts of these later events can be found in post-Homeric sources, notably in the 'Epic Cycle' and in the summary of Greek tradition by Apollodorus. But the tradition that Odysseus turned into a horse is mentioned in neither of these sources, and my unsystematic soundings suggest that it is not widely known even among classicists. Grimal (1982) omits it in his entry on Ulysses (Latin for

Odysseus), though it appears under the obscure figure of Hals. Stanford (1963: 88) slips past it in less than a line – naturally enough, since the theme was to have no future in European literature.

Nevertheless, obscure though it is, the tradition certainly existed: the references are assembled in the large encyclopaedias (Schmidt 1897–1909: 692; Wüst 1937: 1993) and discussed in Hartmann (1917). Three authors are cited.

1. The little-known first-century AD mythographer Ptolemaeus Chennos or Hephaestus (*Novae historiae* 4, pp. 194–195 Westermann).

> In Etruria they say that there is a place called the Tower of Hals, and that it is named after an Etruscan sorceress *(pharmakis)* called Hals, who became a handmaiden to Circe but later absconded from her mistress. When Odysseus came to her [Hals], she reportedly turned him into a horse by means of her magical drugs *(eis hippon meteballe tois pharmakois)*, and kept him with her until he grew old and died. From this story one also has a solution to the puzzle in Homer (where he says that) 'death will come to you [Odysseus] from the sea'(*ex halos* – *Od.* 11.134 [the speaker is Tiresias])

Hals ('Sea', cognate with the English word 'salt') is not mentioned by any other classical sources, and was no doubt invented to make sense of the prophecy by Tiresias. Similarly, the reference to old age *(gērasas)* recalls the continuation of the prophecy: Odysseus will die 'overcome with sleek (or comfortable) old age *(gērai)*'. But Tiresias in no way hints at the metamorphosis. If the latter is to be explained, we need a different approach.

2. In the next century, the sceptical philosopher Sextus Empiricus makes two passing references to the tradition when discussing history and truth. In one passage (*Adversus mathematicos* 1.264), he distinguishes between three sorts of narrative, *historia*, *muthos*, and *plasma*, and exemplifies the second ('legend' in the Loeb translation). This he does by citing two stories of births (of poisonous spiders and snakes from the blood of the Titans and of Pegasus from the severed head of the Gorgon) and three stories of transformations (*metaballō* intrans.): of the companions of Diomedes into sea birds, of Odysseus into a horse, and of Hecabe (Priam's wife) into a dog. A few lines later (1.267), discussing contradictions, Sextus cites three versions of the death of Odysseus. One man says that the hero was killed in ignorance by his son Telegonus (the version found in the Epic Cycle and in Apollodorus), another says that he died when a seagull dropped on his head the spike of a poisonous fish (a fragment of Aeschylus says something similar), and yet another says that he was transformed into a horse *(eis hippon metebale tēn morphēn)*.

3. Two centuries later still, Servius was writing his learned Latin commentary on the *Aeneid* and decided to annotate Vergil's reference to Ulysses in 2.44. He mentions (following no very obvious order) the hero's surreptitious exploration of Troy, his family, his death at the hands of Telegonus, his headwear in paintings, and his post-Troy wanderings, which 'Homer made familiar to everyone'. Then he continues:

> Concerning him another story also is told. For when he had returned to Ithaca after his wanderings, it is said that he found Pan in his home. Pan is said to have been born from Penelope and all the suitors, as the very name Pan ['All'] seems to proclaim. However, others say that he was born from Mercury [Latin for Hermes], who had changed into a he-goat before sleeping with Penelope. But Ulysses, after he saw the misshapen child, is said to have departed (again) on his wanderings. He met his death either through old age, or at the hand of his son Telegonus, being killed by the spine of a sea beast. It is said that when he was just setting off, he was changed by Minerva [= Athena] into a horse.
>
> *(in equum mutatus)*

The two versions of the birth of Pan will occupy us later. The spine or sting of the sea beast *(aculeus marinae beluae)* parallels the sharp spine of the marine stingray *(kentron thalassias trugonos)* in Sextus, though (and this is by far the more common story), it is here wielded by Telegonus, not dropped by a bird. But I cite the passage now for its confirmation of the equine metamorphosis.

The three authors say nothing about their sources, but the differences make it unlikely that the later ones draw on the earlier. More likely, all three drew on lost written sources predating Chennos, and one can reasonably imagine that the first such source was recording an oral tradition. But why should anyone *invent* the story that, towards the end of his life, Odysseus turned into a horse? The idea is odd, and those to whom I mention it are surprised. The hero's previous life hardly suggests that this would be a fitting or natural ending, and one casts around for an explanation. Might the tradition have something to do with the Wooden Horse? Or with the hero's victimization by Poseidon, Tamer of Horses? Recent comparativism offers a more promising lead.

Greek–Sanskrit comparison

I have shown elsewhere that in one part of his career Odysseus closely resembles Arjuna, the central hero of the longer of the two Sanskrit epics [Ch. 2]. The comparison is between the second half of Odysseus' return journey from Troy to Ithaca and the journey that Arjuna undertakes as a penance in Book 1 of the *Mahābhārata*. Shortly after his marriage to Draupadī, Arjuna leaves his young wife to visit the four quarters of India, and in each quarter he encounters females, human or non-human, and then he returns to Draupadī. Odysseus encounters successively Circe, the Straits Monsters (i.e. the Sirens, Scylla, and Charybdis), Calypso, and Nausicaa, before he returns to Penelope. The comparison is not merely an abstract one involving four plus one structural elements; in spite of numerous differences between the two epics, the encounters can be matched one-for-one in respect of many details. Such precise matching excludes independent invention and implies a common origin; and for many reasons, this origin or 'proto-narrative' must have been oral. But as Dumézil showed, the proto-Indo-Europeans possessed a typology of marital unions, and the pattern of encounters in the epics, especially in the Sanskrit, conforms quite well to what one might expect of such a typology. The chances are therefore that the proto-narrative was once told in proto-Indo-European [or better, proto-Greco-Aryan].

If the careers of Odysseus and Arjuna are cognate at one point in their respective epics, it by no means follows that they will be cognate at other points. Perhaps the encounters with females represent an exceptionally conservative structure within two narrative traditions that in other respects were subject to all-pervasive innovation and flux. But perhaps not. It is obviously worth looking at other parts of the two careers to see if they too might be cognate. Moreover, in doing so, one can bear in mind a point of logic. Judgements of similarity between episode *x* in one story and episode *X* in another are apt to seem methodologically suspect: there will always be differences between the two stories, and the weighing of similarities against differences will always involve subjective judgement. But suppose *x* belongs to a biography that includes episodes or characters *d*, *e*, *f*, *g*, *h*, and *X* belongs in one including *D*, *E*, *F*, *G*, *H*, and similarities *d*–*D* and so forth have already been established. In that case similarities between *x* and *X* can be judged more charitably, less sceptically.

So, given that Odysseus becomes a horse, does Arjuna? Certainly not: neither he nor any of his brothers are ever transformed into animals. But towards the end of his career, Arjuna does have an important relationship with a horse, in Book 14 of the epic. Before we come to the details, here is the context.

The *Mahābhārata* centres on the conflict between two branches of a royal dynasty. The Goodies are the five Pāṇḍava brothers, of whom Arjuna is the third by age. Although it is he who wins Princess Draupadī, she is married polyandrously to all of them. The Pāṇḍavas are banished and disinherited, but Kṛṣṇa helps them win a great eighteen-day war, and the eldest, Yudhiṣṭhira, takes the throne. Now comes Book 14, 'The Book of the Horse Sacrifice' [see Ganguli IV]. The remaining four books are relatively brief, and narrate the deaths of the main survivors from the Great War. The epic ends with the deaths of the Pāṇḍavas themselves, as they journey towards the Himalayas and Heaven.

The Horse Sacrifice *(aśvamedha)* is the highest of the royal rituals and establishes the cosmic supremacy of a king. It is a lengthy and elaborate undertaking, lasting more than a year and including a three-day *soma* offering. The details are given in the Vedic texts called the Brāhmaṇas, composed (as we know them) before 500 BC; I shall refer exclusively to the *Śatapatha Brāhmaṇa*. Naturally the epic, which was written down in the centuries surrounding 'year 0', gives little space to ritual niceties, but it states repeatedly that the performance conformed with the scriptures.[2]

Roughly speaking, the ritual can be divided into two parts. In the first, after some preliminaries, a specially selected stallion is released near the capital and wanders at will across the face of India. During the following year, it is accompanied by warriors, whose job is to prevent any interference with it. Assuming none of the challengers are successful, the second part of the ritual takes place back in the capital, in the presence of a large gathering. The horse is sacrificed together with other victims, and (as we shall see) the queens take an active part in the performance.

Let us return to Book 14. A few months after the Great War, Yudhiṣṭhira is still in despair both over the death of his beloved classificatory grandfather Bhīṣma and over his own sins. The sage Vyāsa proposes that the sins be annulled by performance of a Horse Sacrifice. Vast wealth will be needed, and an expedition sets off to obtain it from the Himalayas. Meanwhile, Arjuna's grandson Parikṣit, who is stillborn, is resuscitated by Kṛṣṇa.

When the Himalayan party returns, Arjuna is selected to accompany the horse. While the animal circumambulates India (clockwise, starting in the north), Arjuna has to defeat a number of challengers, his most interesting conflict taking place in the east, in Maṇipura. In Book 1, Arjuna had followed a similar route, going first to the north, where he cohabited with the serpent maiden Ulūpī, then to Maṇipura, where he married Princess Citrāṅgadā. Ulūpī's son had died in the Great War, but Citrāṅgadā's son Babhruvāhana had remained uninvolved and was now king of Maṇipura. Arjuna insists that his son, having been born a warrior, is duty-bound to fight off any encroacher. Ulūpī also appears and urges her stepson to fight.

In the ensuing duel, Arjuna is shot with an arrow and collapses. Shattered by his parricide, the son faints. Citrāṅgadā hears the news and hastens to the scene. On recovering, Babhruvāhana laments his deed, but Ulūpī summons up a magic stone which, placed on Arjuna's chest, revives him. She now explains. During the Great War, Arjuna had used dishonest means to kill Bhīṣma and had been cursed for it. Defeat by his son would lift the curse, and that was why she had incited the duel. Arjuna issues invitations for the Horse Sacrifice and continues his mission.

The horse returns safely to the capital. Three hundred animal victims are tied to sacrificial stakes, and Draupadī is put beside the suffocated stallion. The latter is dissected and offered into the fire, whose smoke purifies the Pāṇḍavas. Largesse is distributed to all present on an enormous scale, and the concourse disperses.

The contrast between the two epic traditions is enormous. The Greek material bearing on the horse is so scanty that I have cited it all, while the Sanskrit is so copious that I have had to summarize ruthlessly (Book 14 has some 2,900 shlokas – say 6,000 lines). Together with a difference in length goes a difference in narrative integration. The Greek gives no hint as to *why* Odysseus was turned into a horse: the motives of Hals are as obscure as those of Athena. In contrast, Arjuna's dealings with the horse make perfect sense. The ritual is a well-established institution; its performance at this point in the epic is well justified; the reasons why Arjuna should accompany the animal are detailed by Vyāsa (71.14–18).[3] To omit the Horse Sacrifice would be to leave the triumph of the Goodies incomplete.

Another difference is that Arjuna is never explicitly identified with the horse. His job is simply to follow it in his chariot and protect it from interference. Nevertheless, his association with the animal is close: a challenge to it is a challenge to himself. When the expedition sets out, crowds gather to gaze at horse and follower *(haya* and *hayasāriṇa)*, shouting 'there goes the son of Kuntī and the glorious horse'

(72.10, 12). When Babhruvāhana invites him into the city, Arjuna declines: his ritual obligation means that he cannot leave the horse even for one night (82.30–31). When the party returns, the proximity of man and horse is again emphasized (89.16).

The association is more than a matter of protection and proximity. As was noted, the second part of the ritual involves the royal wives. The ritual texts list four of them, with separate titles and roles, ranging from chief queen to low-caste wife. The group intervene at a number of points (see Dumont 1927, [also Dumézil 1974: 234–229, 1975: 215–219]), for instance by anointing the horse before it is suffocated, but the most interesting episode occurs after the death. The chief queen lies beside the carcass, a covering is placed over them, and the queen simulates copulation.

Although the epic says rather little about the role of the queens, two points are significant. First, after the sacrifice of the various victims according to the scriptures, the priests cause Draupadī to 'lie beside' the horse (*upa-saṃveśayan* 91.2, cf. *saṃviś-*'approach, cohabit with'). Second, although nothing is said of the other wives' involvement in ritual, they are certainly present. After Arjuna's duel with his son, the two wives are explicitly invited (82.24); when they reach the capital, they meet Subhadrā, who is already there (90.2), and after the ritual is over, the three of them are included in a list of the ladies at court (15,1.21).

In the capital, the 'closeness' of Arjuna and horse takes on a new dimension. When the horse is roaming 'the whole earth' (89.18), the symbolism evidently concerns territorial dominion. But there is more to kingship than military supremacy: a traditional king has cosmic links with a chthonic female principle, and more mundanely, he also has to produce an heir. It is therefore natural that Draupadī, as chief queen, should have a part to play in the ritual, but the interesting point is that Arjuna's conjugal role is here taken on by the horse, albeit post mortem. Draupadī is a dutiful wife, and obviously her ritual act with the horse has nothing to do with adultery. She is miming intercourse with a substitute for Arjuna, who is himself the central and most representative of the Pāṇḍavas.[4]

To sum up so far, Odysseus is physically transformed into a horse, while Arjuna is symbolically associated with one, and the reason for the involvement of horses in the two biographies is that something similar was present in the proto-narrative from which they both derive. My wording is vague, but that is deliberate; for although one can imagine the proto-narrative as closer to the well-integrated Sanskrit than to the scrappy Greek, it would be premature to attempt any precise reconstruction. Instead, I turn to some of the other issues arising from the rapprochement.

Related issues

One puzzle concerns the consequences of the ritual intercourse. One might expect a successful Horse Sacrifice to result in offspring, as indeed the Brāhmaṇa implies (1.9.9).[5] However, Draupadī's five children, one born from each husband, were all killed at the end of the Great War, and neither she nor the husbands produce any more. Yet the line does not die out. For although Abhimanyu, the son of Arjuna and Subhadrā, was also killed in the war, he left his wife pregnant with Parikṣit; and Parikṣit, as already noted, was resuscitated by Kṛṣṇa. But Kṛṣṇa was present at the right moment explicitly because he had been invited for the Horse Sacrifice (51.46, 65.2). Thus, although the survival of the dynasty is ensured *before* the ritual copulation, the two events are not unconnected.

A more important objection to my argument might be that in carrying out her role in the sacrifice, Draupadī is acting not, or not primarily, as the wife of Arjuna, but as the chief queen of King Yudhiṣṭhira, for whom the ceremony is being held. The relation between the two brothers is a fundamental and far-reaching problem which I hope to discuss elsewhere [see Allen 1999a], but one point is very clear. To all intents and purposes, Yudhiṣṭhira has only the one wife Draupadī, while Arjuna does indeed have four. Moreover, unlike his elder brother, Arjuna acquired them by his own acts (he won Draupadī in an archery contest, and she always loves him best). Thus, it is easy to envisage Arjuna as being in some sense the 'real' royal husband of Draupadī, even if Yudhiṣṭhira is the official one. This line of thought lessens the conceptual gap between Arjuna, who is not a king, and Odysseus, who is one (he has of course no elder brother).

The rapprochement can be further strengthened by moving from Odysseus-as-horse to the father–son conflict with which Sextus and Servius associate it. The killing of Telegonus is well attested: in his invaluable notes to Apollodorus, Frazer (1921 II: 303) collected fifteen classical references, and the story has not infrequently been related (as by Katz 1989: 200) to other father–son duels such as Sohrab–Rustam or Cúchullain–Conlaí, as well as to Arjuna–Babhruvāhana. The picture is enriched by another Greek story (recorded by Parthenius *Er. Path.* 3), in which it is the father who kills the son: Odysseus kills Euryalus, his son by Euippe (from *hippos* horse, which is suggestive). Altogether, there must be material for a book-length study, but having previously used the story in arguing for the Calypso–Citrāṅgadā homology, I look at it here only for its bearing on the horse. The relation between the father–son duel and the equine theme varies. Sextus treats the two as alternatives, with a third added for good measure. Servius juxtaposes them but without explaining exactly how he sees the link. The Sanskrit situates the duel as a short episode within the year-long association of hero and horse, which of course presupposes that the duel is not fatal. But in all three cases the two themes are somehow related.

At first sight, Chennos is an exception, since he does not refer to a duel. But the matter is not so simple. Hals starts off as a servant (perhaps a pupil?) of Circe, and she resembles her mistress in being a magician who uses drugs to transform humans into animals, as Circe does in the *Odyssey*. In that sense, she is a doublet of Circe. But Circe, who is regularly given as the mother of Telegonus, is certainly involved in the story of the duel. In Apollodorus [*Epit.* 7.36], it is when she tells her son about his father that he sails for Ithaca, and according to an *Odyssey* scholion (to 11.134) she procures the weapon he uses. Moreover, there are independent grounds for seeing Circe as cognate with Ulūpī, and Ulūpī is several times mentioned as Babhruvāhana's 'mother' in a classificatory sense (she is of course his stepmother), and it is she who engineers the duel. Again, according to the commentary on Lycophron's *Alexandria* (line 805), after Odysseus had been killed by Telegonus, Circe resurrected him with her drugs *(pharmakois)* – compare Ulūpī's resuscitation of Arjuna. Thus, in connecting the equine metamorphosis with Circe, Chennos is indirectly connecting it with the duel.

Servius raises many interesting issues on which I must be very brief:

1 *Wanderings*. Odysseus' return journey from Troy was indeed a matter of wandering *(errores)*, since he was largely at the mercy of wind and wave; but a priori his subsequent departure from Ithaca could have been direct to a fixed destination. Servius' use of the word *errores* here too might perhaps recall the wandering of the sacrificial horse, even if he had omitted the last sentence of his annotation.
2 *Helper deity*. The attribution of the transformation to Athena is natural, given her long-standing association with the hero and her previous transformations of him, for instance into a beggar and back. But in general, Athena as helper deity to the hero corresponds to the god-on-earth Kṛṣṇa, and Kṛṣṇa's role in Book 14 is extensive. He is the first to suggest to Yudhiṣṭhira the idea of a sacrifice (2.3), then, after giving Arjuna a lengthy religious discourse and after visiting his own home town of Dvārakā, he resuscitates Parikṣit, and finally, he is offered the leading role in the Horse Sacrifice (70.21), though he politely declines. The Athena–Kṛṣṇa relationship is potentially a vast topic.
3 *Totality*. According to Servius' first variant, Pan was begotten by all the suitors. Though this accords poorly with the Homeric portrait of the faithful Penelope, similar traditions are known from other sources, and one might wonder if they are somehow related to Draupadī's polyandry. However, I consider here only the folk etymology of the child's name: *pan* is the neuter of *pas* 'all'. The link between Pan and totality is made in a different form in the *Homeric Hymn to Pan* [line 47; Crudden 2001: 84]: the gods called the boy Pan because he delighted the hearts of all of them (*pasin*, the dative plural). But Draupadī's five sons collectively incarnate the Viśvedevas, the 'All-gods' (*viśva* 'all, every, whole, universal').
4 *Goats*. According to Servius' second variant, Pan was begotten by Hermes in the form of a goat. Ignoring Hermes, I focus on the collocation goat-horse. Penelope first has a lover who takes the form of a goat, then a husband who is given the form of a horse; and the Indian ritual involves the same sequence of animals.

As is regularly mentioned (e.g. by Kane 1941 II: 1228), the Indian Horse Sacrifice is first referred to, some centuries before the Brāhmaṇas, in two Vedic hymns (*RV* 1.162–163), which are in fact used in the ritual, and in exalting the horse, both hymns associate it with a he-goat. The first describes a procession: 'This goat for all the gods (the adjective *viśvadevya* relates it to Viśvedeva) is led forward with the racehorse as the share for Pūṣan' (O'Flaherty 1981: 89–90). The goat is the preliminary sacrificial victim, the *Voropfer* (Geldner 1951 I: 222), and when the procession circles three times leading the horse, the goat goes first, 'announcing the sacrifice to the gods'. The second hymn confirms this picture: 'The racehorse has come to the slaughter, pondering with his heart turned to the gods. The goat, his kin, is led in front; behind come the poets, the singers' (O'Flaherty 1981: 88).

The Brāhmaṇa also associates the two animals, albeit less straightforwardly. To the central stake is bound 'the horse, a hornless he-goat and a gayal (?)', and around the horse are tied a whole set of he-goats (2.2.1–10). The horse himself is dedicated to Prajāpati (here treated as the supreme deity), and the 'body-encirclers' are each dedicated to some other god.

The *Mahābhārata* account mentions only bulls and 'aquatic animals' (90.33) and ignores goats, as does the account of the ritual in the *Rāmāyaṇa* (1,13.24). Nevertheless, I suppose that the successive appearance of goat and horse in the biography of Penelope is related to the successive sacrifice of goat and horse in the Indian ritual and that the animals appeared in that order in the proto-narrative.

Two sacrifices

This essay has explored only a selection of the post-Homeric texts and has done so only selectively; but for my final comparison, I return to Homer (11.119–134). Tiresias does not mention horses, but he does mention *two* sacrifices. After killing the suitors, Odysseus is to set out with an oar over his shoulder and travel until he comes among people who know nothing of sea, salt, ships, or oars. When he meets someone who mistakes the oar for a winnowing fan, he is to plant it in the earth and sacrifice a ram, bull, and boar to Poseidon. Then he is to return home and sacrifice sacred hecatombs to the gods, to all of them in sequence *(pasi mal' hexeiēs)*.

The two sacrifices stand in contrast. The first takes place far from home among strangers, it is addressed solely to Poseidon, and it is relatively modest in scale – three victims, and presumably no guests. The second is at home (on the smallish sea-girt island of Ithaca), it is addressed to all the gods (including Poseidon again?), one after another – *hexeiēs* implies a listing, and it is on a large scale, for a *hekatombē* is 'a great public sacrifice'. Even in Homer, as the dictionaries tell us, the number and nature of the victims do not always accord with the etymology (*hekaton* 'hundred', *bous* 'ox'), but the connotations of the word, especially in the plural, are clear enough.

In Book 14, Arjuna is essentially involved in two and only two sacrifices. The second we already know about: the Horse Sacrifice is celebrated in the capital on a quasi-cosmic scale, as regards both human guests and deities. For although Prajāpati is central, the Brāhmaṇa makes it clear that he does not stand alone; he had wanted to keep the ritual for himself, but the other gods demanded their share (2.1.1): 'The horse is the nobility, and the other animals are the peasantry . . . the horse alone belongs to Prajāpati, and the others are sacred to the gods' (2.2.15).

'Seeing that the horse is sacred to Prajāpati, why is it sprinkled for other gods too?' asks the text. It is because all the gods are concerned in the sacrifice (1.2.9). 'The horse is slaughtered for all the deities' (3.4.1). But the pantheon is not honoured simply as an anonymous collectivity. When the omenta are offered up to the gods, the sacrificer 'gratifies them deity after deity (*yathā-devatam* [is repeated six times])' (5.3.1–6). Sometimes the text gives a sequence of divine names: 'Hail to A . . ., Hail to B . . .' (1.8.2–8), or 'Such and such a goat to A . . ., such and such to B . . .' (2.2.3–9).

Arjuna's earlier sacrifice takes place during the Himalayan expedition. The capital is in the plains, and to reach its goal, the party must traverse 'lakes, rivers, forests, and groves' (63.6), which implies a considerable distance; moreover, their northward journey takes them away from the sea. The expedition is sizeable, but compared with the Horse Sacrifice it is modest in scale and involves no guests. Above all, it is directed not to all the gods, but primarily to Śiva, and only secondarily to his associates. The gold was originally buried by a king who obtained it by obeying instructions to go to the mountains and propitiate Śiva (8.12–31); Bhīma urges that they do likewise (62.13) and so they do (64.1–4). Offerings are also made to Śiva's friend Kubera and to other supernaturals, but the expedition is certainly oriented primarily to Śiva, to whom alone offerings are made before both legs of the journey (62.18–19; 64.18). But apart from anything else (it is another vast topic [cf. Ch. 3]), Śiva and Poseidon are both characteristically trident-bearers.

Thus the argument is that Poseidon's sacrifice : hecatomb :: Śiva's sacrifice : Horse Sacrifice.

Concluding discussion

When comparing two things, say two stories, the easiest procedure is to take one as starting point and present the other as diverging from it. Since the Sanskrit epic tradition is copious and coherent, and the area of Greek tradition studied here is scrappy and incoherent, one is tempted to take the Sanskrit as starting point. Diachronically speaking, this is obviously nonsense. There is no possibility that the *Mahābhārata* lies behind the Greek, and if detailed similarities exist, it must be because both descend from a third body of narrative. The latter must have contained some linkage between proto-hero and horse, and presumably the story was indeed more similar to the Horse Sacrifice than to the unmotivated metamorphosis in the Greek.

Comparativists will not be surprised at this conclusion, which relates to a long-running debate: royal horse sacrifice was first postulated as a PIE institution by Schröder (1927). Schröder's brief paper is often referred to, for instance by Dumézil (1975: 216–217) and by O'Flaherty (1980: 338), but what exactly can be reconstructed remains controversial (Polomé 1994a, 1994b; Sergent 1995: 365). The rapprochement presented here provides new material for this already quite complex debate.

What is perhaps more surprising is that the sources used in the rapprochement are so late by Greco-Roman standards. I suppose the lateness is due partly to the loss of earlier writings; but if one is surprised, it is probably more because scholarship has tended to underestimate both the endurance of oral tradition and its ability to bypass the earliest texts so as to surface in later ones. But how could the bypass be demonstrated except by language-family based comparativism?

Notes

1 First published in 1997 as 'Why did Odysseus become a horse?'
2 A historical study of the ritual could include the traces of it identified by Biardeau (1989: 166–241) in contemporary Tamil villages.
3 All *Mahābhārata* references, unless otherwise noted, are to CE Book 14.
4 In the *Harivaṃśa*, the 'appendix' to the *Mahābhārata*, during the Horse Sacrifice held by Arjuna's great-grandson, Indra substitutes himself for the stallion, partly in order to enjoy the beautiful chief wife (118.10 ff.). I cite this Indra-horse link as 'harmonizing' with the Arjuna-horse link.
5 All references to the *Śatapatha Brāhmaṇa* are to Book 13.

5

YOGA

Everyone agrees that a historical understanding of the Sanskrit language is impossible without the framework provided by Indo-European (IE) comparative linguistics, but when we turn to Sanskritic *culture*, the picture is less clear.[1] Ever since Sir William Jones, attempts have been made to develop a field of study that might be called IE cultural comparativism, and to situate Hinduism within it, but how far have we got? Compared with linguists, students of culture have achieved relatively little consensus among themselves and even less acceptance by others. The most eminent IE cultural comparativist of recent times has been Georges Dumézil, but in spite of books like Blaive (1995) and Sergent (1997), his work remains relatively little known and definitely controversial. No wonder so many accounts of Indian religion, if they deal with the IE dimension at all, do so in a couple of paragraphs on the Vedas or in passing footnotes.

Clearly the field is a risky one. Since the death of Dumézil in 1986, I wonder if there is any individual equipped with sufficient cultural and linguistic knowledge to tackle the whole field with confidence – certainly not myself. Even in the best case, the comparativist will seldom know as much about any field he touches on as does the specialist in that field. One can easily go astray and waste everyone's time. Nevertheless, for all the risks, anthropology is meant to be a comparative discipline, and I have found the challenge irresistible. What can we learn about Hindu culture and religion by looking at it within an IE framework?

To explore this question, over the last ten years, I have been pursuing two interlinked ideas: one is that we need to expand Dumézil's notion of the IE trifunctional ideology by recognizing a bifid fourth function that 'brackets' the classical three, so that the ideology is most simply and typically manifested in five-element lists and structures. On the basis of this idea, previous papers have examined materials from Nuristan and from early Roman pseudo-history (Allen 1991, 1996a). The functions may possibly be relevant to some of the five-element lists that will be encountered later, but I shall say no more about them here.

The second idea (e.g. Ch. 2, Allen 2000d) is that much can be learned by comparing Sanskrit and Greek epic, more precisely the *Mahābhārata* and the *Odyssey*. For the decision to focus on the *Mahābhārata*, I am indebted particularly to Biardeau (e.g. 1981), who showed the centrality of that vast and astonishing work for an anthropological understanding of classical Hinduism, and to Dumézil, who convinced me that many of the themes and structures of the 'Fifth Veda' were rooted in the IE heritage. From the comparativist point of view adopted here, the processes by which and the dates at which different parts of the epic were written down (say between 300 BC and 400 AD) are not the central questions. The written texts, in greater or lesser degree, derive their narrative content from an oral heritage to which comparison may give access. Working from reconstructed past towards attested present, the comparativist can envisage a body of proto-Indo-European (PIE) or early IE narrative material being transmitted orally throughout the Indo-Iranian period, bypassing the Vedas proper, and only relatively recently reaching the form in which we now read it.

The Greek epic is a topic on which Dumézil himself worked relatively little, believing that the Homeric narratives (first given written form in the eighth–seventh century BC) had already largely escaped the straitjacket of IE ideology. Here, as over the number of functions, I disagree with the great scholar. As I have argued elsewhere, in parts of their careers, Arjuna and Odysseus show similarities so numerous and detailed that they must be cognate figures, sharing an origin in the proto-hero of an oral proto-narrative. For present purposes, many questions about this proto-narrative can be left unanswered. Was it told in prose or in verse or in a mixture of the two? Was it told in the Urheimat or original homeland (whatever the location and date of that logically necessary zone of space-time), or did it diffuse somewhat after the dispersal began? It does not matter. The similarities cannot be explained either by chance, or by Jungian archetypes, or by diffusion of the Homeric epics from Greece to India, and if they are as striking as I think, then one way or another, they must be due to common origin in a proto-narrative.

I can now explain the aim of this chapter. While looking for similarities between the plots of the two epics, I found that, roughly speaking, Books 5–6 of the *Odyssey* correspond to part of Book 3 of the *Mahābhārata*. In both cases, the hero undertakes a journey. Among much else, Book 3 describes the journey of Arjuna from the Gangetic forests to the Himalayas (the abode of the gods), and then by celestial chariot to the heavenly city of his father Indra, King of the Gods. Books 5–6 of the *Odyssey* describe the journey of Odysseus from Calypso's isle of Ogygia to the capital of the blissful land of Scheria. Not only are the two heroes cognate, so are the two journeys [Ch. 3]; in other words, I proposed, they reflect a single episode in the proto-narrative. But Arjuna's journey is in several senses a yogic undertaking – for a start, the hero is explicitly 'yoked to Indra's yoga'.

In ancient Greece, one finds hints of yoga-like religiosity, especially in Pythagoreanism, but there is nothing obviously yogic or Pythagorean about Odysseus' journey.[2] So if both stories descend from a proto-narrative, there are two possibilities: *either* the proto-journey was like the Greek and contained nothing relating to yoga, in which case the yogic aspect of the Sanskrit story was an innovation that developed in the Indian branch of the tradition, *or* the proto-journey was like the Sanskrit and was quasi-yogic or proto-yogic in character, in which case Greek epic tradition largely or wholly eliminated that aspect of the story. I shall argue for the second scenario, claiming both that the proto-narrative shared certain features with yoga, and also that the telling of such a story makes it likely that there already existed ritual practices ancestral to yoga.

I shall not spend long discussing views on the history of yoga based on other methods of study. In brief, the fundamental philosophical and didactic text, the sūtras or aphorisms of Patañjali, is often dated to around the third century AD (though opinions vary). However, the roots of yoga lie much further back, and most accounts of it mention the references to yoga as such, and to related ideas, in the Upaniṣads (from around 500 BC). Some suppose that yoga was elaborated around that period, perhaps on the basis of quasi-scientific medical ideas as found in Āyurveda (Filliozat 1991: 299–303), while others have wished to go further back still, either rather vaguely to IE or Asiatic shamanism, or more precisely to Mohenjo-Daro, to the pre-Aryan (i.e. PIE) Indus Valley civilization (McEvilley 1981). A complex institution like yoga may draw on multiple roots, and I do not wish to oversimplify. However, I argue that some significant and precisely identifiable features of yoga go back to the culture of those who told the proto-narrative – who, though I do not argue the point here, may well have been PIE speakers.

Structure of the argument

Essentially I limit myself to four main sources: the two epic narratives, Patañjali plus commentaries, and the *Śvetāśvatara Upaniṣad*. No doubt, in a fuller study, other Sanskrit texts could be brought into the argument. Nothing is more confusing than trying to compare more than two texts at once, so all the six comparisons will be binary (cf. Figure 5.1).

To justify the notion of a proto-journey, I have first to compare the two epics. To show in what sense Arjuna's journey is yogic, I concentrate next on the Sanskrit

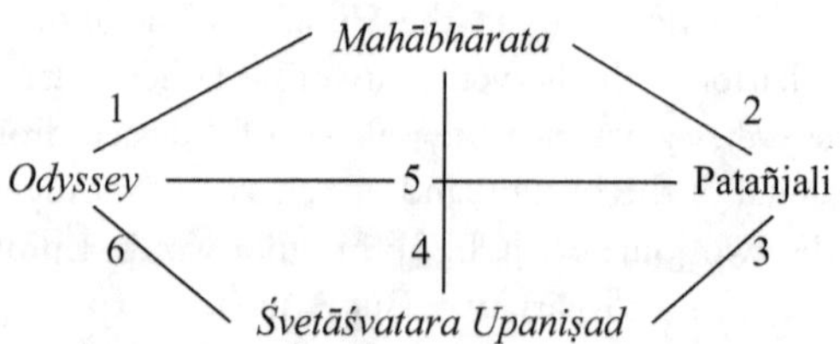

FIGURE 5.1 Sequence of binary comparisons made in this chapter

texts, comparing the epic with Patañjali, and then, moving backwards within the yoga tradition, comparing Patañjali with the Upaniṣad and the latter with the *Mahābhārata*. Only then can we return to the Greek and compare the *Odyssey* first to the later and then to the earlier of the philosophico-ritual texts.

§1. Odyssey – Mahābhārata

I begin by contextualizing the two epic journeys and providing rapid overviews.

Mahābhārata

As is well known, the main plot recounts the conflict between Pāṇḍavas (roughly, the Goodies) and Kauravas (the Baddies). Arjuna is by birth the middle of the five Pāṇḍava brothers, and in many ways the central character of the epic. Although all the brothers have divine fathers, Arjuna's is Indra, King of the Gods. In Book 3, the Kauravas have succeeded in exiling the Pāṇḍavas to the jungle for twelve years, and it is now that Vyāsa the sage arrives with instructions for Arjuna to undertake his journey: the hero will thereby acquire the weapons he needs in order to defeat the Kauravas. He is to receive them from a series of deities culminating in Indra himself.[3]

Arjuna leaves his four brothers and Draupadī and sets out on his journey. First, he goes to the Himalayas and practises severe austerities *(tapas)* directed to Śiva. The great sages are worried and visit the god. Śiva descends to earth, takes the form of a mountain-dwelling tribal hunter, and picks a quarrel with Arjuna. After a duel, Arjuna receives a weapon from the god. The four Lokapālas (deities of the cardinal points) come to visit him, and three of them give him further weapons. Indra now sends his own chariot to take the hero up to heaven. After various adventures, Arjuna receives a thunderbolt. He returns to his brothers, and eventually the Pāṇḍavas complete their exile, defeat the Kauravas, and regain the throne that had once been their father's.

Odyssey

After ensuring the fall of Troy by means of the Wooden Horse, Odysseus sets off for Ithaca. He meets with various delays, and ten years later is still languishing on Ogygia. Athena speaks up for him in the Council of the Gods, and Hermes is sent to start him on the next leg of his return journey, a solo voyage by raft. It is fated that on reaching Scheria he will be safe, but the transit is far from easy. Poseidon, still angry at the blinding of his son Polyphemus, raises a storm that wrecks the raft, and it is with great difficulty, helped by a kindly but unnamed river god, that the hero at last staggers ashore, naked and exhausted. After a night sleeping in a thicket, he accosts princess Nausicaa, daughter of Alcinous king of Scheria, who guides him to the royal city.

At first sight, Arjuna's journey by land and air will probably appear unrelated to Odysseus' journey by sea and land, but I shall now quickly work through the two stories and list twenty-three points of similarity, summarizing a longer analysis still in draft.[4] The rapprochements vary in scale from the very macroscopic (such as the first) to quite small details of the narrative, but such variation has no obvious bearing on the validity of the comparisons.

1 *Larger journey*. For both heroes, as we know, the transit in question is part of a much longer round trip. The Pāṇḍavas set off from their royal capital before their exile and will return there. Odysseus sets off from Ithaca before the Trojan War and will likewise return.
2 *Stasis*. Before the Transit, both heroes are as it were becalmed. The Pāṇḍavas have spent thirteen months in Dvaita forest and show no signs of moving. Odysseus has spent seven years in Ogygia, and Calypso hopes to keep him there indefinitely.
3 *Depression*. The Pāṇḍavas are deeply depressed and lament their situation at length. Odysseus spends his days weeping on the shore of Ogygia.
4 *Visitor with instructions*. Vyāsa arrives unexpectedly (3,37.20) with instructions for the whole party to move on and for Arjuna himself to go to heaven. Hermes arrives unexpectedly with Zeus' instructions for Odysseus to depart (5.77).[5]
5 *Intermediary*. Neither visitor speaks directly to the hero. Vyāsa deals only with Yudhiṣṭhira (Arjuna's eldest brother), Hermes only with Calypso.
6 *Female's farewell*. Draupadī and Calypso both make touching good-bye speeches.
7 *Uneventful start*. Arjuna goes north to the Himalayas, travelling alone and fast until he is well into the mountains. Odysseus sails alone before a favourable wind for seventeen days until he comes in sight of Scheria.
8 *Unwearied*. Arjuna travels night and day without fatigue. Odysseus does not sleep for the seventeen days.
9 *A complex ordeal* (we shall come back to its detailed structure later). Arjuna undertakes four months *tapas*. Following a change of scene while the sages visit Śiva, the story returns to earth for the fight, after which god and hero are reconciled. As for Odysseus, his raft is progressively destroyed by the storm. Then comes a lull. The hero's sufferings resume as he faces the problems of landing, until his final success at the river mouth.
10 *Emaciation*. Though most manuscripts ignore it, some refer, reasonably enough, to Arjuna's emaciation following the *tapas*. The sages worry, but the god reassures them, and they rejoice. During the lull, Odysseus rejoices, and his joy is compared to that of a group of sons worried about their father. The father has suffered a long, emaciating illness, and when at last the gods relent and the father mends, the sons rejoice. This rapprochement, like some others (e.g. §1.13), is between the Sanskrit main story and a Homeric simile [cf. Ch. 3].
11 *Divine enemy and supporter*. When Śiva comes to earth, he initially treats Arjuna as if he were an enemy. When Poseidon becomes aware of Odysseus, he treats him as his enemy. However, in both cases, the divine enemy is balanced by a divine friend, for during his ordeal, Arjuna receives support from Indra

disguised as a Brahmin, and when Poseidon has departed, Odysseus receives help from Athena.

12 *Painful bodily contact.* Arjuna's battle with Śiva starts with an exchange of arrows and progresses to wrestling. Odysseus is thrown by a wave against a rough rock and clasps hold of it as the wave rushes past.

13 *Lump of flesh with injured extremities.* Śiva reduces Arjuna to what looks like a lump of organic matter, a *piṇḍa* (cf. Scheuer 1982: 232ff.), with damaged limbs. The wave that throws Odysseus against the rock rebounds from the cliffs and plucks him off again, stripping the skin from his hands. He is like an octopus dragged from its hole with pebbles adhering to its arms.

14 *Unconscious.* Arjuna falls to the ground unconscious in front of Śiva. Odysseus falls to the ground unconscious on landing.

15 *Prayer.* Arjuna revives and prays to Śiva, begging for forgiveness. Just before he lands, Odysseus prays to the River God, begging for his kindness.

16 *Offering.* Arjuna makes a clay image of Śiva and offers to it a garland, which the god takes and puts on.[6] Odysseus gives to the River God the veil of the goddess Ino, which he has been using as buoyancy aid. The god returns it to Ino, who duly takes it in her hands.

17 *Restoration.* Arjuna is physically restored by the touch of Śiva. Odysseus is physically restored by Athena's hypnotherapy.

18 *Cardinal points.* After his encounter with Śiva, Arjuna meets the four Lokapālas. During the storm, Odysseus is buffeted by the four wind gods, Euros, Notos, Zephyr, Boreas, who are linked with east, south, west, and north, respectively.

19 *Three-plus-one structure* (a point we shall come back to). The four Lokapālas include Indra, but the King of the Gods stands apart from the other three in various ways. Among the four winds, Boreas, who is 'king of the winds' (Pindar *Pyth.* 4.181), stands apart, for when Athena calms the other three winds, she lets Boreas continue blowing until the lull.

20 *City with park.* Indra's heaven contains a divine city Amarāvatī, inhabited by gods, with blossoming trees and a park. The Scherian city (unnamed) belongs to the Phaeacians, who are near kin to the gods (*agkhitheoi gegaasi* 5.35), and it contains Alcinous' park and his ever-fruitful trees.

21 *Wheeled vehicle.* Arjuna goes to the city in a chariot belonging to Indra, its king. Odysseus walks to the city behind the mule-cart that Nausicaa borrowed from her royal father.

22 *Throne.* Arjuna shares his divine father's throne in his palace. Odysseus is seated next to the king on a throne that has just been vacated by Alcinous' favourite son.

23 *Disappointed nymph.* In heaven, the *apsaras* Urvaśī is misled by Indra into thinking that she will enjoy sex with Arjuna, as she desires.[7] Nausicaa is misled by Athena into thinking that she will very soon be getting married, and when she meets Odysseus, she hopes it will be to him.

Although there is much scope for elaboration of the argument, I hope that this straightforward listing of rapprochements suffices to show that the two stories are cognate. The full force of the argument will not be appreciated unless an effort is made to envisage the individual items structurally, that is, as interrelated both sequentially and hierarchically. One needs to compare not only items *n* and *N*, but also *n* with its neighbours and *N* with its neighbours, and *n* regarded as (say) a pre-ordeal feature of a journey within a journey, and *N* regarded similarly. Though individual parallel innovations are always a theoretical possibility, probably all the twenty-three shared features or motifs were present in some form in the proto-narrative.

§2. *Mahābhārata* – Patañjali

In what sense is Arjuna's journey yogic? At its start, the hero is said to be 'yoked to Indra's yoga' (*aindrena yogena* 3,38.27), but what does that mean?[8] Indra-yoga is not a recognized category in the philosophico-ritual literature, but the context suggests that it refers here to the whole of Arjuna's journey from the sorrows of forest exile to the delights of his father's heaven. The journey offers a rough typological resemblance to the spiritual progression of a yogin from the mundane world of suffering to a condition of transcendence, but how close is the similarity?

Before detailing yogic practice, Patañjali describes the obstacles the yogin must overcome. These include languor and listlessness, accompanied by pain and despondency (1.30f., Woods 1988: 63–65; Feuerstein 1989: 45f.), a state of mind which recalls the condition of the Pāṇḍavas before Vyāsa's arrival (see esp. 3,28.1 and §1.3). Yogic practice itself is presented under eight headings called *aṅga* 'parts, limbs', which come in a fixed sequence. The group of eight limbs is split into the five outer or indirect and the three inner or direct. Let us work through the list, asking in each case whether the item in question relates to Arjuna's journey.

The outer aṅga (Pat. 2.29–35)

1 *Yama*. Five forms of self-control or abstentions. Before he sets off, Arjuna is said to be 'disciplined in speech, body and mind' *(yata-vāk-kāya-mānasa* 38.14; *yata* shares its root with *yama)*.
2 *Niyama*. Five observances (positive activities, as distinct from the initial negative group, but the same verb root). The list includes contentment *(saṃtoṣa)* followed by *tapas*. Arjuna is happy *(prīta-manas, ramamāṇa)* at finding a pleasant place in the forest for his *tapas*.
3 *Āsana*. Posture. As we shall see, Arjuna adopts a particular *āsana* for his fourth month of *tapas*.
4 *Prāṇāyāma*. Breath control. The description of Arjuna's posture is followed immediately by a reference to his *prāṇa*. In this particular context, the word seems to mean strength rather than breath, but the choice of the term is suggestive.
5 *Pratyāhāra*. Withdrawal of senses from the outer world. At the end of the fight, Arjuna becomes *sammūḍha*, unconscious or stupefied. This is not the same thing as voluntary sensory withdrawal, but the similarity is again suggestive.

So of the five outer limbs, Arjuna's behaviour certainly relates to the first three and possibly to the last two as well. In the epic, the motifs are not placed in parallel so as to form a recognizable list but the order in which they occur is the same as in Patañjali.

The inner aṅga and the overall structure (Pat. 3.1–7)

The three inner limbs, *dhāraṇā, dhyāna, samādhi*, 'fixation of thought, meditation and enstasy', are psychological activities or states difficult to characterize in words. They in turn lead on to *kaivalya*, 'isolation', the ultimate goal. Though Arjuna does not go through any such mental stages in the course of his journey to heaven, comparison is possible at a more abstract level. The sequence consisting of psycho-physical preliminaries, then three inner limbs, then ultimate goal parallels the sequence of gods who give weapons to Arjuna – Śiva, then three Lokapālas, then Indra. In other words, if we treat the outer limbs as a single element, Patañjali and the epic share the abstract structure of initial element, triad, final element, or 1:3:1.

The comparison would be more striking if the epic structure were 5:3:1, with an initial fivefold element corresponding to Patañjali's outer limbs. Since the hints of the five outer limbs in the epic do not form a list, they cannot be used as evidence of such an element, but there is another sense in which Arjuna's dealings with Śiva are unambiguously fivefold. Their interaction begins with four months of *tapas* addressed to the god, each month under a different regime. According to one of the two versions (3,163.14–16), the regimes are, respectively: roots and fruit, water alone, total fast, and, for month four, standing on tiptoe with arms raised (the *āsana* mentioned earlier). The four months of increasingly severe austerities culminate in the encounter, which constitutes the fifth phase of the interaction. Thus the epic journey does show the 5:3:1 pattern present in Patañjali.

The final element in this pattern is represented on the one hand by Arjuna in heaven with Indra, on the other by *kaivalya*. According to Patañjali's final *sūtra*, Isolation can be conceived either as the involution of the components of nature *(guṇānāṃ pratiprasava)* or as 'the power of awareness grounded in itself' *(svarūpa-pratiṣṭhā citi-śakti)*. The comparison is with Arjuna, earthly incarnation of Indra, who has returned to his origin, being taken into his father's lap and sitting on the supreme throne 'like a second Indra' (3,44.21–22).

Siddhis

Before reaching 'isolation,' the yogin may acquire magical powers *(siddhis* or *vibhūtis)* which, although they are signs of success, are not recommended for those who truly seek salvation. Is this feature of yoga present in the story?

When Vyāsa brings instructions for the journey, he also provides a mysterious entity that seems to be a spell, but which is described as being 'like *siddhi* personified' (3,37.26). With it Arjuna will obtain success, *sādhayiṣyati*, the verb containing the same root as the noun.

More specifically, Patañjali's account of *siddhis* (3.16–18) includes invisibility (21), knowledge of cosmic space (26) and of the arrangement and movement of stars (27–28), the sight of Siddhas or Perfecti (32), and upward flight (39). All of these motifs relate to Arjuna's journey (3,43.26–28). In the course of his upward flight to heaven, the hero becomes invisible to mortals. Having been told beforehand by Yudhiṣṭhira that he will be able to see the entire universe, he sees the stars in their thousands and is told about them by Mātali. He is driven along the Roadway of the Siddhas, and on arrival, those who greet him include Siddhas.

Towards the end of the same section (3.51) Patañjali refers, somewhat oddly, to 'invitations from those in high places', invitations which should not arouse pride or attachment in the yogin. The meaning is clarified by a commentary (Vyāsa's, from around CE 750?) and by Vācaspati Miśra's subcommentary (a century later). Those in high places are the gods, 'like the great Indra', whose invitations may in effect tempt the yogin to deviate from his true purpose – for instance, when they offer 'maidens who are not prudish' (in Woods' translation – literally 'who are compliant', *anukūlā*). But this is just what happens to Arjuna. Soon after his arrival in heaven, Indra arranges for a seductive nymph Urvaśī (cf. §1.23) to visit the hero one evening, done up in all her finery – but the temptation is rejected.

Thus there are connections of many different types between Arjuna's journey and the undertaking of the yogin.

§3. *Śvetāśvatara Upaniṣad* – Patañjali

Any account of the history of yoga (e.g. Hauer 1958; Feuerstein 1989) will mention this latish Upaniṣad, which is also important in the early history of Sāṃkhya. After raising some of the basic philosophical questions, the first section describes the individual soul, which is whirled along in life with five types of suffering, but can be saved by appropriate knowledge and discipline. An invocation of the Vedic god Savitar (2.1–7) leads on to the well-known passage giving brief but explicit instructions on how to perform yoga, where to perform it, and the apparitions (such as mist and smoke) that it will initially produce. The next section begins with a vision of the god Rudra (3.1–6), who remains fundamental in the soteriological reflections dominating the remainder of the text.

The Upaniṣad lacks Patañjali's 5 + 3+1 structure, but it refers to what in classical yoga would be four of the limbs (2.8–9). The practitioner should keep head, neck, and chest erect *(āsana)*; draw his senses into his heart *(pratyāhāra)*; control his breathing *(prāṇāyāma)*; and restrain his mind *(dhāraṇā)*.

The two yogic texts are usually presented in historical order, but the connection between them is so well recognized that I can pass on quickly. However, it is perhaps worth noting their shared theistic orientation. Patañjali gives to Īśvara, the Lord, a significant place in the yogin's undertaking, for instance by making devotion to him the fifth of the *niyama*. On the other hand, he does not associate Īśvara with any other theonym, and it would be risky to assimilate the Lord to Maheśvara = Śiva, and thereby claim a link with the Rudra of the Upaniṣad.

§4. *Śvetāśvatara Upaniṣad – Mahābhārata*

We can skip features that the epic and Upaniṣad share with Patañjali – namely the initial situation of suffering, the explicit reference to yoga, and the four limbs (see §3) – and concentrate on rapprochements involving only the first two texts.

1 The section concerning Savitar is interesting. The god's name, which appears in five of the seven verses, comes from *sū-* 'set in motion, impel, vivify', and is three times linked with other derivatives of the verb (as is common in the Rigveda – Macdonell 1897: 34). In the present context, the god is apparently setting in motion journeys to heaven *(suvargeyāya śaktyā, suvaryato)* and the whole yogic undertaking. But this is just the role of the seer Vyāsa, without whose impulsion Arjuna would presumably never have made his journey.

2 The first five verses of the Upaniṣadic passage all begin with forms of the (uncompounded) verb *yuj-* 'yoke', and the same root occurs seven times in connection with the start of the epic journey (3,38.9–11, 27–28). One notes also that the spell or knowledge provided by Vyāsa is once referred to by Yudhiṣṭhira as an *Upaniṣad* (3,38.9) as well as being called a *vidyā* and a *brahman* (neuter).

3 The Upaniṣadic yogin is to restrain his mind as if it were a chariot yoked with vicious horses (2.9). The image of the person or soul as chariot is quite well known (some Indian instances are collected by Goudriaan 1990), but the comparison here is with the chariot of Indra, yoked with its 10,000 bay horses and driven by Mātali, which carries Arjuna heavenwards from Mount Mandara. Arjuna is of course not restraining the horses – the rapprochement bears only on the occurrence of the image at just this point in both texts.[9]

4 As regards deities, the configuration is not the same as in the epic where, in the present context, the supreme deity is clearly Indra, and the link between Rudra-Śiva and the hero's undertaking is spelled out. On the other hand, the Upaniṣad does resemble the epic in presenting Rudra as a bowman and mountain-dweller (3.5–6), features that, according to Oldenberg (1988: 113), belonged to the original Vedic Rudra. Moreover, just as the Upaniṣadic poet prays that Rudra will show himself in a body that is kindly (*śiva* 3.5), so Arjuna prays to the god for mercy after he has been defeated in the duel.

If we had only the three Sanskrit texts, we might here be tempted to pause and think about their relations. Does the soteriological *darśana* derive from the epic, or has the epic been moulded by the soteriology, or should we think of two-way traffic? But given that this part of the epic story goes back to the proto-narrative, the deeper question is whether the latter was in any sense yogic. Now we know the sort of thing to look for, are there any hints of yoga in the Greek?

§5. *Odyssey* – Patañjali

As Poseidon realizes (5.288–289), once Odysseus reaches Scheria, Fate has decreed his ultimate release from sufferings. Thus, up to a point, the hero's voluntarily undertaken, lengthy solo ordeal at sea resembles the yogin's lonely austerities on land: both experiences ultimately lead to salvation. But the similarity is too general to be very interesting.

Let us look instead at the structure of the ordeal, recalling that the yogin's undertaking starts with the five outer *aṅga*, which correspond to the five stages of Arjuna's dealings with Śiva. Odysseus' ordeal opens with the storm sent by Poseidon, and if we look at his conveyances or modes of progression from this point onward, we find precisely five of them.

1 *The threatened raft*. Poseidon has seen the raft and gathers the storm.
2 *The hulk*. The first great wave strikes, and the raft loses mast, sail, and steering.
3 *The plank*. When the next great wave strikes and shatters the hulk, Odysseus bestrides a single plank.
4 *The veil*. During stage 2, the goddess Ino gave Odysseus her veil. The hero now strips, dives from the plank with arms stretched out, and swims buoyed up by the veil.
5 *Walk on earth*. On landing, he returns the veil and staggers up a hillock on foot.

The four stages on water form a clearly organized sequence. Starting off comfortably on a well-made raft, generously supplied by Calypso with food, drink, and fine clothes, the hero is progressively stripped of all such external supports and reduced in the end to his naked humanity.[10]

If the five stages in the hero's ordeal correspond in number to the five outer limbs, does anything correspond to the three inner ones plus *kaivalya*? The answer was foreshadowed in §1.19: in the Sanskrit epic, the 3 + 1 structure was provided by the three subordinate Lokapālas, plus Indra, and in the Greek by the three wind gods who were quieted, plus Boreas, the north wind, who was not. The 3 + 1 wind gods enter the story at an earlier stage than the Lokapālas and differ also in their minimal individualization; moreover, Boreas lacks a role in Scheria corresponding to that of Indra in heaven. Nevertheless, the abstract pattern is present, and there are also three more concrete similarities.

1 *Light vegetable matter*. When the first wave strikes, Odysseus is thrown into the sea, and it is only with difficulty that he surfaces and regains the hulk of his raft. The latter is tossed hither and thither like thistle plants *(akanthas)* 'which an autumnal north wind [Boreas] blows across a plain, and they adhere to each other in a ball' (5.328–329). For the yogin who masters the *udāna* or upward breath, 'there is no adhesion to water, mud, thorns *(kaṇṭaka)* or the like' (3.39). The idea of adhesion is worth noting, even though it is expressed and used quite differently in the two cases.

Somewhat later, the wave sent by Poseidon shatters the hulk 'as when a strong wind tosses a heap of dry chaff' (5.368). As for the yogin, 'either by controlling the relations between his body and ether *(ākāśa)* or by the coincidence (of consciousness) with light (objects) such as cotton *(tūla)*,' he is able to traverse the ether (3.42). In both passages, a simile refers to dry light vegetable matter that can seem to float in air.

Taken individually, the resemblances are slight, but they need to be seen as a pair (and neither text offers more than two such images): the Greek thistles and chaff parallel the Sanskrit thorns and cotton fibres [– respectively, prickly and non-prickly].

2 *Bodily radiance.* On Nausicaa's encouragement, Odysseus washes the brine from his shoulders and back and the foam from his head, and Athena then makes him taller, stronger, and more admirable; his head and shoulders radiate beauty and grace (6.230–232). Similarly, the yogin who masters *samāna* (one of the 'five breaths') becomes radiant, gaining beauty, grace, and power (3:40, 46). Surprisingly perhaps, the Sanskrit for grace, *lāvaṇya*, comes from *lavaṇa*, 'salt'.

3 *Mist.* Odysseus makes the last part of his journey to the palace enveloped in a mist (*akhlus* 7.41, *aēr* 7.143), so that he is invisible to the populace. In the context of *samādhi*, very close to the end of the yogic undertaking, Patañjali mentions the *dharma-megha* (4.29). Whatever the meaning of *dharma* here (Feuerstein 1980: 100), *megha* means a cloud. One might also recall the yogin's invisibility (3.21).[11]

§6. *Odyssey* – *Śvetāśvatara Upaniṣad*

The following four points bear on successive verses of the Sanskrit (2.8–11).

1 *Raft.* Odysseus crosses the lonely ocean on a raft (even if the account of its construction makes it sound like a boat). The Upaniṣad tells the wise man to cross over fear-bringing streams in his *brahman*-raft (some translators render *uḍupa* as 'boat').

2 *Wheeled vehicle.* We have already compared the mule-cart that Nausicaa borrows from Alcinous with the celestial chariot that Mātali drives on behalf of Indra (§1.21), but we now see that it corresponds also to the chariot image in the Upaniṣad (2.9).[12]

3 *Location.* The place where Odysseus lands seems to him excellent *(aristos)* since it is smooth of stones and sheltered from the wind (5.442–443). It must be essentially the same spot as the idyllic water-meadow close to the shore, where Nausicaa's maidens wash the clothes in abundant fresh water (6.85–95), and where Odysseus washes in fresh water, sheltered from the wind (6.210). But the place recommended for the practice of yoga is pure and level, free from pebbles and gravel, agreeable for its running water and other reasons, and sheltered from the wind.

4 *Mist.* Odysseus travels in a mist (cf. §5.3); the yogin sees a mist *(nīhāra)*.[13]

Presumably the rapprochements between the *Odyssey* and the non-epic Sanskrit texts, like those between the two epics, also indicate features of the proto-narrative.

Concluding discussion

A minimal and conservative conclusion would be that the proto-narrative lying behind the two epics contained a good number of the features that were taken up and elaborated into the ritual and philosophy of yoga when the IE speakers reached India. But the argument can be taken further.

Apart from the proto-narrative, we have discussed three typologically contrasting journeys. That of Odysseus, although it involved the gods, was presumably understood by Homer and his audience primarily as one of a series of adventures such as a hero of old might be expected to undergo – a story that even if it were perhaps open to religious or spiritual interpretation, was in no sense a charter for current ritual practice. The yogin's 'journey', in contrast, is a spiritual undertaking that is presented as lying within the scope of current human beings. Arjuna's journey is typologically intermediate. On the one hand, it is an epic adventure set towards the end of the era *[yuga]* immediately preceding our own, and it is not presented as an undertaking that ordinary humanity could or should attempt to emulate. On the other hand, as Indra-yoga, it is akin to other yogic undertakings such as are constantly recommended in the epic for those with spiritual ambitions, and as we saw in §2 and §4, it has much else in common with those undertakings. The problem is how to relate this typology to a fourth journey, namely that of the proto-hero.

Let us return to the two scenarios sketched at the start of the chapter. One possibility is that the proto-narrative was more like the Greek than the Sanskrit – essentially an adventure story, a sailor's yarn, albeit one in which gods intervened from time to time (§1.11, 15–19, 23). It would follow that, in the East, the story was sucked into the ambiance of one among the various philosophico-religious movements later codified as *darśanas*, and that it acquired its yogic aspects in the process. In short, the proto-narrative was spiritualized by the Sanskrit speakers or their ancestors.

According to the other hypothesis, the proto-narrative was typologically closer to the Sanskrit. In that case, the physical journey of a (fictional) hero was conceived as a spiritual ascent within the cosmos such as could be acted out by contemporaries in a ritual journey of some kind. Such a journey would now more naturally be called 'shamanic' than yogic since (like Arjuna's) it would have been undertaken primarily for the benefit of others rather than for the traveller, and also since it would have been thought of as traversing the external space of the cosmos rather than the inner mental space of the yogin. This second hypothesis assumes that, in the absence of adequate support from mainstream religious institutions, the narrative tradition leading to the Greek epic tended to become more earth-bound and more secular. In short, the proto-narrative was de-spiritualized.

A compromise hypothesis is logically possible (a halfway spiritual proto-narrative was developed in one direction by the Greeks, in the other by the Indians), but I see nothing to recommend it. The second hypothesis – secularization by the Greeks – will probably seem to most readers intuitively more plausible, but it is not clear to me how best to formulate or weight the explicit arguments that are needed to prove it. What follows is a first attempt.

Approaches to the question might be distinguished into atomistic and global. Atomistic arguments focus on particular narrative motifs, which themselves may or may not be demonstrably part of the proto-narrative. Let us take one of the atomistic type: at the end of his journey the hero sits on or by a royal throne (§1.22). One can now ask three sorts of questions. First, is the motif well motivated and well integrated in the Greek narrative as it stands, or would it make better sense in a less secular story? Second, similarly, for the Sanskrit, is the motif puzzling or problematic as it stands, and would it make better sense in a *more* secular story? And third [the diachronic question], is it easier to imagine something like the Greek turning into something like the Sanskrit, or vice versa? In this case, first, it is a little odd for Alcinous to displace his favourite son in favour of a complete stranger. Second, it makes perfect sense for Indra to share his throne with his own son, whose journey was from the start directed towards him. And third, it does seem more likely that the King of the Gods should be naturalized to a proto-Alcinous than that the latter should be promoted to cosmic supremacy. Similarly – to take other examples – is it not more likely that a bout of wrestling with a god should be naturalized into grappling with a rock (§1.12) than vice versa? That the supreme god's chariot should be demoted to a mule cart (§1.21) rather than the converse? All judgements about how oral narratives can change are liable to the charge of being tendentious and subjective, but the atomistic arguments seem to point collectively towards a cosmic and exemplary character for the proto-narrative.

Global arguments too come in various forms. One line of thought focuses on the structure and degree of integration of the two narratives taken as wholes. The Sanskrit, in spite of various minor discrepancies, has a clear overall structure linked to the sequence of five gods with whom the hero has dealings, all of whom are mentioned in advance by Vyāsa in his instructions for the journey. The Greek is in this respect definitely less integrated. One thing after another befalls the hero, and although the reader expects him to arrive safely, no outline of the trip is given in advance. Instead of a neat set of five well-known named male gods, the hero has dealings with Poseidon, the four wind gods, the relatively obscure Ino, Athena, and the nameless River God. Is it not more likely that Greek tradition has seen the clear structure of the proto-narrative give way to a less structured sequence, than that India has forced a disorganized string of adventures into its favoured fivefold framework?

Another global argument focuses not on the epic but on the yogic tradition. Suppose that yoga developed from scratch among Sanskrit (or Indo-Iranian) speakers and lacked any relevant precursor contemporary with the proto-narrative. The rapprochements of §2 and §4 would then be due to the influence of yoga on the

Sanskrit epic. But what about the rapprochements of §5 and §6? They would have to be due to borrowings by the yogic tradition from the epic. In other words, we have to postulate that the philosophico-ritual tradition both borrowed from the epic and gave to it. Some such process of give and take is not impossible, but it is much simpler to suppose that the proto-narrative was already linked with a ritual and spiritual praxis.

This would be in line too with general anthropological expectation. The proto-narrative involved gods and could well be called a myth, but myth and ritual are very commonly intertwined – indeed a ritual very often seems to be the raison d'être of a myth. Thus, independent of all the other arguments, it is a priori quite likely that the account of the proto-hero's journey served as a myth explaining and justifying ritual practices ancestral to yoga as we know it. If it did so, then the journey becomes comparable with those other stretches of the proto-narrative that served, I think, as charters respectively for different types of marriage ritual and for the horse sacrifice [Chs 2, 4].[14]

Notes

1 First published in 1998 as 'The Indo-European prehistory of yoga'. The paper reflects an old interest (Allen 1974).

2 'By practices of asceticism and exercises of spiritual concentration, connected perhaps with bodily techniques, especially with the cessation of respiration, they [the Magi] claimed to collect up and unite the psychic powers scattered throughout the whole individual, deliberately to separate from the body the soul that had been isolated and re-centered in this way, to return it for a moment to its original home so that it could recover its divine nature, and finally to make it descend again and chain itself anew with the bonds of the body' (Vernant 1990: 368–369, cf. 388–389; my translation). Since this chapter focuses specifically on yoga, I avoid discussion of Greek and Indian shamanism. Gold (1996) explicitly avoids the historical questions that I find so fascinating.

3 The relevant narrative comes in Chapters 37–45 of the CE.

4 A few of the comparisons have appeared in Chapter 3, of which this chapter is in part a development.

5 Precise references will seldom be given since they are easily found by following each story as it unwinds.

6 This detail of the story is omitted from the main text of the CE.

7 Like comparison §1.16, this episode too is absent from the CE main text.

8 The passage is not discussed in the substantial article by Hopkins (1901). Van Buitenen (1975: 822) suggests plausibly that 'Indra's yoga' is the spell or secret knowledge that Vyāsa leaves for Arjuna at the same time as he leaves instructions. [Ganguli translates the phrase 'urged by the desire of beholding Indra'.]

9 Mātali congratulates Arjuna on the astonishing firmness with which he withstands the shock of take-off (3,164.37f.), a motif that may relate to the term *dhāraṇā* (from *dhṛ*-, cf. *dhṛti* 'firmness, resolution'). Cf. also the stability *(sthairyam)* included in Patañjali's account of *siddhis* (2.31).

10 An alternative analysis, focusing less on conveyances than on denudation, would identify the fifth phase with the brief period when the hero grapples with the rock and is stripped even of part of his skin.

11 Comparisons can also be made between the Greek epic and the didactic accounts of yoga in the Sanskrit epic. Odysseus remains sleepless for seventeen nights (§1.8), and patient meditation can enable one to abandon sleep (*Mbh.* 12,232.5). The simile of the

octopus with damaged arms (§1.13) might recall the comparison of the yogin with the tortoise who retracts his limbs (*Bh. Gītā* 2.58).

12 The chariot simile also occurs in didactic epic: 'As a heedful charioteer, having yoked good steeds, quickly takes the warrior to the spot he wishes, so the yogin, heedful in *dhāraṇā*, soon attains the highest spot' (12,289.36–37).

13 One might also compare Odysseus with ascetics from traditions other than mainstream Hindu yoga. When he sleeps in his pile of leaves, the Greek hero is likened to a firebrand *(dalon)* carefully kept alight under a heap of ashes (5.487). In a series of Śvetāmbara Jain scriptural stories, a king-turned-ascetic undertakes intense austerities and is likened to 'fire confined within a heap of ashes', *huyāsaṇe viva bhāsa-rāsi-palicchaṇṇe* (Barnett 1907: 57,118, cited by Dundas 1992: 142). If it is accepted, the rapprochement bears on the history of the notion of *tapas* (literally 'heat').

14 [The structure of the yogin's journey (five outer *aṅgas*, three inner *aṅgas*, and finally *kaivalya*) may *also* merit comparison with that of Odysseus' *nostos* as a whole: five pre-Circe landfalls (Cicones, Lotus-Eaters, Cyclops, Aeolus, Laestrygones), three landfalls involving nubile females (Circe, Calypso, Nausicaa), and finally Ithaca. Compare also the journey of the dead soul described in the *Kauṣītaki Upaniṣad* (Allen 2016b): souls heading for the world of Brahmā pass first through the worlds of five Vedic gods. (For a non-comparativist approach to the whole set of episodes that compose the *nostos,* see Lukinovich 1998.)]

6

CROCODILES AND NYMPHS

A careful reader of Bernard Sergent's last book may notice his twenty-line summary of a preliminary article in which I proposed a rapprochement between two epic journeys[1]: that of Arjuna around India in Book 1 of the *Mahābhārata*, and that of Odysseus, especially in the last half of his *nostos* (Sergent 1998: 357 n.205).[2] Similarly, in the previous book by the same author (Sergent 1997: 268, cf. Allen 1999b), one can find two lines dealing with the idea of a quasi-Dumézilian fourth function – an idea that has now occupied me for ten years. Other Francophone writers have reflected on this idea elsewhere (e.g. Sauzeau and Sauzeau 1995), but many of my audience will not have read or noticed these references in the enormous relevant literature, so I shall start with as few assumptions as possible.

The existence of the three Dumézilian functions is now established: it is among the twentieth century's most important discoveries in the human sciences. However, influenced by Rees and Rees (1961), I believe that the three functions did not constitute the global structure of the Indo-European (IE) ideology. Outside the zone of the three classical functions there existed a domain of Otherness – in fact, a double domain. What is 'other', 'outside', or 'beyond' can either be valued (e.g. if it is transcendent) or devalued, rejected, despised. It follows that the framework of IE ideology was in fact fivefold. Above the unit formed by the three classical functions stands the valorized half (or 'aspect') of the fourth function, and below it the half that is disparaged.

Let us translate this somewhat abstract concept into more concrete terms. The socio-structural model of IE society comprises not only priests, warriors, and producers, but also, above them, a king, and below them, slaves and other outcastes. Thus although many trifunctional analyses seem to me perfectly correct, some will need retouching or revising. For instance, sovereignty as such, connected to the king, cannot in the basic model continue to be merged with priesthood, wisdom, and so forth; it belongs under the positive aspect of the fourth function.

But let us turn to the Arjuna–Odysseus comparison and start with India. One knows that Arjuna is, in terms of birth order, the third of the five Pāṇḍava brothers, that is, that he is situated at the centre of the group. In addition, he is the divine son of Indra, King of the Gods, and he often represents the whole group of brothers; he can be described as the central hero of the epic. But no one interested in four- or five-element structures will fail to note his marital history. For a start, following a competitive gathering of princes, Arjuna wins the hand of princess Draupadī, who thereby becomes the shared wife of the five brothers. This first marriage – polyandrous – is no doubt the most important, but he also enters three other unions, and to analyze the crocodiles of the chapter's title, they have to be related to this series of unions. So let us briefly summarize CE 1,200–213.

After their marriage to Draupadī, the Pāṇḍavas settle down in their capital. The seer Nārada comes to visit and warns of the danger of fratricidal conflict, to which their polyandrous marriage has exposed them. To avoid it, the brothers promise never to enter a room if Draupadī is in it together with another brother. But one day Arjuna finds himself obliged to break the agreement, and he then insists on undergoing the consequence – the agreed penalty is a twelve-year exile.[3] The exile takes him to the four cardinal points of Indian geography – north, east, south, west, visited in clockwise order. At each point, he meets female beings, three of them being human: in the north, he meets the magician Ulūpī, who is a snake *(nāgī)*. In the east, he meets princess Citrāṅgadā. In the south, he meets five crocodiles who are metamorphosed nymphs *(apsarases)*, who will eventually regain their condition as nymphs; their leader is called Vargā, (as we shall see). In the west, he meets princess Subhadrā, the sister of Kṛṣṇa. With all of them – except of course the crocodiles in the south – the hero has not only sexual relations but also marital ones (as we learn later in the epic).

Thus, contracted in the course of a journey, what we have here is a triad of marriages. This is of interest to readers of Dumézil's *Mariages indo-européens* (1979), who will recall that, in Dumézil's view, the Indo-Europeans aligned the different types of marital union with the three functions. So the question arises whether Arjuna's three marriages conform to the same pattern.

Certainly, yes! The Ulūpī union belongs to the first function, the Citrāṅgadā one to the third, and Subhadrā's to the second – Arjuna abducts her by force, following the *rākṣasa* mode of marriage. I cannot here repeat the evidence assembled previously [Ch. 2], which seems to me sufficient. But does it follow that the trifunctional analysis is sufficient? Two difficulties arise: first, is it legitimate to separate the three subordinate marriages contracted during the journey from the fundamental marriage with Draupadī? Second, is it legitimate to separate the marriages situated at three of the cardinal points from the relation between hero and crocodiles at the fourth?

In fact, the two difficulties seem to be interlinked by the numerical symbolism. The three trifunctional marriages are monogamous, and as such contrast with the polyandrous Draupadī marriage (with its five males and one female). But the relation with the crocodiles shows the same contrast between unity and plurality, albeit in reverse: it is polygynous (with its single male and five females). Thus, outside the trifunctional triad, we are presented with two elements that echo each other and seem to belong to a single five-element grouping. So can these two elements – excluded from the trifunctional viewpoint – be interpreted as representing the two halves of the fourth function?

The Draupadī marriage is unproblematic. The *svayaṃvara* type of marriage (with its concourse of princes) is not included in the list of types in the code of Manu but is well known from other sources, especially epic ones. It is a royal type, and according to four-functional theory, the king belongs originally or fundamentally to the valued aspect of the fourth function.

As for the problem of the crocodiles, it presents a legal and a narrative aspect. In Manu's list of modes, right at the bottom of the hierarchy – totally despicable, but listed even so – one finds the *paiśāca* mode. It consists in the secret union of a man with a woman who is asleep, drunk, or mad, and it seems well fitted to represent the devalued aspect of the fourth function.

Let us move to the narrative aspect. From a formal point of view, what happens in the south is homologous with what happens at the other three cardinal points, and the numerical echo mentioned earlier reinforces confidence that the series in question is fivefold. But what happens in the south is neither a marriage, nor even a sexual relation. Arjuna has sex neither with the crocodiles nor with the nymphs that the crocodiles become. One cannot say that in the south Arjuna contracts a *paiśāca* marriage.

However, such a negative conclusion is unsatisfactory. We must push the investigation further and take into account four points.

1 Although the crocodiles are neither asleep, drunk, or mad, it seems that in their original form, the apsarases showed youthful folly (details will follow).
2 Although Manu uses the Sanskrit adjectives for 'asleep', 'drunk', and 'mad', the underlying idea could well be that the woman is outside her normal condition, and the nymphs, transformed into crocodiles for a certain period, are not in their normal state.
3 Arjuna certainly does not have intercourse with the crocodiles/nymphs, but he does have bodily contact with them, because he pulls the reptiles out of the water.
4 Arjuna, friend of Kṛṣṇa, is (and this is important) from several points of view, an exemplary figure. So it is totally natural to avoid attributing to him a mode of marriage that is despised. Perhaps the poets eliminated or blurred over such a marriage, which was part of an earlier tradition, or perhaps, all along, the tradition presented the devalued relation not as a sexual union but as something that was equivalent.

Thus although Arjuna does not actually contract a *paiśāca* marriage in the south, he comes fairly close to doing so, and it is very possible to interpret the episode as expressing the negative aspect of the fourth function.

TABLE 6.1 The females in the story of Arjuna's Penance and the corresponding females in the second half of Odysseus' *nostos*

Draupadī	Penelope
Ulūpī	Circe
Subhadrā	Nausicaa
Citrāṅgadā	Calypso
crocodiles	Straits Monsters (see next section)

Those who stick to the trifunctional viewpoint will no doubt prefer to separate the crocodiles episode from the other four and take it to be an *ad hoc* addition, necessitated by the use of the schema of four cardinal points, but this becomes difficult to argue once account is taken of comparison with the *Odyssey*. The comparison must distinguish three aspects: events, cardinal points, and functions.

As regards events, Homer presents us with the same structure as we have in the Sanskrit. The hero, who has left his wife at home, meets a series of female beings in four locations, and the females and their episodes can be put in parallel as in Table 6.1. (At this point, I ignore the ordering within each list.)

As regards cardinal points, what is explicit in the Sanskrit is blurred in the Greek: Odysseus' journey does not follow exactly the scheme of centre and cardinal points. The situation is much the same as regards functions. There are perhaps some scattered hints, but I cannot propose for the Greek story a satisfactory analysis – either trifunctional or quadrifunctional.

How are these similarities and differences to be interpreted? If the common ancestor of the two epics already gave the episode a five-element structure, it is likely that it harmonized events, cardinal points, and functions, which would reinforce the hypothesis of a split fourth function.

Crocodiles and monsters

Up to this point, I have tried to show that the nymphs/crocodiles can be taken to represent the fourth function in its negative aspect. In beginning like this, with the global structure, I hope to have been faithful to Dumézil's fundamental inspiration. But the rest of the chapter will try to deepen the comparison of just a single element within this structure, namely that between the Indian nymphs/crocodiles and the Greek Straits Monsters. Let us start by summarizing the Sanskrit story, creating divisions and subtitles as appropriate.

1 *Warning*. When he arrives in the southern quarter, Arjuna learns from local ascetics that five sacred lakes are inhabited by man-eating crocodiles.[4]
2 *Physical contact*. Despite the ascetics' objections, Arjuna enters a lake. Grabbed by a crocodile, he pulls it onto dry land, and instantly the reptile metamorphoses into a nymph of radiant beauty.

3 *Sin and punishment.* Questioned by Arjuna, the nymph explains that she is called Vargā and that she is the favourite of Kubera, the god of wealth. One day she was travelling with four friends to Kubera's palace when she met a brahmin practising austerities in a forest. Singing and laughing, the nymphs tried to seduce him and distract him from his religious activity. The brahmin puts up with it for a while, but when he has had enough, he condemns the five nymphs to spend a hundred years as crocodiles.

4 *Prophecy.* The nymphs plead their cause: they were young, foolish, and female, and now they repent. They receive reassurance: one of those they attack will pull them onto dry land and let them recover their form as nymphs.

5 *Nārada.* As they travel south, they meet the seer Nārada, who tells them that Arjuna, who will be able to save them, will soon be arriving.

6 *The friends.* At the end of her account to Arjuna, Vargā asks him to free her friends, as he has just freed her. Arjuna happily does so.

7 *Departure.* The nymphs leave for their normal home and Arjuna continues his journey.

In summary, with a little reorganization, the story is as follows. Five singing nymphs try to seduce a brahmin engaged in serious activities. Having been cursed and condemned to a life as crocodiles, they recover their normal condition after physical contact with a travelling hero. One immediately senses the rapprochement between the singing nymphs and the Sirens, and between the crocodiles and Scylla, but we need to proceed methodically, evaluating both similarities and differences.

1 *Unity of the episode.* In the Sanskrit, a separation is possible between what happens at the ponds in South India, and is told to us directly [i.e. by Vaiśampāyana, the main narrator of the epic], and the subsidiary story told by Vargā, of what happened in the forest near Kubera's palace (no doubt in the Himalayas). But Vargā's story is told in the south, and the fundamental unity of the episode is clear enough.

Such unity is less clear in the Greek. First, there is the geographical separation between the islands of the Sirens and the cliffs of Scylla and Charybdis, and second, there is the temporal separation between Odysseus' dealings with Scylla and those with Charybdis. But the geographical separation cannot have been great: everything implies that the journey from the Sirens' island to the start of the Straits lasts at most only a few hours. However, temporal separation is another matter. Odysseus' first entry to the Straits is separated from the second, when he passes close to Charybdis, by the whole episode of the Island of Thrinacia, which itself takes more than a month. At present, I have no explanation to offer for the intercalation of this episode within that of the Straits Monsters.[5] However, this is not an obstacle to the comparison. The conceptual unity of the group formed by Sirens, Scylla, and Charybdis is sufficiently clear in Homer.

2 *Position of the episode in the global structure.* It must not be forgotten that the crocodiles, like the Greek monsters, each constitute one element in a five-element structure. However, the position of the two episodes [among the four occurring on the hero's journey] is different. The crocodiles come third in the series, while the Straits monsters come second.

3 *Types of female being.* The Indian situation is straightforward: there are two types – nymphs and crocodiles. The Sanskrit word for the reptile is *grāha* (masculine, like the French *crocodile*), but one can reasonably imagine that in the story they are female. In any case, the two types are linked by reversible metamorphosis, and the five individuals are barely differentiated. Apart from the pre-eminence of Vargā, the differences appear only in the list of their names and in some details of their respective ponds.

In Homer, the situation is much more complex. The two Sirens on their island attract sailors by their singing. They are located in a meadow, surrounded by the rotting carcases of those who have allowed themselves to be seduced by the false promises in the Sirens' songs. Scylla is a pernicious monster, living in a cave situated halfway up a high cliff. Although her voice is only that of a puppy, she is horrible to look at, with her twelve feet and her six long necks. At the end of the necks, her six maws each contain three rows of close-packed teeth, which she uses to seize sailors and marine creatures. Charybdis, near the opposite cliff, is no less terrifying, but is only a sort of whirlpool. Three times a day, she swallows the sea water, and three times a day, she belches it forth, far away. So there are three well-differentiated types of being.

4 *Number of beings.* Though Homer mentions only two Sirens, most of our sources recognize three, which would make a total of five monsters. Perhaps – but I am not sure – Homer presents a fifth homogeneous element – the Planctae or Moving Rocks.

Let us now consider these rapprochements in greater detail. Without claiming to be exhaustive, we can note the following differences between the nymphs and the Greek being.

1 *Narratological status.* Questioned by the hero, Vargā recounts an episode of her own biography, while it is Odysseus himself who recounts Circe's warnings against the Sirens (and the other dangers), and then recounts his own experience of them.

2 *Victim.* The nymphs try to seduce an anonymous brahmin, who then abruptly disappears from the story, while Odysseus himself is the victim of the Sirens' attack.

3 *Journey.* The nymphs travel while their victim stays still – inverting the movements in the Sirens episode.

4 *Motivation.* The nymphs are young seducers lacking malevolence; the danger they represent for the brahmin is only the collapse of his spiritual ambitions. The Sirens are fundamentally malevolent and murderous.
5 *Resistance.* The brahmin resists the nymphs' blandishments, at first by self-discipline, then by cursing them, while Odysseus resists because, following Circe's instructions, he has himself bound to the mast of the boat.
6 *Other victims?* The brahmin is alone, while Odysseus shares the risks with his companions.
7 *Temptation.* That offered by the nymphs is sensual, that offered by the Sirens is intellectual.

But the similarities between the two epics are no less considerable.

1 The female aggressors belong to a minor category of supernatural beings.
2 The victim they have in mind is a single man (Odysseus' companions have their ears blocked with wax and in that way are safe from temptation).
3 The contact results from a journey, whether that of the aggressors or that of the victim.
4 The aggressors are in the wrong; the victim is blameless.
5 The aggressors use their supreme talent – song – to seduce their victim, but in addition the nymphs laugh and flirt.[6] The Sirens propose extraordinary knowledge.
6 The aggressors fail.
7 A relation of succession or metamorphosis links the singing aggressors with the 'toothy' aggressors (discussed later).

Use of extra-Homeric sources makes it possible to lengthen the list.

8 Homer does not describe the bodily form of the Sirens but, from very early on, vase paintings show them with a woman's head and a bird's body. Apsarases are not normally winged, here or elsewhere, but they travel by air without difficulty. Moreover, they are sometimes able to take bird form – as does Urvaśī in her affair with Purūravas.

This is not everything, but let us for the moment turn to the toothy aggressors, starting with the differences.[7]

1 *Species.* Though it is here rendered 'crocodile', the word *grāha* has in fact a wider meaning: it covers any large fish or marine animal, even the hippopotamus, especially when rapacious; anyway, it is a term from normal zoology. In contrast, Scylla is a monster of unique type.
2 *Physical contact.* Arjuna must use his bare hands to pull the reptile out of the water, while Odysseus, armed with spears and standing in the prow of his boat, does not even touch Scylla.

But here are the similarities:

1 The aggressors live near the water and feed on what they find in it.
2 The aggressors are multiple: the five reptiles correspond to Scylla's six heads at the end of her six necks.
3 The aggressors are killers. The crocodiles eat ascetics[8]; Scylla seizes six victims from each passing boat, as she does from that of Odysseus.
4 The aggressors grab their prey by using their teeth, not for instance by using their arms, or swallowing them like Charybdis, or poisoning them like a snake.
5 In the real time of the narrative, the episode of toothy aggression comes after that of aggression by song.
6 Both texts contain beings who writhe or struggle in the grip of more powerful beings. Vargā writhes in the hands of Arjuna, the six friends of Odysseus writhe in the maws of Scylla. The image is repeated in a Homeric simile: the struggles of Odysseus' friends resemble those of fish caught by a fisherman. English 'writhe' here renders Sanskrit *visphurati* and Greek *aspeirō*; the roots of both the latter verbs are IE cognates. In the references to Vargā and the fish the verbal form is, each time, the accusative singular masculine of the present participle.[9]

In the Homeric text itself, no allusion is made to a metamorphosis, whether undergone by Sirens, Scylla, or Charybdis, but the motif is clearly attested elsewhere. However, the category 'metamorphosis' is too summary – distinctions are needed. What the nymphs undergo is, first, a punitive transformation from apsaras to crocodile, owing to the curse; then the return to their own form – a re-transformation that represents their salvation. So if the whole story is taken into account, one can talk in the *Mahābhārata* of reversible metamorphosis.

The Greek monsters do not undergo reversible metamorphosis, and the idea of salvational metamorphosis is of doubtful relevance. On the other hand, punitive metamorphoses are well attested, even for the singers: in fact, the Sirens were originally ordinary maidens, companions of Persephone. Among the variant versions of their story one can read that the punishment was inflicted by Demeter because the maidens did not resist the abduction of Demeter's daughter, or by Aphrodite because they despised the pleasures of love – see entries in Grimal (1982) or in the *Real-Encyclopädie* (Pauly and Wissowa eds. 1894–1980). In the same way, Scylla is punished for a love affair and Charybdis for her greed – a characteristic she retains when transformed into a monster. After their meeting with Odysseus, two of them undergo further transformations. Scylla is killed by Heracles and resuscitated by her father Phorcys, and as for the Sirens, they commit suicide by throwing themselves into the sea, because of their failure during the passage of Odysseus. This is not for them an absolute end since at least one of them becomes a spirit or minor goddess called Parthenope, who was worshipped at Naples. But although this is a transformation, neither in her case nor in Scylla's can one talk precisely of reversible metamorphosis. In any case, both Sanskrit and Greek traditions contain the idea of punitive metamorphosis.

In conclusion, I hope to have shown that, despite the considerable differences that are of course to be expected, the story of Arjuna with the crocodiles and that of Odysseus with the female monsters have the same origin. This was already suspected, in view of the fivefold narrative structure that we examined at the start, but even so it was necessary to undertake detailed verification (and I do not claim to have said everything that is relevant [cf. Ch. 13].

There are indeed further questions that need to be raised. For instance, I believe that the common ancestor of the two stories was PIE and that, of the two, it is the Sanskrit that has remained closer to the common origin – issues that cannot be discussed here. But finally, let us risk a hypothesis. Is there a particular affinity between metamorphoses and the fourth function in its negative aspect?[10] It is not impossible.

Notes

1 First published in 1999 as 'Les crocodiles qui se transforment en nymphes'; it was originally presented at a conference on metamorphosis held in Brussels in 1998.
2 For a better version of my argument see [Ch. 2], which gives references to the original texts.
3 Or a twelve-month one – the texts vary.
4 *Tīrtha*, here rendered 'lake', covers 'a piece of water, esp. sacred; bathing place, e.g. on pilgrimage; ford'.
5 [Perhaps Odysseus' journey to Thrinacia can be compared to the nymphs' journey from the Himalayas in the north to their place of punishment in the south.]
6 Sanskrit *lobhayantyas*, whose root is cognate with Latin *libido*.
7 My phrase 'toothy aggressors' hints at what the crocodiles share with Scylla. [Cf. also Ch. 13 §3.3.]
8 [The Sanskrit verb is *haranti* 'seize, take away' – *presumably* so as to eat them. Scylla too seized her victims (*heleto*, from *haireō*, and she certainly ate them (12.246, 256)].
9 *Mbh.* 1,208.10 *visphurantaṃ*; *Od.* 12.254 *aspaironta*; from *sp(h)er' (Pokorny 1959).
10 Cf. note 1.

7

MONKEY AND DOG

Specialists in Greek and Sanskrit epic usually take it for granted that the respective narratives grew up in the geographical areas where the deeds of the heroes are set and where the epics were orally recounted before they were written down.[1] But this assumption can be questioned. The two languages go back to a proto-language, and it is increasingly recognized that the proto-language included a poetic language (Watkins 1995) as well as a mythology (Dumézil and followers). So why not postulate a proto-epic? But since questions of form and content are to some degree separable and my focus is on the second, I prefer to talk of a proto-narrative.

How strong is the evidence for a proto-narrative lying behind Greek and Sanskrit epic? The aim of this chapter is not to answer the question in general terms, but to support the hypothesis by means of a comparison between two fairly short stretches of text. Many attempts along similar lines have been made by other comparativists, but since they bear only indirectly on the rapprochement presented here, I limit myself to listing in the bibliography the three most recent attempts by myself. Let us move quickly to the fundamental question of method.

How is one to judge that two narratives are so similar that they must have a common ancestor? There are no easy rules of method. One can only weigh similarities against differences, paying close attention to the primary texts and looking, not for isolated elements (however striking), but for relationships between elements, for sequences and combinations. One fights the constant temptation to tendentiousness and circularity. Secondary non-comparative literature devoted to one or other narrative, however intelligent and learned, is of relatively little help. A convincing case depends on the quality of its argument and on the quantity and interconnectedness of individual rapprochements.

The context

Now to Argos and Hanumān [CE Hanūmān], or more precisely, to the episodes involving them that I think are cognate. An introductory summary of *Odyssey* 17.201–327 can be very brief:

> Returning from the Trojan War, the hero, disguised as a beggar, has been staying for a few days with the swineherd Eumaeus. Together, they walk through the mountains from the latter's dwelling to the palace of Ithaca. En route they encounter first the goatherd Melantheus, who kicks the hero, then Argos, the hero's aged hunting dog, who recognizes his master after twenty years, and promptly dies. In the palace Odysseus kills his wife's suitors and is re-established as king.

As for Hanumān the monkey (still worshipped as a god in India), I am concerned only with the episode in Book 3 of the *Mahābhārata* when the hero Bhīma encounters him on a journey towards the palace of the god Kubera. Here is a slightly fuller summary:

> The heroes of the epic, the five Pāṇḍava brothers, have long been languishing in exile. Arjuna, the central brother, left the others some years back to visit heaven, and they, plus the brothers' shared wife Draupadī, are in the Himalayas awaiting his return. Bhīma, the beefy second brother, is sent off up Mount Gandhamādana by Draupadī to bring her some flowers (3,146.11). (Now comes the encounter.) Bhīma's noisy approach wakes the dozing monkey. Hanumān questions the hero, urging him to turn back. Bhīma arrogantly demands passage, but the monkey says he is too old and sick to move. Declining to jump over him, Bhīma mentions Hanumān who, in the *Rāmāyaṇa*, jumped across the Ocean to Lanka. Invited to pass under the monkey's tail, Bhīma is unable to lift it, and at last learns Hanumān's identity. The two are in fact half-brothers, sons of the Wind God by different mothers. In identifying himself, Hanumān summarizes his role in the *Rāmāyaṇa*, whose events took place in an earlier era. Bhīma wants to see his brother as he then was, and after delivering a disquisition on the eras, Hanumān obliges. After further sage advice and a fraternal promise to help the Pāṇḍavas in battle, the monkey lets Bhīma proceed, and himself disappears. Bhīma finds the pond with the flowers, defeats the Rākṣasas (the local guardian spirits), and is rejoined by the rest of his party.

At this point in the argument a common origin for the two encounters will hardly seem plausible. A hero on a journey to a palace encounters an elderly animal, dialogues with or about it, and passes on. So what? The differences are enormous. One hardly knows how far it is useful to go when listing differences, but Table 7.1 gives some idea of them.

TABLE 7.1 Differences between the Argos and Hanumān encounters

Greek		*Sanskrit*
	formal	
Thirty-eight lines		170 shlokas = 340 lines
two speeches		twenty-two speeches
	animal	
dog		monkey
does not speak		speaks
weak		strong (pretends weakness)
hero recognizes, pretends not to		hero does not recognize
not divine		at least semi-divine
disappears from story		will participate in battle
younger than hero		older than hero
no relative of hero		half-brother of hero
nourished by hero twenty years ago		never met hero
presence needs no motivation		came to help and/or test hero
no effect on journey		first hinders, then helps
	hero	
travelling with Eumaeus		travelling alone
disguised as beggar		no disguise (in hermit garb)
lacks brothers		second of five brothers
	location	
on island of Ithaca		in Himalayas
in front of human palace		in area avoided by humans
at the home of the dog and the hero		at the home of neither

However, an oral narrative transmitted by separate traditions for two or three millennia is likely to develop great divergences – even as regards language, the gap between ancient Greek and Sanskrit is considerable. We must weigh differences against similarities and look closely. I shall consider eighteen similarities, giving each a title. The order in which I treat them and the separations that determine the exact number treated are not fundamental.

1 *Elevated position.* Argos is lying on a large pile of dung (*en pollēi koprōi* 297). Hanumān is dozing on a large slab of rock (*pīne śilātale* 146.64).[2]
2 *Movement of tail.* When Argos becomes aware of the proximity of the hero, he wags his tail (*ourēi esēne* 302). When Hanumān awakes from his doze, the first thing he does is slap his tail on the ground, repeatedly and vigorously (*su-vipulam . . . āspoṭayata lāṅgulim* 146.60).
3 *Aged, afflicted, immobile.* Argos, who is at least twenty years old and flea-ridden, has become too weak to move towards his master (*asson d'ouket' epeita dunēsato hoio anaktos | elthemen* 303–304). In spite of looking nimble as a lightning flash, Hanumān twice claims to be ill (*sarujas* 146.74, *vyādhinā kleśito* 147.7), and

when refusing to move out of the way, he claims that because of old age he lacks the strength to get up (147.16). If the animals could move, Argos would move towards the hero, while Hanumān would perhaps move aside, but the theme of immobility is present in both stories.

4 *Identity questioned.* In his first speech to the swineherd, Odysseus asks whether the dog's speed matched its beauty, or whether it had merely been kept for show. In his first words to the speaking monkey, Bhīma asks who he is and why he has assumed the guise of a monkey (147.2). Later (147.22) he repeats his questions, wondering to what category of supernatural this monkey-like being belongs.

5 *Original athleticism.* Twenty years earlier, when Odysseus left for Troy, Argos was exceptional for his speed and strength: Eumaeus recalls his *takhutēta kai alkēn* (315). The events of the *Rāmāyaṇa* lie in a previous era, and it is more than 11,000 years since Hanumān's famous leap across 100 leagues of ocean (147.38). Both animals have had long lives.

In both cases point 3 precedes point 5 in the text. Taken together in their natural order they imply the physical decline that we all face with age. The theme of decline is underscored in the Sanskrit by the account of the four eras, which start with a golden age lacking death, disease, or senile decay (148.11, 14).

6 *Reference to earlier epic account of abduction and recovery.* The Greek refers twice (293–294, 314) to Odysseus' departure for Troy, which both to us and to Homer's audience implies the *Iliad*. Both Bhīma and Hanumān (147.11, 37) refer to the *Rāmāyaṇa*, and the monkey summarizes its plot. As is often noted, both these previous epics narrate an overseas expedition to retrieve an abducted wife.

7 *Temporary wondrous reclamation of past.* In the Greek, the reclamation is conditional: if Argos were now as he had been once, Odysseus would quickly be amazed at the sight (*aipsa ke theēsaio idōn* 315). In the Sanskrit, the past is re-created: responding to Bhīma's demand, Hanumān expands his body to the dimensions of a mountain. Bhīma is duly delighted and amazed (*visismiye* 149.2–6). But the vision of times past is soon over. After his description of Argos as hunter, Eumaeus returns us to the dog's present plight (*nun d'ekhetai kakotēti* 318). Hanumān contracts (150.1), and the encounter nears its end.

8 *Abrupt termination.* When Eumaeus enters the palace, Argos dies [326]. Having delivered his final promise, Hanumān vanishes (*antaradhīyata* 150.15 – perfectly normal behaviour in a god).

In my next set of similarities, what the Greek attributes to the hero the Sanskrit attributes to the animal. This need not necessarily be viewed as a difference. The Greek hero outranks his dog, while in the Sanskrit, the semi-divine monkey outranks his younger brother, so in both cases, the motifs are attributed to the senior of the two.[3]

9 *Mistreatment of animals*. When he questions Eumaeus, Odysseus suggests that the dog's sorry treatment does not accord with its merits, and his suspicion is supported by Eumaeus. When he opens the dialogue, Hanumān moralizes: humans, endowed with reason, should show compassion to dumb brutes and not rudely awaken them when they are sick and asleep (146.74–76). In the Greek, the mistreatment is the fault of the female slaves and it is real, while in the Sanskrit, it is the fault of the hero and the remark is ironic; but the *theme* is present in both cases.

10 *Pretended ignorance*. Argos and Odysseus both recognize the other, but since the hero is still disguising his own identity from Eumaeus, he cannot reveal his recognition. Thus, in opening his conversation with the swineherd he pretends ignorance of the dog's identity.

It is implied even in the CE text that Hanumān recognizes Bhīma from the start. For his first speech his manner is contemptuous but smiling (146.73–74), reminding one of gods in other contexts who are playing with ignorant humans. The northern manuscripts explicitly say that the monkey came to help his brother (*Bhīmasya kāranāt/rakṣārthaṃ* 146.708* lines 2, 5). Nonetheless, Hanumān pretends ignorance of Bhīma's identity.

11 *Pretended weakness*. Odysseus is pretending to be a miserable aged beggar, needing a staff (202–203). Hanumān pretends to be weak and ill.

12 *Tears*. Odysseus wipes away a tear (*apomorxato dakru* 304) without letting Eumaeus see. After contracting in size and embracing his brother, Hanumān opens his penultimate speech with tears in his eyes *(paryaśru-nayano)* and his voice choked by affectionate weeping (*sauhārdād-bāṣpa-gadgadayā girā* 150.3).

My next two rapprochements compare the speech of Eumaeus with speeches by Hanumān. Both speakers comment on life in general, in the manner of philosophers.

13 *Duties of slaves*. At the end of his speech, Eumaeus blames the slave women for neglecting Argos. But, he implies, what can one expect? When masters are no longer present to exercise control *(mēket' epikrateōsin)*, slaves are no longer willing to fulfil their duties (*enaisima ergazesthai* 320–321).

Of Hanumān's two didactic speeches, the second concerns the duties of different members of society. In its middle it details the duties of the traditional four estates of Hindu social theory, ending up with the serfs or slaves. Their duty, says the god, consists in obedience to the three superior estates (*śuśrūṣā dvijātināṃ* 149.36).

14 *Halving of virtue*. Eumaeus ends his speech with a general reflection: Zeus removes half the virtue of a man *(hēmisu . . . aretēs apoainutai . . . aneros)* when he becomes a slave (322–323). Hanumān's first didactic speech concerns the eras. In each era, dharma (sacred order, virtue, righteousness) is reduced by a quarter so that in the third it is reduced by half (literally by two of its parts – *dvībhāgonaḥ pravartate* 148.26).[4]

My four final rapprochements are grouped together only because their validity may be more debatable.

15 *Awoken by noise.* The Greek does not say that Argos was awoken by noise, but an aged dog lying down in the afternoon is quite likely to be dozing, and the pricking up of its ears might suggest a response to sound. Purportedly, it is Bhīma's noisy approach that wakes Hanumān (146.59, 74).

16 *Dung.* Argos lies on a sizeable quantity of mule and cattle dung. As Bhīma rampages through the forest on his way to the encounter, he frightens lions, tigers, and hyenas, who slink away in fear, discharging urine and dung (146.48). The words for dung, *kopros* and *śakṛt*, are cognate, but even if they were not, the motif seems worth noting.

17 *Lightning.* Regarding the name Argos, the etymologist Chantraine suggests 'originally a notion that expresses the dazzling whiteness of lightning and at the same time its speed' (1968: 104). In a single shloka (146.65), Hanumān is compared to a lightning flash *(vidyut)* no less than four times.

18 *Unprovoked attack.* This somewhat complex rapprochement, meriting a separate heading, necessitates going beyond the hero's encounters with Argos and Hanumān and looking at adjacent stretches of narrative. Let us first recall the context of the Greek encounter.

A complex rapprochement

In line 200 Odysseus and Eumaeus set off from the swineherd's dwelling to go to the palace. Lines 204–253 narrate the encounter with Melantheus, who then enters the palace (254–260). When they in turn come within earshot of the palace, the two travellers make their plans (260–289) and, after the Argos episode (290–327), they too enter the palace, first the swineherd, then (336) Odysseus. So the Argos episode is closely linked with the Melantheus episode; they are the two main events that punctuate a single journey.

Now the Melantheus episode takes place beside a fresh-water spring, and its central act is the unprovoked kick that the goatherd gives to Odysseus (his rightful king) and that earns him an imprecation from Eumaeus. Nothing like this occurs before the Hanumān encounter, but does anything similar occur beside the fresh-water pond that is the goal of Bhīma's journey? I summarize.

> After Hanumān disappears, Bhīma journeys on until, close to Kubera's palace, he comes upon the beautiful pond, which springs from a mountain waterfall (*jātāṃ parvata-nirjhare* 151.2, 152.10). It is surrounded by all kinds of trees and creepers, and its water is nectar or elixir (*amṛta-kalpam* 152.22a). The pond, the play-garden of Kubera, is frequented by supernaturals (151.8) and is guarded by Krodhavaśa demons, who challenge Bhīma and threaten to cook and eat him if he enters the pool. Bhīma promptly slays more than a hundred of them (152.18). Meanwhile, he has been followed by his eldest brother

> Yudhiṣṭhira together with the rest of the Pāṇḍavas, and when the group is reunited, Yudhiṣṭhira reproaches his brother for his recourse to violence [153.26–27].

The pond recalls the location of the Melantheus episode. In the Greek, the fair-flowing fountain is regularly used by the citizens of Ithaca. It is surrounded on all sides by poplars and its cool water flows down *(kata . . . rheen)* from a rock above (*hupsothen ek petrēs* 208–210). Above it stands an altar of the nymphs, the daughters of Zeus, whom Eumaeus mentions in his imprecation, and who regularly receive offerings from passers-by (210–211, 240). Similarly, the Himalayan pond is highly honoured (*paramārcita* 151.7) by deities, Gandharvas and Apsarases, and the latter are celestial nymphs who are fond of water, as their name implies by (*ap* 'water'). One might also compare the cannibalistic threat of the Krodhavaśas with the threatening words of Melantheus, when he says that Odysseus will be pelted in the palace (231–232). On the other hand, the Greek hero silently enduring the kick contrasts sharply with the Indian one killing a hundred demons; so in spite of the comparable locations, not much can be made of this comparison taken by itself.

However, Bhīma's *first* journey up Mount Gandhamādana, which is made in quest of flowers for Draupadī, is scarcely to be separated from his *second*, which is also occasioned by the arrival of wind-borne flowers, is made at the request of Draupadī, and is narrated only a few chapters later (157.14–159.35). Though the second journey makes no reference to Hanumān, in other ways it is so similar that van Buitenen speaks of it as a 'recast' of the first (1975: 201–202). Others have argued that of the written versions the second is the older (Grünendahl 1993, cf. also Brockington 1998: 141–142), but there is no doubting that the two are related. This time Bhīma climbs the mountain and reaches Kubera's palace without encountering any fresh water, though there are beautiful trees of all sorts (157.37).

> Bhīma blows his conch [157.40], and puts to flight various types of supernatural. Halting the rout, Kubera's friend, the Rākṣasa demon Maṇimat, attacks and sorely wounds Bhīma in the right arm, before being felled. Bhīma's brothers follow him, and on arrival Yudhiṣṭhira reproaches his brother for his violence. Kubera arrives as if to take revenge, but at the sight of Bhīma he is delighted. He explains why.
>
> Once he and Maṇimat were on their way to a council of the gods [158.51]. The sage Agastya was engaged in austerities on the bank of the Yamunā, and as they passed over him Maṇimat spat on him.[5] The sage cursed the demon to be killed by a human (i.e. Bhīma), and at the same time extended the curse to Kubera, who had neither prevented nor reproached his friend. The god – sufficiently punished, it seems, by the loss of his troops – is now released from the curse by Bhīma's act.

Kubera's explanation thus refers to an innocent and virtuous victim who suffers an unprovoked and outrageous insult from an evil-doer and responds to it with a curse that in due course is fulfilled. In other words, Maṇimat physically insults the innocent Agastya and is cursed by him but receives no immediate punishment; Melantheus physically insults the innocent Odysseus and is effectively cursed by the victim's friend but receives no immediate punishment. In both cases, the unprovoked assault is stupid. Melantheus acts in his wanton folly (*aphradiēisin* 233), Maṇimat out of folly, ignorance, insolence, and stupidity (158.54).

However, the insult to Agastya belongs to the narrative past, while it is in the narrative present that Maṇimat wounds Bhīma, much as Melantheus presumably leaves a nasty bruise on Odysseus. It is as if Odysseus here corresponds not only to Bhīma, as the Argos-Hanumān comparison already suggested, but also to Agastya – as if he conflated two proto-narrative figures lying behind the two attested figures.

Even if the two mountain journeys of Bhīma are taken together, the comparison with the Greek might seem tenuous were it not for a third journey by the same hero, told only a little later in Book 3 (3.175–178), and again involving a curse imposed by Agastya. This time the sage is insulted, not by the rather minor figure of Maṇimat, but by a far more significant figure. Nahuṣa, father of Yayāti, is the human king who, when Indra went into self-imposed exile, assumed the kingship of the gods. However, he succumbed to arrogance and lust and, as we learn from Book 5,11–17, a scheme was devised to topple him.

> Nahuṣa is induced to order the brahmin seers to carry his palanquin. Then, adding yet further insult, he enters into an argument with them on a point of dharma, and touches Agastya on the head with his foot [3,178.37]; other versions use verbs more violent than 'touch' *(spṛś-)*, verbs like 'kick' *(dhṛṣ-)*, or *abhihan-* (13,102.25, 103.20 – which last passage specifies a kick with the left foot). Agastya (or an unseen being) at once curses the offender to wander the world for 10,000 years as a snake.
>
> While Nahuṣa is under this curse, Bhīma goes on a hunting trip in the forest and is caught by the snake, who prepares to eat him (3,176.15c).[6] But Agastya has set a limit to the curse: the snake will be freed by a mortal who can give precise answers to his questions. Yudhiṣṭhira follows his younger brother to the place where Nahuṣa is holding him, answers the questions, and frees both Bhīma and the snake. Nahuṣa returns to heaven.

Though I cannot explore the parallel in full, the two stories about Agastya are clearly related. In the past, the sage was offended by Nahuṣa and [separately] by Maṇimat accompanied by Kubera and put them under a curse until such and such should happen. In the present, Bhīma is attacked respectively by Nahuṣa and by Maṇimat (then Kubera) but, either directly or via his brother, causes the curse to be lifted. So let us now put together all three journeys made by Bhīma within this relatively short stretch of Book 3, selecting the relevant features for comparison with the Greek.

First Gandhamādana journey: coming to a tree-fringed source of fresh water, Bhīma is attacked by Rākṣasas for ignoring their warnings and entering the pond.

Second Gandhamādana journey: Bhīma challenges the Rākṣasas, including Maṇimat, and thereby lifts the curse laid when Maṇimat insulted Agastya. *Hunting trip*: Bhīma is attacked by hungry snake (Nahuṣa), and causes lifting of curse laid when Nahuṣa kicked Agastya.

Given that the three Sanskrit stories are so closely interlinked, the comparison with the Greek can draw on all of them. Thus, (a) the Odysseus–Melantheus conflict takes place by fresh water, like the first Bhīma–Rākṣasa conflict; (b) Melantheus kicks Odysseus, a stupid and unprovoked insult, which resembles Nahuṣa kicking or spitting on Agastya and also perhaps, though to a lesser extent, Nahuṣa seizing Bhīma (unprovoked aggression, but natural for a snake); and (c) Melantheus is the object of an imprecation uttered by the victim's friend,[7] much as Nahuṣa and Maṇimat (plus Kubera) were the objects of a curse uttered by *their* victim.

A major difference is that the curse uttered by Agastya belongs to the narrative past and its lifting or accomplishment to the narrative present, while the Greek as it were shifts the corresponding events into the present and future. The imprecation, equivalent of the curse, takes place in the present, while the punishment of Melantheus will come during and after the massacre of the suitors. Nevertheless, Greek and Sanskrit share the following motifs: waterside violence, foolish unprovoked aggression, curse or quasi-curse on the aggressor, end-point of the curse when the aggressor encounters the hero (i.e. respectively, Bhīma and Odysseus in his undisguised form). In spite of considerable complexities, one can perhaps add the motif of friendship – Kubera's friendship, first with Maṇimat, then with the Pāṇḍavas, Odysseus' friendship with Eumaeus.

Though rappr. 18, *Unprovoked attack*, is methodologically more complex than 1–17, it merits inclusion for the extra weight it adds to the whole argument. As an overview the following simplified formula may be helpful:

unprovoked attack + Argos encounter = Odysseus' journey //
Hanumān encounter + unprovoked attack = Bhīma's journeys

Opinions may differ on the validity of the rapprochements 1–17, some of which may be dismissed as unpersuasive, or as corollaries one of another. However, I doubt whether even the most determined sceptic could reduce the list by more than a third. Of course, some motifs, regarded individually, may seem sufficiently banal for their occurrence in both epics to be explicable by coincidence. It is pretty common, for instance, for epic characters to question the identity of strangers (rappr. 4) or to pretend to ignorance of someone's identity (rappr. 10). But some of the other motifs are hardly commonplace ones, for example halving of virtue (rappr. 14), and in any case it makes no sense to look at the motifs individually. They compose *episodes*, and it is whole episodes that are being compared. Is it really conceivable that so many detailed similarities could exist between two relatively short passages if they were historically unconnected?

Theoretically, the proto-narrative might have originated at a period considerably later than that of PIE unity, but I doubt it. I cannot here enter on such a wide-ranging question (it is touched on in Allen 1998d). Perhaps one other possible objection should also be mentioned. My previous papers argued that in the parts of the epic traditions that they examined, Odysseus paralleled Arjuna, not Bhīma. That in no sense contradicts the homology presented here. If narrative comparativism were going to be simple, with regular one-to-one homologies extending throughout the whole corpus, no doubt more progress would have been made by now.

Concluding discussion

Let us return to the most obvious difference between the two animal encounters, namely the difference in species. As Ian Rutherford pointed out to me, most theories of the IE homeland locate it where monkeys are not native (cf. also Mallory and Adams eds. 1997: 384–385). Most likely, then, in the proto-narrative scene implied by the detailed similarities, the hero encountered not an aged monkey but an aged dog. Maybe there is even a hint of this in rappr. 2, since tail wagging is more natural in a dog than the same movement by Hanumān is in a monkey.

Tentatively, one can go just a little further. Here is a summary, drawn from the very short Book 17, very close to the end of the epic.

> Clad in bark, the Pāṇḍavas set out on foot for their final journey to Heaven, and are joined by a dog. As they traverse the Himalayas, one by one Draupadī and the brothers die, except for Yudhiṣṭhira. Disregarding the urgings of the god Indra, Yudhiṣṭhira loyally refuses to abandon the dog, who in the end turns out to be his divine father Dharma in disguise. The hero is congratulated on his steadfast sense of duty and is transported to Heaven.

Reading this with the Greek in mind, one notes a hero travelling on foot through mountains, and one who, shortly before reaching his ultimate destination, is involved with a dog; the dog does not speak but is spoken about with a third party. No other passage of the epic involves this canine form of the god, but the god himself is intimately linked with the relevant hero: Dharma was the progenitor of Yudhiṣṭhira, is incarnated in him, and (as Dumézil showed) governs his first-functional personality – which he affectingly displays here in his dharmic loyalty to the animal. The Odysseus–Argos link is also long-standing and intimate (the hero nourished the puppy – *threpse* 293), and arguably there are elements of loyalty on both sides of the relation. More importantly perhaps, both Sanskrit and Greek have the hero travelling on foot in the company of a real or apparent dependent (respectively, Eumaeus and the canine Dharma) and the relationship between the travelling companions involves loyalty.[8]

On all these points the Hanumān episode diverges from the other two. The animal is a monkey who speaks and reappears later in the epic. Although they are half-brothers, Bhīma and Hanumān have not previously met, and Bhīma has been travelling alone. Three-way comparisons are usually complicated, and ideally the two Sanskrit episodes should be compared independently of the Greek. Nevertheless, even at this point, one might wonder whether Argos results from a fusion of two proto-narrative animals whose distinctness is retained in the Sanskrit. If so, the Greek dog would be cognate not only with Hanumān but also, as is suggested in passing by Vielle (1996: 157 n.277), with the canine form of Dharma.

[Although we noted that Arjuna was separated from his brothers at the time of Bhīma's Flower Journeys, this chapter has not addressed some difficult questions bearing on the proto-narrative. For instance, how does its argument for Bhīma // Odysseus relate to the massive evidence elsewhere for Arjuna // Odysseus? Or to the argument in Chapter 20 for Bhīma // Ajax the Great? Or to the suggestion (Allen 2000a: 131) that Bhīma's paired Flower Journeys represent F3 within the set of journeys punctuating Book 3? The humble synchronic task of compiling similarities must precede the temptations of diachronic modelling.]

Notes

1 First published in 2000 as 'Argos and Hanumān: Odysseus' dog in the light of the *Mahābhārata*'.
2 Unless otherwise indicated, all references are to CE *Mbh.* 3, and to *Od.* 17.
3 In similar vein, although the hero's disguise (present in the Greek, absent from the Sanskrit) has been listed earlier as a difference, this is arguably the wrong way to look at it. In a sense, Hanumān the god is 'disguised' as an ordinary monkey. From that point of view, in both cases, the higher-ranking participant in the encounter is in disguise, and what we really have is an acceptable similarity.
4 Russo (1992: 36) thinks that the Greek lines 'have the appearance of a proverbial couplet awkwardly added on'. The rapprochement suggests rather that they are the relic of some more systematic reflection.
5 [Instead of 'spat' (CE *nyaṣṭhīvad*) Ganguli translates 'discharged his excrement on'; it is not clear why.]
6 Cf. the cannibalism contemplated by the Krodhavaśas.
7 It is a prayer and not exactly a curse (which would have unmediated magical effect).
8 Evidently, this last comparison shifts from the homology Argos ~ Dharma to Eumaeus ~ Dharma – cf. the shift made in moving from rappr. 8 to 9.

8

DURGĀ AND ATHENA

The approach to the classical world exemplified in this chapter is that of an Indo-European (IE) cultural comparativist.[1] From this viewpoint, Greece and Rome are just two among the various cultures of IE origin, together with those of early Ireland, Iran, India, and so on. Commitment to exploring this common origin framework does not entail rejecting diffusionist claims any more than it would in linguistics: a linguist interested in genetic comparisons can focus on starred forms and their descendants without in the least denying the existence of loan words. Similarly, my question here concerns the IE origin of a member of the Greek pantheon, but I do not deny the possibility of Middle Eastern influences on that pantheon, or on Athena herself.[2] In historical reality diffusion and common origin interact, but I focus solely on the second.

Within the wider field of IE cultural comparativism, one particularly promising area is the relation between Sanskrit and Greek epic traditions. A number of detailed similarities have already been found between the *Mahābhārata* and the *Odyssey* (plus post-Homeric epic material), and they may exist elsewhere in the two traditions.[3] One such similarity provides my topic. The warrior goddess Durgā intervenes only twice in the *Mahābhārata*, and we shall be comparing her first intervention with one of the many interventions of Athena in the *Odyssey*. The conclusion will be that in her role as warrior Athena is, at least in part, cognate with Durgā. The identity of a deity covers name, icon, cult, mode of action (in this case war), and myth, but I limit myself to myth.

If similarities are found between the two epics and are too substantial to be due to chance, one has four explanatory options. The similarities could be due to some sort of psychological universal (e.g. Jungian archetypes), to independent parallel inventions in societies of similar technology and socio-political structure, to diffusion (from Greece to India or vice versa), or to common origin in an earlier culture. Though it is not the only logical possibility, the most obvious candidate for the common origin is Indo-European. Behind the Greek and Sanskrit languages, there lies a proto-language from which both descend and which accounts for the similarities. Similarly, behind the two epics there could lie a proto-epic from which both descend. However, since the similarities that I examine concern narrative, not for instance metrics or oral formulae, I prefer to speak of a proto-narrative. Very likely the story was told in proto-Indo-European rather than in some later language from the IE family tree, but that question too lies outside my present scope (cf. Allen 2000b).

At the present stage of investigation, it is the primary texts that matter. Homerists and Indologists sometimes provide useful glosses on what these texts say, but insofar as they ignore the comparative dimension (as they usually do), little of their writing is *centrally* relevant. The questions posed here take the form 'To what extent is X like Y?', and however admirable the work of those who discuss X and Y separately, the questions that they address are different from mine.[4] Eventually, one hopes for syntheses embracing comparativists, both sorts of philologist, and archaeologists too, but that is for the future. For the moment, the comparativist can reasonably proceed more or less independently.

As for the comparativist literature, any researcher in this field has to acknowledge the inspiration of Dumézil. I believe that, in his work on ideology, he did not go far enough: the ideology of the IE proto-culture was not simply trifunctional but included a bifid fourth function (Allen 1996b, 1998b). However, I allude to the functions only marginally in the present chapter and cite Dumézil more for his recognition of what I call the 'bypass phenomenon'. He showed conclusively that the *Mahābhārata*, written down in the centuries around the turn of the eras, contains themes and structures from pre-Vedic times that bypassed the Vedas themselves, which date from about a millennium earlier.[5]

The bypass phenomenon bears on the somewhat obscure history of Durgā. 'Durgā' is just one among the various names and forms of Devī 'the Goddess', alongside Pārvatī, Umā, Kālī, and many others. Working backwards, one can say that nowadays Durgā is widely worshipped and that her warrior character is emphasized – she rides a tiger and brandishes a sword. Her celebrity goes back to the Purāṇas (mainly written down between the fourth and twelfth centuries), and especially to the section of the Mārkaṇḍeya Purāṇa called the Devīmāhātmya, which includes an account of Durgā overcoming Mahiṣāsura, the buffalo demon (Varenne 1975).[6] Earlier, in the epic literature, references to Durgā become rarer, and they disappear altogether in the Vedas. The Vedic pantheon is very male dominated, and although various goddesses receive a mention, there is no salient warrior goddess. Thus, if Athena and Durgā are cognate, as I think they are, it can only be by virtue of the bypass phenomenon.

An argument linking two characters drawn from such apparently remote and disparate narratives can scarcely aspire to the cogency of Euclid, but it is by no means wholly subjective. Its task must be to identify a *network* of parallels between the two stories. It means little if element α in the Greek resembles element *a* in the Sanskrit, and the argument begins to take off only if we find narrative sequences such as αβγδ, each element of which resembles the corresponding element in the Sanskrit sequence *abcd*. But a narrative is not simply a linear sequence of elements, and one looks also for parallels of more complex types. For instance, if only α and γ share a protagonist, and so do *a* and *c*, that is good evidence.

One naturally looks first for one-to-one matching of elements in the two stories, but things need not be so simple. Sometimes one stretch of Greek narrative parallels two separate stretches in the Sanskrit, as if the Greek had collapsed or fused what the Sanskrit keeps distinct. Theoretically, the formulation can be reversed so that the Sanskrit is seen as splitting what is unitary in the Greek, but I think that, on the whole, the Sanskrit is the more conservative of the two and the better pointer to the proto-narrative. I shall several times use the language of fusion, so I must emphasize that this is a verbal short cut: in reality of course the Greek has fused not the Sanskrit but the proto-narrative.

The simplest and perhaps the most satisfying comparisons involve quite small units of text. Ideally the Greek is on one side of the desk, the Sanskrit on the other, and one works back and forth comparing motifs, lines, and phrases. But here we shall need to start off by working with larger elements of narrative, exploring the context in which the goddesses intervene. Looked at in isolation, the Durgā-stava, '(The Hymn in) praise of Durgā', the single *adhyāya* (chapter) at the heart of our comparison, is not strikingly similar to anything in the *Odyssey*.

One final caution: in judging alleged similarities, one needs to weigh them against differences. But the undertaking is pointless unless *some* similarities exist, so the similarities have the logical priority, and for reasons of space, my treatment of differences will be skimpy. Of course, large differences are to be expected when two oral narratives have been transmitted separately over a period of millennia and are told in very different cultures.

I start with the highest levels of organization and work towards the details. Both epics say more about mortals than about deities, so to compare the goddesses we must start by comparing heroes.

1. Absence, and return to reclaim throne

Regarded globally, the *Odyssey* is a *nostos*, the return of a hero from the Trojan War: Odysseus comes home after twenty years away, slaughters the suitors, and reclaims his rightful throne. The *Mahābhārata* centres on a similar theme. This time the heroes are plural, for there are five Pāṇḍava brothers.[7] Moreover, the immediate cause of their absence is not some sort of parallel to the Trojan War. They are invited by their enemies to participate in a game of dice: the losers are to spend thirteen years away from public life, and they lose. However, after this absence, the Pāṇḍavas return to slaughter their enemies in a great battle and reclaim their rightful throne. The similarity can be summed up in the formula:

> departure of heroes, absence for period of years, violent return.

2. Triumph preceded by incognito

Between the main period of absence and the resumption of the throne, both epics interpose a liminal period when the heroes are incognito. After the *Telemachy*, the *Odyssey* falls into two parts – the adventures overseas, and the hero's doings in Ithaca. For most of the second part, from Book 13 until close to the end, the hero is incognito: he is physically disguised and assumes false identities. As for the Pāṇḍavas, in accordance with the terms of the dice game, they spend twelve years in jungle and mountain exiled from the capital, experiencing various adventures and encounters, and then they spend one year incognito. They choose to spend this thirteenth year under false identities at the court of King Virāṭa, whence Book 4 of the epic is called the *Virāṭa-parvan*. In both epics, the incognito represents a stage in the process of return: Odysseus is back in his homeland after years overseas, the Pāṇḍavas are back in a royal court, albeit not their own, after years in the wild. The formula is:

absence, partial return with incognito, resumption of throne.

3. Incognito opened by encounter with warrior goddess

Book 13 of the *Odyssey* begins with the hero sleeping on the beach of Ithaca and waking to encounter Athena. The goddess has helped him earlier, but now for the first time in the epic the relationship is overt: by the end of the interview in Book 13, Athena has divulged her identity and promised to help Odysseus regain his throne. In the Sanskrit, near the start of Book 4, Durgā appears for the first time in the epic.[8] The eldest Pāṇḍava brother, Yudhiṣṭhira, praises the goddess in the hope of seeing her face to face, and she duly manifests herself, promising to help the brothers regain their throne.

So in both epics, the incognito period begins with a meeting of hero and warrior goddess. Here is my central point, on which the whole chapter rests. But a minor complication should be noted. The reader of van Buitenen's translation of Book 4 will find no reference to Durgā. That is because the translator renders only the main text of the CE, which relegates the Durgāstava to an appendix (I.4) since it is missing from Kashmiri, Bengali, and southern manuscripts.[9] But the significance of such relegation is debatable and depends on the relation that one posits between oral and written material. Those parts of the epic tradition missing from the earliest reconstructable version are not necessarily of later *origin* than those included in it; perhaps they were simply written down later. This is what my argument implies for the Durgā episode. Thus, in very general terms, the formula is:

absence from capital, meeting with goddess opens incognito, triumph.

We can now look at the material more closely.

4. Incognito preceded by solo journey

At first sight, a major difference between the epics is that Odysseus is alone when left on the shore of Ithaca, while the Pāṇḍavas start their thirteenth year as a group. As already noted, they are five brothers, and they are accompanied throughout the thirteen years by their wife Draupadī. But we need to follow the story backwards from the encounter with the goddess.

Barely more than three weeks previously, Odysseus was still on Calypso's island. Then he undertook his eventful solo voyage to Scheria, ending up in the capital of the Phaeacians. From there, a Phaeacian boat had transported him to Ithaca the previous night. In the Sanskrit, we must go a little further back. In Book 3, in the course of the twelve-year exile, the third brother, Arjuna, departed for five years on a solo journey to heaven, to meet his divine father Indra. In due course, the god's chariot returned him to earth, to be reunited with brothers and wife.

[Ch. 5] argued that Odysseus' journey to Scheria and Arjuna's journey to heaven are cognate narratives, and my point here is that both precede the incognito, either immediately or by a certain gap. The gap is substantial (3,161–299) and not without incident for the Pāṇḍavas. Still, both events belong to the period of absence (§1), and we can reasonably write:

solo journey . . . meeting with goddess.

One way to envisage the comparison is to suppose that Greek tradition omitted or displaced post-reunion adventures present in the proto-narrative (and represented by the ellipses), perhaps prolonging the solo status of the hero. On the other hand (but the approaches could be combined), one might suppose that the Sanskrit produced the gap by filling out this part of the story.

5. Incognito followed by restoration of queen

If §4 built on a previously published rapprochement by looking backwards, this one does the same thing by looking forward. We can take for granted that the proper situation for a queen is to live with her royal husband who rules in his own palace. While Odysseus is incognito, Penelope is living in her palace but without her husband; while the Pāṇḍavas are incognito, Draupadī is living celibately in the same court as her husbands, but they are all servants in a foreign palace, not rulers in their own. In due course, both queens will be restored.

But there are good reasons of various sorts for viewing Penelope and Draupadī as cognate. For instance, Penelope was wedded by Odysseus on the occasion of a concourse of princes suing for Helen (Apd. *Bibl.* 3.10.8) and, more convincingly, she is won a second time in the archery contest against the concourse of suitors in Ithaca. Draupadī is won in an archery contest at a concourse of princes who have gathered to sue for her (*Mbh.* 1,174–181). And that is not all. A more elaborate argument for seeing the queens as cognate can be built on the four-function theory of IE ideology [Ch. 2, also Ch. 9].

6. Slaughter of queen's suitors

Odysseus' main enemies in Ithaca are the 108 suitors, who hope that one among them will marry the hero's wife and thereby take over his kingdom, as they have already started to do. But they are killed towards the end of the incognito. More precisely, their leader Antinous is killed before Odysseus' identity emerges, the others immediately afterwards.

In the Sanskrit, the Pāṇḍavas' main enemies are their cousins, the Kauravas. During the dice match, the Kauravas attempt (unsuccessfully) to disrobe Draupadī, doubtless with a view to violating her sexually. They are about to take over the kingdom, and at first sight might seem to provide the parallel for the suitors. But it is not as simple as that. First, the Kauravas are not massacred until the great eighteen-day battle of Books 6–10 – long after the incognito has ended, and second, around the end of the incognito, two other violent episodes occur.

In the final weeks of the incognito, Kīcaka, King Virāṭa's marshal, becomes infatuated with Draupadī and tries to seduce her.[10] She calls on Bhīma, the second brother, who kills Kīcaka at night without betraying his own identity. When the 105 followers of Kīcaka, the Kīcakas or Upakīcakas, try to take revenge, Bhīma by himself kills them too. So Antinous plus the other suitors parallel Kīcaka plus the Upakīcakas. Unlike the Homeric suitors, the Upakīcakas include no individuals who are named or otherwise distinguished; it is only their leader who attempts seduction, and none of them realize who is their killer. Nonetheless, the attempted seduction, the number of victims, the nocturnal setting, the separation made in the text between the fates of leader and followers – all these are clear similarities.

The second conflict that needs to be mentioned comes even closer to the end of the incognito. Learning of the marshal's death, the Kauravas and their allies the Trigartas plan a concerted attack on Virāṭa's kingdom with a view to plundering cattle. The Pāṇḍavas help Virāṭa beat off the raiders, and the humiliation of the Kauravas foreshadows their later annihilation during the Great War. Unlike the homogeneous Upakīcakas, the enemy coalition contains at least two separate groups and many named individuals, thereby resembling the Homeric suitors, who come from Dulichium, Same, and Zacynthus, as well as Ithaca. Perhaps the Greek can be thought of as fusing the two battles that Book 4 distinguishes, and perhaps also as drawing in the definitive conflict with the Kauravas. In any case, near the end of the incognito, the Sanskrit has something like a mnesterophonia.

7. A set of lies

As part of his incognito, Odysseus gives five different false accounts of his identity to five different individuals – first to Athena herself on the beach, then in succession to Eumaeus, Antinous, Penelope, and Laertes. Similarly, each of the five Pāṇḍavas gives a false account of his identity to King Virāṭa, and Draupadī gives hers to Virāṭa's queen Sudeṣṇā.

One major difference concerns the addressees of the lies – multiple in the Greek, single in the Sanskrit. Another concerns timing. Odysseus spreads his lies throughout the second half of the epic (Books 13, 14, 17, 19, 24), while the Pāṇḍava lies are all told to the royal couple immediately when the group arrives in the capital, and they form a single block of text.[11]

On the other hand, in both epics, some or all of the false accounts allude to the true hero(es). Odysseus three times makes his false persona allude to his true self,[12] and all the Pāṇḍavas [except Arjuna] claim to have served the Pāṇḍavas.[13] Moreover, in both epics, the lies contain elements of 'truth'. In his tale to Eumaeus, Odysseus includes a shipwreck echoing the one he himself experienced, and his false account of Thesprotia partly echoes his real experiences in Scheria.[14] Compare Draupadī's tale addressed to Sudeṣṇā: the disguised queen claims to be married to five princes of the Gandharvas (a category of supernatural), who will protect her against would-be seducers.[15] This echoes her real polyandrous marriage to five incarnations of supernaturals.

8. Fun

More generally, one can compare the tone or atmosphere of the incognito periods. The impression is given that Odysseus enjoys using his skill at lying and deception – that is surely Athena's implication when she congratulates him on this skill (13.393–395). Certainly, the Pāṇḍavas enjoy themselves. When announcing the choice of Virāṭa's kingdom for Year 13, Yudhiṣṭhira lays down that they are to take jobs and to amuse or divert themselves.[16]

But it is not only the heroes who have fun. No doubt both the Greek poets and their audiences savoured the many openings for irony that arise from Odysseus' incognito, and when introducing CE Book 4, Raghu Vira (1936: xvi) says that this is the most popular book in the Epic. Dumézil thought that in this book the poets had given themselves a sort of recreation which permitted them 'to amuse themselves while amusing us' (1968: 84); van Buitenen elaborates on the 'distinct tone of hilarity' with which the book opens (1978: 6); Brockington mentions the 'carnival-style inversion of roles, with its rich possibilities for the comic' (1998: 143).

This comparison between Greek and Indian incognito periods is far from complete. It could be filled out by comparing Odysseus' conflict with Irus with Bhīma's defeat of the local champion wrestler Jīmūta (*Od.* 18.1–116; *Mbh.* 4,12.12–25) or by comparing the staggered ending of the incognito in the two epics. But perhaps it suffices to establish the general similarity of the two stretches of narrative, and hence to lay the ground, at last, for comparing the two opening episodes and the warrior goddesses.

9. A sleeper, a tree, and storage

Seen in isolation, these three motifs could be dismissed as commonplace; their argumentative force comes from their combination.

During the voyage from Scheria, Odysseus sleeps deeply on the bedding laid out for him in the stern of the boat. The Phaeacians sail for the natural harbour of Phorcys, at whose head stands an olive tree next to a cave sacred to Naiads. They lift the hero, still sleeping on his bedding, carry him from the boat, and leave him on the sand. Then they unload his treasure, put it for safety by the olive tree, which stands aside from the path, and depart (13.70–125).

The Pāṇḍavas plan their disguises, are given some parting advice by their family priest on how to behave at court, and set off on foot. As they enter Virāṭa's kingdom, Draupadī complains of tiredness and, on Yudhiṣṭhira's instructions, Arjuna picks her up and carries her onward. As they approach the city, he puts her down, and discusses with Yudhiṣṭhira where to hide their weapons, which would betray their identity. He proposes a *śamī* tree on a hilltop by a desolate cremation ground. The tree stands in a patch of forest away from paths and infested by wild beasts. The Pāṇḍavas unstring their five bows, each of which receives individual mention, and lay them down together with their swords, quivers, and arrows.[17]

So in both stories, at the start of the incognito, a sleepy or sleeping human being is carried by others, and this motif is juxtaposed to references to a tree that stands somewhere out of the way.[18]

Beside this tree valuable property is temporarily deposited before being moved elsewhere for safe storage. Odysseus counts his treasures, which are briefly listed, and on his request, Athena helps him to hide them in the cave (13.217–218, 230, 363–371). Nakula volunteers to climb the *śamī* tree and tie the weapons to the branches.[19] In both cases, too, a final measure is taken for security. Athena sets a stone at the door of the cave; the Pāṇḍavas tie a corpse in the tree, pretending to some country folk that it is their traditional method of corpse disposal (13.370; 4,5.27–29).

10. Prayer and response

During his interview with Athena, Odysseus makes various requests. On first meeting her in her shepherd guise, he prays 'as if to a god', asking her to help safeguard himself and his treasure and to tell him where he is. Later, when Athena dissipates the mist, he greets the Naiads with prayers, promising them gifts if Athena protects himself and Telemachus – which is a sort of indirect prayer to her. Finally, he asks the goddess directly for help in defeating the suitors (13.231, 359–360, 386–391).

As befits a hymn of praise, most of Yudhiṣṭhira's invocation of Durgā consists in recitation of her attributes and allusions to her mythic deeds, known to us from other texts. Unlike Odysseus, he does not need to ask his whereabouts, but he does ask the goddess to be merciful, auspicious, and on the side of truth, and to grant victory, boons, shelter, and protection (Appx I 4D 30, 32, 50–51). The similarities to Odysseus' requests are somewhat vague. When epic hero meets warrior goddess, prayers for help in battle can be expected, and indeed both goddesses promise such help. Athena will be beside her protégé when the suitors' blood and brains bespatter the earth, and it is by Durgā's grace that Yudhiṣṭhira will kill the Kauravas en masse and, with his brothers, rule over the whole earth in health and happiness (13.393–6; Appx I 4D 55–59). But without being specifically asked, both goddesses go on to do something less predictable. Athena promises to make her hero unrecognizable, and Durgā promises that by her grace neither Kauravas nor local inhabitants will be able to recognize them.[20]

11. Shepherds and partly hidden royalty

When Athena first approaches Odysseus, it is in the form of a young man, a shepherd (or perhaps herdsman more generally), and at the same time delicate *(panapalos)*, as princes are, and with a doubly folded cloak over his shoulder (13.222–224). In other words, although she appears as a man of the people, her disguise barely hides her exalted origin (she was born directly from the King of the Gods).

When the Pāṇḍavas tie the corpse in the tree, the locals to whom they explain their act (adding the further lie that the corpse is that of their 180-year-old mother) are cowherds and shepherds (*gopāla*, *avipāla*, 4,5.29). Only two shlokas later, the CE moves us directly to Virāṭa's court, where Yudhiṣṭhira arrives with his dice fastened under his armpit in his cloak. From his appearance, Virāṭa judges that the newcomer is not a brahmin (as he pretends to be) but a lord of the earth or anointed king (4,6.1, 5–6). Virāṭa expresses similar doubts about the others, notably Sahadeva, who claims to be a cowherd, and Nakula, who claims to be an expert on horses. In other words, the Pāṇḍavas present themselves in relatively lowly disguises, but their royal birth almost shows through. This alone would make a reasonable comparison, even without the Sanskrit references to sheep and cloak.

12. Deity in disguise

Comparison 11 ignores one major difference: in the Greek, it is the deity that is disguised, in the Sanskrit, it is the mortals – when Durgā shows herself to Yudhiṣṭhira there is no reference to disguise. But a disguised deity does intervene in the last minor *parvan* of Book 3,[21] and yet again the Greek seems to bring together what the Sanskrit separates.

> Yudhiṣṭhira's divine father is the god Dharma (Religion or Cosmic Order personified). Dharma takes the form of a deer and runs off with a brahmin's fire-drilling sticks in his horns. The Pāṇḍavas pursue the deer but lose it. Suffering from thirst, they lament their plight. Nakula climbs a tree and locates a lake. One by one the younger brothers go to fetch water, but they disobey the orders of an anonymous voice and collapse in a sort of death-like trance. Finally, Yudhiṣṭhira goes to the lake, which is adorned with piles of gold. He, at last, obeys the orders of his father, who pretends to be a crane but has in fact taken the form of a large Yakṣa (a type of supernatural), who is tall as a palm. Dharma questions his son, is well answered, admits his identity,

and apparently reveals himself in his true form.[22] He explains his aim (which was to test his son), and gives boons, including that of unrecognizability in Virāṭa's city.

Even this brief summary suggests many links with the start of Book 4. Nakula climbs a tree, members of the party lie as if asleep, Yudhiṣṭhira speaks with the manifestation of a boon-giving deity, and unrecognizability is guaranteed. But what matters here is the comparison with the Greek. Odysseus is depressed and laments past failures and decisions, just as the Pāṇḍavas do (13.198–206; 3,295.15–296.4). Both heroes express unjustified suspicions: Odysseus at first blames the Phaeacians for dumping him in a foreign land, while Yudhiṣṭhira at first blames the leader of his enemies for the apparent death of his brothers (13.209–10; 3,297.5–7). Athena takes the initiative in arranging the meeting, as does Dharma. The goddess seems to be testing her protégé, the god is explicitly testing his son. Both meetings take place beside water and in the presence of gold. Both heroes end their first speeches with factual questions: Odysseus asks where he is, Yudhiṣṭhira asks who is his interlocutor. By their verbal behaviour, both heroes impress deities and receive praise from them. Even the double assurance of success in the incognito has a parallel in the Greek. Long before she gets to work with her wand, Athena covered the hero with a mist to render him temporarily unrecognizable even to wife, friends, and townsmen, and although she later scatters the mist, that is to allow him to recognize where he is. One need not assume that it cancels her earlier magical act.[23]

In short, whatever is made of the Sanskrit–Sanskrit comparison, it is clear that, even if attention is limited to the start of the Greek incognito, the Greek–Sanskrit comparison is not simple. As a war goddess who promises victory, Athena parallels Durgā, but in her male disguise, she is closer to Dharma. There is a general lesson here. Life would be easier for comparativists if comparisons were regularly one-to-one – a single Greek character or episode corresponding to a single Sanskrit one, but that may well prove the exception. More specifically, this particular Greek 'fusion' of male and female hints at ways of approaching other aspects of Athena's paradoxical nature.

Concluding discussion

No particular significance attaches to the number of headings under which the two narratives have been compared. The similarities reviewed here number many more than twelve, and to this virtual total can be added the relations between motifs. For instance, §9 not only compares two trees and two accumulations of valuables but also uses the spatial and narratological juxtaposition of the motifs. Again, the supplicant in §10 is husband of the queen in §5 and §6.

Since it is not easy to keep in mind two complex stories at once, let alone the relations between them, here is a rough formula to serve as overview: in conflating the Pāṇḍava brothers under the abstract figure of hero, it does not prejudge whether the protagonist in the proto-narrative was singular or (as is perhaps more likely) plural. It is presented as a simplified aide-mémoire, not a reconstruction:

> Hero departs and is absent for years. He undertakes a solo journey, is approached by a male deity or deity in male disguise, finds himself beside a religiously significant tree, encounters a warrior goddess, receives boons from her, enjoys himself telling lies as part of an incognito, kills his queen's suitors and restores her.

The density and interlinking of the similarities, reinforcing those presented in previous papers, demands historical explanation. Moreover, though I cannot argue the point here, the rootedness of both epics in their local cultures, taken with their general conformity to IE ideological patterns, strongly suggests explanation in terms of common origin. From this, it follows that the two warrior goddesses are cognate.

However, this finding needs to be put in its context. We are talking only about one strand in the complex figure of Athena. There is much more to her than a role in myth or epic, and even there one must not oversimplify: Athena intervenes often in Homer (cf. Wathelet 1995), Durgā only twice in the *Mahābhārata*. In other epic contexts, the role of Athena parallels that of Indra, King of the Gods, or that of Kṛṣṇa, as whose sister Durgā is sometimes presented.[24] The scope for further comparative work is immense.

Notes

1 First published in 2001 as 'Athena and Durgā: warrior goddesses in Greek and Sanskrit epic'.
2 As suggested by Teffeteller (2001).
3 [Ch. 4] and my other relevant papers cited later; also Vielle (1996).
4 Cf. for instance Karanika (2001), especially her concluding discussion of the Athena–Odysseus encounter in *Od.* 13.
5 Dumézil 1968, part 1; the same volume (pp. 580–586) presents his well-known trifunctional analysis of the Judgement of Paris, [which he considered a 'literary game' and 'evidently not an authentic religious combination' (1958: 58 = 1992: 150).] His analysis seems to me to omit the roles of Zeus and Eris – cf. Allen (1996a: 22–23).
6 Durgā as *mahiṣāsurā-mardinī* [killer of the demon] is a very common scene in Hindu iconography.
7 The names will be useful: (from older to younger) Yudhiṣṭhira, Bhīma, Arjuna, and the twins Nakula and Sahadeva. Their shared wife is Draupadī.
8 I ignore her second appearance, when Arjuna invokes her just before the *Bhagavad Gītā* (6 Appx I.1). Similar to the first, it does not tell against my argument here.
9 The Durgāstava is translated by Ganguli (1993) II: Book 4: 10–12; and (omitting lines 59–67) by Péterfalvi (1985–6) I: 274–276.
10 4,13–23. The timing is not totally clear. The story begins (4,13.1) when there are two months to go, climaxes when a month and a half remains (20.13), and ends when only thirteen days are left (23.27).
11 4,6–11, one chapter for each lie. The Pāṇḍavas discuss their disguises in advance in 4,1.19–3.18. The disguises are important in Dumézil's analysis of the brothers in 1968 – cf. also Allen (1999a). I have not been able to match up the Greek and Sanskrit false personae.

12 14.321–330, 19.185 ff., 24.309.

13 Arjuna says he will mention this if asked (4,2.26), but does not in fact mention it.

14 14.301–333, cf. especially 12.403–450.

15 4,8.27–31. Draupadī attributes the killing of Kīcaka and followers to her Gandharva husbands.

16 4,1.14. The verb *vihṛ-* 'amuse oneself' appears five further times while the disguises are being planned, and the verb *ram-* 'enjoy' twice.

17 Root *nidhā-* 'lay down' – 4,5.15, 24. I presume they were first laid on the earth.

18 The olive is *ektos hodou* – 13.123, while the *śamī* grows in forest which is *utpatha* (*ud* out of, away from, apart; *patha* way, path, road) – 4,5.13. Draupadī's weariness is inconsequential and has no obvious symbolic significance, but presumably the proto-narrative not only juxtaposed the motifs but also gave them a raison d'être.

19 4,5.25. The southern manuscripts have a variant version, summarized by Raghu Vira (1936: xix).

20 13.397 *(agnōston)*; Appx I 4D 68–69 *(na prajñāsanti)*. The verb roots are cognate but too common for this to be interesting. Lines 60–67, a *phalaśruti* (statement of the benefits derivable from the hymn) are absent from some manuscripts. If they are ignored, the *matprasādāt* 'by my grace' in line 68 clearly parallels the same phrase in 59 and the similar one in 56. The three Sanskrit promises are doubtless trifunctional: victory F2 (i.e. second functional), joy and health F3, and unrecognizability (belonging to the magical or cognitive domain) F1. In any case, the unrecognizability comes last, as in the Greek.

21 3,295–299, 'The Drilling Woods' or 'The Firesticks'. A minor *parvan* is a division of a *parvan* or book.

22 3,298.22. There is no suggestion that, either in his *yakṣa* or other form, Dharma is here particularly royal or princely in appearance.

23 13.189–193 (*agnōston* again, as in note 28), 352, 429. In the southern manuscripts, before meeting Virāṭa, the party visit the Ganges, where Yudhiṣṭhira obtains from Dharma in an instant the clothes and ornaments needed for the new roles (Raghu Vira 1936: xix; Appx I 5). This parallels Odysseus obtaining from Athena the appearance and accoutrements of a beggar.

24 Athena ~ Indra: [Ch. 3, §2, agent G]. Athena ~ Kṛṣṇa: [Ch. 2] (the deities bring together the hero and Nausicaa/Subhadrā). Kṛṣṇa ~ Durgā: *Mbh.* 4 Appx I 4D 7, and later texts. One needs to ask whether Athena has expanded her epic role, Durgā has contracted, or both.

9

DRAUPADĪ AND PENELOPE

Right at the start of his *Genèse de l'Odyssée* [1954], Gabriel Germain proposed a comparison between Homer's Penelope and Draupadī, the heroine of the *Mahābhārata*.[1] Penelope regains her husband Odysseus after he defeats the suitors in an archery competition, and Draupadī chooses her favourite husband, Arjuna, after he defeats the other suitors in an archery competition. So each epic heroine makes a 'marriage by concourse' [Sanskrit *svayaṃvara*]. Germain thought that the two traditions derived equally from a prehistoric tradition that could well have been Indo-European. I think he was right, and I hope today to make his comparison somewhat deeper and fuller.

Naturally, numerous differences can be found between the two stories. Above all, one should note that for Penelope the event is a repetition of her first marriage more than twenty years earlier, while for Draupadī it is truly her first marriage. This is why Penelope is living in the palace of her husband, while Draupadī is living in the palace of her father Drupada, and Penelope already has a son, while Draupadī does not. Moreover, Penelope's marriage is monogamous while Draupadī's is polyandrous – to the five Pāṇḍava brothers.

Rapprochements

Here are the similarities that I shall be emphasizing. I have given them numbers and invented titles.

1 *Disguise*. Odysseus is disguised as an aged beggar, Arjuna (like his brothers) as a brahmin. Both have been disguised for some while: Odysseus since Athena transformed him on the beach at Ithaca, the Pāṇḍavas since they arrived at Ekacakrā (1,145.2–5).[2]

2 *Begging*. One expects that a beggar will beg. But a brahmin possesses knowledge, of ritual and other matters, and could probably survive without begging. Even so, the Pāṇḍavas live by collecting alms, first at Ekacakrā, then at Drupada's capital, Śiśumāra (176.7. . .).

3 *Humble lodging*. During his first nights in Ithaca, Odysseus stays with Eumaeus, a swineherd; and when he arrives at the palace in Ithaca, he refuses a comfortable bed (19.336–342, 20.2). The Pāṇḍavas lodge in the house of a potter, sleeping on the earth (137.15).

4 *Is the hero dead?* Many in Ithaca think that Odysseus is dead – Eurymachus, an anonymous suitor, Eumaeus (1.183, 333; 14.68), Melanthius, Penelope, Eurycleia among others: the 'day of his return (*nostimon ēmar* 1.168) is destroyed'. But the Pāṇḍavas too are believed to be dead, incinerated in the lacquer house (136.4–12, 180.21, 185.12); their funeral rituals have even been performed (137.15).

5 *May the hero still be alive?* Just a few individuals remain who believe that the hero still lives. Interpreting a bird omen, Halitherses says that Odysseus will soon be home (2.163–176). Theoclymenus is equally confident (17.154–161). At Śiśumāra, Kṛṣṇa is not taken in by the disguise and recognizes his cousins (178.10, 181.32, 183.2).

6 *Gathering of suitors*. Here is a substantial difference: the Greek suitors seem to have assembled spontaneously while the Indians are responding to the widespread public announcements ordered by Drupada. On the other hand, (a) both sets of suitors have similar intentions. (b) In each case, the gathering is separated chronologically from the archery competition. The Greeks assembled at the palace more than three years before the competition (2.89), the Indians sixteen days before (176.29). (c) In the interval, the household of the bride has incurred considerable expense. In Homer, the extravagance is attributed to the suitors – it is one of their sins. In India, Drupada spends generously, and no doubt his largesse is regarded as meritorious – he enjoys unsurpassed wealth (176.29). In Greece, the expenditure mostly concerns the domestic animals killed for feasting; in India too, apart from gifts and spectacles, Drupada donates cows, food, and delicacies (175.14). But (d) the gathering is not simply a secular event. The day of the competition, which is associated with lunar cycles, is the festival of Apollo (20.156, 21.258, 276–278); and the gathering at Śiśumāra is also described as a festival (*devotsava* 175.11, 20). A learned brahmin opens the ceremony with an oblation of butter to Agni (176.31–32).

7a *Suitors' character*. The wooers of Penelope are full of arrogance *(huperphialos)*, and so are those of Draupadī (*ahaṃkṛtena, samṛddha-darpā* 178.1–2). If the Greek suitors are sinners whom Odysseus can kill in the name of justice, the list of the Indian suitors opens with the Kauravas (Duryodhana, etc. 177.1), who are incarnations of demons (161.80–84) and behave in a manner befitting their origin.

7b *Suitors' names listed.* Among the 108 suitors, a few are named in passing by Homer, but a 136 are listed by Apollodorus (*Epit.* 7.26–30). The Sanskrit text gives a hundred and eleven names or titles, albeit mentioning that there were 'many others' (177.1–21).

8 *Divine planning.* Right from the start of the *Odyssey*, the reader knows that Athena is promising the return of the hero, and that Zeus approves of it. One can imagine that, even at this point (1.91), Athena has in mind the death of the suitors, which she does not explicitly announce until much later (13.376). In any case, it is she who gives Penelope the idea of the archery competition (21.1–4). But it is equally the will of the gods, or Destiny, that establishes not only the victory of the Pāṇḍavas over the Kauravas, but also the polyandrous marriage of Draupadī. Already at Ekacakrā, the seer Vyāsa tells the Pāṇḍavas the story of Draupadī in a previous incarnation: she five times repeated to Śiva her prayer for a husband, and she will indeed receive five husbands. She is now the 'predestined' wife of the Pāṇḍavas (157.6–14, cf. 189.41–47). To Drupada, Vyāsa also gives an explanation of the polyandrous marriage, but a different one, according to which it conforms to the decree of Nārāyaṇa (= Viṣṇu) as well as that of Śiva (189.1–34).

9 *Presence of deities.* Zeus and Athena do not merely decree the sequence of events from afar; they are also closely involved in them. As we shall see later (§18), Zeus celebrates the success of Odysseus in the competition, and his daughter participates in the massacre of the suitors. Three Sanskrit shlokas (178.6–7, 13) list the categories of supernaturals present at Śiśumāra.

10 *Proclamation.* In Homer, terms of the competition are announced by Penelope (21.68–79), in India, by Dhṛṣṭadyumna, Draupadī's brother.

11 *Failure of suitors.* Both in Greece and India, they are unable even to bend the bow (21.144–187, 245ff; 178.15–17).

12 *Finally, the hero comes forward.* Antinous proposes to put off continuing with the competition until the next day, but Odysseus wants to have his turn straightaway. He demands the bow (21.275–84), and Eumaeus gives it (21.359–79). Once the princely suitors have withdrawn, Arjuna stands up among the brahmins (179.1).

13 *Protestations and responses.* Making threats, Antinous protests against Odysseus, but Penelope defends him. Eurymachus restates the suitors' case in a moderate manner, but Penelope does not yield. Dismissing his mother, Telemachus authorizes the giving of the bow to his father, in spite of the outcry raised by the suitors, who roundly reproach Eumaeus (21.360).

The brahmins make a similar hubbub. Some protest against the presumption of a young brahmin trying to outdo well-known warriors, while others defend him and approve of his attempt.

14 *The debate.* Eurymachus expresses his fear of humiliation: if the beggar succeeds, the Greeks of lower social classes will laugh at the suitors (21.324). At Śiśumāra, the protestors express a similar fear: if Arjuna should fail, the brahmins will be laughed at by the kings (179.6–8).

On the other side, Penelope praises the physique of the stranger: he is tall and well-built (*megas ēd' eupēgēs* 22.334). The Indian defenders of Arjuna do the same: the young man is sturdy, like the trunk of the King of elephants; his shoulders, thighs, and arms are massive (179.9).

15 *Hero's [treatment of] bow*. Odysseus studies the bow minutely, turning it over repeatedly in his hands *(anastrōphōn)*, so as to see it from all sides (21.394, 405). Then he strings it with as little effort as a lyre-player fits a new string to his instrument. Arjuna, on foot, circumambulates the bow in the auspicious [clockwise] direction, bowing his head as a sign of respect (179.15).
16 *Musical sounds*. [The hero's manipulations culminate in a Homeric simile.] Taking the bow in his right hand, he plucks the string, which sings like a swallow (21.411). In the Sanskrit, the bending of the bow is immediately followed by the discharge of the arrow, which produces reactions both in heaven and on earth. On earth, music can be heard and praises are sung by troupes of bards and praise-singers (179.19).
17 *Reaction of spectators*. The hero's success causes the Greek suitors great distress *(akhos mega)*, transforming the colour of their cheeks (21.412–413). In India [the spectators show great emotion, waving their clothes in the air and giving vent to exclamations] (179.18ab).
18 *Reaction of deities*. As a sign, Zeus thunders, thereby encouraging Odysseus (21.413–415). In India, the air resounds with a loud noise *(nāda)*, and a god [not named] causes a rain of divine flowers to fall on the head of Arjuna (1,179.17–18).
19 *The shot*. From his seat, Odysseus discharges the arrow, which passes through the twelve axe handles. Arjuna, aiming through a wheel (?), hits his target with five arrows and shoots it down (176.34, 179.16). The technical details are not entirely clear, either in Greece or India.
20 *Test of identity*. In both epics, the hero's triumph is followed by violence – the massacre in Greece, a conflict that ends without fatalities in India. But the victor's identity remains uncertain, at least for some of those present. In Homer, Penelope shows herself particularly suspicious. She resists the revelations of Eurycleia (23.62), and even when face to face with her husband, she does not accept him. Odysseus thinks of an identity test – an idea that Penelope takes up by giving Eurycleia instructions concerning the conjugal bed (23.177–180). Her husband's response at last convinces her.

When Draupadī leaves with Arjuna and Bhīma for their lodgings at the potter's house, Drupada still does not know the identity of his son-in-law. Dhṛṣṭadyumna follows his sister and brings back to the king a report of his secret observations. But Drupada resists his son's revelations. At first, he sends his chaplain to ask direct questions, but then this step is supplanted by a non-verbal test. The Pāṇḍavas are invited to a banquet at which varied objects are put on display, relating to different modes of life (186.5–6). The brothers interest themselves only in objects relating to warfare, which wins them the approval of the royal circle.[3] Now Drupada puts his question face-to-face and is at last satisfied by the answer.

21 *Transfiguration.* Before his intimate conversation with Penelope, Odysseus is transfigured by Athena; she makes him larger and more handsome, surrounding him with a halo (23.156–163). The transfiguration of Odysseus is presented by Homer as an objective event, while in India, what Vyāsa does is more subjective. He gives Drupada a miraculous vision of the Pāṇḍavas in their divine Indraic form. In other words, they appear to be radiant, as they were in their previous life (189.35–40).

Of these twenty-one rapprochements, Germain already recognized nine (§§1, 2, 6, 10–13, 15, 19). In addition, he proposed one other that I have not accepted:

11a? *Competitor debarred in advance.* Responding to Antinous, Penelope announces that, even if the stranger should succeed in bending the bow, he would not become her husband – he himself would not expect to do so (21.314–319). All she would do would be to give him gifts and let him depart (338–342). After the failure of the other Indian suitors, Karṇa takes the bow and bends it straightaway. Before he can shoot, Draupadī announces that in any case she will never accept him as a husband, because of his low birth. So Karṇa gives up.

This incident (1827★) is rejected from the text of the CE, but the difficulty lies not there but in the narrative. Germain seems to believe (pp. 13, 17, 26) that Penelope angrily disqualifies Odysseus more or less as Draupadī angrily disqualifies Karṇa. But it seems to me rather that she is objecting to the refusal of Antinous to allow participation by the beggar. If one wants, even so, to include the Karṇa episode in the comparison, it would be better to consider a rapprochement with Telemachus. Having set up the axes for the competition, Telemachus tries to bend the bow and desists only because of a sign made by his father (21.124–129). If this rapprochement is accepted, it might be called '11a. Participant dissuaded'. [As regards *agents*, the implications (Karṇa // Telemachus, and Draupadī // Odysseus) are 'fleeting' and insignificant; the significant rapprochement is between *actions* and seems to me acceptable.]

Wider context

In any case, reasons for seeking a common origin of the two stories are much more plentiful than was recognized by Germain. But Germain – the pioneer – was limiting his study to the theme of marriage by concourse. He supposed that the Greek poet, having found this theme among the stock of traditional stories, fitted it in to the plot of his epic. But perhaps what was present in the traditional stock was a story of far greater scale, in which marriage by concourse was just one element among others? That is what I believe. Aspects of the question have been discussed elsewhere, and what follows is only an extremely concise précis.

1 *Series of liaisons.* Penelope and Draupadī are the chief wives of their heroes, but they are not the only ones. Developing a little the trifunctional theory of Georges Dumézil, I have tried to show that each of these females has a place within a pentadic structure, and that the Greek and Sanskrit elements of these structures correspond to each other. For instance, Circe corresponds to Ulūpī, and the group of monsters stationed near the Straits corresponds to a group of five crocodiles/nymphs [Chs 2, 6].

2 *Children linked to idea of totality.* According to a post-Homeric tradition, Penelope has sexual relations with the suitors and gives birth to Pan, whose name was understood by the Greeks as the neuter of *pās* 'all'. Draupadī has sexual relations with her five husbands and gives birth to the five Draupadeyas, incarnations of the Viśvedevas – a name which means 'All-the-Gods'.

3 *Husband associated with horse.* According to other post-Homeric traditions, towards the end of his life, Odysseus is transformed into a horse. But Draupadī ritually imitates a sexual act with the horse that Arjuna has accompanied for a whole year (for 2 & 3, see [Ch. 3]).

4 *Death of female's would-be lovers.* Just as the 108 suitors of Penelope are massacred by Odysseus and his helpers, so the 105 Kīcakas, and their leader, Kīcaka himself, who tries to seduce Draupadī, are massacred by Bhīma, Arjuna's brother [Ch. 8].

So the two texts are not only similar in that each deals with a marriage by concourse. In spite of the differences that one expects, the biographies of the two queens present other similarities – showing that Penelope and Draupadī have common roots *as heroines of an epic narrative*. But to finish with, here is a rapprochement that some may hesitate to accept but that is at least worth raising.

22 *Trickery, weaving, and alternation.* When the suitors put pressure on Penelope, she gains time by means of a trick. She claims the right to weave a shroud for her father-in-law, but what she weaves by day she undoes at night. Finally, her ruse is revealed, and she abandons it (2.93ff, etc.).

Having won the dice match by trickery, the Kauravas have reduced the Pāṇḍavas to the condition of slaves (Book 2,60–61). Draupadī is dragged into the Great Hall, and a violent attempt is made to strip her. But now comes a miracle. Each time her dress is removed, it is replaced by a similar one. Eventually her persecutor realizes that his attempt is futile, and he abandons it.

So both stories show alternation: fabric is woven, undone, and woven again. . .; a dress is worn, stripped away, and worn again. . .

Whatever one makes of this last rapprochement, I hope to have assembled additional demonstration in support of the great insight of Gabriel Germain. There are certainly other comparisons that will eventually make their contribution to the prehistory of the Homeric narratives.

Notes

1 First published in 2002 as 'Pénélope et Draupadî: la validité de la comparaison' in a book celebrating the work of Germain.

2 References are to the Sanskrit text (CE), and enable one to find the relevant pages in van Buitenen's translation [1973]. Sometimes the French version used the translation of Péterfalvi [1985–6]. Since [nearly] all the Sanskrit references come from the first book of the Great Epic, that book number will henceforth be omitted. [Greek references are all to the *Odyssey*.]

3 The reader will recall Achilles/Pyrrha on Scyros [Hyginus *Fab*. 96].

10

BHĪṢMA AND SARPEDON

In the days of Max Müller, the polytheism of the pre-Christian Indo-European (IE) speakers was a central topic in human studies and attracted much attention.[1] However, the results proved disappointing, and in the first half of the last century, IE comparativism contracted: when not being misused by Nazi racists, it was mainly pursued by comparative philologists, whose centre of gravity was purely linguistic. In the last half century the field has been revived by Georges Dumézil, and this present chapter, like my other papers in this area, is, broadly speaking, Dumézilian.

Dumézil's central concern was how far the linguists' model can be transferred to extra-linguistic culture: if IE languages can be analyzed in terms of divergent historical descent from a proto-language, how far can IE cultures, especially early ones, be understood in terms of divergent descent from an original proto-culture? Dumézil's famous three functions are just one among the many proposals that arose from asking the central question and will be mentioned today only in passing. The central question itself is a perfectly sensible one, which can of course be asked of any language family. However, for various reasons, Dumézil's work is still regarded as controversial. Among the good reasons are weaknesses internal to his arguments (weaknesses which necessitate, I think, a shift of focus from triads to pentads). Some of the reasons are bad ones, for example blindness to structure, or misrepresentations ultimately motivated by the desire of narrower specialists to defend the borders of their own fields. Some are just matters of fact, for example the relative paucity of those who are, or think they are, equipped to handle Latin, Greek, and Sanskrit materials on the same footing, and the difficulty of coming to terms with an oeuvre on the scale of Dumézil's. But, as I hope to show here, not only is the central question reasonable, but the field is an exciting one. It may be too philological for most anthropologists, too cultural for most linguists, too comparative for the narrower philologists, but it offers scope for unexpected findings.

Linguists long ago established that Latin Jupiter, Greek Zeus, and Sanskrit Dyaus (or Dyu) are cognate: these three theonyms (and there are others) must descend from a common origin, which can be reconstructed as PIE *Dyēus. *Dyēus must have been a father, must have meant 'sky', and was surely an important god, perhaps even a sovereign, as are Zeus and Jupiter; but it was difficult to go further (Dunkel 1988–90). The myths do not help. The major Roman gods have little surviving indigenous mythology, and although many Vedic deities are well supplied with it, Dyaus is not. Zeus of course has myths in plenty, but one cannot reconstruct using a single source.

Dumézil, prompted by Stig Wikander, showed the way ahead. Although he has some divine relatives, Dyaus practically never appears in Vedic narrative, but a millennium later, in classical Sanskrit, Dyaus does appear in one story in the *Mahābhārata*. Together with his seven [or eight] brothers, he is cursed to be born on earth, and his human form or incarnation is the hero Bhīṣma. Bhīṣma is a major figure right from his birth in Book 1 up to his death in Book 13 (90% of the way through the epic), and as Dumézil showed, in certain respects Bhīṣma resembles the Scandinavian god Heimdall. The resemblance is close enough to point to a common origin for the narrative features in question, and Dumézil concludes (1968: 190) that they were originally part of the mythology of *Dyēus; they then descended to Dyaus and his human form.

In his mature work, Dumézil usually avoided comparisons involving Greece,[2] but his discovery is suggestive. If we can learn about the mythology of *Dyēus by comparing Dyaus' incarnation Bhīṣma with a *Norse* god, can we learn more by comparing him with *Greek* gods? I have attempted this elsewhere [Ch. 11]. It turns out that Bhīṣma can be compared not only with Dyaus' etymological cognate Zeus but also with his semantic cognate Ouranos (which, like Dyaus, means 'Sky'). These rapprochements, like the Norse one, link a Sanskrit *hero* with non-Sanskrit *gods*. But does Bhīṣma resemble any Greek *heroes*? This question brings us to Sarpedon.

Bhīṣma and Sarpedon

Greek gods sometimes take human form for short periods, but they do not incarnate for a whole human life-span, as Indian gods often do; so we cannot expect an incarnation of Zeus parallel to the Indian incarnation of Dyaus. But the conceptual gap between being a god's *incarnation* and being a god's *son* cannot be great, if only because the Pāṇḍavas, the Winners in the *Mahābhārata*, are presented in both ways.[3] Now Zeus, though he lacks incarnations, has numerous human sons, born of mortal women (unlike Ouranos, who has none, and need not concern us further).

A salient fact about Bhīṣma is that he is a major leader on the losing side in the Great War that dominates the Sanskrit epic. The Great War that dominates Greek epic is at Troy, the Losers are the Trojans, and one of the major Trojan leaders is Sarpedon, son of Zeus. So let us explore a Bhīṣma–Sarpedon rapprochement.

Winners and losers

The two sides in the Sanskrit are the Pāṇḍavas and Kauravas. The Pāṇḍavas are the Winners; they represent the gods as opposed to the demons and are the side with which the audience fundamentally identifies. In Homer too, the Winners, the Greeks or Achaeans, are the side with which the Greek audience should ultimately identify. It is therefore striking that the human form of the old IE sky god fights for the opposition, for the Losers – one is tempted to say the Baddies.[4] One might of course wonder whether in other respects Pāṇḍavas correspond to Greeks, Kauravas to Trojans. The question is complicated, for comparison can also be made with the other Sanskrit epic, the *Rāmāyaṇa*, where Rāma represents Winners/Goodies and Rāvaṇa Losers/Baddies. But the complication does not invalidate a Bhīṣma–Sarpedon comparison.

Important loser leader

Bhīṣma is not just a major Kaurava warrior. He is the first in a set of five successive Kaurava marshals – one of the pentads I mentioned in passing [see esp. Ch. 24, 'Five phases']. On Day 10, he is shot down and disabled; he lives on for two months but is succeeded by three other marshals in turn, each of whom dies on the battlefield. Since the whole war lasts only eighteen days, Bhīṣma holds office for longer than all his successors put together.

Similarly, Sarpedon is not just a major Trojan warrior (12.101); he leads all the *epikouroi*, the allies who have come from outside Troy and its immediate environs. No Homeric heroes live on immobilized like Bhīṣma, and Sarpedon is straightforwardly killed (by Patroclus).

Forms pair with loser supremo

Supreme authority among the Kaurava warriors lies not with the marshal *(senāpati)* but with the crown prince, Duryodhana, who appoints the marshals and is himself a great warrior. Thus, during his ten days as marshal, Bhīṣma is effectively paired with his supremo; they are the two leaders par excellence. Duryodhana's father, King Dhṛtarāṣṭra – blind and indecisive – is a non-combatant, who stays in the royal city.

Among the Trojans, the warrior supremo is of course Hector, until he is killed by Achilles. Hector is the eldest son of the aged non-combatant king Priam, who stays in Troy and can be compared with Dhṛtarāṣṭra, and in several ways Hector and Sarpedon form a pair. Consider the two passages that enumerate the Trojan forces. In 2.876, the list of seventeen contingents starts with the Trojans themselves led by Hector, and ends with the Lycians led by Sarpedon and Glaucus. Similarly, in 12.88, the list of five companies starts with the 'biggest and best', led by Hector and Polydamas, and ends with the allies, led by Sarpedon; so in both cases, these two names come effectively first and last. Or take the fact that only this pair inflict damage on the Greek defences: Sarpedon pulls down some battlements, then Hector shatters a gate (12.398, 461).

A fourth argument builds on the generally recognized pairing of Patroclus and Achilles – paired for instance because of their long and close association, because Patroclus in Achilles' armour leads Achilles' troops, and because they alone when they die are honoured by funeral games. But the most important enemies of *this* pair – namely Patroclus and Achilles – are respectively Sarpedon and Hector.

Thus, in both epics, the human form of Dyaus/Zeus not only fights for the Losers but also does so as a leader subordinate only to his side's supremo.

Critical of loser supremo

Although Bhīṣma renounced marriage and had no children, he is regarded and referred to as the grandfather both of Duryodhana and of his opposite numbers, the five Pāṇḍava brothers. He often criticizes Duryodhana's immoral behaviour (e.g. 1,195) but his wise advice is ignored. But towards the Pāṇḍavas, he shows genuine affection and respect, which is reciprocated.

At his first appearance in the narrative (as distinct from the *Catalogue*), we find Sarpedon strongly criticizing Hector for lack of dynamism (5.493). Hector is energized, but a little later he pointedly ignores a pitiful plea from Sarpedon, who has just been badly wounded by Tlepolemos (5.689).

Sarpedon's uneasy relation with Hector is clear enough though, unlike Bhīṣma, he does not show any particular affection for the Winners. On the other hand, he has a sort of doublet in his Lycian compatriot and first cousin, Glaucus: for instance, after Sarpedon's death, it is Glaucus who criticizes Hector for lack of valour and lack of gratitude (17.140). So it may be significant that Glaucus provides the only clear instance of friendship between warriors on opposite sides. During Diomedes' *aristeia*, it transpires that he and Glaucus are ritual friends (6.224), and their intended duel turns into an amicable exchange of gifts.

Active over three generations

Bhīṣma's warrior prowess, already apparent in his fight with Paraśurāma following his brother's wedding (5,180.19 ff.), is undiminished when as 'the grandfather' he becomes marshal two generations later. Homer's Sarpedon is not presented as aged, but Apollodorus (*Bibl.* 3.1.2) tells us that this hero received from Zeus the privilege of living for three generations. The statement is often understood as a secondary rationalization of the fact that Sarpedon is the name of another son of Zeus (the brother of Minos and Rhadamanthys) born two generations earlier. But in view of the other Sarpedon–Bhīṣma similarities, it is more likely that here (as quite often) Apollodorus preserves an ancient tradition – that is of vigour persisting over three generations.

Bloody rain

When Bhīṣma is appointed as marshal, a bloody dirty rain appears in a clear sky,[5] accompanied by other fearsome portents. When Zeus is persuaded by Hera that

Sarpedon must die, just before the fatal fight with Patroclus, he honours his son by pouring down bloody raindrops (*haimatoessas psiadas*, 16.459). Since in both traditions bloody rain occurs in a few other contexts as well, the comparison is not 'biunique'; nevertheless, it is worth noting.

Even if the last two headings are omitted, the similarities between Bhīṣma and Sarpedon are too solid to be dismissed as coincidence, and there must once have existed a proto-narrative concerning the human form of *Dyēus – let us provisionally call him the 'proto-figure'. Naturally, divergence has been considerable, and one could assemble a systematic list of differences by working through the dossiers of Bhīṣma and Sarpedon. But an obvious one is simply the relative size of the two dossiers. Bhīṣma is far more important in the Sanskrit epic than Sarpedon is in the Greek, and we need to consider two possibilities. If the Greek is the more conservative, a Sarpedon-like proto-figure has expanded to produce Bhīṣma, perhaps simply by invention of new narrative, but perhaps – more interestingly – by absorbing other figures. If the Sanskrit is the more conservative, a Bhīṣma-like proto-figure has contracted to produce Sarpedon, either simply by the elimination of certain features or episodes or – more interestingly – by losing them to other figures. Intuitively, the son of an important sky god *ought* to have a larger role rather than a smaller one, and for many reasons I prefer the hypothesis of Sanskrit traditionalism. I have already mentioned the argument that Bhīṣma, the incarnated god, corresponds in some features to the Greek gods Zeus and Ouranos. Expressed in diachronic terms, this *could* mean that the proto-figure lost parts of his dossier to the two gods, but whether or not this is the case, we cannot assume that all the surviving dossier that was attached to mortals was attached to Sarpedon. We need to ask whether Bhīṣma resembles any other warrior.

A rapprochement was briefly made earlier between the two loser supremos, Duryodhana and Hector, eldest sons of the non-combatant king, but here too we cannot assume that the comparativist's task is simple. It will be recalled that Hector and Sarpedon are closely linked (as Homerists recognize),[6] and in at least two respects Bhīṣma parallels Hector, not Sarpedon.

Bhīṣma and Hector

Sequence of four battlefield leaders

Bhīṣma, as we know, is the first of the five Kaurava marshals, but the fifth, Aśvatthāman, is heterogeneous, for example in fighting by night and in an enclosure, not on the battlefield; there are only four 'battlefield marshals'. But extra-Homeric sources tell us that after Hector is killed by Achilles, the Trojans are led successively by Penthesilea, Memnon, and Eurypylus; so the Trojans too have four battlefield leaders [Allen 2002b]. The three leaders just mentioned all come from areas at some distance from Troy, and I suppose that at earlier (unattested) stages of Greek tradition the sequence began with Sarpedon the Lycian (or an earlier form of that figure), who then lost to Hector the position of first overall battlefield leader.

It is as if Bhīṣma lost to Duryodhana the position of *senāpati*, while remaining the second most important leader among the Losers.

We can perhaps see a hint of the shift in Homer. In Book 12, Hector is the first to leap into the Greek camp (entering through the gate he broke, 12.457–466), but after he kills Sarpedon, Patroclus says that his victim was the first to do so (16.558).

Killed by winners' champion with female help

Bhīṣma is shot down by two warriors acting together: Arjuna, supreme champion of the Pāṇḍavas, and Śikhaṇḍin, who is involved largely because he was born a female (Bhīṣma has vowed not to fight anyone who counts as female). This is the only death in the Sanskrit Great War that crucially involves a female or 'quasi-female'. But Hector too is killed by two figures acting together: Achilles is the supreme Greek champion but he is helped greatly, even unfairly, by Athena.

This feature too, I suppose, originally belonged to the death of Sarpedon (or his proto-narrative equivalent) but was transferred to Hector alongside the battlefield supremacy. If the proto-narrative here resembled the Sanskrit, the loser supremo survived until after the death of the fourth loser battlefield leader.

Concluding discussion

The body of this chapter has presented a rapprochement between Bhīṣma and Sarpedon: the two heroes are to be seen as divergent reflexes of a proto-figure, the son of the PIE god *Dyēus. Towards the end I briefly suggested that the Sanskrit was the more conservative tradition and that, as the Greek tradition diverged, a more or less Bhīṣma-like proto-figure lost parts of his persona to at least one other hero. In this case, Hector, the recipient of the lost parts, no doubt derives his core features from a different proto-narrative human, but such a process cannot be taken for granted: rather than being transferred, fragments of a proto-figure could, as it were, simply become free-standing. A number of logical possibilities can be envisaged for the process of divergence, which may well have been very complex. To factor in the other traditions, for instance the Norse, will multiply the complexities.

Nevertheless, something has been achieved. In particular, we now know, as we did not previously, that *Dyēus had a human form (whether son or incarnation), who participated with the Losers in a more or less epic proto-narrative. Of course, *Dyēus provides exceptionally favourable opportunities for the comparativist since the etymological picture is so clear. But serious comparisons can be undertaken even between deities whose names lack a common origin. Examples might include Dumézil's Dyaus–Heimdall comparison or my own [Ch. 8] between Durgā and Athena. In spite of the complications, the history of the IE pantheon is less unknowable than has usually been thought.

Notes

1 First published in 2004 as 'Dyaus and Bhīṣma, Zeus and Sarpedon: towards a history of the Indo-European sky god'.
2 Except when discussing Plato and Heracles; [but see also Dumézil 1982, 1985a: esquisses 12–15, 51–58.]
3 Sons most fully in 1,114–115; partial incarnations in 1,61.84–85 (e.g. 'King Yudhiṣṭhira was a portion of [the god] Dharma').
4 As regards Dyaus and Bhisma, Dumézil recognizes the puzzle (1968: 254) but has only the most tentative answer to it. My own answer needs a wider comparative framework than can be attempted here.
5 *Anabhre varṣaṃ rudhira-kardamam* (5,153.28).
6 Zeus is very fond of both. Sarpedon is described by Zeus as the 'dearest of men', *philtatos andrōn* (16.433), while Hector is also described by Zeus as a 'dear man', *philon andra* (22.168) and the 'dearest of men', *philtatos andrōn* (24.67) – dearest of the Trojans to the gods in general.

11

HESIOD'S SUCCESSION MYTH

This chapter, like [Ch. 5], belongs to the field of research that I call 'Indo-European (IE) cultural comparativism',[1] but while the earlier paper took off from a comparison between the *Mahābhārata* and Homer's *Odyssey*, this one turns to Homer's approximate contemporary, Hesiod. The assumption is again that, if similarities between the Sanskrit and the Greek narratives are sufficiently numerous, detailed, and well structured, then they indicate a common origin, very possibly in a narrative that was already current at the time when the languages separated. During many centuries of oral transmission, the 'proto-narrative' would have diverged or branched, alongside the languages in which it was expressed.

The Sanskrit narrative studied here centres on Bhīṣma and comes primarily from *Mbh.* 1, especially *Upaparvans* 6–7. In the CE (used consistently here) these sections occupy chapters *(adhyāyas)* 54–123, but only about a dozen chapters will be closely relevant. As for Hesiod, his *Theogony* ('Birth of the Gods') is a poem of 1,022 lines, of which the last hundred or so are often taken to be a later addition. It was written down, in roughly the same metre and diction as the two Homeric epics, around 700 BC. Interspersed among much genealogical matter, the poem tells the story of three gods linked by filiation – Ouranos (= Latin Uranus), Cronus and Zeus – each of whom dominates his own generation. The same story, with differences of detail, is covered by Apollodorus (first–second century AD) at the start of his compendium of Greek mythology (1.1–6).[2] The story of the three gods has come to be known as the Succession Myth (West 1966) but is sometimes subsumed under the broader title 'Kingship in Heaven' (Littleton 1970).

One good reason for exploring this particular comparison is that Bhīṣma is the incarnation of Dyaus, and Dyaus is etymologically cognate with Zeus (both names, like that of Roman Jupiter, derive from a reconstructed *Dyēus – Polomé et al. 1997). Moreover, when it is not used as a theonym, *dyaus* means simply 'sky, heaven', which is also the meaning of Greek *ouranos*. Since none of these facts is obscure or newly discovered, one might expect the IE comparative literature to be unmanageably large, but it is not. This is partly because most IE comparativists, being linguists by background rather than mythologists, focus on the earlier Vedas rather than on the later classical Sanskrit epic, and cultural comparativists are relatively few and academically marginalized, but there may be a more specific reason. It is widely accepted among classicists (e.g. Walcot 1966; Kirk 1974: 256; Griffin 1986; West 1997), in light of Hittite, Syrian, and Mesopotamian material, that Hesiod's Succession Myth derives from non-IE West Asia, and the conclusion has been accepted by some IE mythologists (e.g. Puhvel 1987: 24–31), though not by all (Wikander 1952; Sergent 1997: 334).[3] The myth could of course combine motifs from different origins, as Briquel (1980) rightly notes, but the argument for a West Asian origin complicates the picture for IE comparativists and may have inhibited curiosity.

For comparativism involving Bhīṣma, the basic reference is Dumézil (1968: 176–190), which draws on an article of 1959 (reprinted, with retouches, as 2000: 169–188). As Dumézil acknowledged, this work merely applied to Bhīṣma the discovery made by the Indo-Iranian comparativist Stig Wikander in 1947 of the analytical importance of the links between individual Pāṇḍava brothers and the gods of whom they are the children or incarnations.[4] However, during his mature phase, Dumézil avoided India–Greece comparisons (for reasons he explained in 1987: 157–166). In fact, he regarded the etymological link between Dyaus and Zeus as disappointing for comparativists: 'In Vedic Dyaus, the "sky" is quite differently oriented from Greek Zeus or Roman Jupiter and the rapprochement teaches us almost nothing' (1968: 11). Instead, his comparison linked Bhīṣma with the Norse god Heimdall, focusing among other similarities on their respective birth stories. Although the comparison is convincing,[5] the present chapter concentrates on the Sanskrit and Greek, barely alluding to the Scandinavian material; I also refer only briefly to the important topic of Bhīṣma the match-maker (Dumézil 1979: 66–71, Allen 2007a).

Dumézil's general position is that stories about human agents in the *Mahābhārata* are transpositions of Vedic or pre-Vedic myths about deities – myths which may or may not survive in the Vedic literature we possess. Thus the Bhīṣma–Heimdall similarities arise because Bhīṣma is a transposition of Dyaus, who was cognate with the Norse god. We too will be exploring similarities between Sanskrit epic figures and non-Sanskrit deities, but now that similarities, both of structure and detail, are beginning to accumulate between Indian and Greek *heroes*, there is less reason than previously to think in terms of a god-to-man transposition occurring in India. In fact, since so much more evidence exists than can be mobilized here, I do not even try to decide whether the stories applied to gods before they applied to men. Similarly, fundamental though it is, and relevant in certain ways, I scarcely have space to mention three- or four-functional theory (Allen 1999b).

Writing in 1952, before Dumézil's work on Bhīṣma and Heimdall, Wikander proposed a brief but lucid comparison between the Greek and Hittite gods in the Succession Myth and three figures from the Iranian king-list – a comparison that merits further attention.[6] The classicist-comparativist Dominique Briquel wrote three closely linked papers (1978, 1980, 1981) of which the second bears most

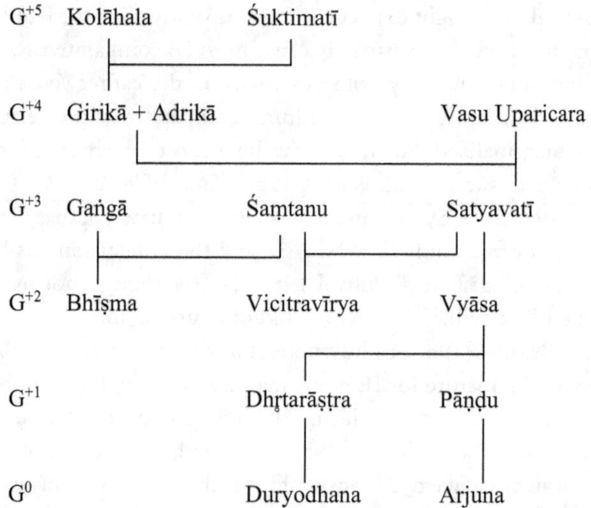

FIGURE 11.1 Skeletal genealogy of selected characters from the *Mahābhārata*

Note: The generations are numbered from the point of view of the central protagonists in the Great War.

closely on the Succession Myth. Briquel's papers rely heavily on Dumézil's analysis (1968: 145–175) of Pāṇḍu and his brothers in terms of the Mitra–Varuṇa opposition and the theory of the 'Minor Sovereigns', and a proper assessment of them would involve us in this murky topic, which lies outside my present scope.

This chapter involves many individual characters (especially in the Sanskrit), and for readers unfamiliar with the Indian epic, Figure 11.1 presents a selection of them in their genealogical relationships. The figure is primarily for reference and need not be assimilated all at once. Roughly speaking, we shall work from the top downward.

Since the subject matter of *Upaparvans* 6–7 is equally complicated, I summarize it by chapters (again for reference):

53–56: Preliminary. Reference to frame stories, brief summary of plot, virtues of the epic.

57: (a) Vasu Uparicara. (b) Some incarnations, with cursory narratives and genealogical information.

58: Earth's complaint to Brahmā.

59–60: Divine genealogies.

61: Partial incarnations of supernaturals in humans who are involved in the Great War.[7]

62–88: Stories of Bhīṣma's remoter ancestors: (a) Śakuntalā, (b) Yayāti.

89–90: Human genealogies, starting from (a) Yayāti's son, (b) the god Dakṣa.

91–100: Birth of Bhīṣma and of the father and uncles of Arjuna.

As for the *Theogony*, after its proem, the poem can be dissected into pure genealogical matter and narratives; among the latter, the Succession Myth is interrupted by digressions (West 1966: 16–18). Ignoring the interruptions, the myth can be summarized as follows:

> Ouranos ('Heaven') and Gaia or Gē ('Earth') together have a series of children, of whom the youngest is Cronus. Hating his children, Ouranos stops them exiting from Earth. Gaia encourages them to rebel, and after castrating his father, Cronus becomes King of the Gods, marrying his sister Rhea. Learning from his parents that he is fated to be defeated by his own child, Cronus swallows his children one by one, immediately at birth. His children are the three goddesses Hestia, Demeter and Hera, followed by three gods, Hades, Poseidon, Zeus. But Zeus is not in fact swallowed. Appalled at the treatment of her children, Rhea, when about to give birth for the sixth time, complains to her parents, who advise her to go to Crete and hide the infant; meanwhile she tricks Cronus by wrapping up a stone and giving it to him in place of the infant. When Zeus is old enough, Cronus is induced to vomit up what he swallowed, starting with the stone, which becomes sacred. After a ten-year war, helped by some of his father's brothers, Zeus defeats Cronus and the Titans, and relegates them to Tartarus. It only remains for him to defeat the monstrous Typhoeus, ensure that he himself is not displaced, and produce his own children.

The myth is narrated roughly by generations, as shown in Figure 11.2.

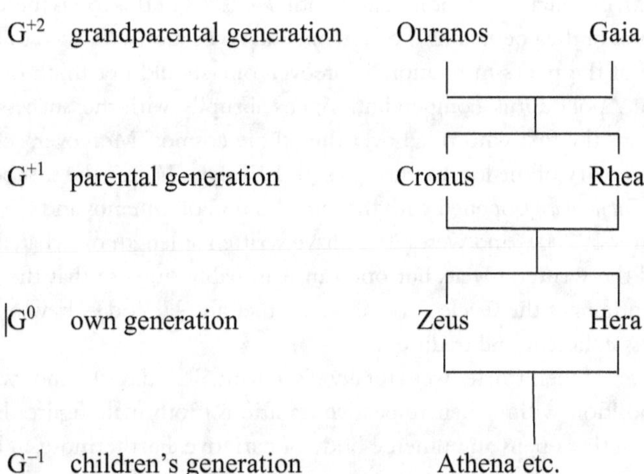

FIGURE 11.2 Marriages in successive generations in Hesiod's Succession Myth

Note: The generations are numbered from the point of view of the King of the Gods.

Vasu Uparicara and Ouranos

We can start with the male in G^{+4} of Figure 11.2. Gaṅgā's father, the sage Jahnu (1,92.49) or Bhagīratha (e.g. 1,2.78), is omitted from the figure as being less interesting here than King Vasu Uparicara, the father of Bhīṣma's stepmother Satyavatī.[8] Uparicara means 'moving or walking above or in the air'; *upari* is cognate with English *over*, and the verb root *car-* means 'go' (the name alludes to an airborne chariot in which Vasu can ride aloft like a god – one of several gifts he receives from Indra). Since Ouranos simply means 'Sky/Heaven', both figures in this section have names that connote altitude.

Position within the tradition

Although the account of Vasu's career does not come until 1,57 – so quarter-way through Book 1 – what precedes consists largely of frame stories, which tell how the main story of the epic came to be told. Moreover (1,1.50), some narrators who learned the epic started only from the story of Uparicara, which does indeed open the causal chain leading to the Great War. Accordingly, Biardeau (2002 I: 189) subtitles this section of her summary *Entrée en matière*, 'Entry into the substance of the story', and the final chapter of the whole epic (18,5) repeats several verses from 1,56 . . . 'which evidently was regarded by its author as the beginning of the work' (Brockington 1998: 136). Both the tradition itself and subsequent writers have proposed other starting points. For instance, an editorial comment by V.S. Sukthankar claims that 'the story proper' begins in Chapter 91, with the descent from heaven of Bhīṣma's parents. The same view is taken by van Buitenen (1973: xvi).[9]

The birth of Ouranos is not narrated until *Th.* 127, but this too is misleading: the first 115 lines of the poem consist of a hymn and invocation addressed to the Muses, the source of the poet's inspiration. Moreover, one should not think of the poem in isolation. Apollodorus' compendium opens abruptly with the Succession Myth: 'Ouranos was the first who ruled over the whole cosmos.' Moreover, according to Photius' summary of the lost Cyclic epics (fr. 1 Evelyn-White), the first book in the cycle, the *Titanomachy*, opened with the fabled union of Ouranos and Gē. Hellenists such as Burgess (2001) and West (2013) have written at length on what, if anything, lay behind the written Cycle, but one can reasonably suppose that the somewhat shadowy authors of the Cycle – as well as Homer and Hesiod – drew on a mass of more or less coherent oral tradition.

Thus, even if their stories were totally discrepant, Vasu and Ouranos would share a primal position within their respective traditions. Both male figures head a line of succession that opens an immense body of narrative. Furthermore, in both cases, their story is located close to passages consisting wholly of genealogical information about supernaturals, and such passages intervene before we reach the birth of Bhīṣma and Zeus two generations later.

Two genealogical features

My first point is essentially negative: neither Vasu nor Ouranos receive named fathers – an absence that helps to reinforce their primordial character. Apart from his name, nothing clearly connects Vasu with the group of eight Vasus whom we shall meet later, and Vasu equally lacks a mother.

In Hesiod (*Th.* 116–122), the first generation (G^{+3}) simply comes into being (verb *gignomai*) and consists of Chasm, Gaia, Tartarus (in the plural), and Eros (Love). Earth then produces Ouranos, followed by mountains, nymphs and sea, all without a partner. Only then, with Ouranos as partner, does she give birth to Ocean and eleven other children, the Titans, who include Cronus, and finally (at this point in the story) to two triads – the Cyclops and the Hundred-Handers.

My second point concerns the wives of our two figures. Nothing is said about the mother or mothers of Vasu's five sons, but we do learn a little about Girikā:

> The river Śuktimatī is raped, impregnated, and imprisoned by the (personified) Mount Kolāhala. Vasu kicks a passage through the mountain, and the river, grateful to her liberator, gives him the twins she bears. The male twin becomes Vasu's general, while the female, Girikā, becomes his wife.

So while Vasu apparently lacks parents, we have the names of his wife's parents – a mountain and a river. As for Gaia, it is not clear that she has parents but, as well as being the wife of Ouranos, she is also his mother (*Th.* 115–116, 126–127), and as such goes back to G^{+3} – a generation earlier than her partner. The name Girikā is from *giri* 'mountain', the noun applied to her father. Whether or not the earthy quality shared by Girikā and Gaia is significant, one notes the naturalism – sky, water (fresh or salt), mountain – of most characters at the start of both our texts.

Unusual birth of daughter

> One day, when about to make love with Girikā, Vasu is asked by his ancestors to break off and go hunting. In the forest, still feeling amorous, he ejaculates and, catching the semen in a leaf, gives it to a kite to convey to his wife. Attacked by another kite, the bird drops the semen into the River Yamunā, where it is swallowed by a fish. The latter is in reality an *apsaras* called Adrikā, who is under a curse. She is impregnated, and when she is later caught and cut open by a fisherman, she is found to contain twins. Vasu takes the boy, who becomes King Matsya ('Fish'), and gives the girl twin, the virtuous Satyavatī, to the fisherman.
>
> When Cronus cuts off his father's genitals he throws them behind him. The blood that drips from them is received by the Earth, who eventually gives birth to Erinyes (goddesses of retribution), armed giants and a category of nymphs. The genitals fall in the sea and, after floating for a while, give rise to white foam, in which there forms a maiden called, among other names, Aphrodite (*aphros* means 'foam'). She approaches Cythera, but lands in Cyprus. Her business, both among gods and men, is seduction and erotic activity.

Thus, on land the severed genitals emit blood, whence come two sorts of aggressive being, and in the sea they give rise to foam, whence the non-violent Aphrodite. The contrast is clear enough to suggest an expansion. If the red blood comes from the cut end of the genitals, the white foam could well come from the other end, in which case it represents semen – the foam–semen linkage was made by a number of ancient authors or commentators (West 1966: 212–213). Anyway, whether via semen or via generative matter in some vaguer sense, Ouranos is here presented as fathering Aphrodite in an unusual manner. But Vasu's fathering of Satyavatī is also unusual. We must look more closely.

Within the reproductive process, we can distinguish the release of semen from its subsequent transmission and development. While Vasu ejaculates normally (albeit in the absence of his partner), all we are told about the castrated Ouranos is that the foam 'began to grow from the immortal flesh' (of the severed member – *Th.* 191). Vasu dispatches his semen to his wife via a bird, while Ouranos' semen, contained in the genitals, is thrown away by Cronus, who does not even look where he is throwing it. Nevertheless, in both cases, normal love-making is replaced by generative matter travelling through the air. Passing at first over land, it then falls into water – whether river or sea.

In some respects Girikā and Adrikā are doublets – if *giri* means 'mountain', *adri* means 'stone', and both are in different ways partners to Vasu. The well-loved Girikā, daughter of the raped river, is Vasu's wife in an ordinary sense and provides the erotic stimulus leading to the birth of Satyavatī; Adrikā never even meets Vasu. She is a celestial nymph who, for reasons not stated, has been cursed by Brahmā to live as a fish until she gives birth to human twins, and on being cut open, she rejoins the nymphs (among whom she will dance and sing at the birth of Arjuna – 1,114.50). In contemporary parlance the nymph/fish is the surrogate mother of Satyavatī, her ovum- and womb-provider – as distinct both from her biological father's wife Girikā, and from her nurturing or adoptive mother, the unnamed wife of the Fisher King.

The blood and semen of Ouranos are both generative, but in different ways. The blood is received (*dexato*, *Th.* 184) by Gaia, Ouranos' normal partner, while the genitals and semen are carried (*phereto*, 190) by the sea, which Ouranos himself never meets. Although the sea is not here personified, as is Adrikā, both traditions mention a period of 'gestation': the fisherman catches Adrikā in the tenth month of her pregnancy, and the genitals float for 'a long time' (*poulon khronon*, 190).

In short, Girikā, as terrestrial and normal wife at home, parallels Gaia (= Earth), while Adrikā, as aqueous and one-off partner at a distance, parallels the sea. As for the males, both suffer interruption of their amorous advances, and both are producing their last offspring.[10]

Finally, both stories contain a curious reference to shellfish. Vasu's mother-in-law takes her name Śuktimatī from *śukti* 'pearl oyster, oyster shell', and depictions of Aphrodite's birth from the fourth century BC onward show her rising from or riding in an opening scallop shell (Carpenter 1991: 69; illustrations can be found in *LIMC*). This comparison connects Aphrodite not with Satyavatī but with her grandmother, but even so, the sharing of such a relatively rare motif is striking.[11]

Bhīṣma and Ouranos

A grandfather

To Arjuna and his generation, Bhīṣma is the grandfather par excellence: the kinship term *pitāmaha* 'paternal grandfather' is applied to him regularly – for instance, some twenty times in the last five chapters of Book 6. Of course, since he has no children, the term is being used not biologically, but in what anthropologists call a 'classificatory' manner; he counts as, or is regarded as, grandfather to the biological descendants of his half-brothers' half-brother Vyāsa.[12]

As is shown in Figure 11.2, Ouranos is grandfather to Zeus at least as emphatically as Bhīṣma is to Arjuna: he is not only Zeus' father's father, but also Zeus' mother's father. The genealogical similarity reinforces the ontological/semantic one: the Dyaus incarnate in the human grandfather means 'Sky/Heaven', just as does Ouranos.

Lose both kingship and virility

Bhīṣma's father Śaṃtanu rules at Hāstinapura as a member of the Bhārata dynasty, and the expectation is that Bhīṣma will succeed him. However, Bhīṣma's career has two dramatic turning points, two events that I shall call 'falls'. The first is non-violent and occurs when, as heir apparent, he renounces throne and marriage. The second is violent and happens on the battlefield when he is shot down by Arjuna and Śikhaṇḍin. The career of Ouranos has only one such 'fall', but it can be compared with both of Bhīṣma's:

> After his birth and childhood (treated later), the hero settles in Hāstinapura and becomes crown prince. Śaṃtanu spends four years without a partner (1,94.40) but then falls in love with the beautiful Satyavatī who, though biologically the daughter of Vasu, has been adopted by the Fisher King. At first, the latter resists the marriage proposal, but he yields when Bhīṣma, of his own volition, swears two oaths. First, the prince renounces the throne, so that Satyavatī's son will succeed, and second, he renounces marriage, lest any resultant sons contest the succession. The Fisher King now gladly assents and the heavens applaud, giving the prince his new name Bhīṣma, 'the Awesome'.
>
> Ouranos detests his children and gladly hides them away in the darkness of the Earth. The Earth groans, tightly pressed inside (*steinomenē*, *Th.* 160) and decides to resist. Creating a legendary metal (adamant), and from it a reaping hook, she urges her children to punish Ouranos. When Cronus volunteers, Gaia gives him the sickle and puts him in an ambush. Approaching his wife to embrace her, Ouranos is castrated by Cronus.

Although Hesiod does not state that Ouranos was a king, the god clearly has the power to confine his children, and we learn later that the successor Cronus wants to monopolize the royal office (*basilēida timēn* 462). Apollodorus, in his first sentence, simply presents Ouranos as the first ruler of the universe *(prōtos . . . edunasteuse).* In effect, then, Ouranos resembles Bhīṣma in losing kingship and virility *on the same occasion.* However, Ouranos' oppressive treatment of Gaia does not resemble Bhīṣma's respectful treatment of Satyavatī, and to find a parallel to Gaia, we must turn to the female involved in Bhīṣma's second fall.

Incur hostility of female

The story starts with Ambā, a princess from Banaras. Bhīṣma wants to continue the dynasty by finding wives for his half-brother Vicitravīrya, so he goes to Banaras and abducts Ambā, together with her two younger sisters; however, before the wedding, Ambā admits that she was already engaged to a rival suitor. She is allowed to return to him, but the former fiancé now rejects her, and she cannot return to Hāstinapura. After reflecting, she blames her plight on Bhīṣma and seeks revenge. Her first attempt fails (5,173–186), but she undertakes powerful austerities with a view to killing him in her next life. Reincarnated as the female Śikhaṇḍinī, she undergoes a sex-change and, as the male Śikhaṇḍin, participates crucially in mortally wounding Bhīṣma and ending his tenure as Kaurava marshal.

So – albeit unintentionally – Bhīṣma incurs the hostility of Ambā by causing the collapse of her engagement and rendering her an embittered spinster. Ouranos incurs the hostility of Gaia by impregnating her repeatedly, while preventing the emergence of the resulting offspring – even rejoicing in doing so (*Th.* 156–159).

Gaia's predicament is in a sense the opposite of Ambā's for she has too many offspring, even if they are not properly born. Another difference is that Bhīṣma did not know, and probably could not know, how his abduction and release of Ambā would affect her, whereas Ouranos presumably knew what he was inflicting on Gaia. In any case, both the 'heavenly' males rouse the anger of females with whom they deal.

Suffer at hands of female's reincarnation/offspring

Śikhaṇḍinī is the daughter of King Drupada's wife, not of Ambā, but she is also Ambā reborn; Ambā is, as it were, the spiritual mother or soul-mother of the youth who effects the vengeance that Ambā longed for. Whatever terminology is used, the avenger parallels Cronus, the youngest son of Ouranos and Gaia, who volunteers to carry out his mother's wishes and punish his father. The avengers use different weapons (bow in India, sickle in Greece) and inflict different forms of harm (mortal wounding, castration), but both leave their victims alive. The following schema attempts to summarize:

G^{+2} male	*Hostile female*	*Her avenger*
Bhīṣma	Ambā	Śikhaṇḍin(ī)
Ouranos	Gaia	Cronus

Śikhaṇḍinī's sex change raises another line of thought. Ambā's reincarnation is reared as a male, but when the time comes for a wedding, problems naturally arise, and the maiden contemplates suicide. However, the marital difficulty is solved by a kindly *yakṣa* spirit, who exchanges his male sexual organs for her female ones (5,193.7). The *yakṣa* helping the maiden recalls the earlier Sanskrit episode of Bhīṣma helping his father to escape a marital dilemma. Presumably, in order to effect the exchange, the *yakṣa* has to castrate himself, while Bhīṣma merely takes his vow of chastity. But the reaction of the supernaturals is so enthusiastic (they let fall a rain of flowers) that one wonders whether the Sanskrit tradition has bowdlerized. If an earlier version of Bhīṣma's first fall involved his autocastration, this would reinforce the similarities with the Greek.[13] However, such speculation is not essential to my overall argument.

Subsequent collaboration with female

Although Gaia is definitely hostile to Ouranos before the castration, this attitude is not consistently maintained afterwards. Sometimes the two collaborate, notably when issuing joint prophecies or advice. For instance, the pair inform Cronus of what is fated and, on learning that he will be defeated by his own child (*Th.* 463–464), he responds by swallowing his children as they are born. His wife Rhea is desolated, and when pregnant with the future Zeus, she begs advice from her parents: how is she to save her infant and punish Cronus? They tell her what is fated and how to react (468–480). Third, much later, when Zeus has defeated his enemies and supplanted Cronus, he marries Mētis, who is pregnant with Athena. His grandparents again prophesy. Learning that he risks being supplanted in his turn, Zeus swallows his first wife (886–900). These three occasions do not exhaust the interventions of Gaia (advisory or other), but they provide the basis for a rapprochement.

Bhīṣma's interactions with Ambā soon become hostile, but his relationship with Satyavatī is consistently amicable and cooperative. Again and again (there are more than a dozen such passages), he obtains the consent of his stepmother, fulfils her wishes or proposals, and keeps her informed; she approves, congratulates, and blesses him. When King Vicitravīrya is still a child, in effect the pair act jointly as regents. At this time Bhīṣma attributes the peace and prosperity of his kingdom to himself, Satyavatī, and her premarital son Vyāsa (1,96.1, 103.3).

In summary, then, after his first fall, Bhīṣma's collaborative dealings with Satyavatī find a parallel of sorts with the joint activity of Ouranos and Gaia after the castration. One difference concerns generations: as so far presented, the Greek pair and Bhīṣma belong in G^{+2} while Satyavatī belongs in G^{+3}. But Gaia is not only the wife of Ouranos; as we saw, she is also his mother. Of course, Bhīṣma's mother is Gaṅgā, and Satyavatī is his stepmother, but the English distinction can be ignored in Sanskrit. In his very first words to Satyavatī, Bhīṣma addresses her as *mātar* 'mother' (1,94.91), and both he and Vaiśaṃpāyana (the narrator) use the same term to refer to her (1,96.4; 5,187.12). Reciprocally, she addresses Bhīṣma as *putra* 'son' (5,171.3).

It is easy to assemble other differences. Among the most glaring are that the Sanskrit story is about humans while Hesiod's is about gods; the Sanskrit lacks brother–sister marriages; Bhīṣma is not the biological grandfather of Arjuna as Ouranos is of Zeus; Bhīṣma has no biological offspring while Ouranos has plenty, both before castration and (from his severed member) even afterwards. But the differences are counterbalanced by the similarities, which themselves need to be taken together as a set, and as just one set among the others in this chapter. If one supposes the Sanskrit double-fall structure to be close to the proto-narrative, one can hypothesize that Greek tradition took the simultaneous loss of kingship and virility from the first fall and the involvement of angry mother and violent offspring from the second.

Bhīṣma and Zeus

To follow up the etymological link between Dyaus (incarnate in Bhīṣma) and Zeus, we must start from the birth (or pre-birth) story of Bhīṣma. The Epic tells it in two versions, which I call A and B for convenience. Both are told by Vaiśaṃpāyana, but he tells Version B via the words of Gaṅgā. Version A, the longer (1,91–92), opens with an assembly in Brahmā's heaven (absent from B), and tells how Bhīṣma's parents come to earth, meet, and reproduce. Version B (1.93) is told when Gaṅgā responds to a question asked by Śaṃtanu, just before the couple part. The following outline applies to both.

> Dyaus belongs to an eight-member group of gods called Vasus. One day the Vasus offend the seer Vasiṣṭha, who curses them to be born as mortals. Whether it happens by chance or design, they meet Gaṅgā (the divinized River Ganges), and an agreement is reached that she shall become their mother. The Vasus wish to leave earthly life as quickly as possible, and Gaṅgā agrees to drown them at birth. However, her last son is to survive, and becomes Bhīṣma.

Versions A and B differ both as to the offence committed by the Vasus and as to the special status of the last-born. In A, the Vasus pass by the sage while he is meditating at twilight and fail to notice him, but in B, the offence is less trivial:

> Accompanied by their wives, the Vasus are wandering in the forest near the seer's hermitage when Dyaus' wife sees the holy man's milk-cow. Drawing the animal to Dyaus' attention, she learns that its milk confers lasting youth. She persuades him to steal it for the sake of a certain princess, a friend of hers, and the other Vasus participate in the theft.

As for the last-born, in A, the goddess herself proposes to the Vasus that Śaṃtanu be allowed to keep one son from his union. The Vasus each undertake to leave behind one eighth of the sperm (i.e. in the womb) to contribute to the birth of the survivor, who thus draws on eight ejaculates.[14] When Śaṃtanu first met

Gaṅgā, she insisted that she would leave him at once if she was criticized. Having borne eight god-like sons, she drowns each of them at birth (92.43–44), but when the eighth is born (*sic*, 92.46), the king can restrain himself no longer. His reproach prevents the drowning, but Gaṅgā now reveals her divine identity and departs, leaving the child.

In B, the Vasus try to pacify the sage, and it is he who then distinguishes two levels of the curse: the Vasus in general will spend only one year on earth (he must be referring approximately to the length of pregnancy), while Dyaus, more deeply implicated in the theft, will spend a long time. In this version, Gaṅgā takes the infant away with her, only to return him later (1,94.22–36), as a well-educated teenager.

Birth stories

Both stories present what might be called 'serial infanticide', within which different motifs can be distinguished: (a) The 'killer' is one or other parent – mother Gaṅgā or father Cronus, and the act takes place virtually at birth. Gaṅgā throws the children in the water as each is born (*jātaṃ jātaṃ* 92.44), while Cronus swallows each child as it comes from the womb to the mother's knees – the parturient Rhea is envisaged in kneeling position (*Th.* 459–460). (b) The victims form an unbroken sequence of siblings, respectively eight males, and three females plus three males. In both cases, although he almost becomes a victim, the youngest sibling survives. Probably the females are listed first because Cronus' vomiting, which amounts to a rebirth, reverses the order of the swallowing (West 1966 *ad* 454, 497). The numerical matching of the Greek gods and goddesses recalls the matching of Vasus with their wives, though the latter receive mention only as indicated earlier. (c) Both killers dispose of their victims into their own bodily substance. The anthropomorphic Gaṅgā drowns the infants in the river Ganges – her own divine form (1,92.44, 93.41). Cronus puts them in his own stomach. (d) Śaṃtanu is not pleased at the drownings (92.45), but because of the prenuptial arrangement he cannot object, until eventually his grief overcomes him. Rhea suffers terrible grief at the swallowing (*penthos alaston*, *Th.* 467) but takes no action until her sixth birth.

After the birth

When she leaves Śaṃtanu, Gaṅgā takes Bhīṣma away to educate him (Version B). Rhea removes Zeus to Crete to save him from being swallowed. Both the last-born 'survivors' renew contact with their fathers only when they are mature.

The time spent by the Vasus in the womb and as infants is presented as a disagreeable spell of imprisonment imposed by the sage as a punishment.[15] Afterwards, they resume normal celestial life, and even Bhīṣma, the long-stay prisoner on earth, finally rejoins the Vasus when his soul flies up to heaven (13,153.44, 154.5). The five Greek deities are not being punished, but after their confinement in Cronus' belly they too regain the freedom that deities normally enjoy; even the stone (Zeus' substitute) becomes an object of worship. Incidentally, like his siblings and substitute,

Zeus too is in a sense confined: Rhea hides him in a remote cave where he is nurtured by Gaia, the Earth.

Participation in the human Great War

Despite obvious contrasts, such as mortal-immortal or bachelor-uxorious, Bhīṣma and Zeus share one important feature that may seem surprising. Both, whether permanently or temporarily, support the losing side in the Great War (cf. Ch. 10 here). During his ten days as marshal, Bhīṣma fights bravely for the Kauravas, until he is shot down. Choosing not to die at once, he lies painfully on his 'arrow-bed' (his *śara-talpa*), like a fakir on a bed of nails. The arrows sticking into his body support him so that he does not touch the earth (*dharaṇīṃ nāspṛśat* 6,114.84; *medinīm aspṛśaṃs* 115.8).

A Greek parallel occurs in *Iliad* 14. Responding to the request of Thetis, Zeus has been favouring the Trojans; Hera, as always, favours the Greeks. After elaborate preparation, she gets her husband to make love and then fall asleep, thereby helping her protégés. When Zeus embraces his wife, 'beneath them the divine earth made fresh-sprung grass to grow, and dewy lotus, and crocus, and hyacinth, thick and soft, that upbare them from the ground' (*apo khthonos hupsos' eerge*, 14.349).[16]

Thus, in both epics: (a) At a certain point the losing side finds its most prominent protagonist, human or divine, abruptly rendered inactive. (b) This inactivation is due to the participation of an ex-female or female (Śikhaṇḍin // Hera).[17] (c) The inactivated male is recumbent, but his posture does not bring him into contact with earth; he is raised above it either by arrows alone or by plants (or, depending on coital position, by Hera also). Both arrows and plants possess a natural direction of movement (point of an arrow // growing tip) and here the arrows point upward – as do the plants that the divine earth causes to grow similarly (*hupo-phuen* 347).

In her first attempt to punish Bhīṣma, Ambā persuades Rāma Jāmadagni to fight him (*Upaparvan* 60). This section offers two relevant comparisons. The first is another instance of the 'don't touch earth' motif. On the fourth day of the duel, Bhīṣma is shot and falls. But eight radiant brahmins appear, crowd around him, and hold him in their arms so that he does not touch the ground – as he puts it, *nāhaṃ bhūmiṃ upāspṛśam* (5,183.13; although the point is only hinted at, e.g. in 184.9, the octet must be a manifestation of the eight Vasus). The second concerns drops of fluid. The wounded Bhīṣma is as if asleep in mid-air but on being sprinkled by the octet with drops of water (*jala-bindubhir ukṣitaḥ*), he soon recovers. The Greek couple are hidden from view within a cloud of gold, from which there fall drops of glittering dew (*stilpnai apepipton eersai* – 351).[18]

The obvious differences between hero on bed of arrows and god on bed of flowers are outweighed by the combination of the etymological link of Bhīṣma/Dyaus with Zeus and the conceptual link of Dyaus with Earth. A deeper analysis might even show that Bhīṣma's separation from earth relates to the motif of Heaven collapsing onto Earth, as mentioned in *Th.* 702–703. But let us move to a more obvious comparison.

Arjuna and Zeus

As one descends the generations, the size of the dossiers increases. Vasu Uparicara's was small, Bhīṣma's was much larger, and Arjuna's is enormous, just as there is far more to say about Zeus than about Ouranos. Selection and concision become even more necessary for an analyst.

Within the G^0 of the Bhārata lineage, it is clear that Arjuna, so closely linked with Kṛṣṇa, is the most salient hero, just as Zeus is the most salient deity in G^0 of the Succession Myth. We already know how much Bhīṣma shares with Ouranos, and just as Arjuna is classificatory grandson to the former, so Zeus is grandson to the latter. But it would be unsatisfying to move from G^{+2} to G^0 while ignoring G^{+1} (as I did in 2004).[19] We have already met comparisons for Cronus (with Śikhaṇḍin the avenger and with Gaṅgā, the absorber of infants), but he needs to be seen also as the genealogical link between grandfather and grandson. As such, he could well parallel Pāṇḍu – as proves to be the case. Just as Cronus succeeds G^{+2} Ouranos, Pāṇḍu succeeds G^{+2} Vicitravīrya, but both reigns are broken off. Cronus is defeated in the Titanomachy and confined in Tartarus, far below the earth; Pāṇḍu, subjected to a curse obliging him to chastity, is deprived of his virility (*vīrya-varjitaḥ* 1,110.20d), whereupon he and his wives dedicate themselves to asceticism in remote forests. He sends his royal apparel back to the capital (110.36–37), where Dhṛtarāṣṭra becomes king.

Although the two reigns are interrupted in different ways, the story of the curse on Pāṇḍu confirms the rapprochement:

> While hunting, Pāṇḍu shoots with five arrows a pair of deer who are copulating. Before dying, the male explains that he is a human ascetic called Kiṃdama, who (with his wife) has taken animal form. Blaming Pāṇḍu for killing him during love-making, he issues his curse: Pāṇḍu will die similarly. The curse is fulfilled: one day, when the forest is in bloom, Pāṇḍu's resolution gives way and he dies while trying to make love with Mādrī (his second wife).

So, in brief, Cronus violently interrupts the sexual interaction of Ouranos and Gaia, Pāṇḍu interrupts that of Kiṃdama and his wife. Epic Kiṃdama lacks the primal quality of an Ouranos, but a fuller study would include the Vedic story of the archer-god Rudra interrupting the love-making of Prajāpati and his daughter – both of whom were in the form of deer (e.g. O'Flaherty 1975: 29–30, translating *Aitareya Brāhmaṇa* 3.33–34). In any case, the Pāṇḍu-Cronus parallel suggests we should compare their wives. Rhea, as we saw, bore three daughters, then three sons of whom Zeus was the last. After his curse, the childless Pāṇḍu encourages his first wife Kuntī to use a spell she possesses and summon gods as partners. She has no daughters, but as wife she bears just three sons, of whom Arjuna is the last. Both last-born sons stand apart from their elders in their birth stories: Zeus escapes being swallowed, Arjuna receives by far the greatest welcome (1,114). For each Pāṇḍava neonate, a disembodied voice utters a prophecy: for Yudhiṣṭhira son of Dharma the voice utters two shlokas, for Bhīma son of Vāyu less than one, and for Arjuna seven.[20]

However, a pentadic analysis of Pāṇḍu's wives' divine partners and the five Pāṇḍavas would take us too far from Hesiod (cf. Allen 1999a, [Ch. 20 here]), and I shall counter only one possible objection. Despite his etymological identity with Dyaus, Zeus is typologically closer to Indra (e.g. O'Flaherty 1987), but Indra is King of the Gods, and Arjuna, though son of the King of the Gods (or his incarnation, 1,189.25), is never himself a king. When the Pāṇḍavas enjoy sovereignty, the throne belongs to his oldest brother. The Pāṇḍava birth order is a rich topic, but one relevant factor is that Arjuna so often represents the five brothers as a set – for instance when he wins their shared wife Draupadī. Because of this 'totality aspect', his position in the birth order is not inappropriate; it should be seen less as 'third' than as 'central'.

Two modes of conflict

Different phases of the Great War involve three different modes of fighting: long-drawn-out day-time engagement of large armies on the open battlefield, nocturnal massacres of sleepers within an enclosure, and a quick final day-time contest between named individuals [Chs 17, 24]. Roughly speaking, the first type occupies *Mbh.* 6–9, the second 10,1–9, the third 10,10–18 (= *Upaparvan* 79). Absent from the second, Arjuna wins major victories in the first and third phases. On the Kurukṣetra battlefield, after helping eliminate the first Kaurava marshal on Day 10, he kills Karṇa, the third marshal, on Day 17, and on Day 19 he and Kṛṣṇa, acting together, counter the supernatural weapons launched by the fifth marshal, Aśvatthāman.[21]

In the Succession Myth, Zeus fights and wins two battles, the second apparently continuing the first. After Zeus expels the Titans from heaven and imprisons them in Tartarus, Earth (with Tartarus) bears as her youngest child the snake-headed Typhoeus (*Th.* 830–825, the Typhon of later sources). The ten-year Titanomachy involves two large hosts, the Typhonomachy is a duel. In other words, the Kauravas, children of the elder brother Dhṛtarāṣṭra, correspond to the Titans, the older generation of gods (G^{+1}), while the Pāṇḍavas, the junior branch, correspond to the Olympians (G^{0} and G^{-1}), and Aśvatthāman corresponds to Typhoeus.

Multiple unions

Apart from the shared Draupadī, each Pāṇḍava has an individual wife, and with each wife (including Draupadī), begets one son; the names are listed in prose in 1,90.81–89. The five Draupadeyas have only minor roles in the epic, and most of the others have no role at all. However, two unions are more important: Arjuna's with Subhadrā, Kṛṣṇa's sister, who bears Abhimanyu, and Bhīma's with Hiḍimbā (which is listed last, as if to make up the explicit total of eleven).[22] However, the list fails to mention two other unions. In the course of his 'pilgrimage' [Ch. 2], Arjuna begets two further sons, Irāvat and Babhruvāhana, whose mothers, Ulūpī and Citrāṅgadā, attend the Horse Sacrifice in Book 14 as his wives.

After the Typhonomachy, Zeus establishes his regime (*Th.* 881–885), and the text at once starts listing Zeus' unions, of which the seventh, with Hera, is explicitly the last. Three further unions are mentioned in 938–944, but 'probably they are not regarded as regular marriages' (West 1966: 411). In any case, the listing is incomplete: Grimal (1982: 480) tabulates twenty-three of the god's unions, fifteen of them with mortals. Apparently no other deity is so well supplied with partners.

So Arjuna has five wives and five sons – two more than any of his brothers, and Zeus has numerous fertile unions, producing both sons and daughters. It is not clear whether the comparison can be taken much further than this, except as regards Abhimanyu and Sarpedon. Both these mortals die in the Great War, the former on Day 13, the latter in *Il.* 16.502. Though Abhimanyu fights for the Victors and Sarpedon for the Losers, it is striking that both Arjuna and Zeus are deeply affected by the death in battle of sons they love dearly.[23]

Concluding discussion

In focusing on the texts mentioned at the start, numerous questions have been consciously skirted, and others may well have been missed inadvertently; a full comparison would certainly be longer and more complicated. Thus, in organizing the analysis in terms of generations, we have ignored a stylistic similarity between the traditions: each is internally repetitive (e.g. in the premarital births of Vyāsa and Karṇa or in the Greek sibling marriages). Cronus has been briefly compared with Śikhaṇḍin and with Pāṇḍu but not with Iranian Azhdahāk (Wikander 1952); and we have ignored the long-noted and important comparison between Earth complaining to Brahmā about overpopulation (1,58), and Earth making the same complaint to Zeus (scholion to *Il.* 1.5) – see, for example de Jong (1985), Vielle (1996: 40–46, 115–123). The aim has not been to exhaust the comparison, but to argue that the start of the *Mahābhārata* main story and the Hesiodic Succession Myth are sufficiently similar to imply a proto-narrative.

Although a definitive model of the proto-narrative will need much more work, I offer some preliminary reflections. A regular problem in comparativism is to decide which of two cognate narratives to treat as synchronically basic and/or diachronically closer to the proto-narrative. As Figure 11.3 suggests, there are perhaps two key issues.

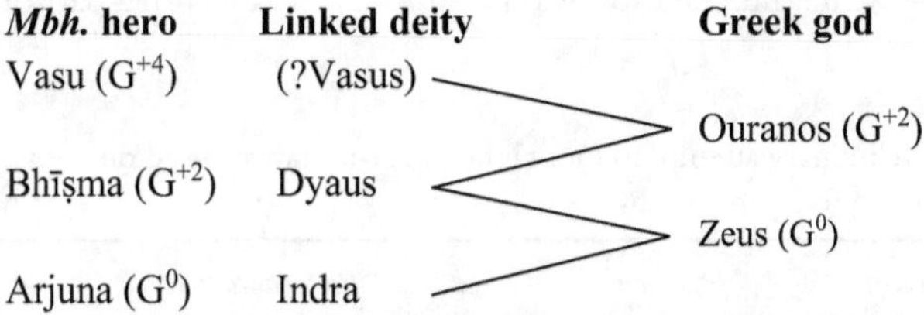

FIGURE 11.3 Overview of the four main comparisons

Note: If the proto-narrative resembled the Sanskrit, its five-generation pattern was compressed to give the three generations of the Greek—one reads the diagram from left to right. For the alternative hypothesis one can either reverse the figure or read the present one from right to left. The diagram could also be drawn rotated 90° clockwise (or counterclockwise).

Were the proto-narrative agents primarily human incarnations of the gods, as in the Bhārata lineage, or were they simply gods, as in the Succession Myth? On the hypothesis of Sanskrit conservatism, presumably Greek tradition simply lost the theme of gods incarnating as mortals.[24] But one also wonders whether the narrative matter was originally spread over five generations, as in India, or over three, as in Greece; and again I prefer the hypothesis of Sanskrit conservatism.

This preference is based partly on previous experience and partly on the Heimdall comparison, or more precisely, on the sociogony narrated in the *Rígsþula* (Dumézil 1973b: 118–125, tr. Larrington 1996: 246–252). Here Heimdall is involved successively in the marriages of 'Great-grandfather', 'Grandfather', and 'Father', and he is then involved in a different way with Konr ungr in the next generation. Similarly, Bhīṣma arranges the marriages of his father (G^{+3}), his half-brother (G^{+2}), and his nephews or classificatory sons (G^{+1}) but not those of Arjuna's generation.[25] This comparison, which I hope to elaborate elsewhere [see Allen 2007f], suggests that the proto-narrative involved more than three generations.

If the five-generation Sanskrit schema is provisionally taken as the older, it makes sense to identify the proto-narrative figures by using the Sanskrit names. The main conceptual problem seems to concern proto-Bhīṣma, who was presumably already linked (if not identified) with *Dyēus. As Figure 11.3 suggests, this proto-figure must have had a grandson, the proto-figure behind Indra (or his incarnation) and Zeus; moreover, in the Greek branch of the tradition he must in some sense have split, since he contributes to both Ouranos and Zeus. The point is expressed in another format in Table 11.1.

The approach and results offered here differ from those of philologists. For instance, Euler concludes (1987: 51–52) that the original Indo-Europeans lacked a pantheon with a clear genealogical structure and that their deities, associated with features of the natural environment, possessed only the germs of kinship relationships. While recognizing a nuclear family within the proto-pantheon, Dunkel (1988–90) sees Indra as deriving much of his content from Parjanya, a thunder god, who himself derives from one of the epithets applied to *Dyēus. This chapter suggests rather that the PIE family of gods included two important males who were two generations apart (see Figure 11.4). The grandfather, called *Dyēus, personified heaven or sky, while the grandson was presumably linked with a part of the cosmos

TABLE 11.1 Preliminary attempt to model the proto-narrative, based on the assumption that it had five generations

	Sanskrit	*Greek*	*Proto-narrative*
G^{+4}	Vasu	Ouranos	*heavenly founder
G^{+3}	Satyavatī	Aphrodite	*founder's water-born daughter
G^{+2}	Bhīṣma	Zeus+Ouranos	*infanticide birth story+adult fall
G^{+1}	Pāṇḍu	Cronus	*interrupter of sexual embrace
G^{0}	Arjuna	Zeus	*king with two styles of combat

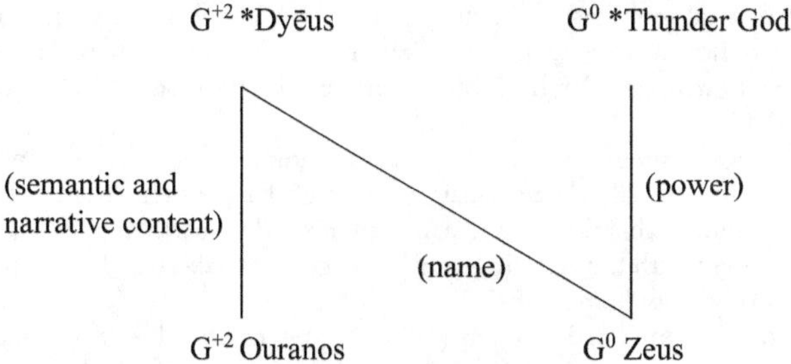

FIGURE 11.4 Relationship between, on the one hand, Sanskrit and Greek 'grandfather' gods and, on the other hand, their 'grandsons'

that was less remote (Indra is regularly associated with the atmosphere, understood as situated between heaven and earth). Within the myth, the grandfather was in some sense replaced by the grandson, who became King of the Gods.[26] However, during the history of the Greek tradition, the grandson took over the grandfather's name – cf. Figure 11.4, which uses Dunkel's notation.

Whatever the final conclusions on these matters, and whatever we make of the West Asian rapprochement (*some* similarity is undeniable), it becomes ever clearer that we shall never properly understand the roots of European culture without taking account of India's Great Epic, and that we shall never understand the roots of Hinduism without tackling IE cultural comparativism.

Notes

1 First published in 2004 as 'Bhīṣma and Hesiod's Succession Myth' but now somewhat rewritten and expanded [Ch. 5 had appeared in the same journal].

2 For translations, see, respectively, van Buitenen (1973), West (1988a), and Hard (1997).

3 Sergent refers to his later book (1998: 193–235), which explores trifunctional interpretations of the *Theogony*, but though it draws on the *Śatapatha Brāhmaṇa*, the later chapter makes no reference to Bhīṣma or the epic.

4 Strictly speaking, these are distinct ways of linking gods and men, but the text sometimes blurs the distinction.

5 *Pace* Hiltebeitel (2001): 274 n.52.

6 The comparison proposed by Skjaervo (1998) between Bhīṣma and Rostam in the Iranian epic leaves me unconvinced.

7 The incarnations are 'partial' so that, even while incarnated, gods can continue to live and operate in the divine realm.

8 Vasu is discussed by Dumézil (1971: 301–315), within an Indo-Iranian context.

9 Chapters 57 and 91 both begin with variants of the story-opening formula 'Once upon a time there was a king named... 'This opening phrase is well recognized as such by IE comparativists (e.g. Watkins 1995: 25; West 2007: 94–95). Other instances occur in *Mbh.* 3 at the openings of the Nala and Rāmāyaṇa Upaparvans.

10 In Homer (*Il.* 5.370–371) and Apollodorus (*Bibl.* 1.3.1), Aphrodite is a daughter not of Ouranos but of Zeus, by Dione.

11 Good reasons exist for seeing Aphrodite as cognate with the Vedic Dawn goddess Uṣas (Boedeker 1974; Friedrich 1978; Dunkel 1988–90: 8–11), and my argument for an additional Aphrodite–Satyavatī rapprochement does not controvert them.

12 Vyāsa, the physical grandfather, born on the Yamunā, needs to be seen in relation to Bhīṣma, the honorary (spiritual?) grandfather, born of the Ganges. Among gods, the grandfather *par excellence* is Brahmā, but to explore the Brahmā–Bhīṣma link would take us too far afield.

13 'In about 20 [*RV*] passages the word *dyaus* is feminine, sometimes even when personified' (Macdonell 1897: 22; the dictionary entry is under the stem *div*, *dyu*). Linguists have explained this remarkable fact by the pairing with *pṛthivī* 'earth' in a *dvandva* compound and/or by analogy with the rhyming word *gaus* 'cow' (Wackernagel 1925: 68), but might Bhīṣma's loss of virility be relevant?

14 The gloss comes from van Buitenen (1973: 455) – cf. also 1,2.78–79 and 57.77. The numbers show a certain discrepancy. When 1,60.16–17 names all the eight Vasus (sons of Prajāpati, himself son of Grandfather Brahmā), it ignores Dyaus, but birth story B presents him as one of the octet. However later, when he is fighting Rāma, Bhīṣma is visited three times by a set of eight brahmins, who must represent his eight Vasu brethren (5,183–186). [Moreover, when praising the moribund Bhīṣma, Kṛṣṇa mentions that he is regularly reckoned by seers as a (or the) ninth Vasu (12,50.26).] The eight-plus-one pattern is important in Dumézil's Heimdall comparison but also occurs elsewhere in India: a king's body is made from particles of the eight Lokapālas (*Manu* 5.96, 7.5).

15 On temporary humanization as a punishment for errant Greek gods, see West (1966: 374). A recent non-comparativist book on Bhīṣma (McGrath 2018) ignores his birth story.

16 Tr. Murray (1976–8). The 'lotus' is a species of wild fodder (Janko 1992: 206). The allusion to fertility, clear in the Greek, is absent from the Sanskrit here.

17 At some point, Bhīṣma has taken an oath not to fight a female or ex-female (5,193.62), so he does not resist when attacked.

18 The dew drops may hint at semen as well as fertilizing rain. I here ignore the possible comparison with the cloud that envelops Satyavatī when she couples with the brahmin Parāśara and conceives Vyāsa.

19 The next two paragraphs draw on Allen (2009d), a sort of postscript to the main article.

20 If Zeus and Arjuna enjoy the highest value within their respective series, what about the lowest valued? A Hades–Yudhiṣṭhira comparison is worth thinking about (the title Dharmarāja applies both to the Pāṇḍava and to Yama god of Death), and one might try comparing Rhea's daughters (devalued as females) with Karṇa son of the Sun, Kuntī's first-born (devalued as premarital and illegitimate).

21 The symmetries are explored in Allen 2012a, where for *moins marqués* (p. 198 line 2) read *plus marqués*.

22 Perhaps the figure echoes the total of eleven Rudras.

23 See further Chapter 10 here. Arjuna losing his son *also* parallels Achilles losing his intimate friend Patroclus.

24 Even in the Sanskrit, the status of this theme is curious: asked why the godlike warriors were born on earth, Vaiśampāyana says that even to the gods the matter is truly a mystery (*rahasya* 1,58.3).

25 When Duryodhana abducts his bride, he 'counts upon' the support of his seniors (*Bhīṣma-Droṇāv-upāśritaḥ*, 12,4.13), but nothing suggests that Bhīṣma arranges the match.

26 Contrary to what one might expect, succession to a grandfather's position is probably more archaic than succession to the father's (Allen 2004a).

12

FIVE ELEMENTS

Massive similarities exist between ancient Greek and ancient Indian philosophy, and a massive study such as McEvilley's was needed to assemble the materials and grapple with them.[1] One has to applaud the scope and ambition of the book. Naturally, anyone who undertakes an interdisciplinary study on a grand scale risks making mistakes and misjudgments, and McEvilley sensibly anticipates criticism (2002: xxxi) – which has not been lacking. For instance, at the lowest level, the diacritics are appallingly slapdash, and the French accents are little better.[2] However, my aim is not to criticize the book piecemeal but rather to respond to it constructively at a level commensurate with the scale of its undertaking. I shall address a systemic problem that is built into the initial assumptions.

The missing dimension

McEvilley argues that the similarities between Greek and Indian philosophy are due to diffusion, that is, to historical contacts. More precisely, for the earlier period the choice lies between Mesopotamian ideas spreading both east and west, and Indian ideas spreading west via Greece–India encounters within the Achaemenid empire. From Alexander to the Fall of Rome, the predominant flow was eastwards, whether via the Greek presence in the north-west of the subcontinent, Roman coastal trading ports, or Indian visits to the Mediterranean world. Though not well equipped to judge them, I thought the evidence for contact in the later period was good. However, for the earlier period, the argument neglects an alternative explanation of the similarities, namely Indo-European (IE) common origin.

In principle, the difference between the two modes of explanation is sharp. Since the very notion of Indo-European comes from linguistics, let us draw on that discipline. If a word in one IE language resembles a word in another, and the resemblance cannot be due to chance, then it may either be because one language has borrowed the word from the other (or both have borrowed from a third language, related or not), or because the words descend independently from the ancestral language. In the former case, the word was once foreign to the borrowers, in the latter, it was never foreign to the speakers of either language. In practice, the distinction may not always be easy even for the linguistic comparativist, and usually the latter faces an easier task than the cultural comparativist. Nevertheless, if we wish to attribute similar philosophical ideas in Greece and India to diffusion, we need to be sure that the explanation by common origin is impossible. Otherwise, the similar ideas could merely be continuations of an old idea that was current among those who spoke the common ancestor of Greek and Sanskrit.[3]

The shared IE background of Greece and India does receive brief mention in the foreword (p. xxiv). The trend emphasizing this background 'culminated in the work of Georges Dumezil [sic] and others who have articulated parallelisms in the social structures of different Indo-European-speaking cultures' (reference to Littleton 1982). By 'social structures', McEvilley is thinking of the varṇa system in Manu, the classes in Plato's *Republic*, and the social organization of early Latin peoples. 'But in order to account for striking comparative details such studies must be supplemented by postulates of historical influences.' Neither Dumézil nor the relevant others are cited, and the topic scarcely surfaces again.

This treatment of the IE background denatures Dumézil's work, reducing it to just one of its components, and oversimplifying even that. Social structure was important in the genesis of Dumézil's breakthrough in 1938, and it was the functions performed by the three twice-born varṇas that led to the label 'trifunctionalist', which is now attached to his work. However, for Dumézil and those working in his tradition, the three functions form an ideology, a mental framework which patterns many social phenomena in addition to social structure – pantheons, rituals, legal procedures, narratives of various types (myths, epics, pseudo-history, tales). Moreover, the reference to social structure is itself too simple.

> A decisive step forward was taken on the day when I recognized, around 1950, that the 'tripartite ideology' is not necessarily accompanied, in the life of a society, by the *real* tripartition of society, as in the Indian model; that on the contrary, where it is to be found, it is possible that it is nothing but (is no longer anything but, perhaps never was anything but) an ideal and, at the same time, a means of analysing and interpreting the forces that ensure the course of the world and the life of men.
>
> *(Dumézil 1968: 15)*[4]

Elsewhere the same recognition is expressed in different words. Between 1938 and about 1950, overinfluenced by the role of the varṇas in his breakthrough, Dumézil had assumed that manifestations of the ideology, wherever they occurred, indicated the concurrent or earlier existence of a real division of society into distinct functional classes, but he now saw that it was not legitimate 'to move from the ideology to conclusions about practice, from a philosophy to conclusions about social organization' (1973a: 338).

Thus Dumézil's enterprise was an effort to recognize in the available facts the survival of the ideology or philosophy current among early IE speakers.[5] Linguists sometimes argue about the ontology of the starred forms they reconstruct, and Dumézil was usually cautious in his wording, but in effect he reconstructs an IE proto-philosophy. It follows that a comparative philosopher has three options. The best is to take account of the IE common origin of Greek and Indian tradition and incorporate the findings of the Dumézilian enterprise. Another is explicitly to write off the enterprise, preferably by alleging serious reasons and not simply citing 'authorities'. The third, a compromise, is to try and drive a wedge between the reconstructed proto-philosophy and the attested Greek and Indian philosophers. This might be attempted by claiming that the former is not real philosophy (e.g. it is too limited in scope or too close to myth); or that, if it is philosophy, it does not connect historically with the attested philosophies; or that, if such connection does exist, it is too tenuous to account for striking similarities of detail. McEvilley apparently espouses some form of the compromise argument, and we need to ask how valid it is.

In thinking about continuities and connections between early IE speakers and attested texts, a problem to be confronted head-on is the relationship between the dating of texts and the dating of their contents. The dating of texts (or of their stabilization within an oral tradition) is a topic for specialists and obviously worthwhile, albeit often intractable. But it is all too easy to slide from this to the dating of contents. Other things being equal, one assumes that form and contents go together, so that an earlier text contains ideas current at an earlier period, and a later text from the same tradition contains ideas that, insofar as they differ from the earlier ones, were developed later.

However, once comparison enters the picture, other things are seldom equal. When a later text contains an idea or theme that is strikingly similar to one in another branch of the same tradition, then the common origin explanation needs consideration *even if the idea is absent from the earlier texts*. The earlier absence can be explained in several ways. The idea may have been known to the composers of the earlier text but passed over as inappropriate to their genre or excluded as esoteric (a 'Mystery'); or it may have been unknown to them but known to other social categories inhabiting the same area (e.g. unknown to priests but known to warriors); or it may have been known within the same social group but in another area. Thus, the absence may be ascribed to genre, social category, or geography. But whatever the explanation, ideas can bypass earlier texts to surface in later ones. Because the motive for invoking such a bypass often comes from comparison, history as envisaged or written by comparativists is likely to differ from histories of the same cultures produced by non-comparativists, and since, for the present, comparativists are few in number and most of the history that is written is by non-comparativists, bypass phenomena will often be ignored.

These considerations bear directly on the a priori possibility that an IE proto-philosophy lies behind both Greek and Indian philosophizing. If particular philosophical ideas are absent from the Vedic hymns or the Brāhmaṇas, or from Homer and Hesiod, this does not prove that they were absent from society as it existed when those texts were stabilized; the ideas could have bypassed the earliest texts in one of the ways we mentioned. For instance, a variant of the geographical explanation might envisage different waves of Indo-Aryan–speaking migrants carrying different components of the tradition, as has been proposed for Vedic India by Asko Parpola (2004–5: 27–28). In the Greek case, the dating of texts is usually more precise, but the bypass problem is no less real and applies even within the tradition. It is usually assumed that the ideas of Socrates and his pupil Plato are later than those of the pre-Socratics, and it takes a certain effort to set aside so deeply rooted an assumption. But although the texts are later, the ideas need not be [Allen in press].

An Indo-European proto-philosophy

Plato is particularly relevant here because, while the mature Dumézil wrote relatively little about Greece and even less about Greek philosophy, he was very aware of the IE heritage in the *Republic*. Soon after his breakthrough, he raised the possibility of Plato's ideal city being 'in the strictest sense an Indo-European reminiscence' (Dumézil 1941: 275), and he reverted to the topic several times; thus, he talks of the *Republic* as containing 'remarkable expositions of the tripartite ideology' (Dumézil 1982: 256 n.3). His main account (Dumézil 1968: 493–496) occurs in a discussion of the intelligence that Ossetic folklore attributes to the Nart hero Batraz: the political psychology in play is close to the one that Plato expounds, 'certainly on the basis of very old trifunctional speculations'. Having summarized the correlations between the classes in the *Republic* (philosopher kings, warriors, and commoners – farmers and artisans being grouped together), the virtues (wisdom, courage, and prudence), and the metals (gold, silver, then iron and bronze), Dumézil comments that, since Pythagoras, and no doubt before him, Greek philosophers had speculated a lot on social tripartition; it was a concept they retained no doubt from the IE past, even if Plato in Athens could observe a few survivals of the scheme (e.g. in the three archons – for fuller discussion see Bodéüs 1972).

However, Dumézil does not, here or elsewhere, present a precise comparison between Plato and Indian philosophy. On the one hand, he is comparing the political psychology in Plato with that in the Caucasian folklore (the Ossetic language belongs to the Scythian branch of Indo-Iranian). On the other, he is saying that Plato's philosophical discourse about classes and virtues (and he also has in mind Plato's three-soul doctrine) belongs to a tradition going back to the old IE proto-philosophy, or more precisely, to the application of that philosophy to the ideal organization of society. It is the same source that lies behind the varṇa doctrine, itself so central to aspects of *dharma*. We are certainly dealing with continuity.

Dumézil also provides answers to the problem of 'striking comparative details'. In spite of the long stretches of time and space involved, he often shows that quite small details in attested materials go back to a common origin. Numerous examples of this can be found in his comparison between one of the myths attached to Indra and the pseudo-history of the third king of Rome (Dumézil 1985b, followed up by Allen 2003b). But for the moment I leave Dumézil (who died in 1986) and take up more recent work, focusing first on the functions.

Evidence is accumulating that three functions are not enough. Many of the hierarchized triads that Dumézil and followers have recognized are in fact situated within larger pentadic structures: the triad forms a coherent core, but this core is enclosed or bracketed by one element that is hierarchically superior and another that is inferior. The triad 'priests, warriors, producers' is in many cases bracketed by the king at the top and the serf or slave at the bottom.[6] To make a long story short, I think that the proto-philosophy was pentadic. For the core functions Dumézil's definitions can stand, except that sovereignty should be excised from the first function. The two extremes are covered by a fourth function, defined as relating to what is other, outside, or beyond relative to the core, but the fourth function has two aspects, one valued positively, the other negatively. The notion of positive and negative value will cover a variety of phenomena depending on context, but its application to king and slave is obvious. In terms of ideology, whether or not an individual king happens to be good or bad, he represents the society qua totality and is positively valued in the same sense as is a whole relative to its parts. As for the slave, however valued he may be as an individual, in a traditional hierarchical society, his status is so devalued that he is barely part of society. In the religious domain, the equivalents of king versus slave are Creator versus Devil, or Salvation versus Death/Destruction. In the annual cycle, they are the New Year (taken as a whole) and the Old Year or its closing phase.

A case study: the elements

The case for the pentadic theory depends primarily on the number, wide distribution and cultural importance of the contexts to which it relates, and on the rigour of the arguments supporting this relation. Let us for the sake of argument assume that the schema is well founded and ask how it might apply to Greek and Indian philosophy. Since the schema has four functions and five slots, one obvious target is McEvilley's chapter on the elements (pp. 300–309): both Greece and India recognize four elements, sometimes adding a fifth.

McEvilley's tentative conclusions are as follows:

> The doctrine of the four elements would seem to have arisen in a single source, perhaps in India, where the developmental sequence is clearer than in Greece, and to have entered Greece in different versions, partly conflated with the Doctrine of the Five Fires and Two Paths. Some Near Eastern background, which can only be vaguely discerned, may have been in effect. The doctrines of the fifth elements, *ākāśa* and *aither* [*sic* for *aithēr*] surely are cognate concepts. . . . Most likely the Indian concept was imported into Greece

> in a later phase of the same general wave of Upaniṣadic influence which brought the transformations of [concepts of] matter.
>
> *(pp. 308–309)*

In the present context, a case study cannot be developed at length, but at least I hope to show that an IE ancestral doctrine offers a rival hypothesis to diffusion.

The four elements are essentially the same in the two traditions: fire; air, wind, or breath; water; earth. This is the standard order in Greece (sometimes reversed) and seems to follow the order of the functions. The standard order in India differs in that air regularly precedes fire (as also happens in Heraclitus). For various reasons, I draw mainly on Indian or Indo-Iranian data.

Fire *(agni)* provides a good starting point since in Vedic India Agni is the priest of the gods – more precisely, its *hotar*. Though Agni shares priesthood with Bṛhaspati, fire is the only *element* to enjoy this status. Since the attributes of any one Vedic deity tend to be shared with several others, passages can be cited that constitute exceptions to almost any theological statement, but the priestly role of Agni is such a standard feature of introductions to Vedic religion that citing details would be pedantic. Moreover, the role makes good sense in that [as in many cultures] it is the fire on the altar, together with the priests around it, that links men to gods. The association between fire and priesthood is equally clear in Zoroastrianism, with its sacred fires entrusted to fire-priests in fire temples, so it is surely at least Indo-Iranian. Fire is thus a strong candidate for interpretation as first-functional (F1), provided that all the other elements can be linked to other functions.[7]

Air is represented in India by wind *(vāyu* or *vāta)*. Unlike Agni, Vāyu is a minor figure both in the Vedic and later Hindu pantheons, but he has one important role in the *Mahābhārata*. He fathers Bhīma, the second of the five Pāṇḍava brothers, the one who for half a century has been associated by comparativists with the second function (F2), which pertains to physical force and war.[8] Bhīma is indeed the largest and most muscular of the brothers: he once picks up the whole family and carries them with the speed and force of the wind (1,136.16–19, 137.23). In his 1968 analysis of Bhīma, Dumézil presents Vāyu as an old Indo-Iranian war god, who has largely bypassed the Vedas. Moreover, the association between wind and force makes good sense – one has only to think of a hurricane. Thus, as an element, wind is a reasonable candidate for F2.

Dumézil himself (1973b: 77, 1985b: 30, 2000: 121–138) connects water with the third function, for instance when writing on the Norse god Niord and his links with the sea.[9] Water, whether from rain or irrigation, is essential to the fertility of the peasant's fields, and fertility is an important component in the definition of this function (together with wealth, abundance, fecundity, large number, health, sexuality). It is of course needed not only for the growth of plants and crops but also for the well-being of herds (often a measure of wealth), not to mention the health of humans. Fertility and well-being are more directly linked to water than to wind or fire, and one need hardly mention the common assimilation of water and semen (as when rain is viewed as heaven inseminating earth). Water is intrinsically an excellent candidate for F3.

As for earth *(pṛthivī)*, the first question is whether it stands apart from the other elements. In mentioning that in the Atharva Veda fire, water, and air or breath (or life-force, *prāṇa*) are each in different passages treated as the ultimate principles, McEvilley (p. 302) implies that earth is not. Similarly those early Greek philosophers who derived everything from a single element made their choice from the same triad and (as Aristotle noted) never selected earth as an *arkhē* or ultimate principle. However, in general, the texts align at least the four elements, and the heterogeneity of earth, if it exists, must be sought among its taken-for-granted qualities or in narratives. One obvious quality is immobility – in a traditional world, view earth does not normally move, let alone spread, blow, or flow. Moreover, earth is the only element unambiguously personified not by a god but a goddess. As regards cosmogony, Pherecydes of Syros derived fire, breath, and water from the seed of Time, while Zeus, Time, and Earth always existed (p. 306), and in epic, both Pṛthivī and Gaia complain of being overburdened and thereby initiate the Great War (e.g. Vielle 1996: 116).

If earth stands apart from the other elements, is it in any way devalued? Let us try to correlate elements (the division of matter) and human activities (the division of labour). If the priest uses his sacred fires for rituals, the warrior emulates the speed and force of the wind, and the producer exploits the fertility of water, then who relates most intimately to earth? Dumézil (e.g. 1985b: 30) combines earth with water under the third function, implicitly relating the element to the agriculturalist. But from a four-functional viewpoint, a better answer is the miner or quarry worker, the blacksmith or stone-mason. It is they who extract and use 'the bones of the earth', and in the caste system, they belong among the Untouchables, the F4– component of society (Allen 2007g).

As for the fifth element, the quintessence (which can be called ether) – in Vaiśeṣika philosophy as in Aristotle – it is 'kept carefully separate from the others' (525). It relates to matter so rarefied as to resemble mere space, and it 'is characterized by sanctity.' Its non-appearance in the earliest texts may reflect this very heterogeneity – it does not *need* to have been a later addition to the four. In both traditions, it (rather than any other element) is linked with the cosmos, that is, the totality of things, and hence can represent F4+.

Entities representing the two aspects of the fourth function stand apart from those representing the core functions, and the ways in which they differ from the core may or may not themselves differ (in addition to contrasting as superior and inferior), but quite often representatives of the two aspects, taken by themselves, have points in common. In this case, ether often shares in the effective immobility of earth, and in India at least it perhaps shares to some degree in earth's femininity. *Ākāśa* is semantically close to *dyu* or Dyu (Heaven), with which Vedic *pṛthivī* or Pṛthivī is usually coupled, and *dyu* is feminine in about twenty passages, sometimes even when personified (Macdonell 1974: 22, 88).[10]

This cursory account of the elements in Greece and India can be complemented by a glance at the Zoroastrian Bounteous or Beneficent Immortals, the Aməša

Spəntas. By the post-Gāthic period, these six or seven spiritual beings came to constitute a more or less standardized list. Each Immortal was correlated with a material entity, and among the entities are some of the familiar elements. This theological structure was analyzed trifunctionally by Dumézil (1977: 37–51; his tabulation in 1992: 60 is particularly neat). Replacing the Avestan names with the English translations in Boyce (1975: 203), we can present the analysis as follows in Table 12.1, printing in bold the correlations that are most relevant here.

Although he cites the row V correlation in his analysis of Niord, Dumézil ignores the row II correlation when discussing Agni, but both accord with our functional analysis of the elements. Similarly, the Immortals in rows V and VI, Haurvatāt (or Health) and Amərətāt (or Non-Death), have names that are similar both in morphology and semantics; the pair are convincingly compared by Dumézil with the twins so typical of the third function, and as we noted earlier, their material correlates fit well with the F3 notion of fertility.

On the other hand, row IV runs counter to the idea that earth represents F4−, and Dumézil's F3 interpretation has to be questioned. Since V and VI gain their feminine gender from the abstract-forming suffix *-tāt* and were probably originally male (Dumézil 1977: 45–46), Bounteous Devotion (Spənta Ārmaiti) is the only Immortal who is straightforwardly female, which sets her apart from the other Immortals and suggests comparison with Pr̥thivī and Gaia.[11] Moreover, when the list contains seven Immortals, it may open with Bounteous Spirit (Spənta Mainyu, correlating with man) and place Bounteous Devotion last (Varenne 1981: 582b). Spənta Mainyu is conceptually close to and sometimes identified with Ahura Mazdā, the sovereign Creator, so one suspects that Ahura Mazdā and Spənta Mainyu represent F4+, and Spənta Ārmaiti and the Evil Spirit (Aŋra Mainyu) represent F4−.

Critics of Dumézil often object that the evidence for the three functions in the Vedas, and especially the hymns, is less plentiful than one might expect. According to Dumézil, the typical or canonical expression of the trifunctional pattern in the Indo-Iranian pantheon is Mitra-Varuṇa (F1), Indra (F2), and the Aśvin twins (F3), and the pairing of the first two and last two gods is reflected in the pairing of the first two and the last two Immortals. This pattern can be found both in the

TABLE 12.1 Trifunctional interpretation of the Aməša Spəntas, together with their material correlates

	Bounteous Immortal	*Function of Bounteous Immortal*	*Material correlate of Bounteous Immortal*
I	Good Intention	F1	bovine
II	Best Righteousness	**F1**	**fire**
III	Desirable Dominion	F2	metal
IV	Bounteous Devotion	**F3**	**earth**
V	Wholeness	**F3**	**water**
VI	Life	**F3**	**plants**

hymns (Dumézil 1977: Appx 1) and the Brāhmaṇas, but it cannot be said to dominate them; Agni and Soma (both of them visible entities as well as gods) are more prominent than Mitra-Varuṇa and the Aśvins, as Dumézil recognizes (1968: 58). But if Agni represents F1, as we have argued, Soma could represent F3. Like Agni, Soma has a large and complicated dossier, but if Agni is saliently a priest, Soma is saliently king of plants or herbs and lord of waters – the same conjunction as we found for the correlates of the paired F3 Immortals.

In this connection one might think of the triadic classification of Vedic ritual based on the main oblation: situated between offerings into the fire of dairy products or cereals and libations of soma, one finds *paśubandha*, the sacrifice of animal victims, where 'control of the breath [of the victim] is of paramount importance' (McClymond 2003: 235). Since breath or life-force, like air, relates to F2, the classification seems trifunctional. If so, it supports both the general Dumézilian argument for the pervasive presence of the core functions, and the link proposed here between the elements and the four functions.[12]

Of course, even if one rejects their link with functions, the elements are not unrelated entities that just happen to be juxtaposed in a certain order. However one understands the ordering of air and fire, the overall sequence from ether to earth is one of condensation and descent, while its reversal implies rarefaction and ascent. Both traditions used these unifying principles not only in their cosmogonic speculations but also in their eschatologies, when describing the path of the reincarnating soul that dies and is reborn (41). If the proto-philosophy did really associate functions and elements, perhaps it too used the association to think about changes or transformations of macrocosm and microcosm alike.

The previous argument needs to rebut at least two counterproposals. First, the similarities might indeed be due to use of the four-functional ideology to analyze materiality, but the application might have been carried out independently in the East and West. However, even if the old ideology was sufficiently alive in sixth century Miletus, it is unlikely that the results of the application within two such different cultures would be so similar. Second, if the application *was* made only once, but at some point in the history of the Indian tradition, this does not rule out the east–west diffusion envisaged by McEvilley. To answer this objection, we must broaden the discussion and return to the question of whether common origin can account for striking similarities of detail.

Similarities of detail

Apart from the idea of a split fourth function, another development since the death of Dumézil has been the clearer idea of an early IE proto-epic or proto-narrative, features of which can be reconstructed by Greco-Indian comparison (e.g. Vielle 1996). It is now hard to doubt that a substantial epic tradition bypassed the Vedas to surface around the turn of the eras in the *Mahābhārata*. Whatever may be the scope for comparing Greek traditions with the Vedas, the scope for comparison between the two epic traditions is immense. Such comparisons may involve macrostructures such as the five phases of the wars at Troy and Kurukṣetra, but they may also relate to tiny details. One instance is the use in cognate contexts of the masculine accusative singular of the present active participle of a verb that is cognate in the two languages [Ch. 6 n.9].

Of course, as in philosophy, the hypothesis of diffusion raises its head, but here too it faces numerous difficulties, which are discussed in several of my papers. In brief, the following seem to be the main problems: (a) the difficulty of envisaging a context for the encounters (where, when, in what language); (b) the fact that in some respects the *Mahābhārata* parallels closely not only Greek epic but also other IE traditions such as Roman pseudo-history (Allen 2005b); (c) the deep embedding of each epic within its local religious and cultural traditions (much deeper than is usual with folktales) – neither 'feels' like a borrowing; (d) in world-historical perspective, the correlational style of thinking manifested in the IE ideology (a 'primitive classification') has been losing ground over the millennia, yet its patterning effect is apparent in both epic traditions. It is easier to suppose that it operated on a proto-narrative than that it operated twice, independently, in the two branches of the tradition.

The more one accepts the idea of a proto-narrative lying behind the epics, the less reason there is to resist the idea of a proto-philosophy, for the two genres turn out to be much less separate than one might anticipate. The last part of this chapter introduces three philosophical topics that can be studied at least in part via epic.

McEvilley gives plenty of attention to yoga, suggesting tentatively that an early Mesopotamian doctrine diffused in both directions, and that the Indian variety, after elaboration, spread back west to Greece in the sixth century BC (p. 287). But the network of similarities between Arjuna's ascent to heaven in *Mahābhārata* Book 3, Odysseus' passage to Scheria in *Odyssey* Book 5, and the yogin's undertaking in *Śvetāśvatara Upaniṣad* and Patañjali [Ch. 5] suggests that the proto-narrative told of a cosmic/shamanic journey, presumably relating to shamanic practice, that somehow fed into yoga. It is not clear at what stage or stages the shamanic tradition underwent the interiorization that characterizes yoga, where this occurred, or whether it was a process that essentially occurred just once or one that occurred in parallel in different branches of the tradition. Even so, discussion of the shamanism–yoga complex needs to take account of the IE common origin hypothesis which, here again, can relate to striking details. For instance, the references to thistles and chaff in the *Odyssey* passage are cognate with Patañjali's references to thorns or cotton fibres.

If yoga is treated repeatedly by McEvilley, Sāṃkhya, the *darśana* with which yoga is traditionally paired, is virtually ignored – despite its pervasiveness in Hindu culture (including the *Mahābhārata*), and despite the various tempting comparisons with Greek thought. One such comparison concerns the use of numbers in Sāṃkhya and Pythagoreanism, particularly the use of five (for the Greek, see, e.g. Mattéi 1996: 108–117). Arguably (Allen 1998a), in Sāṃkhya the emanational sequence of twenty-five *tattvas* or principles opens with a set consisting of Puruṣa (associated with cosmogony), the three guṇas *(sattva, rajas, tamas)*, and *ahaṃkāra*. The guṇas, which have been described [by Dasgupta 1992: 244] as intelligence stuff, energy stuff, and mass stuff, respectively (i.e. F1, F2, F3 – cf. Sergent 1995: 339), constitute *prakṛti* ('primal nature'), and the overall one-three-one structure might recall the fragmentary text of Pherecydes cited earlier. If the analysis is right, the initial pentad incorporates a manifestation of the four functions, and the final pentad in the sequence consists simply of the five gross elements *(mahābhūtas)* – our familiar set, in the standard Indian order ending with earth.[13]

Between the first five principles and the last five come three other pentads – the five sense-capacities, the five action-capacities, and the five subtle elements. These three 'core' pentads show a degree of correlation: thus, the first member of each is respectively hearing, speaking, and sound, while the second is feeling, grasping, touch. But rather than pursuing the details and asking if or how these individual principles relate to the functions, we can view the pentads as units. The first core pentad, the *buddhīndriyas*, relates to the cognitive domain, while the second *(karmendriyas)* relates to action, and these domains qualify for F1 and F2 (action being a philosophic substitute for dynamism or force). The label for the third, *tanmātras* ('only so much or little, rudimentary, trifle' – Larson 1979: 187) suggests its lower standing, but the main reason for taking it as F3 lies in its origin. Whereas the two sets of *indriyas* emerge from *ahaṃkāra* in its *sattva* mode, the subtle elements emerge from it in its *tamas* (F3) mode (the structure F1 + F2 versus F3 is familiar in the trifunctionalist tradition). While the core pentads are held together by their origin from *ahaṃkāra*, the final pentad has a separate origin, namely from the subtle elements. I take it to be devalued by virtue of its materiality as well as its position.

In other words, Sāṃkhya appears to manifest the four functions in at least three ways. On the global level, the pentads themselves show the characteristic one-three-one hierarchy. Only the first pentad is linked with creation, and within it we can probably recognize another but interrupted manifestation – compare the anomalous ordering in most lists of Bounteous Immortals. Finally, the last pentad presents the functionally organized elements.[14]

Since enlightenment and related ideas are so important in both Indian and Greek philosophies, McEvilley naturally returns to them frequently, and one might think that here at least is a purely cognitive topic, to which studies of epic can hardly contribute. However, if one compares the biographies of Arjuna, Odysseus, Cúchulainn, and the Buddha (Allen 2005d), in each case one finds, following a period of privation or asceticism, some sort of breakthrough to another and better world, whether it is conceived in terms of cosmology, poetic geography, or soteriology. Arguably, all these events are cognate and go back to a single story in a proto-narrative.

Concluding discussion

More could be said, even on the basis of comparative work already published (e.g. on cosmic time), and it is only when the approach has been taken further, and its limitations emerge more clearly, that we shall be well placed to see how and where to call on the other cultural inputs referred to by McEvilley – Egypt, Mesopotamia,

Indus Valley, Dravidian substrate. One way ahead might be to take the ideological framework, as elucidated so far, and speculate on possible applications to philosophical topics. For instance, one can reflect on dualisms:

F4+ The Absolute, Ultimate Being, Totality, Infinity
F4− (The opposite) non-being, unreality, nothingness, the infinitesimal

Such contrasts between the aspects of the fourth function may, somehow, underlie the Vedantic Brahman–Ātman equation. But one can also play with triads: the transcendent One (F4+), the realm of structure (F1–3), meaningless multiplicity, or devalued oneness (F4−), or again with pentads, or the 'vertical' scales that underlie them. This proposal is of course only a heuristic, a way of generating ideas to explore.

My main aim has been to identify a gap in the problematic within which McEvilley works – and not only McEvilley, for the gap is equally obvious in many other writers. Practitioners of IE cultural comparativism have a vast task ahead if they are to modify the academic landscape to the point where their contribution to historical understanding is taken seriously across the disciplines. The task is not only intellectual but also concerns the sociology of academe. Anticipating opposition to his approach, McEvilley talks briefly of 'issues of turf', and it is true that neither classicists nor Indologists are likely to welcome being told that certain questions relating to their fields can only be answered by going outside it. But I would rather end on a positive note. Those like McEvilley who are willing to invest the time and take the risks can enter an exciting and sparsely cultivated comparative field where, despite the pessimists, scientific progress *is* possible.

Notes

1 First published in 2005 as 'Thomas McEvilley: the missing dimension' in a Review Symposium on McEvilley (2002). Unattributed page numbers in Chapter 12 refer to this book.
2 Another detail: among the 750 or so references, admirers of Marcel Mauss will miss Mauss (1927).
3 According to one estimate, the common ancestor of Greek and Sanskrit was spoken before 2300 BC, the common ancestor of Mature ('Brugmannian') Indo-European was spoken before 2800, and the common ancestor of PIE proper (i.e. including Hittite) was spoken before 3500 [West 2007: 7–11].
4 This well-known passage is cited again in Dumézil (1985b: 321n).
5 [He sometimes equates the two abstractions – e.g. 1968: 26.]
6 For the complications of the Indian case, see Allen (2007g). As for Plato, the king has been effectively merged with the philosophers, and arguably the artisans from the bottom have been merged with the farmers. To put it briefly, the three functions are the bundles of associations attaching respectively to priests, warriors, and producers, though there is more to the third function than productivity.
7 Though Dumézil mentions the priesthood of Agni (1968: 204), he does not emphasize it: 'Among the individual male gods Agni is the one who is most obviously trifunctional and the only one who is constantly so' (ibid.: 119). But he is not examining the elements as such.

8 Trifunctionalists maintain that Arjuna too represents F2, but if he does, it is in a less straightforward sense than Bhīma: as son of Indra, King of the Gods, Arjuna, though not himself a king, is better seen as representing F4+ [Ch. 15].
9 When connecting waters with F3, he writes of them as 'fécondantes, nourricières, guérisseuses, nettoyeuses' (providing fecundity, nourishment, healing, and cleansing – Dumézil 1985b: 30).
10 Since Dyu is etymologically cognate with Zeus, and Zeus is sometimes equated with *aithēr*, it is interesting that *aithēr* too can be either masculine or feminine. For some ramifications of the Zeus–Dyu comparison see [Ch. 10 and Allen 2018a].
11 The enlargement of Spənta Ārmaiti (= the earth) in *Vidēvdāt* 2 is cognate with the enlargement of the earthen container of Matsya in the Indian Deluge story (Allen 2000d: 292). [Narten 1982 totally ignores Dumézil.]
12 Conceivably the *agnicayana*, with its bricks, relates to earth, but the whole topic needs deeper study [cf. Allen 2015b].
13 I take the translations from the convenient diagram in Larson (1979: 236 – misspelled by McEvilley). Is there not a remote connection between the genealogical framework of Sāṃkhya and that of Hesiod's *Theogony*?
14 Curiously, when discussing the gross elements, Frauwallner (1973: 228) presents them in the standard Greek order, which accords with none of the three *Mahābhārata* texts he is citing.

13

RINGS AND ROTATIONS

The Tibetan image

The painting called the Wheel of Existence or Wheel of Life appears regularly as a colourful wall painting in porches of Tibetan temples but is sometimes also realized in other forms.[1] Figure 13.1, specially drawn by the artist in black and white, shows the design.

The central part consists of a hub or core, surrounded by concentric bands. The hub itself shows three animals, a bird (dove or cock), a snake, and a pig, symbolizing three evils that are discussed later. Next to this is a thin band, divided into black and white halves. On the white half, human figures are ascending towards heaven or better incarnations, while on the black, they are descending towards hell. The large and very crowded band consists of six sectors representing the different worlds into which one may be reborn: sin will lead to worse rebirths, merit to better ones. Heaven and hell are at the top and bottom in larger sectors. The worlds are inhabited by the following beings (from the top, working clockwise): gods, titans or *asuras* (who are at war with the gods), *pretas* or tormented ghosts, those suffering in hell, animals, and humans.

The outermost band, less crowded, shows twelve little scenes, mostly involving one or two figures. Without the help of informants or texts, their meaning would be obscure, but in fact they represent the twelve links in the chain of causation (the twelve *nidānas*). This is a philosophical insight that came to the Buddha in the course of his Enlightenment and explains how, on an individual level, one thing leads to, or is led to, by another; we worldlings are thereby caught within the round of births and deaths *(saṃsāra)*.

The wheel as a whole represents the ordinary human condition, dominated as it is by suffering, craving, or frustration *(duḥkha)*, and the being who grasps it so firmly is the Demon of Impermanence or Death, who has various names, including Māra. He has a third eye, a chaplet of skulls, and a snake across his shoulders, and he wears a tiger skin. The top right corner shows a small figure of the Buddha, who represents the possibility of *nirvāṇa*, of escape from *saṃsāra*.

FIGURE 13.1 The Wheel of Existence (Tibetan *srid-pa'i khor-lo*, Sanskrit *bhavacakra*)

Note: This is taken from Snellgrove (1987) plate 3 (it is also shown, slightly smaller, in Snellgrove 1957, plate 2). It was drawn by a Sherpa artist in Solu Khumbu (Nepal) in 1954, and I thank Professor Snellgrove for permission to reproduce it.

Specimens of the Wheel vary considerably in their details. Some omit the Bodhisattva (Avalokiteśvara), who is here shown in each sector. Others omit the innermost band, or merge gods and asuras to give a five-sector design. A Japanese specimen (Thomas 1901) puts the Buddha in the hub with the animals, locates the sectors immediately next to the hub, and shows the *nidānas* dispersed in the space outside the bands. However, despite such variation, the image seems sufficiently standardized for its identification never to be in doubt. Buddhism of course originated in India, and Waddell (1892) identified a fragmentary Wheel of Life painted in a fifth-century Buddhist cave at Ajanta (near Mumbai).

There also survives from early Buddhism a related textual tradition, attested by three documents. Two of them, the *Divyāvadāna* in Sanskrit (Foley 1894) and the *Mūlasarvāsti-vādin Vinaya* (in Chinese – Przyluski 1920) ascribe to the Buddha himself instructions for making the painting. The third is a fragmentary Sanskrit document from Central Asia (Pauly 1959). I summarize the Chinese text:

> The Buddha was in the Bamboo Wood at Rājagṛha with (Mahā-) Maudgalyāyana, who often visited the four other realms of the cosmos, observing with compassion the sufferings of their inhabitants (even gods suffer – at the prospect of their future fall). Maudgalyāyana preaches about this to large audiences and with great success. Since his pupil will not always be on earth to perform this role, the Buddha instructs the monks how to draw the Wheel on monastery porches. Choosing an appropriate diameter, they should draw the hub and the five sectors, with hell below, men on their four continents, and gods above. At the hub they should draw a white circle, the Buddha, and in front of him, the three symbolic animals. Around this will be a water wheel (as used for irrigation) with figures exiting from the buckets (being born) and plunging into them headfirst (dying). For the outermost band the Buddha lists the *nidānas* with their symbols, then describes the open-mouthed demon who grips the whole. Above the demon, a round white mound symbolizes *nirvāṇa*, and beside his head are written two verses of scripture (two *gāthās*). A learned monk is to expound the meaning of the whole painting.

Despite the various discrepancies between texts and images – for instance, the waterwheel (Sk. *ghati-yantra*), which corresponds to the innermost band in Figure 13.1 – the texts must have promoted the relative standardization of the image. In fact, the two, taken together, constitute a single verbal/visual tradition, which summarizes many of the fundamental doctrines of Buddhism.

For completeness, I mention one other Sanskrit tradition, namely that the Buddha devised the painting so that King Bimbisāra of Rājagṛha could give it as a countergift to King Roruka of Pāṭaliputra (Bleichsteiner 1937: 219). There is also a Tibetan oral tradition that the Buddha himself first drew the image on the ground (Gordon 1963: 19; Waddell 1895: 108).

Very soon after it was first discovered, the image at Ajanta was compared, by one Mr Ralph, to the Shield of Achilles in *Iliad* Book 18 (Prinsep 1835: 559). Let us follow up Ralph's idea.

First Greek comparison: wheel and shield

While Achilles is refusing to fight for the Greeks, his arms are borrowed by Patroclus who, at his death, loses them to his killer, Hector. Achilles' mother Thetis then goes overnight to Olympus and persuades Hephaestus to make another set. The shield is described in a well-known passage (an ecphrasis)[2] of 131 lines. Instead of showing the fearsome figures typical of shields, the decoration presents a sort of microcosm of human life.

> At the centre are the heavens. Around them, distributed probably in concentric bands, maybe four or five, there is a city at peace in which two events are taking place – a wedding and a lawsuit. Then comes the city at war, with a siege, sortie and battle, followed by a set of five rural scenes. The first three concern ploughing, grain harvest and grape-harvest, the last two concern cattle and sheep. Presumably the next scene, a dance, occupies a whole band, as does the Ocean around the outer edge.[3]

Comparing Wheel and Shield, one can note the following similarities:

1 *Concentric design*. Both images are based on concentric circles. Clearly this pattern is so common, for instance, in cosmograms or on ceramics, that the similarity is interesting only when combined with others.
2 *Image and word*. Both traditions show a complex interplay between a depiction – a wall painting, a decorated shield – and the words that relate to it. Of course there are differences. The Wheel, made by humans, exists and may be seen by the tourist or in photographs, while the Shield, made by a god, has to be imagined; the one relates to religious salvation, the other to the events of an epic poem; and while the Buddha both prescribes and explains, Homer only describes. On the other hand, both textual traditions refer to the process of production as well as to the outcome, and in oral tradition, the Buddha, like Hephaestus, makes a unique original.[4]
3 *Microcosm*. Buddhologists and Homerists both accept that their respective artefacts have a microcosmic character: quite small artefacts represent the whole of human destiny or human life. This is obvious in the Tibetan case, and as for Homer, many scholars have cited Lessing's remark from 1766: the poet makes his shield *zu einem Inbegriffe von allem, was in der Welt vorgehet*, an epitome of everything that goes on in the world (1990: 135–136). Lists have also been made of topics missing from the Shield, for instance female domestic work, illness, trade, and fishing, but Marg is surely right when he says that the selection of scenes *represents* a whole: '[A]nd this whole is humanity, or rather humans as they live with each other on the wide earth' (1971: 31).

If one asks why human life should be represented on a warrior's shield, Homerists point out *(inter alia)* that the description forms part of a welcome interlude between scenes of slaughter, and also, more strikingly, that the shield represents the (on the whole) enjoyable existence that Achilles chooses to sacrifice in exchange for revenge and glory.

4 *Multiple scenes*. In both cases, human life is represented by multiple scenes of individual or group activity. Thus, Giorgi (1762: 488), the first Westerner to publish a picture of the Wheel, describes the human sector as showing 'the Tibetan king, subjects bringing tribute to the king, a yeoman farmer, a carefree nobleman sitting out of doors, soldiers, a butcher, drinkers, a female weaver, a muleteer – representing the various types of human life'. The individual scenes in the sectors were apparently not specified by the Buddha (unlike the individual *nidānas*) but were introduced in the second century AD by the monk Nāgārjuna, drawing on similes used by the Buddha (Waddell 1895: 108). In some sectors, certainly in hell with its horrific tortures, the scenes are no doubt drawn from texts other than those I have cited (cf. e.g. Mus 1939: 219–243). Overall, the Tibetan images are less coordinated and less elaborated than the Greek ones but have the same representative function. One might expect that societies of similar cultural level would represent human life with similar figures – for example kings, cooks, soldiers, ploughmen, cattle – so my argument does not draw on the details of the scenes (which might or might not repay separate study).

5 *Functional ideology*. I come finally to what originally drew me to the topic (during a visit to Darjeeling in 2000). Little introduction is needed here to the Dumézilian view of the early Indo-European (IE) speakers as organizing their world view according to a triadic form of classification. Roughly speaking, under the first class (or function) fall people or things linked with knowledge of the sacred (religion, law)[5]; under the second function falls what relates to physical force and war; and under the third, what relates to fecundity and prosperity. For mnemonic purposes one can think of the three functions as relating to priests, warriors, and producers.

The evils represented by the pig, snake, and bird on the hub are respectively *moha*, *dveṣa*, and *rāga* – delusion, enmity, and passion – evils that relate to religious knowledge and cognition (first function), conflict or war (second), and desire or sexuality (third); though apparently not noted by Buddhologists, the fit with the classical three functions is good.[6] But for many years I have been arguing that, in addition to Dumézil's triad, we need to recognize a split fourth function, pertaining to what is other, outside, or beyond relative to the core functions; it is split since its valued or positive aspect comes at the top of the hierarchy, and its devalued or negative aspect comes at the bottom. In the present case, outside the *saṃsāra* in which we wander so frustratingly, prey to the three evils, two figures are presented: the Buddha manifesting the positive aspect of the fourth function, the Demon its negative aspect. If the Buddha is sometimes shown right at the heart of this *duḥkha*-dominated world rather than as far from it as possible, this may parallel the fact that the two aspects of the fourth function – the top and bottom of the hierarchy – are not infrequently juxtaposed (especially in cyclical contexts, cf. Allen 2005a).

Although the symbolic animals and their evils have no close parallel on the Shield, the classical functions that they represent *are* unambiguously present on the Shield, albeit in quite a different form.

After a preparatory reference to earth, heaven, and sea (line 482), the account of the Shield begins with the sun, moon, and four constellations in heaven, but neither of these triads accords with the functions. It was the 'human' part of the shield that was analyzed trifunctionally by Yoshida (1964). Though his paper is regularly dismissed or ignored by Homerists, the core of its argument is sound. One needs to focus on lines 497–589. This stretch of text opens in the juridical realm: two disputants are arguing in the agora before the elders, who are seated in a sacred circle *(hierōi eni kuklōi)*. The next scene, precisely delimited, concerns warfare, and it is followed by the three agricultural scenes and the two pastoral scenes. Sacred law, warfare, production of food and wealth – these three types of activity, presented by the text in the standard or canonical order of the classical functions, manifest them unambiguously. The problem arises with the scenes that precede and follow this sequence – the urban marriage and the dance. But whatever is made of these, the trifunctional analysis of the core sequence remains unscathed. As for the heavens at the centre and the Ocean at the edge (or their implicit inhabitants or personifications), I leave open whether or not they represent F4+ and F4−, respectively.[7]

In summary, Wheel and Shield share a concentric design and a presentation simultaneously in visual *and* verbal forms. Both present world views, and do so via multiple scenes of human life. Both show clear traces of the old Indo-European form of classification – at any rate of the three classical functions.

Second Greek comparison: wheel and straits monsters

In *Odyssey* Book 12, the hero Odysseus is wandering the world, trying to find his way back from Troy to his home in Ithaca. After leaving Circe he encounters, in what amounts to a single episode, three monstrous types of female one after another – the Sirens, Scylla, and (after the disastrous visit to Thrinacia) Charybdis. The Sirens are singing temptresses who try to lure mariners to their deaths. Scylla, who inhabits a cliff on one side of the Straits, is a polycephalic monster who seizes and eats six of the hero's companions. Charybdis, who lives by the cliff on the other side of the Straits, is a destructive whirlpool.

1 *Cosmic journeys.* My first comparison draws on two features of the Wheel tradition. First, in the myth of origin, Maudgalyāyana travels around the cosmos observing the sufferings of its various inhabitants, and second, over countless rebirths, a moral being wanders among the worlds that make up *saṃsara*. But Odysseus too is a wanderer, who visits Hades as well as many other realms, even if his movements are determined by winds, currents, and the will of deities, not by his moral behaviour in successive lives or his sense of compassion.

2 *Rotation, especially of water.* The idea of rotation is already implied by the Buddha's reference to the painting as a wheel, a *cakra*, and the observer should envisage the rotation both of the hub and of the six worlds (Waddell 1892: 135). But the idea is expressed even more clearly by the waterwheel, whose buckets carry reincarnating beings upward towards heaven and downward to hell. Admittedly, the theme of rotation is not absent from the Shield: the celestial bodies rotate, the Ocean may be viewed as a river flowing round the earth, the agricultural year cycles through the seasons, and the circle of dancers periodically revolves like a pot on the potter's wheel. However, shields themselves do not rotate, and the rotations just listed lack both the salience and negativity of *saṃsāra*, whereas in the *Odyssey*, Charybdis is both salient – she forms the climax of the whole episode – and as negative as one could wish. Moreover, like a *ghatiyantra*, she involves specifically the rotation *of water*.

Furthermore, Charybdis is said to suck down the sea so as to reveal the sea-bed and then to belch it forth (i.e. upward). This duality compares both with the upward and downward movement of water on the waterwheel and with the Buddha's instructions for drawing the *nidānas*, which is to be done both *anuloma* and *pratiloma*. The latter terms contrast two directions of movement – literally with the hair (as when one strokes an animal) and against it, and they may well echo events immediately after the Enlightenment. For when the Buddha discovered the law of causation, he worked through it first in one direction, then the other, *anuloma* and *pratiloma* (as it were, clockwise and anticlockwise, though this is not said). In addition, he did so three times in the course of the night, while Charybdis repeats her double action three times a day.

3 *Large, static, toothy monster.* If the wheel is tightly clutched by the more or less static Demon, the whirlpool is only a bowshot away from Scylla, whose midriff appears to be anchored in her cave (*Od.* 12.93). Moreover, if the Demon has prominent teeth (shown biting the top of the shield), so has Scylla – three rows of them, close-packed and full of black death, in each of her six heads (12.91–92) – in contrast to Charybdis, who swallows her prey rather than crunching it. Again, just as the demon is bigger than the wheel, so Scylla's cliff is larger than that of Charybdis. Finally, in one text, the demon is three-headed (*triśīrṣam*, Pauly 1959: 238) – cf. Scylla's six heads; if the demon is sometimes wreathed with snakes (Gordon 1963: 21), Scylla's long and flexible necks seem snake-like, and some sources make the Demon a *srin-mo*, that is, as female as Scylla (Bleichsteiner 1937: 219). However, I am not sure what to make of this last point, for Scylla and Charybdis are opposites in so many ways that one might try to align them symbolically with opposite sexes. One need not be a committed Freudian to feel that Scylla, projecting aggressively from her cliff, is less feminine than Charybdis, who sucks things into her circular hole.

4 *Triads and multiples.* Both our comparanda favour triads. The Buddhist tradition has thrown up three symbolic animals, a three-headed demon, and three

meditations on the chain of causation, while the Bonpo variant adds a triple-headed cow at the hub (Kvaerne 1981). In the Greek, we have already met the three types of hostile females (Sirens, Scylla, Charybdis), the three rows of teeth, and the triple repetition in Charybdis' activity, and we can add the three Sirens (typical of extra-Homeric sources), the three locations (Sirens' Isle and the two cliffs), and the three hazards mentioned by Circe (after 12.39) – the Sirens' Isle, the Wandering Rocks, and the cliffs taken as a unit.[8] But the two traditions share not only a liking for triads but also multiples of that number: Scylla's six heads and twelve legs parallel the six worlds and twelve *nidānas* on the Wheel. Is this mere coincidence?

5 *Animals and monsters.* Among the triads the most interesting comparison relates the three types of monster in the Greek to the three hub animals on the Wheel. I consider first their form. Greek depictions of Sirens usually show them winged (i.e. like birds), which recalls the dove or cock; and we have already noted the snaky character of Scylla's necks. But Charybdis herself is not depicted, and the text does not relate her overtly to a pig. Originally a greedy young woman, she was metamorphosed by Zeus for her gluttony when she stole and ate some cattle belonging to Hercules (Serv. *ad Aen.* 3.420), but I do not know if pigs were associated with greed in India, as they are in English, so the comparison remains inconclusive. Let us therefore turn from forms to functions.

On the wheel, the bird was linked with passion (F3), the snake with hatred (F2), and the pig with delusion (F1). Now the danger posed by the Sirens comes from the knowledge they offer: their appeal is addressed to the hero's curiosity. This orientation towards cognition places them under the first function. As regards Scylla, with her snaky extremities and aggressive nature, Odysseus ignores Circe's warnings and tries to ward off her attack by donning armour and taking up spears (12.288), as if she were an enemy warrior. But if Scylla operates in the realm of F2, Charybdis is notably greedy – *voracissima*, says Servius – and consumption falls under F3.

Thus, the classical functions are manifested as much in the attributes of the Greek Monsters as in the evils symbolized by the animals on the Buddhist hub. Admittedly, the analyses by form do not accord with those by function, the Buddhist bird being linked with the F3 evil, the bird-like Sirens with the F1 threat. But such anomalies need not disconcert us, since they are rather common where multiple correlations are involved (as in the Brāhmaṇas).

Our analysis of the Wheel went beyond the three animals to embrace the Buddha and the Demon, representing F4+ and F4−. In the Greek, the fourth function is, I think, represented by the supernaturals most closely involved in the hero's wanderings, even though they do not intervene explicitly in this episode. The hero is helped by Athena, harassed by Poseidon (angry at the blinding of his son, the Cyclops Polyphemus). It is no surprise that some late sources make Poseidon the father of Charybdis and involve him in the metamorphosis of Scylla into a monster.

Thus, the second comparison uses the following shared features: wandering; rotation (especially of water); large, toothy monsters; theriomorphic triads; multiples of three; tri- and quadrifunctionality. But it gains its full force only when placed in a broader narrative context.

6 *Narrative context*. Although the stories of the origin of the Wheel do not explicitly situate the episode within the Buddha's biography, the references to Maudgalyāyana and Rājagṛha imply a time well after the First Sermon. However, the ideas expressed in the whole painting (and not only in the outermost band) are essentially those attained by the Buddha at his Enlightenment. Thus, although the five or six worlds available for rebirth are not listed in the main accounts of the Enlightenment, two of the three types of knowledge gained by the Buddha at that point concern previous births, respectively of himself and of all living beings, and in this context he mentions heaven and hell, that is, two of the extra-terrestrial realms shown in the painting. The third type of knowledge the Buddha gains is of his own release from *saṃsāra*, which is of course also implicit in the painting. Now for quite different reasons, I have argued elsewhere (Allen 2002a, 2000c) that the narrative surrounding the Enlightenment draws on the same early IE traditions as lie behind the second half of Odysseus' *nostos*, and the present argument will be easier to dismiss if one ignores this wider setting. Though individual rapprochements are of course open to individual criticisms, what I propose is really a single package: either Buddhist tradition is cognate with the *Odyssey* or it is not.[9]

Moreover, within the story of Odysseus' return, the Straits episode as a whole represents the fourth function negative (F4−) in a sequence of episodes [Ch. 6], while the hero's reunion with Penelope back at Ithaca represents F4+. The negativity of the Straits episode can be compared with the negativity that dominates the Wheel – apart from the Buddha himself (who is not always shown).

We must now bring together the three elements of the chapter.

Wheel, shield, and straits

My underlying hypothesis, here as in previous papers, is that there existed in early or PIE times a fairly lengthy and coherent proto-narrative, from which Greek epic, Sanskrit epic, and Buddhist sacred biography all derive much of their narrative substance. But how exactly would this idea link the Buddhist tradition with the two Greek texts?

Two simple models present themselves. Model A postulates that the Buddhist tradition (including its narrative component) is highly conservative: something like a proto-wheel episode existed at a very early period (long before the historical Buddha), and this bifurcated, giving rise to the two Greek passages. Model B postulates that the Greek duality is conservative. 'Originally' there were two distinct proto-narrative episodes, one relating to a circular object, the other to a set of monsters, and Buddhist tradition has synthesized them.

Model B is far more plausible and finds support in the comparisons I have published between Homer and the *Mahābhārata*. These show that the proto-narrative contained a pentadic story about the journey of a proto-hero, a journey concerned with marriages (not war) and including an encounter with a set of five female monsters [Ch. 2]. Nothing suggests that the tradition of a concentric design containing microcosmic vignettes belongs in this section of the proto-narrative. On the contrary, since the proto-narrative also recounted a Great War ancestral both to the Trojan War and to the central conflict of the *Mahābhārata* (Allen 2002b), it is probably with this part of a proto-hero's career that we should link the proto-Shield.

Model B is not intended to imply that, in constructing the Wheel, Buddhist tradition drew *only* on the two sources.[10] For instance, little has been said here about the sequence of twelve *nidānas*, which may constitute a polemic against Vedic cosmogonic thinking (Jurewicz 2000). The waterwheel on the innermost band reflects the influence of agricultural technology (Coomaraswamy 1931: 283), and ideas of hell have their own history. No doubt the Wheel absorbed and synthesized ideas from multiple sources.

One such possible source merits fleeting mention. The Wheel is first painted as a result of the other-world journeys of Maudgalyāyana; the shield is created as a result of Thetis' journey to Mount Olympus; the Straits episode is part of a hero's journey to the extremities of the earth and includes a journey to the Island of the Sun. But the notion of travel to other worlds suggests shamanism; shamans use drums, which are usually circular; and the drums often have paintings on them, sometimes images of the cosmos. Sometimes the drum's myth of origin, as well as the journey it makes possible, are narrated in the chants that constitute most of the séance (de Sales 1991, [Ch. 12]).

Whether or not the Wheel relates specifically to shamanism, many non-literate peoples preserve culturally important traditions by using visual aids – not writing, but pictures accompanied by exposition (Severi 2003). One implication of the present chapter is that the early Indo-Europeans used images similarly: they depicted the human condition by using themes common to the Wheel and Shield. Comparativists have more often tried to reconstruct features of prehistoric rituals than of prehistoric designs, but the latter project need not be impossible.

Notes

1 Published in 2006 as 'The Buddhist Wheel of Existence and two Greek comparisons'.

2 'The verbal representation of a visual representation' (Heffernan 1993: 3). Becker (1995) distinguishes four levels of representation in an ecphrasis: the referent, the physical medium (here metallic), the creation (by Hephaestus), and the response to the work (by bard and/or audience).

3 [For one of many attempts to illustrate the shield, see the one by David Jones and Sarah Jones in Alden 2011: 795.]

4 In the *Divyāvadāna* (Cowell and Neil 1886: 300) the gerundive *kartavya* (from the ordinary verb *kṛ-* 'to make or do') appears eight times, the only other relevant verb being *lekhitavya*, gerundive of 'to write' (i.e. the stanzas). Homer uses indicative past tenses of

four different verbs to describe what Hephaestus does, one of them (used twice) being *poieō* 'to make', which is as ordinary in Greek as *kṛ-* is in Sanskrit.

5 Dumézil – mistakenly, I believe – also included 'sovereignty' under the first function.

6 This by no means controverts the view that the three evils are an allusion to the three fires in Vedic sacrifice (Gombrich 1996: 66), since the fires themselves are trifunctional (Dumézil 1974: 319–321).

7 [Ch. 14 argues that they do and presents the functional analysis more fully.]

8 Triads are not prominent on the Shield. Apart from its triple rim, it has only the triple ploughing and the three binders of sheaves (the three functions being implicit). There are four herdsmen and nine dogs, but the salient number is two (cities, litigants, talents; armies, scouts, herdsmen; lions, tumblers).

9 One easily overestimates the remoteness of a sacred biography from a heroic one: the Buddha has to *vanquish* Māra, and Achilles' choice of fame over long life is an eschatological or soteriological one.

10 Nor, for that matter, that the Charybdis scene derives *only* from the episode in the marital journey of the proto-hero.

14

ACHILLES' SHIELD

When Patroclus borrows Achilles' arms and loses them to Hector, Achilles needs a new set, and his mother goes to Mount Olympus to get it made by Hephaestus.[1] The decoration of the new shield is described by Homer at some length (126 lines) and falls into a number of discrete scenes, no doubt disposed in concentric circles around a hub or boss. The question addressed in this chapter concerns the subject matter of the different scenes: to what extent do the subjects form a coherent structure, and to what extent does this structure reflect early Indo-European (IE) patterns of thought?

The shield as a whole

An IE background to the shield was first proposed by Atsuhiko Yoshida in a classic paper (1964), which we shall need to recall. But Yoshida's analysis draws on Dumézil's account of the three functions that provide the framework to IE ideology, and it may be useful to begin by recalling what is meant by a function in this context, and how each function is defined.

Some world views, including that of the early IE speakers (but not, for instance, that or those of the modern West) are 'partitional': the partitions or compartments that they recognize cross-cut contexts (contexts such as the components of social structure, the gods or heroes in a particular narrative, a list of priestly offices, the objectives of a particular ritual). In one context after another, one finds that the entities recognized by the culture fall unambiguously into one or other of the compartments, which have become known as functions. The analyst needs to be able to label the compartments or functions, and the numerical labels – first, second, third – have become current for two reasons. First, if one analyzes the entities occurring in a given context, the compartments into which they fall tend to follow a standard order. Second, this same order tends to correlate with rank, the highest-ranking compartment coming first, the lowest last. We can now define the three functions. The first relates to the intellect, to the management of the sacred, and to what is morally binding; the second to physical force and war; the third to fecundity, abundance, wealth, and related ideas, such as sexuality and nourishment. For reasons I have discussed elsewhere, my definition of the first function is deliberately narrower than that of Dumézil, for whom it also covers 'sovereignty'.

With this in mind, we can turn to the shield. The description starts in 18.483 at the boss and progresses to the rim (18.609). The boss is occupied by cosmic entities – earth, heaven, sea, sun, full moon, constellations (four are listed), and the rim is occupied by the ocean.[2] Between boss and rim are scenes of human activity, and it is these that Yoshida analyzes in terms of the three functions. The 'city at peace' shows cheerful wedding processions (six lines), then a lawsuit in the assembly (twelve); law being divinely sanctioned, this city represents the first function. Next, the city at war (thirty-two lines) straightforwardly represents the second function. Finally, agricultural productivity relates to wealth and nourishment, so the five scenes of rural life (forty-nine lines), plus the round dance (16 or 17), represent the third function.

Yoshida's analysis has generally been endorsed by comparativists (e.g. Littleton 1980: 147; Sergent 1998: 62–68) but ignored or rejected by classicists (cf. Edwards 1991: 209). The classicists are not altogether unjustified. The round dance has youths and maidens in their best clothes in a lovely dance (*perhaps* a fertility dance), watched by cheerful spectators, and may be acceptable as third-functional under the rubrics of sexuality, beauty, and (perhaps) fertility, but the arguments for treating the wedding processions as first-functional seem to me unpersuasive. The sequence litigation–war–agriculture is a straightforward trifunctional set in the standard or canonical order: if any text manifests the three functions, this one does. But as some Homerists have noted (e.g. Redfield 1975: 188), the weddings and dance have a lot in common – song, whirling young men (*edineon* 494, *edineuon* 606), music, onlookers – and the scenes may perhaps be seen as an instance of ring composition, framing the trifunctional pattern but originally independent of it.[3]

Whatever is made of the weddings and dance, the cosmic entities at the centre and rim, which come respectively first and last in the text, clearly form a frame that stands outside the human activities. We must now introduce an idea that Dumézil knew of but never seriously entertained – that of a fourth function in IE ideology. As I have argued elsewhere (e.g. Allen 1999b, 2000a), the fourth function pertains to what is other, outside, or beyond, relative to the classical or 'core' functions, and it has two aspects. One aspect, the superior and/or transcendent one, precedes and outranks the first function, while the other, inferior and often in some sense excluded, follows and ranks lower than the third function. There are reasons, which I need not discuss here, for avoiding the obvious idea of a fifth function and preferring to recognize a split fourth function.

The cosmic entities fit reasonably well under the fourth function. The firmament, as transcendent as anything material can be, would represent the positively valued aspect of the fourth function. The outer ocean, which Odysseus has to cross to reach the dreaded Other World of Hades, would represent the devalued or negative aspect.[4] If this interpretation is accepted, the five compartments of the ideology are manifested on the shield in their standard or canonical order.

Dumézil's rules for trifunctional analysis require the representatives of the functions to be homogeneous, and in four-functional analyses, the additional entities have to be homogeneous with the others *to some degree*. Firmament and ocean are in fact not wholly unlike human beings. In some contexts, the cosmic entities are animate beings, endowed with agency, beings whose names can be written with capital initials. From this point of view, Earth and Heaven can be seen as Gaia and Ouranos, the Hesiodic primal couple; similarly, Ocean can be seen as the figure who ignores Zeus' summons in *Il.* 20.7 and who is said by Homer to be the source or origin of all the gods (*Il.* 14.201, 246).[5] Even in the present context, one constellation 'keeps his eye' on another – the Bear watches Orion (*dokeuei* 488). Thus, the cosmic entities show just that combination of homogeneity and otherness that four-function theory looks for.

The weak point in the analysis is the interruption of the solidary sequence by the wedding procession and (perhaps) the dance, but such interruptions in functional sequences occur elsewhere, for instance in the Nuristani pantheon and (I think) in the Ynglingasaga king-list (see Allen 1991, 2005a). One possibility is that they were elaborations introduced into the oral tradition at a time when the old partitional ideology had ceased to dominate the creative imagination of the bards. In any case, the Homerist literature, from Lessing in 1766 onward to Schadewaldt, Marg and Taplin a generation back, emphasizes that the shield constitutes a whole (*ein Ganzes*, a microcosm), and four-functional analysis reflects this holism better than trifunctionalism.

Another comparativist chapter [Ch. 13] argues that Achilles' shield is cognate with a well-known and frequently painted Buddhist image called the Wheel of Life. This image may show the Buddha in the centre, and around the centre are disposed concentric rings showing vignettes of human activity, while the wheel as a whole is gripped by a demon representing death (cf. the Ocean on the shield). The comparison not only provides a measure of support for the four-functional analysis of the shield but also suggests that it has a long prehistory. With this prehistory in mind, let us concentrate attention on the third-functional part of the shield.

The agricultural scenes: (A) taxonomy

The five agricultural scenes depict the following activities: ploughing, grain harvest, grape harvest, cattle rearing, and sheep farming. The first four scenes each average around eleven lines in Homer, while the sheep receive only three. All that is actually said is that Hephaestus depicted a pasture in a valley with sheep, pens, and huts. Following the preceding and far more elaborate descriptions, these three lines have been judged rather feeble, and certain Homerists, including Heyne (1802), Leaf (1900–2), and Taplin (1980), have thought of dismissing them as interpolations.[6] But from a comparative point of view, their presence makes excellent sense.

It is now clear that within the field of livestock rearing, the early IE speakers made a distinction between larger and smaller domestic animals. For the Roman material, one can start in 1962 with Dumézil's analysis (based on Varro, Vergil, and Columella) of the two Roman goddesses called Pales, who protect respectively *le gros bétail* and *le petit bétail*, or *pecus maior* and *pecus minor*, *armenta* and *greges*, herds and flocks. Without referring to Dumézil, Benveniste (1969 I: 40) touches on the same distinction when examining Greek lexical material, while Watkins, following Benveniste, treats the topic systematically (1979, summary in 1995: 209–213). None of the three refer to the shield.

Watkins (1979) starts from the Hittite phrase NAM.RA GUD UDU,[7] which means roughly 'deportees, cattle, sheep', that is, mobile wealth taken on a raid; but the words for cattle and sheep, GUD and UDU, constitute a merism, by which he means 'a bipartite noun phrase serving to designate globally an immediately higher taxon'. Thus, the two species, bovine and ovine, represent livestock in general, as distinct from the human deportees or slaves. Since English lacks convenient expressions, Watkins refers to the two livestock categories using the German words *Großvieh* and *Kleinvieh*, and he assembles further evidence for the distinction from Indo-Iranian. If we were right to recognize an IE background to the overall design of the shield, the chances are that the separation of cattle and sheep scenes also reflects an early IE distinction.

Watkins then goes on to situate this particular distinction within a wider folk taxonomy of wealth, conceived in terms of binary semantic features such as ± human, ± large, ± equine; but I summarize without using this device. The crucial point is that non-mobile organic wealth (i.e. vegetable wealth) is expressed by the merism 'grain and grape'. Apart from Hittite, Watkins draws into his analysis (1995: 197–206) an early Roman prayer to Mars reported by Cato (*Agr.* 141.1 ff.), where the two units of the merism appear doubled: grains and corn, vineyards and brushwork or shrubwork *(fruges frumenta vineta virgultaque)*, the brushwork serving as support for the vines. This line is followed by a reference to shepherds and cattle *(pastores pecuaque)*, and its relevance for us is of course the parallel with the sequence of scenes on the shield – grain harvest and the grape harvest followed by the two livestock scenes.[8]

Watkins' fullest taxonomy derives from a list in the Old Hittite *Merchant Epic*, which spells out the components of 'plenty and abundance'. In this text, the forms of wealth we have touched on so far are followed by a list of inorganic materials – precious metals and jewels, then iron, copper, tin (less precious). The Hittite list is compared by Watkins (1979: 285–286) with three lists of valuables that include metals or metal artefacts and that occur elsewhere in the *Iliad* (23.259–261, 549–550; 7.467–475). On the shield, the taxonomy is not presented in full since the deportees or slaves are missing, but what about inorganic wealth?

Obviously, metallic wealth does not receive a discrete section of the description, but it is not absent either. The reader or listener is constantly reminded that the shield is being made by Hephaestus, the divine metalsmith, and some of the reminders consist of references to the materials he is using. Moreover, such references are particularly frequent in the section of text relating to the third function: the forty-nine lines contain eight of them. The god uses gold for the ploughed field, for the vineyard and the herders; silver for the vine supports, blue enamel for the trench, tin for the fence, gold and tin together for the cattle. In the remaining seventy-seven lines, only one reference occurs that is certainly comparable: in the war scene, Ares, Athena, and their clothes are in gold. A few further cases are ambiguous in that we are not told whether the objects depicted by Hephaestus are made from the relevant metal (this applies to the gold talents, the gold daggers in the dance, and to the bronze-tipped spears). The god's craftsmanship is so wonderful that, although the ploughed field is crafted from gold, the viewer sees it as black; so we cannot be certain that the bronze spear-tips are made of bronze. If we take account only of the unambiguous passages, we can say that nearly all the references to inorganic wealth come in the third-function section of the shield.

If we are on the right track, the shield reflects an IE classification of wealth that includes inorganic wealth as well as grain and grapes, cattle and sheep. Admittedly, while metals are present in the account of the shield, it is not in the same sense as the organic forms of wealth: the latter are depicted, the metals are used to depict.[9] We shall later suggest an interpretation of the difference.

Watkins' paper also prompts the question of how the ploughing scene would fit in a taxonomy of wealth. In his final sentence, he refers to 'the complete absence of any reference to land tenure as a form of wealth despite its documented economic significance in Mycenean Greek and Old Hittite times'; so might the gap be filled by the ploughing scene, with its reference to 'soft fallow-land, rich tilth and wide'? The idea seems too narrow, too exclusively economic – Homer does not present the ploughed field as anyone's property. We need a broader frame of reference.

The agricultural scenes: (B) functions

To make sense of the ploughing scene, we must leave Watkins with his lexical pre-occupations and return to Dumézil with his interest in ideology: in anthropological parlance, we leave ethnoscience and return to classifications that cross-cut contexts. When Dumézil links the paired Roman goddesses Pales with the *Großvieh/Kleinvieh* distinction, he remarks that such pairing is typical of the IE theology of the third function; for instance, it recalls the twin gods called Nāsatyas or Aśvins, and their *Mahābhārata* incarnations, the Pāṇḍava twins Nakula and Sahadeva.[10] Dumézil's remark raises the question whether correlations exist between scenes and functions and also suggests that to answer it one might look for the Roman deities who best fit the scenes.

For the grape harvest, the obvious Roman deity is Liber; for cereals, Ceres; for the Earth itself, Tellus (corresponding to Greek Gaia or Ge). Now the sequence Tellus, Ceres, Liber, Pales may sound familiar to students of Roman religion: it opens, indeed dominates, the section on the third function in one chapter of Dumézil's *Religion romaine archaïque* (1975: 375–394). He sums up this set of deities as 'defining the ordinary field of peasant activity . . . they are, roughly speaking, the articulated and solidary principles of the third function' (ibid: 389). This remarkable insight is not developed elsewhere; usually, for instance in *Les dieux souverains* (Dumézil 1977: 10), Dumézil presents the third function as 'by its nature recalcitrant to systematization'. He was certainly not thinking of Achilles' shield when he wrote about this sequence of gods, and the fit with Homer's scenes is all the more remarkable.

We must now ask whether this 'articulated and solidary' sequence, correlating so neatly with the Homeric scenes, relates to the functions. We are of course operating *within* the third function, but one functional set can perfectly well be involuted within another. For instance, as kṣatriyas, the Pāṇḍavas are all second-functional at one level of analysis (i.e. in terms of the varṇa schema), but at another level, regarded as individual brothers or half-brothers, they form an involuted four-functional set.[11] In our present case a functional interpretation is attractive, though not totally compelling.

Following Dumézil's rules of method (1979: 77), we may note that the scenes of rural production constitute a set of units that are 'distinct, solidary, homogeneous, and exhaustive' (the round dance, not being clearly related to rural production, need not be considered). But the second rule demands that it be 'evident' that the units relate to the functions, and this is more debatable.

First come Earth and ploughing. Now the earth produces not only cereals and grapes but also the pasturage needed for livestock, the *nomon* referred to in both livestock scenes (575, 587). The earth is thus the ultimate origin of the growing things, both vegetable and animal (not to mention the inorganic wealth it may contain), and in that sense it subsumes them. Representatives of the valued fourth function, such as kings, often somehow embody synthetically the totality that is then covered analytically by the other functions. Moreover, as we noted, Earth in the form of Gaia can be read as the Creatrix in the Hesiodic cosmogony,[12] and the gap between creator and creation is one of the common modes of heterogeneity that separates representatives of the transcendent half-function from representatives of the rest of the ideology.

Now comes the harvest scene. Among the rural scenes, this one contains the only clear reference to religion, namely the ox sacrifice of 18.559. This provides a link, albeit a slender one, with the first function.

As for the grape harvest, Indian evidence, mainly relating to the heads of the monster Triśiras, links alcohol *(surā)* specifically with the warriors and the second function, in contrast to the sacred beverage soma, which is linked with the brahmins and hence the first function (Allen 2003b: 166–168). The argument is again less direct than one would like, and the question of the place of intoxicants in IE ideology is complicated (Dumézil 1975: 87–107); compare also the reference to wine in the ploughing scene (18.545). However, it is worth noting Dumézil's proposal (1975: 126 n.3) that, at least in India, 'it may be that there were originally three drinks related [respectively] to the functions and classes: soma, surā, madhu' [mead].

The connection between the paired livestock scenes and the third function was our starting point for this section of the chapter, but it raises the broader question of why pairing or twinning is such a salient feature of the third function. The usual answer has been that the pairing reflects the abstract notion of abundance, which is so prominent in definitions of that function. However, it may also express the more concrete notion that wealth in livestock is of two basic types.[13]

Three further observations are relevant at this point. First, as regards the relative status of the two types of livestock, presumably the *Kleinvieh* rank lower than *Großvieh* – which may go some way towards explaining the brevity of the sheep scene. Second, as regards the relative status of cultivation and livestock rearing, the proposed allocation to functions implies that cultivation was originally the higher-ranking, and this in turn raises questions that archaeology may be able to answer about the relative economic importance of the two forms of production in the proto-society. Third, as Yoshida might have noted, in the sequence litigation–warfare–production, the duality within the last item (i.e. cultivation versus livestock) can be seen as a typical third-functional pairing. Again the element that comes earlier in the text and presumably ranks higher is treated in greater detail: (9 + 11 + 12=)32 lines for cultivation versus (14 + 3=)17 lines for livestock.

Having argued that the third-function scenes relate to four of the five slots in the ideology, we need at least to raise the question of the remaining slot. Of course, it does not *have* to be filled: no relevant scene appears on the shield and consequently no correlated Roman deity was suggested. But this is the point to recall the earlier discussion of the place of metals at the end of Watkins' taxonomy of wealth.

Being inanimate, metals are in a sense dead, and death and the Other World regularly fall under the negative aspect of the fourth function. Moreover, those who work with metal tend to belong to that devalued social class that in India is represented by Untouchables, who belong to the same category (Allen 2006b). Another line of argument draws on the connections one often finds between representatives of the positive and negative aspects of the fourth function (compare the cosmic entities on boss and rim, as noted earlier). Whereas grain, grapes, and livestock all grow on the surface of the earth, ploughing means penetrating that surface, as does mining. But ploughing is a respectable ritual activity quite often performed by kings, for example by Romulus when founding Rome (Plutarch *Rom.* 11.2) or by a modern-day 'ploughman king' in Rajasthan (Balzani 2003: 157–162), while mining, in contrast, is typically a task for slaves. If Homer had allocated a third-functional scene to metalwork, it would fit well under the devalued aspect of the fourth function.

Thus, there are several reasons why metallic wealth would fit well within the fifth, apparently empty, slot. If the other forms of wealth are represented by scenes of human activity, while metalwork is represented only by the activity of Hephaestus, this heterogeneity may itself be a mark of the fourth function. Perhaps the absence of a scene devoted to this compartment of the ideology reflects not only its low rank in the hierarchy but also, more precisely, an associated inauspiciousness.

Concluding discussion

The shield of Achilles is a delightful piece of poetry, providing welcome relief after the long battle scenes surrounding the death of Patroclus, but it has been treated here solely as a reflection of early IE patterns of thought. The argument rests on the theory of a split fourth function bracketing the traditional three. The theory is already supported by much evidence, assembled from several areas and many contexts in the IE-speaking world, and I have tried to add to this.

We have seen that the pentadic pattern relates to the shield at two different levels of analysis. It is expressed in Homer's account of the shield as a whole, even if the small amount of text devoted to the weddings and dance (18%) may be extrinsic to the pattern, and it is probably expressed again, though less clearly and completely, within the part of the shield devoted to the third function. Moreover, we have encountered one further expression. Watkins' work has here been used as a source of assistance in analyzing the poetic artefact of the shield, but the perspective can be reversed. If the analysis of the third-function scenes on the shield is correct, then the IE folk taxonomy of wealth that he reconstructs was itself partly patterned by the old ideology.

By way of overview, it may be worth presenting the argument as Table 14.1, despite the inevitable simplifications intrinsic to this format. Thus, the table does not show the different degrees of confidence attaching to different rows (the interpretation of the whole shield is more secure than that of its third-function part), and only in the last row does it show the tendency to pairing in the third-function column.

Immense scope remains for further work to establish in just how many contexts traces of the ideology can be detected. It may turn out to have been surprisingly pervasive. On the other hand, we should remember that the old IE partitional ideology was doomed to transform itself into, or give way to, the non-partitional ideologies of the modern world. Nowadays our world views no longer recognize compartments that systematically cross-cut domains such as social structure, pantheons, philosophy, narrative. So we need not be surprised if, even in sources as early as Homer, the fit between reconstructed ideology and text is less than perfect.

TABLE 14.1 Summary of the argument

Functions	*F4+*	*F1*	*F2*	*F3*	*F4−*
their foci	valued otherness, transcendence	knowledge, including law/ritual	physical force	fertility, fecundity, wealth	devalued otherness, exclusion
whole shield	firmament	lawsuit	combat	production	ocean
its F3 part	ploughing	grain harvest	grape harvest	livestock	metals?
Watkins' taxonomy	--	grain	vines	livestock	metals
Dumézil's list	Tellus	Ceres	Liber	Pales I, II	--

Notes

1 First published in 2007 as 'The shield of Achilles and Indo-European tradition'.
2 The last constellation, the Bear, is mentioned as not bathing in the ocean (18.489). The reference to the ocean in the first and last scene is an instance of ring-composition.
3 Vanderlinden (1980: 122) criticizes specifically Yoshida's interpretation of the weddings and dance but does not realize how strong the trifunctional interpretation becomes if these two elements are omitted. As quite often happens, the representatives of the first two functions are linked to each other (as the 'two cities' of line 490) and stand apart from the representatives of the third (the rural scenes). Note also the multiplicity ('abundance') of the third-functional scenes, which are not explicitly interlinked.
4 It seems to be a widespread cultural rule that centre contrasts with periphery as valued with devalued: kings belong in the centre of the ordered cosmos, barbarians outside it.
5 That Homer's Ocean and Hesiod's Ouranos are both primal figures relevant to the origin of the gods exemplifies one of the sorts of argument in favour of keeping the two aspects of the fourth function together rather than positing a fifth function.
6 One of Taplin's reasons is that he links the first four scenes repectively with the four seasons, starting with spring, and has no season left for the sheep. Among other problems, the link between herding and winter is not obvious, but Taplin is right to sense that the sequence of scenes has a rationale.
7 Written in capitals because the phrase consists of sumerograms. The individual letters do not represent Hittite phonemes and the Hittite reading of the phrase is debated.
8 Like Cato's prayer, the Iliadic grape-harvest scene mentions supports for the vines. The grain–grape merism covers food and drink in general and might perhaps bring to mind the bread and wine of the Eucharist.
9 In referring to 'metals', I include the enamel.
10 I hope to show elsewhere [cf. Ch. 20 on *Od.* 22] that an even better comparison is with the servants who help Odysseus on his return to Ithaca: Philoetius is a cowherd *(Großvieh)*, Eumaeus is a swineherd *(Kleinvieh)*.
11 Dumézil analyzes them as a three-functional set: brother I as F1, brother II and Arjuna (III) as F2, the twins (IV and V) as F3. But a better analysis (Allen 1999a) associates Arjuna primarily with the F4+ slot and includes the quasi-outcaste Karṇa, Arjuna's elder half-brother and arch-enemy, in the F4− slot.
12 Moreover, the ploughed land on the shield is *eureia* 'broad' (18.542). The Vedic Earth, so often coupled with Dyu or Dyaus 'Sky', is called Pṛthivī, which means 'the broad one' – a locution that goes back to the proto-language (Dunkel 1988–90: 12).
13 On this interpretation, grain and grape relate to different functions, while cattle and sheep relate to a single one, but I do not see this as problematic.

15

DUMÉZIL AND DUMONT

Doit-on vraiment aller en Inde pour comprendre nos propres problèmes?
– *Stern (1984: 57)*

Louis Dumont (1911–1998) ranged widely across anthropology and sociology, but if one had to summarize his orientation in two lines, one might do worse than describe him as a continuator of Durkheim and Mauss who undertook to compare the ideologies (or 'configurations of values') of India and Europe.[1] His work on India culminated in the controversial but classic *Homo Hierarchicus* of 1966 (second edition 1979), and the insights he gained from India were then applied and carried forward in his work on the history and ideology of north-west Europe – see *Homo Aequalis* I (1977), *Essais sur l'individualisme* (1983), and *Homo Aequalis* II (1991).

The comparison of India and Europe was not his only comparative undertaking. Within Europe, he compared the French and German varieties of the modern ideology of individualism (see especially Celtel 2005), and when studying kinship, he compared South Indians both with North Indians and with Australian aboriginals. He also compared two theoretical approaches to the study of kinship. But the India–Europe comparison is at the heart of his life's work.

The idea thus suggests itself of comparing Dumont with another towering figure from the same French academic milieu. Georges Dumézil (1898–1986) compared India and Europe using the framework provided by Indo-European (IE) linguistics, but his interest was less in language as such than in culture or ideology. Of course, IE embraces many languages other than the Sanskrit-derived Indian ones and those of north-west Europe, and Dumézil did not ignore them. However, he regarded the two extremes of the IE world (Indo-Iranian and Italo-Celtic plus Germanic) as the most conservative and the most useful for his purposes – more useful for instance than Greek. In the East, India received the most attention, and it has even been claimed (though I disagree) that his work as a whole gives excessive weight to the Subcontinent (Dubuisson 1993: 115–120). Thus, if the present chapter gives more space to India than Europe, this reflects not only the bias of my own knowledge but also the special place of India in the work of both comparativists.

Both these scholars wrote a lot, sometimes polemically, and their work is quite demanding to read. Obviously, a full comparison between them would amount to a large undertaking, for which an essay such as this can only offer pointers. I hope others will take up topics neglected here and look, for instance, at the two men as individuals, and at the reception of their work.

Comparing comparativisms

We should recognize at once the different orientations of the two enterprises. To put it very crudely, Dumont looks forward from India while Dumézil looks backwards. Dumont wants to understand how and why the modern West, from an anthropological point of view, is such an anomalous civilization. To do this, he starts from the holism and hierarchy of India, which he takes, in this regard, as representative of the pre-modern world, and contrasts those values with the individualism and equality developed and proclaimed by the modern West. In contrast, Dumézil seldom addresses the modern West, his primary aim being to identify in the cultures of the earlier IE speakers the heritage of their common origin. As I say, this is a crude and introductory contrast. In practice, Dumézil avoids discussing the IE-speaking proto-culture. His emphasis is not on the proto-culture as such (its date, location, archaeological remains, etc.) but on cultural forms attested in different areas, which show similarities best explained as resulting from common origin. When he devotes a book to archaic Roman religion (1974), he follows the religion forward in time, not backwards. Nevertheless, just as the notion of a proto-language provides a constant background to the work of IE comparative philologists, so the notion of a proto-culture provides the background to Dumézil. Its pervasive presence means that naturally Dumézil puts more emphasis on East–West similarities than differences – without of course ignoring the latter (e.g. 1974: 128–130). Dumont's concern with divergence makes him stress the differences, and his references to Dumézil and the common origin are scanty.

One might expect the main contrast between the two scholars to lie in the disciplinary frameworks within which they operated. Dumont was explicitly trying to continue the tradition of the *Année sociologique* (a tradition within which the contemporary distinction of social anthropology from sociology was meaningless – Durkheim's aspiration was a science of social phenomena). In contrast, Dumézil claimed that, within the Republic of Letters, his place was among the historians, 'according to the most traditional definition' of the profession (1973a: 10, 14). The difference cannot be dismissed. Obviously, the one brings to his work a far deeper knowledge of sociology (including, for instance, the literature on kinship), while the other comes from philology and ancient history. Dumézil even admitted to an aversion towards the *Année* school, at any rate towards Durkheim (1981b: 18–19, 1987: 47–48).

However, the differing disciplinary backgrounds should not be exaggerated. Dumont studied Sanskrit,[2] and when working on the history of ideas in Europe, his method was to focus on the texts of individual authors who articulated the ideas in exemplary fashion rather than trying to elicit the collective representations of their period. On the other side, although Dumézil disapproved of Durkheim and had an awkward relationship with Hubert, he developed great affection for Mauss (*'j'ai aimé cet homme'*), and he frequently acknowledged his debt to Granet. Granet himself was deeply influenced by the *Année* and, as I have argued elsewhere (2000: 40–41), it was very likely the influence of Durkheim and Mauss (1903), mediated by Granet, that led to Dumézil's 'breakthrough' in 1938.

In any case, Dumézil's lack of a sociological education by no means implies lack of interest in social phenomena. His best known idea, first glimpsed in 1938, is of course that of the three functions in IE ideology: the first, second, and third functions relate, roughly speaking, to the sacred, to force, and to abundance, respectively. Originally he used the term 'function' to refer to the work of those who specialized in these domains, that is, priests, warriors, and producers, or more narrowly, the corresponding social estates *(varṇas)* recognized by ancient Indian tradition. However, the meaning of the term was soon extended to the domain in which the specialists operated, so that in Dumézilian parlance a function is nowadays a zone or compartment within the ideology. But originally it referred to the division of labour within society. Moreover, the ideology itself is a social fact in Durkheim's sense, and so are most of the cultural forms in which it becomes manifest – the myths and other narratives, the pantheons, rituals and invocations, the laws and institutions. Thus, the disciplinary background of the two comparativists casts only a limited light on their differences.

A more illuminating approach is to consider how these two students of ideology envisage what they study. To put it very crudely again, Dumont thinks in terms of binary oppositions, Dumézil in terms of a triadic framework.

Dumont's interest in oppositions derives from at least three sources. First, oppositions were a favourite mental tool of the *Année* school – one might think of collective and individual, sociology and psychology, mechanical solidarity and organic, sacred and profane, and Hertz's right and left (1909). Second, Lévi-Straussian structuralism, building via Jakobson on Saussure, operated essentially in binary mode, and Dumont was aware of Lévi-Strauss' work before he went to India. Third, the South Indian Tamils, among who Dumont carried out his first fieldwork, and who seemed to him 'born sociologists', organized much of their culture, including their elegant kinship system, in terms of oppositions. It was only gradually that Dumont came to develop his own brand of structuralism, in which the emphasis was less on binary oppositions as such than on the notion of hierarchical opposition (Allen 1985; Parkin 2003, 2006). The difference between equistatutory (or complementary) opposition and hierarchical opposition is that the latter also involves a notion of levels. At the lower level, A contrasts with B (cf. man versus woman), but at a higher level, A encompasses B (cf. 'mankind').

Someone who knows of Dumézil only from the pages of *Homo Hierarchicus* could easily be misled about the contrast between the two scholars. When introducing the Indian system of varṇas, Dumont says:

> Thanks to Hocart and, more precisely, to Dumézil, one can view the *varṇa* hierarchy no longer as a linear order but as a series of successive dichotomies or involutions. The whole consisting of the four *varṇas* divides into two: the lowest ranking category, the Shudras [= Śūdra, Serfs] stands in opposition to the bloc formed by the first three, whose members are twice-born in the sense that they undergo initiation, a second birth, and hence can participate in religious life in general. These twice-born in their turn divide into two: the Vaiśyas [Producers or Commoners] stand in opposition to the bloc formed by the Kṣatriyas and Brahmins, who in their turn divide into two.
>
> *(1979: 94, cf. also 351–352)*

This summarizes accurately the gist of Dumézil (1948: 76, cf. also 189–190) although, in starting with the whole set of varṇas, that is with the three versus one opposition, Dumont reverses the order in Dumézil, who starts with the brahmin at the top of the hierarchy. Dumont also omits mention of Dumézil's presentation of the series as 'more or less Hegelian in type'.

> The priest, warrior and stockman-farmer are not to be enumerated 'one, two, three' . . . First of all, the brahmin is defined in opposition to the kṣatriya. Then the two of them come together and collaborate in a new notion of 'power' . . . which is defined immediately in opposition to the vaiśya . . .; in its turn, this opposition is resolved by synthesis in the *dvija*, 'the twice-born', which is then confronted by the appearance of the Śūdra.

In fact, Dumézil [1948: 77] even suggested that a further step might be added at the start of the hierarchy. Before the term *brāhmaṇa* came to cover the first estate as a whole, the series could have begun with the couple king-brahmin.

However, if Dumont's presentation of Dumézil's position is misleading, it is less because his summary in incomplete than because the passage in question is not representative. After 1948, this interpretation of the varṇa schema is dropped; certainly by 1959 Dumézil has changed his mind.

> Some of the philosophers who even today depend on the colossal Hegel, including several structuralists, find it difficult to tolerate the intrusion into their worldview of a system having three homogeneous terms and make an effort, not without doing violence [to the facts] – in the West as well as in the USSR – to reduce two of the three to a unity so as to be able to recover the familiar and comfortable binary opposition.
>
> *(1973a: 339)*

In fact, Dumézil recognizes a number of contexts where representatives of the first two functions stand together in opposition to those of the third (e.g. the Aesir gods versus the Vanir gods in Scandinavian myth), but in general he treats the three functions as forming a homogenous series. One wonders what Dumont made of Dumézil's change of mind, if he was aware of it.[3]

The numerological approach we have just explored – as if one could write Dumont : two :: Dumézil : three – is of course both superficial and crude. Dumézil's interest is not in triads as such, but in manifestations of an ideology which, as he sees it, falls into three compartments. But occasionally a compartment can be empty, and very often it contains more than one representative. For instance, the Vedic gods Varuṇa and Mitra both belong in or under the first function, of which they are said to represent different 'aspects', and the third function is often represented by twins. The attested sets which manifest the triadic ideology certainly need not contain precisely three members, and it is better to think of Dumézil's style of analysis as non-binary.

In any case, a numerological labelling of the contrast makes the two analytic approaches seem more similar than they are. At a more empirical level of operation, Dumont recognizes a multiplicity of dualisms, whose interrelation is subject to analysis in each case. For instance, in India, pure and impure, kingship and priesthood, worldly religion and world-renunciation, or in the West, equality and hierarchy, political power and economic success, and at a more abstract, panhuman level, he recognizes the superior (or encompassing) and inferior poles of hierarchical oppositions. Dumézil is interested in a single triadic ideological structure, whose clarity of outline is lost at different rates in different areas and in different domains of life; and his work on ideologies focused only on the traditional IE speakers.[4]

Nevertheless, despite their differences, the two comparativists share much more than admiration for Mauss and an interest in the ideologies of India and Europe. Above all, they both think structurally. Thus, Dumont attacks the atomism of J.H. Hutton and presents the introduction of the idea of structure as 'the capital event of our time' (1979: 53, 61). Dumézil became irritated at being lumped together with 'structuralists' when the term was in vogue (1973a: 14–15), but he repeatedly emphasizes the system, structure, or *ensemble* within which elements need to be understood (1987: 116–119; Desbordes 1981: 51–52). For instance, within a polytheism, a god, even the most important god, can in general be clearly defined only in his relations to a certain number of other gods, through his place in an ordered whole *(ensemble)*, through his role in one or several mechanisms of which he is only one component (Dumont 1977: 207). Dumézil makes the same point, less abstractly, when he criticizes Wissowa, and even more Kurt Latte, for their failure to explore the archaic triad of Roman gods (Jupiter, Mars, Quirinus) as an *ensemble*: the facts they give about the individual gods are dispersed, and the triad is not examined as such (1974: 153–155). His rejection of *pointillisme* (1979: 89) corresponds to Dumont's rejection of atomism.

In addition, the two scholars share a concern, not only with articulated wholes but also with hierarchy – and in the full sense of that word that draws on its etymology (Greek *hieros* = holy). Obvious in the case of Dumont, the interest is less emphatic in Dumézil, but the latter quite often introduces lists of the three functions as 'hierarchized'. A typical list will open with the words 'magical and juridical sovereignty' (sometimes associated with 'a sort of maximal expression of the sacred' – Dumézil 1974: 173). Thus, the label 'first' for this particular function is natural and appropriate within Dumézil's conception.

Combining comparativisms

Since Dumont and Dumézil both approach ideologies in terms of structure and hierarchy, the question arises whether and how their approaches can be brought together.[5] Their interests are closest when they talk about traditional India and diverge chronologically (into early and modern) when they talk about Europe, so it makes sense to start with India. Since both refer to the varṇa schema, that provides the obvious point of entry.

Dumont's focus is on the caste system as observed and understood by anthropologists and sociologists, and his interpretation is based on the religious value of purity as opposed to impurity. The brahmins at the top of the system are associated with purity (with its spectrum of connotations), while the untouchables are associated with impurity. Thus, the system as a whole, with all its complexities (variable numbers of castes and subcastes, regional differences, etc), is oriented by the pure-impure opposition. However, between the two extremes, a purer caste does not invariably outrank a less pure one. For instance, vegetarianism is purer than meat-eating, yet a vegetarian merchant ranks below a meat-eating warrior. The anomaly is to be explained, says Dumont, because the Hindus readily envisage the caste system (in which they actually live) in terms of the ancient varṇa schema, which is pervasive in the classical Sanskrit scriptures, and the merchant, being a Vaiśya or Commoner, ranks below the Kṣatriya. In the middle ranges of the hierarchy, purity gives way to power.

On this point Dumont's position seems to me unnecessarily complicated, and later we shall attempt to simplify it. But let us ask first how Dumézil's schema can accommodate impurity. The simple answer is that it cannot. Impurity, with its spectrum of connotations (social exclusion, repulsiveness, death, corpses, excreta, dirt, evil spirits, etc.), does not fit comfortably under any of the three functions. But such undesirable or negative aspects of the human condition are too important for any plausible ideology to ignore them. Were they really ignored by the original IE speakers, or by the Indo-Aryans who brought the language family to India?

It may seem odd that Dumézil gave so little attention to the Śūdra or serfs, whom the texts present, not exactly as impure, but certainly as devalued and ritually excluded. The reason is that he interpreted the fourth varṇa as historically secondary, as a development of the triadic sociostructural schema when it became necessary to recognize the social incorporation of the aboriginals who inhabited India before the coming of the Indo-Aryans. But this interpretation is only one possibility. A priori, it is more likely that a devalued category already existed in the ideology of the Indo-Aryans before they immigrated, and empirically plenty of comparative arguments can be mustered in support.

In other words, Dumont's emphasis on the place of impurity in Hindu ideology, at least since the Code of Manu (written down around the turn of the eras), suggests that Dumézil's triadic hierarchical schema needs to be extended at its bottom end. Without expatiating on the empirical arguments, I here answer two possible objections. First, I am not *equating* the Serfs in the varṇa schema with the Untouchables in the caste system. The point is simply that, regarded structurally, both forms of hierarchy include on their lowest rung a category that is devalued and in some contexts excluded. Second, the question arises why, if the proposal is well founded, it was not obvious long ago. Too many factors are involved for a systematic answer to be attempted here, but I cite one of Dumont's insights (1979: 58). What is observed in a society consists, he says, of two components (note the characteristic dualism): that which is fully conscious and ideologically elaborated, and a residue – all the rest. He sums up the point in the formula $o = i + r$, that is, observation equals ideology plus residue. *One* of the reasons why Dumézil's schema does not cope with impurity is that the ideology, as reflected in the early texts, tends to leave impurity in the shadows, that is, in the residue.

If Dumont can be used to extend Dumézil's hierarchy at one end, one wonders about the other. It seems to me that both authors have difficulties with the top end. Dumont's approach is to distinguish two aspects or (later) two 'levels' within the relationship of king and priest (1979: 354, 1983: 244–245). Spiritually and absolutely, that is, as regards ultimate values, the priest is superior, but temporally, materially, or 'practically', he is inferior. Such reversals are characteristic of the move between hierarchically superior and inferior levels. Dumont recognizes that the ambiguity in the relationship is unusual in comparative perspective, that kings are usually supreme religiously as well as temporally (1979: 356), and explains the Indian king's exceptional situation as due to an early process of secularization. The notion of secularization has been much criticized, but it has also been defended (Parry 1998), and we shall come back to it. At this point, I simply emphasize the importance that Dumont attaches to the priest–king opposition.

Dumézil naturally regards king and priest as filling different roles, but he usually subsumes both under the first function. In some contexts, for instance in the analysis of the early Roman king-list, Romulus and Numa fall respectively under the Varuṇa and Mitra aspects of that function (referred to earlier). However, a different solution, which comes to the fore in Dumézil's later texts, sees the king not as first-functional but as transfunctional, as representing a synthesis of the three functions. But this shift (seldom emphasized) is not accompanied by a corresponding redefinition of the first function. When defining or listing functions, Dumézil avoids a standard form of words and occasionally he offers a brief pointer such as *puissance sacrée* (1969b: 179), but usually, even in later texts, he refers to *souveraineté*.

The situation seems to me to demand three steps. One is to change the definition of the first function, by dropping the reference to sovereignty and confining the domain to 'the administration of the sacred' (Dumézil 1969b: 214). The second is to situate the king and his sovereignty in a function other than the first, and finally, this latter function must be given a place within the hierarchical ideology considered as a whole. The most obvious move is to posit a fifth function at the top of the hierarchy, but for various reasons (presented elsewhere), I prefer to adapt Dumézil's idea that a function may be split into two aspects. Thus, I posit a fourth function whose negative aspect comes at the bottom of the hierarchy and whose positive aspect comes at the top. The extremes have in common that, seen from within the three core functions, they pertain to what is other, outside, or beyond, whether it be more highly valued than the core or less highly. The preference for four functions rather than five is not merely a matter of analytic nomenclature since, by implying a certain affinity between the valued and devalued extremes, it affects the hypotheses one explores.

The idea of the valued fourth function has been introduced here via a discussion of the king, since this seems the easiest way into the topic, but other routes are possible. The king represents the whole of society, and one could start from Dumont's notion of holism (defined at 1983: 273), which no doubt goes back to the category of totality so prominent in the work of Mauss and Durkheim.[6] It would certainly be a mistake to limit the valued aspect of the fourth function to kingship or sovereignty, which are only the sociostructural manifestations of this domain of the ideology. Perhaps the most useful term with which to approach it is 'transcendence'. If kings transcend their subjects, creators transcend their creation. In the myth of origin of the varṇas, Puruṣa, with his whole body, transcends the four estates that derive from his dismembered body parts; their internal hierarchy is expressed both in time and space – the brahmins originate first and issue from the highest part. In general, in Dumézil's work, creator figures such as Dyu, Puruṣa, Prajāpati, and Brahmā are not allocated to a function, and had Dumont been asked to react to this, he might well have recalled his remarks on transcendence on the last page of *Homo Hierarchicus* (1979: 403). He there suggests that 'the central and constant effort of modern thought has been and is directed against transcendence in all its forms' – an idea that accords with the lack of a special place for transcendence in Dumézil's schema.

So far, the second part of this chapter has proceeded by using Dumont's ideas on India to expand and clarify Dumézil's ideas on IE ideology (of which early India, with its enormous literature, offers such a good example). Of course the hypothesis of a pentadic IE ideology cannot be based solely on Indian evidence, and I have elsewhere tried to support it by using material from Greece, Rome, Iran, Arthurian tradition, and so forth. But my point here is that the combination of the two comparativists need not be unidirectional. If Dumont helps us to revise Dumézil, the revised Dumézil may help us rethink Dumont. At least some of Dumont's dualisms can be brought together within the pentadic framework – thereby both unifying his views and simplifying them.

Dumont's king–priest opposition has already been presented as one expression of the opposition between the fourth function (positive) and the first function – now purged of its association with sovereignty. But his pure-impure opposition is embodied in the relation of brahmin to untouchable, and this in turn is to be interpreted as the relation between first function and fourth (negative). This not only brings together Dumont's two dualisms into a more unitary conception of the ideology but also simplifies the explanation of the ranking of the vegetarian merchant. It is no longer necessary to think of the varṇa hierarchy as supplementing and distorting a caste hierarchy that is otherwise pervaded by considerations of purity. Both hierarchies express the pentadic ideology, the varṇas in the context of myth and stereotype, the castes in the context of everyday social interaction. In either context, the warriors, theoretically, use force not only to fight enemies but also to kill the animals they eat, and they represent the second function. The merchants' role focuses on wealth, and whatever they eat, they belong under the third function. The ranking derives from the functions. The shift from a dualistic viewpoint to a pentadic one slightly relativizes the importance of the pure-impure opposition and eliminates what seemed to be an anomaly.

To interpret king–priest–warrior as representing the functions 4+–1–2 is neat from an IE comparative point of view, but from a Dumontian point of view, it is too simple. As we saw, Dumont argues that it is only in the temporal domain that the king outranks the priest; in terms of ultimate values, that is, the religious ones that encompass the temporal, the ranking is reversed. In pentadic terms, it is as if the representative of the valued fourth function has lost his position in the spiritual hierarchy and been demoted or secularized so as to fall among representatives of the second function. Some such process, taking place in certain contexts, seems to me plausible, though perhaps it was accompanied by promotion of the representatives of the first function. Brahmins are sometimes referred to as 'gods on earth', as if they were taking over the sacredness the kings were losing. In any case, we are dealing with a historical change in the old ideology, as Dumont sensed.

An interesting question is whether Dumont's opposition between priest and renouncer, between this-worldly religion and world-rejection, can be interpreted in terms of the pentadic ideology. The priest must again represent the first function. But the renouncer becomes an outsider to ordinary social life, and may even, symbolically speaking, perform his own death ritual while still alive – that is, in a sense he transfers himself to the other world. This suggests that he belongs under the fourth function, and since renunciation is recognized and approved as the final stage in a brahmin's life, it must be under the positive aspect of that function.

It may seem paradoxical that the propertyless renouncer and the owner of the whole kingdom fall under the same function, but it is worth reflecting on the Buddha. Although the Buddha followed the Middle Way and rejected extreme asceticism, he was certainly seen as a renouncer, as was the reputed founder of Jainism. According to one account, the sage Asita examined the Buddha when he was an infant and prophesied on the basis of his bodily signs that he had only two possible careers – as a universal king or as a fully enlightened Buddha (Thomas 1949: 40); so the two are alternatives. In addition, there are independent reasons for interpreting the Buddha as representing the positive aspect of the fourth function [Ch. 13].

Moreover, Dumont himself goes some way towards linking renouncer and king. The Indian renouncer, as he argues in 1979 (Appx B), makes his own choice to renounce society and represents the individualism for which the world of caste offers no place.[7] But the king too is emphatically an individual, and not only in the obvious sense that at a given moment a society usually only has one king. In addition, the Indian king is expected to pursue his personal interest *(artha)*, an orientation that is contrasted both by the texts and by Dumont with *dharma* (roughly religion). Dumont refers to the theory of *artha* as being 'not without links with the individualism of the renouncers and their negation of Brahmanic values' (1979: 373), and connects this individualist or subjective perspective with the secularizing trend mentioned earlier (366). This view of human kings can be compared with Dumézil's emphasis on the uniqueness, independence, and autonomy of Indra, King of the Gods, and the frequency with which his Vedic epithets begin with *sva-* 'self-' (1985b: 74–79).

A full treatment of these complex issues would need to cover Indian philosophico-religious thinking, not only about the classification of human behaviour within which *artha* has its place but also about the contents and composition of the cosmos.[8] But the aim here has only been to show, rather briefly, that by combining ideas from Dumont and Dumézil, one can envisage an ideology that is both richer and better articulated than the models proposed by each of them individually. But if the pentadic ideology helps us rethink Dumont on India, it should also help us rethink Dumont on Europe.

We can end by trying in a preliminary way to envisage the outcome of such rethinking. The aim would be a history of European thought, starting from the pentadic ideology. I used to suppose that this would be the history of an ideology that simply faded away, losing ground in one context after another, faster in some geographical regions than others – with a few survivals lingering on here and there. But if we take seriously Dumont's call for a historical understanding of Europe informed by anthropological comparativism, together with the examples he gives of the sort of analysis that can be attempted, a different view becomes possible.

The history of the ideology would largely be one of increasing abstraction. During this process, the functions would undergo transformation into 'rubrics', such as religion, politics, and economics, or 'areas' of social life.[9] Such areas, and the relations between them, would wax and wane in importance, and the sharpness of the boundaries between them would decrease while their contents underwent other transformations. We are perhaps inclined to exaggerate our remoteness from the pentadic ideology. We still have kings or their successors; specialists in religion, law, and forms of knowledge; the military; those who devote themselves to production and money-making; and those who are effectively excluded from society. The UK polity still consists of monarch at the one end of a hierarchy and voters at the other, with parliament in between; and parliament (cf. Hocart 1970: 279) falls into two Houses, the Lords and the Commons, the former consisting of Lords Spiritual (archbishops and some bishops) and Lords Temporal (originally warrior aristocrats). The processes leading from the pentadic ideology to modern ideology find a smaller-scale analogy in the history of thought leading from Plato to modern philosophy, and indeed the changes in ideology must *include* the changes in philosophy. But such questions could hardly arise without the help of India.

Notes

1 First published in 2007 as 'Dumont e Dumézil: una comparazione e una combinazione'; English version previously unpublished.
2 As a prisoner of war in a camp near Hamburg, he was able to make weekly tutorial visits to the German Indologist Walther Schubring (Galey 1988: 14).
3 Soon after World War II, Dumont consulted Dumézil when choosing a doctoral topic, and in 1986 he received from his hands the *Légion d'honneur*, but the two were probably not frequently in contact.
4 As a linguist or philologist, he worked also on Caucasian languages and on Quechua, and he sometimes pursued IE cultural themes beyond the language boundaries, for example in the Caucasus or Finland.
5 For more detail on the Indological material relevant to this section, see Allen (1999a) and (Allen 2006a).
6 Dumont (1983: 18) laments the lack of appreciation of hierarchy by the *Année*, but they were not entirely blind to it. Apart from their interest in *totalité* and religion, they were interested in ordering and thereby ranking the different kinds of social phenomena, and in how much weight each kind should receive. In his *Manuel* (1947), Mauss moves explicitly from the more material to the more spiritual (cf. also Allen 2000a: 101–116).
7 Female renouncers exist but are fewer and less typical than male.
8 For instance, I do not attempt here to link the argument that individualism falls under the valued fourth function with the idea that in Sāṃkhya philosophy Puruṣa and the 'ego-maker' *(ahaṃkāra)* both fall under F4.
9 Note the sequence – global framework, religion, politics, economics – in Dumont (1983: 25). If economics does represent a transformation of the third function, Dumont's argument about its genesis (1977) would need some rephrasing.

16

YUDHIṢṬHIRA AND AGAMEMNON

At the start of his analysis of the *Mahābhārata*, Dumézil (1968: 35–36) introduces us to the two sides involved in the Great War that forms the core of the Sanskrit epic: the Pāṇḍavas are 'les bons', the Kauravas are 'les méchants'.[1] Following Dumézil, in English one might talk of Goodies and Baddies or of Heroes and Villains, but since neither side is unmixedly good or bad, I here prefer the terms Victors and Vanquished (despite the occasional reversals in the fortunes of war). Thus, in an attempt to compare the Indian epic with the *Iliad*, one approach is to look for rapprochements between the Victors in the two traditions – Pāṇḍavas and Greeks, as well as between the Vanquished – Kauravas and Trojans.

It is well known that the *Iliad* does not tell the whole story of the Trojan War. As we learn in its opening lines, the epic focuses on the wrath of Achilles and what follows from it. Thus, it starts with an account of the quarrel that caused the wrath – the quarrel between Achilles and Agamemnon, leader of the Greeks. So the question arises whether anything similar occurs among the Pāṇḍavas. In fact, a parallel was noted by von Simson (1984: 216), albeit only in passing, and in an article whose main purpose was not Indo-European (IE) comparison. To begin with, then, we shall fill out his observation, but thereafter we shall find that two other quarrels in the *Mahābhārata* need to be brought into the picture.

Agamemnon versus Achilles (*Iliad* Book 1)

Though the story will be familiar to many readers, a summary may be convenient. As throughout the chapter, I shall summarize and paraphrase.

Agamemnon has received Chryseis, daughter of Chryses, as part of his war booty. Chryses, priest of Apollo, tries to ransom the girl, but is rudely rebuffed by the king. The priest prays to Apollo on Mount Olympus to punish the Greeks, and the god accordingly sends a plague that (envisaged in the form of his arrows) kills many of the besiegers. On the tenth day, prompted by Hera, who favours the Greeks, Achilles calls an assembly:

Achilles: Let us consult a diviner.

Calchas: I can do the job, but will you promise to defend me if my answer angers the king?

Achilles: Yes.

Calchas: Apollo is angry that Agamemnon rebuffed Chryses and will only end the plague when we return the girl without a ransom and offer Apollo animal sacrifice at her home.

Agamemnon (furious): You enjoy prophesying against me! I prefer Chryseis to my proper wife Clytemnestra. Even so, to end the plague, I'll give her back. But I demand a replacement.

Achilles: That's greedy. We can't provide a replacement until we sack Troy.

Agamemnon: If I don't get a replacement of equal value, I'll come and seize your woman or some other leader's – whoever provides the replacement will be angry. But let's leave that decision till later. The first thing is for one of you leaders to take back Chryseis.

Achilles: Why should anyone listen to you? I have no quarrel with the Trojans. You don't appreciate the help we are giving you. It is I who win the victories and you who scoop the best booty. I'm off home.

Agamemnon: Off you go then! Others respect me, including Zeus. You always love fighting. You may be a good warrior, but I can do without you. To teach you and everyone else a lesson, I shall come myself and seize your Briseis as my replacement.

Achilles is just drawing his sword when Hera sends down Athena to stop him. Achilles recognizes her and asks why she has come.

ATHENA: Hera loves both you and Agamemnon and sent me to stop you fighting. Instead, you can insult him.

Achilles accepts the advice and the goddess departs.

Achilles (to Agamemnon): You are a cowardly, arrogant drunkard, and if your subjects knew how to stand up for themselves they'd kill you. I swear solemnly that you will all miss me, and many of you will be killed by Hector. You'll be sorry you insulted me – the best of the Greeks.

Nestor tries to reconcile the disputants.

Agamemnon: This Achilles wants to be king himself.
Achilles: I'll take no more orders from you. I won't fight over Briseis, but just you try and take any other property of mine!

The assembly breaks up. Odysseus takes charge of the boat that returns Chryseis, and the army purifies itself, sacrificing to Apollo. Agamemnon sends his heralds to fetch Briseis. Achilles tells Patroclus to hand her over, and she departs unwillingly. Achilles withdraws to the shore and prays to his mother Thetis, who arrives and hears an account of the quarrel. Recalling that Zeus owes her a favour, Achilles asks her to persuade the god to help the Trojans, and thereby punish Agamemnon. Thetis agrees to put the request to Zeus when he and the other gods get back from visiting the Ethiopians in twelve days' time. Meanwhile Achilles is to hold entirely aloof from the battle.

Odysseus completes his mission successfully. When Zeus returns, he worries at the prospect of Hera's reaction but commits himself to granting Thetis' request. Hera questions Zeus accusingly, but Hephaestus, son of Zeus and Hera, prevents a quarrel, and the gods feast till nightfall.

In essence, then, in the course of the greatest war recounted by Homer, the greatest warrior among the Victors becomes disaffected and ceases to serve his commander. We can now turn to the Sanskrit passage mentioned by von Simson (I use the CE).

Quarrel 1: Yudhiṣṭhira versus Arjuna

The Great War on the battlefield of Kurukṣetra (Books 6–9) lasts only eighteen days, not ten years, as at Troy. In the afternoon of Day 17, the situation for the Pāṇḍavas looks grim. True, they have eliminated the first Kaurava marshal, Bhīṣma, who is now lying disabled on his 'bed of arrows', and by means of a trick they have killed the second, Droṇa. But on Day 16, Karṇa took over as the third marshal and is proving a formidable opponent. He has wounded Yudhiṣṭhira (the eldest of the five Pāṇḍava brothers and King of the Victors), forcing him to withdraw from the battle. Arjuna, the supreme warrior among the Pāṇḍavas but the third of the brothers in seniority, discusses the situation with his charioteer, Kṛṣṇa, the divine incarnation, who describes the retreat: the king is being pursued by Duryodhana (the Kaurava supremo) and by the other sons of Dhṛtarāṣṭra. For a moment it seems that Yudhiṣṭhira may even have fallen – his standard can no longer be seen – but no, he *is* alive, and Bhīma (the second brother) is leading a rally. Even so, Yudhiṣṭhira has been seriously wounded by Karṇa's arrows and, accompanied by the youngest Pāṇḍavas (the twins Nakula and Sahadeva), is retreating towards the camp. When his horses and those of Nakula are killed by Karṇa, Yudhiṣṭhira mounts the chariot of Sahadeva, sending the twins to support Bhīma. Arjuna asks Kṛṣṇa to find Karṇa. Instead, Kṛṣṇa proposes ascertaining the condition of Yudhiṣṭhira. Arjuna

> questions Bhīma on the subject, but the latter refuses to leave the field, fearing to be reproached for cowardice.[2]
>
> Reaching the camp, Arjuna finds Yudhiṣṭhira lying on his bed. Thinking that Arjuna brings news of Karṇa's death, the king congratulates him. Arjuna explains what has happened, promising to kill Karṇa today. Yudhiṣṭhira blames him bitterly for leaving Bhīma to bear the brunt of the fighting, and suggests that he hand over his bow (which is named Gāṇḍīva) to someone who will make better use of it. Arjuna has taken an oath to kill anyone who suggests that he part with Gāṇḍīva, so he draws his sword to behead his brother. Kṛṣṇa intervenes, narrating two stories concerning truth and morality. Arjuna still feels he should keep his vow, but Kṛṣṇa tells him that to insult someone counts as killing them. Arjuna insults his elder brother by using the familiar and disrespectful second person pronoun *tvam*, instead of the respectful *atrabhavat*, but by the end of his long and insulting speech he feels so upset that he contemplates suicide. Kṛṣṇa says that self-praise is a form of self-destruction, so Arjuna now begins to boast. After this, he begs Yudhiṣṭhira's pardon, promising to kill Karṇa and rescue Bhīma. Yudhiṣṭhira too grieves, saying that Bhīma should be king. Kṛṣṇa comforts him, persuading him to forgive Arjuna and himself.
>
> Arjuna returns to the battlefield intending to relieve Bhīma and kill Karṇa. Events move towards his climactic duel with Karṇa.

Ignoring for the moment the massive differences between the Greek and Sanskrit quarrels, both in context and content, let us concentrate on the similarities. Globally, von Simson was clearly justified: both quarrels set the Victors' overall leader against their best warrior. The similarity can be expressed as follows:

Commander	Yudhiṣṭhira	Agamemnon
Subordinate	Arjuna	Achilles

Moreover, both quarrels take place in the Victors' camp. But the real interest lies in the details. I number the rapprochements in such a way as to suggest their grouping.

1.1. Commander is high-handed

Yudhiṣṭhira starts the meeting on the wrong note, having jumped to a false explanation of the arrival of Arjuna and Kṛṣṇa.[3] When he is gently corrected, instead of apologizing for his embarrassing misunderstanding, he launches into a swinging attack on Arjuna who, he says, should never have been conceived or should have aborted *in utero*. He shows no interest in hearing Arjuna's side of the story. Being an incarnation of the god Dharma (Sociocosmic Order), he is usually just, intelligent, unaggressive, and pious, and his behaviour in this episode is uncharacteristic and surprising.

Agamemnon starts the whole affair when Chryses comes to the Greek camp to ransom his daughter. The priest politely expresses the hope that the Greeks will sack Troy, and the army wants to accept the ransom and show the old man proper respect. But Agamemnon refuses him offensively (*kakōs*, 25), threatening violence if he persists or returns; in short, he humiliates or dishonours him, *ētimēse*, as Calchas puts it (94). He is equally ungracious when he is told the truth by Calchas, whom he calls a prophet of evil *(kakōn)*, one who delights in delivering evil prophecies (*kaka*, 106). He continues in aggressive mode to Achilles, threatening that if he is not satisfied with what the Greeks offer him, he will seize the hero's prize (i.e. his slave-girl).

1.1.1. Commander accuses subordinate of cowardice

Yudhiṣṭhira accuses Arjuna of dishonourable behaviour and, in particular, of having left Bhīma and retreated to the camp because he was afraid of the battle and of meeting Karṇa. When Achilles threatens to sail off home (169), Agamemnon says, 'Flee, if that is what you feel like doing.' Although the Commander goes on to admit that a god made Achilles a mighty warrior (*karteros*, 178), the use of the verb *pheugein* 'flee' is an implicit accusation of cowardice.

1.2. Subordinate to hand over something he values

Yudhiṣṭhira tells Arjuna to hand over Gāṇḍīva to someone who will use it better: if Arjuna had given it to Kṛṣṇa earlier, Karṇa would be dead by now (48.14, *683). Agamemnon at first (138) mentions Achilles as just one among his subordinates who might have to give up their prize, but later he decides definitely to take Briseis (184). The bow is of course not actually handed over while the slave is, even though Agamemnon returns her without having used her in a sexual sense. The bow is to be given to a third party, the girl to the Commander himself, but both transfers concern property of emotional value to the Subordinate.

1.3. Subordinate draws sword

Because of his vow, Arjuna sees no alternative to killing his brother. Achilles envisages two alternatives. He may draw his sword, break up the assembly and kill the king, or he may contain his anger. When Athena arrives, he has presumably decided on the former since he is unsheathing his sword (194).

1.3.1. Divine mediator prevents violence

Kṛṣṇa asks Arjuna why he needs his sword – Bhīma is dealing elsewhere with Duryodhana and his brothers. When Arjuna explains, Kṛṣṇa tells him to avoid anger and follow the scriptures, of which he is ignorant. Any killing is a sin, but killing an elder brother who is not even fighting would be worse than lying (i.e. worse than ignoring an oath). The oath was foolish anyway. After hearing the edifying anecdotes, Arjuna still wants advice, and Kṛṣṇa resumes his argument. Yudhiṣṭhira had been angry and disappointed, and his insults were intended merely to provoke Arjuna against Karṇa. Anyway, fratricide is not the solution.

Athena's intervention is rather different. Invisible to everyone but Achilles, she stands behind him, pulls his hair, and looks fiercely at him. Her speech, only eight lines, is much shorter than Kṛṣṇa's to Arjuna. She tells him she is acting on Hera's initiative, that he should re-sheathe his sword, and that he will eventually gain wealth as compensation for his humiliation.[4] When Achilles accepts her advice, she disappears back to heaven.

Despite the differences, both mediators stop the Subordinate using his sword, and both are divinities – moreover ones who correspond in certain other contexts (Kṛṣṇa's closeness to Arjuna resembles Athena's closeness to Odysseus).

1.3.2. Mediator successfully recommends verbal attack

Kṛṣṇa says that Arjuna can 'kill' (*nihan-*, 8,49.67) Yudhiṣṭhira by using insulting language to him. Athena tells Achilles not to kill his commander but to blame or reproach him in words (*epesin . . . oneidison*, 1.211). Both Subordinates explicitly accept the mediator's advice. Arjuna applauds (*praśams-*, 49.72) the suggested mode of 'killing', and Achilles recognizes, more grudgingly, that however angry they are, mortals do best to obey gods (216–218).

1.4. Subordinate insults commander

Arjuna goes well beyond insulting forms of address. 'Lying here, two miles behind the fray, you are in no position to chide me, as Bhīma could. You are more like a brahmin than a warrior, and your language is harsh and insensitive. It was your addiction to gambling that caused all our troubles.'

Achilles too offers a broad indictment. Agamemnon is a drunkard (*oinobares*, 225), a coward (in spite of his arrogance), and an oppressive ruler.

1.4.1. Despite other attributes, commander is not a real soldier

Among his insults, Arjuna recalls the saying that the strength *(balam)* of Brahmins lies in their words *(vāc)*, while that of Warriors (Kṣatriyas) lies in their muscular arms *(bāhu-balam)*; Yudhiṣṭhira has the former (he is *vāg-balo*, 49.81). This echoes Kṛṣṇa's earlier remark that Yudhiṣṭhira, excessively emaciated by (religiously motivated) fasting, possesses brahmin power *(brāhme bale)*, not kṣatriya might (*kṣatro 'tibale*, 43.17). Diomedes similarly describes Zeus' ambiguous endowment of Agamemnon (9.37–39): 'He gave you the sceptre and the honour that goes with kingship, but he did not give you the valour *(alkē)* that underlies real authority *(kratos)*.' So in both epics, during this particular quarrel, the point is made that, in spite of his high status, the Commander is defective as a soldier.[5]

1.4.2. Trifunctional insults?

Arjuna's indictment of his Commander may relate to the three core functions: lack of martial prowess, F2; insensitive use of the brahmin's speciality, F1; and addiction to gambling (i.e. misuse of property), F3. Achilles' indictment may also be trifunctional: gross appetite (for alcohol), F3; cowardice, F2; and unjust response to a dissenter in a public political forum, F1. Neither analysis seems to me entirely cogent, but the second provides an interesting comparison with the interpretation of Agamemnon's persona presented by Blaive and Sterckx (1988) and summarized approvingly by Sergent (1998: 84). In line with Dumézil's schema of the three sins of the warrior, the Commander is indicted on the following counts: sacrilege against Chryses (punished by Apollo's plague), F1; insistence on his right to booty and especially to Briseis (punished by Achilles' withdrawal), F3; neglect of the warrior ethic in his defeatist moments (punished by rebukes from Diomedes and Odysseus), F2. While the two trifunctional analyses of Agamemnon are not mutually incompatible, the second is weakened by the textual dispersal of the sins and the heterogeneous character of the related punishments. In addition, I think, the Sanskrit comparisons make it harder to view the sins as forming a sufficiently homogeneous series.

1.5. Subordinate is depressed

Having insulted Yudhiṣṭhira, Arjuna repents, sighs, is deeply grieved *(anutepe, niḥśvasan, su-duḥkhita)*; he draws his sword again, with suicidal intent (49.88–90). Kṛṣṇa asks what it is all about this time, observing that suicide is a sin even worse than fratricide. The solution he proposes is again casuistic: Arjuna should 'kill' himself by indulging in self-praise.

For a Greek parallel, we must jump ahead a little. After the assembly disperses, when Patroclus takes away Briseis and gives her to Agamemnon's heralds, Achilles bursts into tears and goes off to the beach by himself to pray to his mother. A passage of eight lines (357–364) contains five references to his tears, grief, and groaning. Here it is Thetis, not Athena, who corresponds to Kṛṣṇa and carries the story forward.

1.6. Subordinate boasts

Following Kṛṣṇa's instructions, Arjuna 'kills' himself by boasting to Yudhiṣṭhira along the following lines: 'There is no bowman like me, apart from Śiva, and even he respects me. It was I who got you your *rājasūya* (inauguration ritual) and your palace. By myself I have killed half the enemy army.' He ends by promising that he and Kṛṣṇa will soon kill Karṇa (49.92–97).

For a satisfactory Greek parallel, we must follow the quarrel further ahead still to the time when the Greeks, forced back to the walls of their camp, attempt a reconciliation with Achilles. When the Commander's envoys arrive, they find the hero as obdurate as ever. Achilles supports his position by recalling his warrior exploits with pride: the twelve cities he sacked on naval expeditions and the eleven others around Troy (9.328–329). It was he who had kept Hector at bay, indeed who had once almost killed him (9.351–355). Both boasters mention their archenemy, respectively Karṇa and Hector.

1.6.1. Elongated objects of wood and/or metal

Immediately after the account of Arjuna's boasting, the CE omits a stanza (731*) which opens: 'Dropping his weapons for striking and throwing *(vimukta-śāstrāstra)*, letting fall his bow *(visṛjya)*, and quickly putting his sword back in its sheath,' Arjuna formally apologizes to Yudhiṣṭhira. Unlike the verb used a few lines earlier (*dhanur vināmya*, 'lowering his bow', 49.92), the verbs *vimuñc-* and *visṛj-* both imply dropping on the ground rather than just lowering.

Immediately after his final speech abusing the king (1.225–244), Achilles throws to the ground (*bale gaiēi*, 245) the staff studded with golden nails that he has been holding while speaking. He has already noted that the staff (*skēptron*, 234) is held by Greek judges when they deliver solemn verdicts, but his reason for mentioning it is his oath that the Greeks shall come to regret Agamemnon's insults to himself. The oath shall be as true as the fact that the staff, long ago stripped of its leaves and bark, will never again put forth green leaves or shoots.

Thus, in both epics, a moment comes during the king-champion quarrel when the champion throws or drops on the ground one or more elongated objects; like the bow and spears (taken together), the staff and nails combine wood and metal – albeit the order of events is different.

Arjuna blames Yudhiṣṭhira, then praises himself, then drops his weapons (all in Book 8).	Achilles blames Agamemnon, then throws down his staff (Book 1); later, he praises himself (Book 9).

1.7. Commander regrets failure

When Arjuna asks Yudhiṣṭhira for forgiveness for his verbal attack and for boasting, his brother sadly confesses his mistakes. 'Please behead me! I am a useless human being. I shall retire to the woods, and Bhīma can take over as king. After the insults you have heaped on me, what good is kingship or life to me?' (8,49.102–105).[6]

As a consequence of Agamemnon's quarrel with Achilles, the Greeks fare badly, and several times the Commander expresses his regrets and apologies. The first occasion is at the start of Book 9, before the failed embassy to Achilles, when the king weeps copiously and bitterly. 'Zeus ensnared me: he promised me success but is not keeping his promise. Let us give up and go home' (9.27). Soon after, when Nestor observes that the root of the problem lies in the quarrel with Achilles, the king concedes that he has been blind and foolish (115–116). By Book 14, the situation is even worse, since the wall of the Greek camp has been breached and nearly all their elite warriors are now wounded. Agamemnon again proposes giving up (14.75–81). Third, in Book 19, when Achilles has decided to rejoin the fray, Agamemnon gives a long speech. He puts the blame on Zeus and supernatural forces rather than on himself, but he admits that he was blinded (14.88) and would like to make amends. Perhaps the best parallel to the Sanskrit is given by *Iliad* Book 9, though all three Greek passages convey the Commander's sense of personal failure.

1.7.1. Commander is encouraged to persist

Kṛṣṇa bows to Yudhiṣṭhira and explains how he himself advised Arjuna to utter the insults: 'We both beg mercy. Karṇa will indeed die today' (8,49.110–112). Yudhiṣṭhira is mightily relieved and does not retire from his position as leader.

Agamemnon's defeatist attitude in Book 9 is countered first by Diomedes: 'You, and others, can go home; but I, at least, will fight on until we win.' While supporting the young man, Nestor then lays the ground for his later proposal of an embassy to Achilles. In Book 14, Agamemnon's defeatism is rejected abruptly by Odysseus, and Diomedes then suggests that, in spite of their wounds, they should go to the battlefield to encourage others. In 19.185, Agamemnon rejoices at Odysseus' proposals for ending the quarrel. The upshot is of course that he continues the war, and eventually Troy falls.

1.8. Reconciliation

On Kṛṣṇa's urging, Arjuna puts his head on the Commander's feet and begs forgiveness (8,50.9–10). Raising and embracing his younger brother, Yudhiṣṭhira forgives him. Arjuna renews his promise to kill Karṇa.

Following the death of Patroclus in Book 16, the quarrel is formally ended in Book 19, when Agamemnon returns Briseis, admits he was foolish at the start of the quarrel, and gives Achilles the wealth Athena promised him. The reconciliation is less emotional than in the Sanskrit, partly because the Greek quarrel is not between brothers, partly because Achilles is so impatient to begin fighting. The Commander's speech, which is quite long (19.78–144), is rather clearly articulated by subject matter. Though the first seven lines contain some puzzles, they are introductory: they are about speech-making and about this particular speech. Then come three themes, treated at unequal length.

First (85–138), Agamemnon argues that although the Greeks have often blamed him for the quarrel with Achilles, the responsibility really lies with Zeus, Fate, and Erinyus, who afflicted him with the personified Ate, 'Blindness, Criminal Folly', on whom he expatiates. Admitting his error, he is happy to make generous recompense. Next, line 139 consists of two brief imperatives: 'Rouse yourself for battle and rouse the others!' Finally, the end of the speech (140–144) concerns gifts. The king is willing to hand over all that the envoys offered in Book 9, and if Achilles can wait a little, the squires will bring them from the king's ship and show them to him.

Thus, the first section is about responsibility and liability, which are jural issues, and about interaction with the gods – F1. Line 139 is about fighting – F2. The final section opens with the word *dōra* 'gifts' and concerns their amount and adequacy. Although the gifts might be regarded primarily as a jural prestation (*apoina*, 138), they include the sexual object Briseis and can reasonably be construed under F3. If so, whatever one makes of the introduction, here again a speech is organized trifunctionally.

The similarities between the two quarrels must of course be balanced against differences, but a full account of differences is scarcely practical. Here are a few major ones, listed but not elaborated. To start with the Subordinate, Arjuna will survive the war, Achilles will not. As for the Commander, Yudhiṣṭhira has been forced by wounds to leave the battlefield, while Agamemnon, so far unwounded, has no doubt been in camp during the plague.[7] The Indian quarrel is between brothers and more or less private, while the Greek quarrel takes place in an assembly, between disputants who are not relatives. The ostensible cause of the quarrel is in the one case a bow, in the other a woman.

The placement of the episode within the course of the war raises complex issues. Both quarrels come chronologically towards the end of their respective conflicts – Day 17 out of eighteen, start of tenth and final year – but if the course of the war is measured by the changes in the marshals who lead the Vanquished, we meet a discrepancy (cf. Allen 2002b: 171–172, 2006a: 248–249). The third Kaurava marshal, Karṇa, corresponds to the third Trojan leader, Memnon, while the first marshal, Bhīṣma, corresponds to Hector, but in the quarrel, as we saw, Karṇa corresponds to Hector. Indeed, in both cases, the quarrel is very soon followed by the death of these two heroes at the hands of the Subordinate. The discrepancy does not invalidate either analysis but illustrates the complexity of the comparative task.

Perhaps the most striking difference is one of scale and narrative weight. In the Sanskrit, the quarrel proper lasts minutes rather than hours – certainly not days. It is all narrated within five *adhyāyas* (8.46–50), and seems not to be referred to subsequently. In the Greek, the quarrel lasts for weeks and, together with its direct consequences, dominates the whole of Homer's epic. However, in compensation for its brevity, the Sanskrit quarrel exhibits a neat dualistic structure. Accused by his elder brother, Arjuna is advised to 'kill' him by blaming him; then, feeling suicidal, he is advised to 'kill' himself by self-praise. The explicit pairing of praise and blame is well recognized by IE comparativists (Dumézil 1969b: 103–108; Nagy 1979: 222–242). Because the Subordinate's boasting in Book 9 is separated by so much text from his blaming in Book 1, the symmetry shown by the Sanskrit is not apparent in the Greek.

Since in India the event is so brief and inconsequential, one is curious as to why it is present at all. Part of the answer may lie in the events of Day 16 when Śalya is acting as Karṇa's charioteer. Śalya attempts to demoralize Karṇa by both insulting him and praising the enemy. So the quarrel among the Victors can be seen as balancing the scene among the Vanquished on the previous day. The underlying idea in both episodes may be that efforts need to be made to rouse the fighting spirit of the two champions before their crucial conflict – compare Agamemnon taunting Odysseus and Diomedes in 4.326–421. In any case, Śalya repays further attention.

Quarrel 2: Yudhiṣṭhira versus Śalya

Śalya is a close relative of the Pāṇḍavas. Pāṇḍu, the human father of the Pāṇḍavas (as distinct from their five divine fathers), had two wives, of whom the second was Mādrī, mother of the twins, and Śalya was Mādrī's brother. When Nakula visited him before the *rājasūya* (2,29.13), the uncle formally accepted the authority of Yudhiṣṭhira, and he was the first ally to be invited to join the Pāṇḍavas at the start of the war (5,4.8, 11). Accordingly, he sets out from his home intending to join them. However, in the course of his journey, he is induced to change his mind, being seduced by Duryodhana's hospitality. Even so, before he joins the Kauravas, Śalya goes to the town where Yudhiṣṭhira is residing with his brothers and informs him of his plans (5,5.8).

Thus the scheme to be explored is:

Commander	Yudhiṣṭhira	Agamemnon
Subordinate	Śalya	Achilles

Arjuna in the previous schema has simply been replaced by Śalya.

At first sight, the comparison seems unpromising. The Subordinates themselves differ greatly in military prowess: Śalya is not exceptional in this respect, while Achilles is. Śalya fights and dies for the Vanquished, while Achilles, however disaffected, never actually changes sides. Finally (despite my subheading), Śalya's meeting with Yudhiṣṭhira barely qualifies as a quarrel: it apparently involves no anger on either side, and hence there is no call for a mediator or for reconciliation. Even so, we are dealing with an estrangement between the Victors' Commander and someone whom he could reasonably expect to be a Subordinate. Moreover, the Commander learns of the change of sides at a face-to-face meeting in his own lodgings. Finally, as in the Greek, the Subordinate's withdrawal of services lasts for weeks, not minutes, and leads on to his own death – Achilles is fated to die soon after Hector, and Śalya dies the day after Karṇa. This is perhaps enough to justify the comparison, but two further points are of interest.

2.1. An ambivalent opponent

When Yudhiṣṭhira talks to his (classificatory) uncle, he accepts the uncle's change of sides but makes a proposal. When Śalya becomes charioteer for Karṇa (something both of them expect to happen), he should try to demoralize him. Agreeing, Śalya fulfils his promise on Day 16. Whether his words to Karṇa have any long-term effect remains unclear, but they imply that he has not totally abandoned the family loyalty with which he set out for the war. An episode the next day points in the same direction. According to some of the manuscripts, when Karṇa is pursuing and harassing the fleeing Yudhiṣṭhira, Śalya feels pity for his nephew (8 Appx 1.18, line 97), and persuades Karṇa to go off and attack Bhīma instead.

On Day 18, after only half a day as marshal, Śalya is quickly dispatched by Yudhiṣṭhira, a death that corresponds to that of Eurypylus in the Cyclic tradition (Allen 2002b: 172–173). But the present rapprochement concerns the previous period when Śalya occupied a curious middle ground between Victors and Vanquished, a position whose ambivalence is not unlike that of Achilles. It is curious, but perhaps coincidental, that Śalya's ambivalence lasts for seventeen days of fighting, and that Achilles' complete non-participation lasts the same number of days.

2.2. Role of wealth

Śalya changes sides because he appreciates the luxurious accommodation provided for him by Duryodhana, and his enjoyment of wealth is only one of the many features that link him with the third function (Dumézil 1968: 70–76; Allen 2005b: 27–28). This raises the important question of whether or to what extent Achilles can be related to the same function. Because he is such a supremely good soldier, this may seem unlikely a priori, but he is also the handsomest among the Greeks (2.673–674) – which is already suggestive. Moreover, if Agamemnon corresponds to Yudhiṣṭhira, who represents the first function, and Ajax corresponds to Bhīma, who represents the second, then it is not out of the question that Achilles should (at least to some degree and in some contexts) represent the third. A proper argument along these lines would demand a whole paper, or more [cf. Ch. 20], but it is worth bearing the idea in mind as we look more closely at the role of wealth in the causation of the Greek quarrel.

The Agamemnon–Achilles quarrel is certainly political – it concerns power, prestige, and status, but it is also about sex, and above all, about booty. The Commander wants to retain Chryseis because he prefers her to his own wife (1.113), and Achilles' feelings for Briseis are comparable: although she is a captive, he loves her as Menelaus loves Helen – she is his darling wife (*alokhon thumarea*, 9.336, 343). The Subordinate also feels strongly about material booty. His first hostile speech to the Commander calls him the most greedy of men (*philokteanōtate pantōn*, 1.122), and his next speech mostly concerns the distribution of prizes or booty (*geras*, 161, 163, 167) after the sack of a city, and ends by asking why he should toil to increase Agamemnon's stock of goods and wealth (*aphenos*, *plouton*, 171). So as one might expect in view of her intelligence, Athena is talking in the right register when she mollifies Achilles by promising him not rank but plentiful glorious gifts (*aglaa dōra*, 1.213). Whatever one says about Achilles and the functions, he resembles Śalya in feeling very strongly about wealth.

Quarrel 3: Bhīṣma versus Karṇa

If our first Sanskrit quarrel involved two Victors, and our second involved one Victor and a Subordinate who joins the Vanquished, our third involves two of the

Vanquished. The comparison may again seem surprising, but we must be guided by the evidence.

Commander	Bhīṣma	Agamemnon
Subordinate	Karṇa	Achilles

When Bhīṣma becomes marshal just before the start of the war, he insults Karṇa, who is so angry that he refuses to fight so long as Bhīṣma remains marshal. Bhīṣma responds, but Duryodhana patches things up (5.165–166). However, Karṇa sticks to his refusal and enters the fray only after Bhīṣma's fall. Some Kauravas want him to follow Bhīṣma as marshal, and he provisionally agrees, but when he returns from making his peace with the fallen Bhīṣma, he himself proposes Droṇa, who holds the position until he dies on Day 15 (7.1–5).

Since Quarrel 3 takes place among the Vanquished, not the Victors, it is natural that the Commander dies (more precisely, he is mortally wounded on Day 10 but chooses to die about two months later). Among further differences from the Greek, one notes that in this case neither sex nor wealth is relevant, nor does the Commander run any real risk of losing prestige. As for the similarities, they begin with the high-handed behaviour of the Commander in his own camp near the start of a major episode of the epic tradition. This behaviour offends a Subordinate who is the best warrior in the whole army and causes him to withdraw his services for more than a week. The withdrawal ends following a prominent 'death' among the Vanquished – in other words, the elimination of Bhīṣma as a combatant corresponds from this point of view to the death of Patroclus. Again, it is not clear that the quarrel affects the outcome of the war as a whole. But let us turn to details.

3.1. Exchange of insults

When Duryodhana asks him to assess the strength of the armies, Bhīṣma reviews his major warriors. He begins with himself and Duryodhana, whom he calls king (*rājendra, pṛthivīpāla*, 5,162.17), and evaluates about thirty Kaurava warriors individually before finishing his list with Karṇa. The others are described as *rathas* or *atirathas* – ordinary or superior chariot-warriors, but Karṇa is classified as only a half-*ratha*; furthermore, he is described as boastful, arrogant, and stupid. Karṇa loses his temper, retorting that Bhīṣma is senile. The unexpected and humiliating verbal aggression of Bhīṣma, which seems to come out of the blue, recalls that of Agamemnon against Calchas and Achilles.

3.2. Limited range of the quarrel

Direct attempts to limit the quarrel are made by Duryodhana and by Nestor, but beyond this abstract level, the two attempts are not particularly similar. Two other points are more striking. First, despite their passionate reactions to insult, neither Subordinate goes so far as to change sides (as Śalya did). Karṇa is in fact approached by Kṛṣṇa, who proposes that he fight for the Pāṇḍavas till Bhīṣma falls, but he is far too loyal to Duryodhana and firmly refuses (6,41.85–87). He simply abstains from fighting for the ten days. Achilles goes further in that, via Thetis and Zeus, for a time he indirectly helps the Trojans. However, having sent Patroclus to get news from Nestor (11.610), eventually Achilles authorizes him to help the Greeks. At no point does he look forward to a total Trojan triumph; indeed he even envisages himself and Patroclus taking the city (16.100).

3.3. Timing of quarrel

Bhīṣma makes his evaluations just before the battle starts, while Agamemnon's rejection of Chryses takes place at the very beginning of the *Iliad* (1.11). Although the rejection supposedly occurs around the start of the tenth year of the Trojan War (2.134), neither Homer nor the Cyclic epics have much to say about the previous years of the siege, and according to Apollodorus (*Epit.* 3.34), it is only after nine years have passed that the Trojan allies assemble. The victories that Achilles has been winning (1.164) have been against outlying cities allied to Troy and, as is well known, some early parts of the epic (notably Book 3) make much better sense if one imagines them happening near the start of a siege.[8]

As for the end of the quarrel, on the morning of Day 11, Karṇa goes to find the fatally wounded Bhīṣma on his bed of arrows and is privately reconciled with him (6.117). Henceforth he fights vigorously for Duryodhana and the Kauravas. The comparison is with Achilles when, on the morning after the death of Patroclus, he goes along the shore to reconcile himself publicly with the wounded Agamemnon.

3.4. Commander's association with sky god

Although the god never intervenes in his life, Bhīṣma incarnates Dyu or Dyaus ('Sky'), whose name comes from PIE *Dyeus and is cognate with Zeus [Ch. 11]. But the Greek Commander too has a special link with Zeus. Agamemnon claims that, whatever Achilles does, he himself will enjoy the honour of others and especially of wise Zeus (1.174–175). Moreover, the sceptre he owns once belonged to Zeus (2.100–108, cf. 1.279).

3.4.1. Death of human counterpart of sky god and end of quarrel

Let us, for brevity, refer to the mortal Bhīṣma as the human 'counterpart' of the immortal Sky God. In the *Iliad*, Agamemnon is not the only Commander closely associated with Zeus: Sarpedon, Commander of the Trojan allies, is the beloved son of Zeus and so can be called Zeus' human counterpart in a slightly different sense. In other words, in the context of this particular rapprochement, I am assimilating incarnation of a god and filiation to a god [Ch. 10]. Whatever terminology is preferred, the point is that the death of this Commander is causally related to the end of the quarrel. Bhīṣma's fall (equivalent to his death) enables Karṇa to start fighting for the Kauravas. Sarpedon's death at the hands of Patroclus so enrages Hector that he kills Patroclus and thereby causes Achilles to rejoin the Greek army. The causal chain is longer in the Greek, but it is unambiguous.

Concluding discussion

Now that the time has come to try and draw the chapter together, my main feeling is that the attempt is premature. The facts presented are complicated enough, but they are as nothing compared to the complexities that would arise in a full comparison. The disputants need to be treated in greater depth, and many more figures need to be drawn into the picture, together with their multiple interactions and relationships. The supernaturals incarnated in the Sanskrit disputants may need attention, for instance Dyu and Sūrya in Quarrel 3, and more account needs to be taken of the IE functions. A satisfactory comparison, the precondition for a serious prehistory of the two epic traditions, lies in the future. Even so, a tentative start can be made with the material assembled here.

We began the survey of the *Mahābhārata* with the Yudhiṣṭhira–Arjuna quarrel. No doubt among the three Indian quarrels, this is the closest to the Greek, both as regards participants, both of whom are Victors, and in its detailed development. Like the others, it is resolved following a 'death', though in this case there are two successive deaths, both of them symbolic in the sense that they are accomplished by words alone. Arjuna, the Subordinate, 'kills' first his Commander, then himself. On the other hand, in contrast to Homer, Quarrel 1 is situated right at the centre of the epic, in the middle one of the five books devoted to the Great War. Moreover, it can hardly last more than an hour or so.

Quarrels 2 and 3 in the Sanskrit, Yudhiṣṭhira-Śalya and Bhīṣma-Karṇa, provide a much better temporal match with the Greek. First, both last for more than a week. Indeed, in Quarrel 2, the duration of the estrangement seems to be exactly the same as in the Greek (although in neither case is the duration stated explicitly – the number of days has to be calculated from the narrative). Second, both quarrels begin at the start of the Great War, somewhat as the Agamemnon–Achilles quarrel forms the start of the *Iliad*. As for the disputants, both the Subordinates (Śalya and Karṇa) will, like Achilles, die during the war – indeed before the nocturnal attack with which it concludes, but unlike the Greek champion, they will die fighting on the side of the Vanquished. One difference between them is that Śalya changes sides, while Karṇa, despite being a half-brother of the Pāṇḍavas, remains a staunch partisan of Duryodhana, as he has been ever since their first meeting in Book 1.[9] As regards the comparison of narratives, Quarrel 2 (more an estrangement than a quarrel, as we noted) may seem to have least to offer, but since it is the only one to emphasize the economic aspect – so fundamental in the Greek – it cannot be neglected.

A complex issue is that of the death or deaths that precede and lead to the end of the quarrel. In Quarrel 1, we have the symbolic deaths of both disputants, that of the

Subordinate coming second. Quarrel 2 has no reconciliation so the relationships are different, but the death of Karṇa may qualify. In Quarrel 3, the relevant death is the 'partial death' of the Commander – his elimination from active service and from the role of marshal. In §3.4.1 we compared this 'death' with that of Sarpedon, on the grounds that Bhīṣma and Sarpedon are both human counterparts of the Sky God. However, earlier in the third comparison, we had compared Bhīṣma's death to that of Patroclus, not because the two characters are ontologically similar but simply because Bhīṣma's 'death' ends Karṇa's estrangement, while Patroclus' death ends that of Achilles. The two arguments are not incompatible, and my first idea was that they merely illustrate the complexity of Greek–Sanskrit comparison. However, there is more to it. Sarpedon, son of Zeus, is in his own way a Commander (namely of the Trojan allies), and he dies first. Patroclus, usually and reasonably taken as an alter ego to Achilles, is from that point of view a Subordinate, and he dies second, the last important death before the reconciliation. Thus, the duality in the Greek (Sarpedon, Patroclus) parallels the symbolic killing first of the Commander, then of the Subordinate in Quarrel 1. One recalls that, according to Kṛṣṇa, the second, the quasi-suicide, is the more serious sin.

Finally, an even more complex question concerns the diachronic relationship between the single Greek story and the three Indian ones. At the present stage of research I doubt if it is worth exploring the topic in detail, so I simply repeat the hypothesis to which previous studies have inclined me. I suggest that here, as elsewhere, the Sanskrit tells a story that is closer to the early IE proto-narrative than the *Iliad* is. If so, Greek tradition has woven together separate elements from three quarrels, independently of whether they originally took place among Victors or Vanquished (which itself raises questions), and has distributed them across a single epic. Most of the narrative material has gone into *Iliad* Book 1, but elements from later in the story, from the Subordinate's boasting onward, appear in Books 9, 14, and 19, and in a sense the story pervades the whole epic. This interweaving of originally separate stories may contribute to the remarkable richness and semantic density of the Homeric epics.

Notes

1 First published in 2009 as '*Iliad* and *Mahābhārata*: the quarrel among the victors'.

2 [After this contextualization, my summary of the brothers' quarrel draws mostly on CE 8,46–50; if no book is given, the reference is to this passage; for a translation, see Bowles 2008: 123–204; his introduction does not comment on the quarrel. References to the Greek are to Book 1, unless otherwise specified.]

3 The comparison might start with a feature of the context: the arrows of Karṇa, son of Sūrya, the Sun God, may parallel the arrows of Apollo, who in later texts is identified with the Sun. But this chapter focuses on the disputants.

4 Trifunctional (F1, F2, F3), with Hera showing intelligent planning?

5 Greece of course lacks a hereditary priesthood comparable to the Brahmins.

6 Yudhiṣṭhira's comprehensive self-accusation may be an incomplete expression of the functions. He is a killer of his own family, the lowest of men, a sinner (*kulāntaka, adhama-puruṣa, pāpa*, F4–); stupid and idle *(vimūḍha-buddhi, alasya)* – *not* obviously F3; cowardly (*bhīru*, F2);

lacking in respect for the elderly and harsh in his language *(vṛddhāvamantṛ, paruṣa)*, hence deficient in *dharma* (F1); and unsuitable to be king (F4+?).

7 But somewhat later (11.248–283) the Greek Commander does receive a painful wound and has to withdraw on his chariot, leaving Ajax (a plausible parallel to Bhīma) as the main Greek defender.

8 For the Trojan War as lasting *ten years*, compare the marshalship of Bhīṣma, which lasts *ten days*.

9 Quarrels 1 and 3, taking place among Victors and Vanquished respectively, can be viewed as offering a deliberate contrast, but I leave the point for future study.

17

KAURAVAS AND SUITORS

Nowadays it can be taken for granted that the Homeric epics are the outcome of many centuries of oral transmission.[1] So when an anthropologist like myself studies the *Odyssey* it is in the hope of contributing to the understanding of orality. One would like to grasp the processes that led up to this foundational text in European literature. Without denying the importance of other aspects, such as metrics or the sociology of the art of poetry, I limit myself here to narrative processes.

To explore this topic, three main methods are available. One can confine oneself to the study of Greek facts and attempt internal reconstruction – as do many Hellenists (see, e.g. Willcock 1997 or Burgess 2001). Alternatively, one can enlarge the field of study and take account of stories coming from anywhere in the world – the folkloric approach, in the manner of Frazer. Between these two extremes stands Indo-European (IE) comparison. Since all the IE languages derive from a common source, it makes sense to hypothesize a similar origin for the cultural productions expressed in those languages. But to enter this field of study one has to select a starting point. No doubt the most obvious challenge is to compare Greek and Sanskrit epics, and of the two Sanskrit epics, a good choice is the *Mahābhārata*, as it is about four times as long as the *Rāmāyaṇa*, of which it even includes a shortened version. On the Greek side, the choice of the second half of the *Odyssey* arises mainly from my current research.

Before starting, a word is needed about the unrivalled leader of IE cultural comparison in the twentieth century. As is well known, in the writings that start from his period of summing up (his *phase du bilan*), that is, since 1966, Dumézil gave rather little space to Greek material. For instance, in his *Myth and Epic* trilogy, he includes only his trifunctional analyses of the Judgement of Paris, of a passage in Plato's *Republic*, and of the life of Hercules (1968: 580–586, 493–496; 1971: 117–130). Elsewhere only sparse references can be found to the Greek corpus. This lover of Greece found the Greeks to be 'ungrateful lovers', and as for Homer, 'he had already escaped the IE straitjacket' (1987: 161–166). Even so, both during the lifetime of Dumézil and after his death in 1986, a number of researchers (e.g. Rose 2006) have again taken up the question of the IE heritage in Greece.[2] Dumézil approved: 'The misuse of Greek material had so often led me astray before 1938 that I later became excessively cautious. I am happy that younger scholars are using it' (Dumézil 1987: 163).

For the present chapter, we need a quick reminder of the relevant books of the *Mahābhārata*.[3]

1 Birth and marriage of the main figures. 'The Goodies' (to use a [Dumézilian] label that is over-simple, but useful) are the five Pāṇḍava brothers – Yudhiṣṭhira, Bhīma, Arjuna, and the Twins. The Baddies, their cousins, are led by Duryodhana. The Goodies already begin to suffer from the jealous hostility of the Baddies.
2 Following a fraudulent dicing match, the Pāṇḍavas have to leave for a twelve-year exile, followed by a year to be passed incognito.
3 The Exile.
4 The thirteenth year, spent among the Matsya.
5 Preparations for the Great War.
6–9 The Kurukṣetra War, won by the Goodies.
10 The nocturnal attack. Aśvatthāman, a Baddy, with two companions, massacres the Goodies (except for the Pāṇḍavas and two of their friends), while they are asleep. The next day sees the end of the war.
11–18 Consequences of the War. Copious didactic material. Death of the main characters.

The most relevant books here will be 1, 3–4, and 10.

1. Comparisons already published

The comparisons surveyed here are labelled according to the locations where the comparable events unfold.[4]

1.1. Ithaca ~ Kāmpilya

Owing to Germain (1954: 11–54), this comparison is fairly well known. Kāmpilya, aka Śiśumāra, is the capital of the kingdom of Drupada, father of Draupadī. It is here that Arjuna wins Draupadī in a concourse of princes (who include the Kauravas); he triumphs in an archery competition. So the comparison is between the marriage of Arjuna and the 'remarriage' of Odysseus, and between the two competitions themselves (*Mbh.* 1,174–82, *Od.* 21).[5]

The similarities are naturally accompanied by differences, of which I shall emphasize two. First, for the youthful Arjuna, this is his first marriage (he will have others later), whereas for Odysseus, it is the resumption of the marriage that he interrupted twenty years earlier by leaving Ithaca for the Trojan War; as a consequence, the social and psychological situations of the two women are also different. Second, Odysseus' marriage is monogamous, while Arjuna's is polyandrous – Draupadī becomes the shared wife of the five brothers.[6]

Nevertheless, the two stories are distinctly similar. Penelope corresponds to Draupadī, and not only here: her position in the series of female beings with whom her husband has (more or less sexual) relations during his *nostos* corresponds to the position of Draupadī in a comparable Sanskrit series [Ch. 2]. Similarly, the Arjuna ~ Odysseus correspondence in the context of the (re-)marriage is supported by the comparison between the two heroes when they ascend to heaven [or equivalent] (Allen 2005d). Clearly, the Greek suitors correspond to the Suitors assembled at Kāmpilya, and at a more abstract level, in both cases they assemble for the same sort of event – a marriage following a concourse of princes, such as in Sanskrit is called a *svayaṃvara* ('the choice made by oneself'). This aspect of the comparison has been well studied by Stephanie Jamison (1999), who is less interested in relating narratives than in relating institutions (IE systems of law and ritual). But the most convincing rapprochements appear not at this level of generality (hero, his wife, the mode of union, etc.), but at the level of details – of which, following Germain, I listed around twenty [Ch. 9]. In this sort of research, quantification can only be approximate: one often hesitates between splitting up the elements of a rapprochement or, conversely, conflating two or several such elements. However, I emphasize the importance of concrete details. Serious critics of the comparative enterprise cannot simply stay at the level of generalities.

1.2. Ithaca ~ Vidarbha

This comparison (Gresseth 1979) uses one of the numerous independent stories that interrupt the main plot of the epic. During the Pāṇḍavas' exile in the forest they are visited by a seer, and Yudhiṣṭhira asks him if anyone else has ever suffered such misfortune. In reply, the seer recounts the romance between the prince Nala and Damayantī, daughter of the king of Vidarbha. Their idyll starts off cheerfully with a *svayaṃvara* in which the gods participate, but after twelve happy years of marriage, Nala, possessed by an evil spirit, loses a dice game (as Yudhiṣṭhira has done). The royal couple depart as exiles, but Nala abandons his wife. After many ups and downs, Damayantī finds herself back with her father, while Nala, transformed into a hunchback, has become charioteer to the King of Ayodhyā. Kept informed by the brahmin-spies that she has sent out, Damayantī suspects the hunchback's identity, and sends to Ayodhyā (without telling her father) the announcement of a second *svayaṃvara* – this time a fictive one. Following the instructions of the King of Ayodhyā, Nala hastens to Vidarbha where, via her servant Keśinī, the princess continues to probe his identity. Finally, after irrefutable evidence has emerged, Nala regains his normal body, and the couple embrace. Their separation has lasted three years.

At Kāmpilya, as we saw, the hero was marrying for the first time, and the union was polyandrous. In contrast, at Vidarbha, the husband is re-joining his faithful wife after a separation, and there is no question of polyandry. In these respects, Nala parallels Homer's Odysseus. However, here again, major differences separate the Greek and Sanskrit stories. The second *svayaṃvara* at Vidarbha (invented by Damayantī!) involves neither an archery competition nor rival suitors. The reunion of the couple takes place at the palace of the wife's father, not at that of the husband, and the throne is regained without violence.

As in the Ithaca ~ Kāmpilya comparison it is not enough to recognize only the obvious rapprochements – Odysseus ~ Nala and Penelope ~ Damayantī. One needs above all to consider what these figures do and what happens to them at each moment and to consider the other roles. Examples include those of the supernatural beings who transform the hero's bodily appearance (Athena ~ Karkoṭaka), the males who set off on journeys to seek the absent husband (Telemachus ~ brahmins), and the maid-servants who help establish the hero's identity (Eurycleia ~ Keśinī). In all, Gresseth presents about fifteen rapprochements.

1.3. Ithaca ~ Indraprastha

It is not only in one of the independent stories that an Indian hero returns from a long journey to be reunited, not without difficulties, with his faithful wife (1,204.27–213.21). Soon after his marriage, Arjuna leaves Draupadī at Indraprastha (the Pāṇḍava capital) and undertakes a journey to the four quarters of India – a journey that is variously said to last either twelve months or twelve years [see Ch. 2]. This episode parallels the journey of Odysseus, who leaves Penelope at Ithaca, where he returns twenty years later. Since the comparison mainly concerns the first half of the *Odyssey*, I do not summarize it here but merely note the temporary awkwardness of the protagonists at the start of their reunion. Arjuna brings back from his journey an additional wife – Subhadrā, sister of Kṛṣṇa – and has to counter the initial jealousy of Draupadī. Of course, Odysseus does not bring back any equivalent of Subhadrā, but the rapprochement concerns the reaction of the wife (the failure to recognize ~ the awkwardness) in the final episode of the comparable journeys.

1.4. Ithaca ~ Gandhamādana

The return of Odysseus must not be reduced to its climax in the palace. One of my comparisons [Ch. 7] concerns the journey on foot that takes the hero from the home of Eumaeus to the palace and the emotive meeting between Odysseus and Argos, his aged dog (17.200 ff.). The Sanskrit parallel is with the journey on foot that takes Bhīma from a Himalayan hermitage to the palace of Kubera, God of Wealth, and Bhīma's meeting with his half-brother Hanumān, the divine monkey. At this point Arjuna is absent (he is in heaven, visiting his divine father Indra), but his return is eagerly awaited; compare the diffuse atmosphere of expectation in the *Odyssey*.[7] As always, the differences are considerable – between the dog (with its naturalistic portrayal) and the divine monkey, between the contexts, between the Greek concision and the Sanskrit prolixity – the latter is nine times as long; but eighteen detailed rapprochements can be found. For instance, Eumaeus talks of the duties that are neglected by the slaves, Hanumān of the duty of obedience owed by the Śūdra (the social category at the bottom of the Hindu social hierarchy), and both refer to the loss of one 'half' of virtue (of *aretē* 17.322, of *dharma* 3,148.26). A less obvious comparison links the kick received by Odysseus from Melanthius with certain cases of unprovoked aggression in the Indian story.

1.5. Ithaca ~ Matsya

While comparison 1.4 concerned a fairly short passage in Homer, 1.5 is on a much larger scale. After the twelve-year exile in the forest (3,298.18), the Pāṇḍavas have to spend one year incognito; if they fail, they must repeat the exile. Under their disguises they live in the kingdom of Virāṭa, King of the Matsyas (*Mbh.* 4). To Book 4 one can add the final part of Book 3, in which Yudhiṣṭhira receives a promise from Dharma, his divine father (disguised as a stork): the brothers' identities will not be discovered while they reside with the Matsyas (3,298.18). This promise, recalled in (4,1.2, 7), can be treated as part of the Matsya episode.

Homerists are well aware that a comparison (a Greek–Greek one!) connects the Ithaca episode and the Scheria episode: the hero arrives by himself on the shore, receives the help of Athena, hides his identity for a considerable period, proceeds to the capital, and so on. So might an Ithaca ~ Matsya comparison imply a Scheria ~ Matsya one? I think it does, but leave the question unexplored.

At a more abstract level, the progression of Odysseus (journeys to the edge of the cosmos, return home under a hidden identity, complete restoration) corresponds to that of the Pāṇḍavas (their wanderings in the forests and mountains, their return in disguise to the life of a royal court, their partial restoration); indeed, at the end of Book 4, they temporarily seat themselves on thrones in Virāṭa's great hall (4,65). But we need to follow events more closely. This comparison has been sketched elsewhere [Ch. 8], but I now list a selection of rapprochements in the Sanskrit order, which simplifies the presentation.

1.5.1 Divine promises

As we know, the god Dharma promises Yudhiṣṭhira that their disguise will be successful, but a little later Durgā, the warrior goddess, makes him a similar promise (4 Appx 1.4D, 68–69).[8] When Odysseus arrives in Ithaca, he meets Athena and speaks with her (13.221–440); she promises to render him unrecognizable (397), and fulfils her promise by changing his bodily form and dressing him in the rags of a beggar.[9] During their meeting, she takes two human forms of opposite gender: she disguises herself first as a young shepherd, then becomes a tall and beautiful woman – cf. the male Dharma followed by Durgā.

1.5.2. Fictive autobiographies

After careful planning for the meeting, each of the Pāṇḍavas introduces himself to Virāṭa under a fictive identity, and Draupadī does the same to the queen; the topic is discussed by Dumézil (1968: 70–73), but from a different point of view. Odysseus gives himself five fictive identities, but each of them he addresses to a different individual (starting with Athena). The symmetry is striking: five brothers present themselves to a single individual in a single place; a single individual presents himself to five interlocutors in five different contexts. Remarkably too, the majority of the eleven fictive presentations make references to the actual heroes, Pāṇḍavas or Odysseus – a device of obvious literary interest.

1.5.3. Concealment of property

To preserve their incognito, the Pāṇḍavas hide their weapons in the branches of a tree (4,5.29; Arjuna will retrieve them later). The Phaeacians hide the gifts they gave to Odysseus near an olive tree (13.122–124).

1.5.4. Wrestling

Bhīma defeats Jīmūta, an impressive wrestler (412.12–24). Odysseus defeats Irus, the aggressive beggar (18.1–109).[10]

1.5.5. Suitors: leader and followers

Kīcaka, the Matsya marshal and brother of the queen, falls in love with Draupadī and gives her a nocturnal assignation, but Bhīma takes her place, hides in the bed, and kills the marshal with his bare hands. The Kīcakas or Upakīcakas, friends or brothers of the dead leader, want to burn Draupadī along with their leader (as if she were a *satī*), but Bhīma kills 105 of them and saves his wife.

At Ithaca Antinous, the leader of the suitors, is the first of them to die (22.15–21), as is Kīcaka, and unlike his followers, he dies without knowing the identity of Odysseus. The Upakīcakas correspond to the other Greek suitors: according to Telemachus (16.246–252), they number 107 – not far from 105.[11]

1.5.6. Conjugal union or reunion

After the death of Kīcaka and followers, the Kauravas and their allies undertake an unsuccessful attack on the Matsyas, but I skip the rapprochements suggested by this episode and move straight to the end of year 13. On learning the identity of the Pāṇḍavas, Virāṭa offers his daughter [Uttarā] to Arjuna. The hero declines the offer for himself but accepts the princess as daughter-in-law. This is the union that will eventually enable the continuation of the Pāṇḍava royal line; the wedding is celebrated with great pomp. The marriage of Arjuna's son Abhimanyu parallels the reunion of Odysseus and his wife; both epics end of the period of incognito with a sexual union.

2. New comparisons

The comparisons indicated earlier, in conjunction with the relevant publications, show in a preliminary way the breadth and depth of the narrative correspondences between the two texts, but they certainly do not exhaust the possibilities of comparison. Let us take the question of the massacre of Penelope's suitors – starting with a summary of the hostilities mentioned so far.

1.1: At Kāmpilya, after the triumph of Arjuna, the disappointed suitors attack him and Bhīma, but they are defeated, apparently without any fatalities. 1.2: At Vidarbha, Nala defeats his brother (who had driven him from the throne) at a dice game. 1.3: Arjuna's return to Indraprastha is immediately followed by the Khāṇḍava forest fire; he and Kṛṣṇa massacre the beings of all species (demons, animals, birds, serpents, etc.) who live there (1,214 ff.). 1.4: At Gandhamādana, after the meeting with Hanumān, Bhīma kills more than a hundred rākṣasas near Kubera's lake (3.152.18). 1.5: At Matsya, Bhīma kills Kīcaka and the Upakīcakas, and the Pāṇḍavas, helped by the Matsyas, repel the attack of the Kauravas and their allies.

So, in a general way, one can compare the massacre of the suitors with various conflicts in the Sanskrit epic.[12] But none of these conflicts is really close to that in the *Odyssey*, not even that between Bhīma and the Kīcakas, which is the closest. First, Bhīma is acting by himself, while Odysseus has his little team of well-individualized helpers. Second, the locations are very different: Kīcaka dies in a dancing hall used during the day by the maidens of the palace, while his followers perish at the cremation ground. Neither of these locations resembles the Great Hall of Odysseus' palace. So let us turn to the greatest of all the *Mahābhārata* massacres [that vast block of text that describes the Great War].

2.1. Great Hall ~ Kurukṣetra

The massacre of the Kaurava army at Kurukṣetra stands right in the middle of the epic; at the end of Book 9, this enormous multitude is almost annihilated. But this multitude is gathered around the 100 Kaurava brothers, of whom Duryodhana is the eldest. Do they correspond to the Greek suitors? At Kāmpilya, as we saw, the Kauravas in this narrow sense attend the *svayaṃvara* just as do the other princes, and they continue to lust after Draupadī. After the first dice game it seems that Yudhiṣṭhira has gambled away his wife, and Duryodhana exposes his left thigh to show it to her (2,63.11). This gesture implies a sexual advance (cf. 1,92.10), for which he will pay with his death when Bhīma kills him by breaking his thighs (end of Book 9). In the same way, Jayadratha, sister's wife to Duryodhana and a Kaurava supporter, tries to abduct Draupadī during the exile (3,248–256) but ends up humiliated by Bhīma. Moreover, at the symbolic level, Draupadī represents what is truly at stake in the war, namely sovereignty (Hiltebeitel 1976: 143–191; Brockington 1998: 69) – just as does Penelope.

Given the correspondences between the victims of the great massacre (Greek suitors ~ Kauravas) and of the queen who is the object of such desire (Penelope ~ Draupadī), the question arises of those who commit the massacre. The great army of the Pāṇḍavas is gathered around the five brothers, whose trifunctional analysis, developed by Dumézil (1968), explicitly goes back to the discoveries of Stig Wikander. So could the five brothers correspond to Odysseus' team?

This question raises another, of much greater significance. For reasons that are above all empirical – being based on the analysis of a considerable number of cases, I believe that the theory of an IE tripartite ideology needs to be enlarged: what the texts so often give us is a fivefold or pentadic structure, enclosing the Dumézilian triad. At the ends of the hierarchical triad two further categories need to be added, one at the top, one at the bottom, and the Dumézilian first function needs to be made narrower and more precise. Losing its reference to 'sovereignty', this function retains wisdom, priesthood, and justice, the administration of the sacred and the use of intelligence. Compared with the classical functions, the additional ones are defined by their alterity. But the notion of alterity has two aspects or poles. One is valorized or positive, being manifested particularly by entities that are transcendent, for instance a creator, a founder, or a king (the personification of the totality of a society). The other pole is devalued or negative, and covers what is set apart (what representatives of the classical functions exclude, despise, hate, fear, etc.) – for instance outcastes, slaves, enemies, demons. In spite of a certain clumsiness in the analytical vocabulary, I think the best solution to the problem of nomenclature is to propose a fourth function, but to distinguish positive and negative poles within it.

From the four-functional [or pentadic] point of view, the trifunctional interpretation of the five Pāṇḍavas needs to be revised according to the following schema (Allen 1999a):

trifunctional theory		F1	F2	F3	
trifunctional theory		Yudhiṣṭhira	Bhīma, Arjuna	twins	
four-functional theory	Arjuna	Yudhiṣṭhira	Bhīma	twins	Karṇa
four-functional theory	F4+	F1	F2	F3	F4−

Trifunctional theory follows the birth order, which puts Arjuna in the middle of the series of brothers (actually half-brothers – the twins have a different mother). However, according to my theory, the birth order should be left on one side so as to give greater weight to the alterity of Arjuna: he alone wins Draupadī, is son of the King of the Gods, visits heaven, etc.[13] The other pole of the fourth function is represented by Karṇa (Dumézil 1968: 125 ff.). The elder half-brother of Arjuna (they share a mother), Karṇa is among the suitors at Kāmpilya and is a fanatical supporter of the Kauravas.[14]

We are now ready to compare the team who commits the massacre at Ithaca with those responsible for the massacre at Kurukṣetra. It is immediately obvious that the two groups have in common a leader who stands apart from the others (Odysseus ~ Arjuna, the correspondence we have so often met earlier), and also that the lowest position is shared by two individuals who are distinctly similar to each other. The two stockmen, Eumaeus, who rears pigs, and Philoetius, who rears cattle, correspond to the twins Nakula and Sahadeva who, during year 13 of the exile, adopt the roles of groom and cowherd. The humble occupation of the Greek pair, their connection with food, their pairing itself – all support their interpretation as third-functional.

In Odysseus' team, we have still to deal not only with Telemachus but also with Mentor. One might easily overlook him: he is not recruited by Odysseus, he is not armed by Telemachus (22.101 ff.), he does not join in until fairly late in the massacre (22.205), and he soon leaves it; Above all, ontologically, he is not a normal male – he is the human form adopted by Athena to help her protégés, father and son. But Athena's choice is an interesting one. The human Mentor appears only once *in propria persona* (2.225), when he rises in the assembly to denounce the passivity of the populace in the face of the outrageous behaviour of the suitors. Being a friend of Odysseus, he accepted the task of overseeing Odysseus' property when the king left for the war. Like the elderly prophet Halitherses (2.157), Mentor showed his moderation and justice in the warnings he addressed to the Ithacans (24.451). He too is elderly (a *gerōn*), even though Odysseus addresses him his age-mate (*homēlikiē* 22.209), and his characterization as a wise councillor accords with his name (from the root **men* 'think'). All in all, the human form chosen by Athena fits well with the first function.[15] In support of the rapprochement with Yudhiṣṭhira, it is worth noting that Mentor-Athena does not kill any named victim among the suitors: what he does is encourage and provoke Odysseus and sow terror among the hero's enemies (22.448). Yudhiṣṭhira does kill a number of named victims, but in spite of being the king, 'he does not like fighting, an activity in which he shows himself, technically, only just acceptable' (Dumézil 1968: 60).

There remains the question of Telemachus and the second function. From the hierarchical point of view, he outranks the stockmen and is outranked by his father, and perhaps also by Mentor. As for his functionality, there is no doubting his warrior endowment: to speak in the assembly he puts on his sword (2.3), he knows how to string Odysseus' bow (21.128), and he aspires to maintain the heroic tradition of his family (24.511), but one would not say of him, as one would of Bhīma, that he is characterized by strength. What dominates in the Homeric portrait is rather his youth and a certain lack of confidence.

To sum up, a correspondence exists between the two teams, each of which has five members, including a leader and a pair of lower standing. The two other members do not fit perfectly with the functional schema. Mentor would fit well if he were a mere mortal and therefore homogeneous with Telemachus and the stockmen, but he is not, and Telemachus is not the Strong. Although the manifestation of the functions is not complete, the rapprochement between the two pentads is worth proposing. Thus, the following line could be added at the bottom of the previous schema.

Odysseus	'Mentor'	(Telemachus)	paired stockmen	Antinous

2.2. Great Hall ~ Pāṇḍava camp

Let us return to topography. So far we have lacked a Sanskrit massacre carried out within an enclosure, that is, a space comparable to the Great Hall at Ithaca. But the battlefield massacre at Kurukṣetra (an open space) does not conclude the war, which continues until the end of Book 10. [By the end of Book 9] the Kaurava army has been reduced to three warriors, and during the long-drawn-out death of the [fatally wounded] Duryodhana, Aśvatthāman and his two companions launch a nocturnal attack on the camp containing the victorious army.[16] The five Pāṇḍava brothers, with Kṛṣṇa and Saṃjaya, are elsewhere, but the remainder of their army is annihilated, apart from a single chariot driver who conveys the news to the brothers.

One major difference is striking. The victims at Ithaca are the Baddies, the victims in India are the Goodies. Such a difference cannot be minimized, but it needs to be relativized, in light of the following rapprochements.

2.2.1. The leader's oath

On the eve of the massacre, Odysseus, still disguised, is talking with Penelope when he takes an oath (*horkia* 19.302), calling on Zeus. He swears that the return of Odysseus is imminent – it being understood that, when the hero does return, he will kill the suitors.

A few hours before the massacre, during his conversation with Duryodhana, Aśvatthāman takes an oath, calling on Truth and on his own religious merits (9,64.34–35). He swears that this very day he will kill the Pāñcālas, that is, Dhṛṣṭadyumna (who is Draupadī's brother and the Pāṇḍava marshal), together with his people.

2.2.2. Leader's insomnia

Responding to Odysseus' oath, Penelope instructs her servants to make up a comfortable bed for him (19.317–319), but the hero rejects such luxury. He lies down on the skins spread on the earth outside the Great Hall and spends the hours in a restless state (20.6, 24), furiously pondering his vengeance; presumably, he is suffering from the bruises inflicted on him by Melanthius and Antinous. It is only with the aid of Athena that he falls asleep.

With his two companions, Aśvatthāman leaves his king and enters a forest near the camp. Suffering from their wounds, they stop under a banyan, and stretch out on the earth. The companions fall asleep, but Aśvatthāman does not sleep, hissing with rage (10,1.17, 30–33).

2.2.3. Bird omens

After the episode with Eurycleia, Penelope resumes her conversation with Odysseus. She narrates her sufferings and asks the stranger to interpret the following dream (19.536 ff.). There are twenty geese whom she loves and who feed in her dwelling. An eagle with a curved beak slaughters them and flies off, leaving the bodies piled up in the Great Hall. In her dream, the queen is lamenting over this event when the eagle comes back and, perching on a beam, explains that he is Odysseus and the geese are the suitors. The stranger supports this interpretation.

In his forest, Aśvatthāman sees on the banyan thousands of crows who are sleeping calmly. A fearsome owl, with a very long beak, attacks and slaughters them. Their bodies are piled up around the tree, and the owl rejoices (10,1.34 ff.). Aśvatthāman understands that he is to follow the example given by the owl – and does so. The Sanskrit story is the simpler in that the slaughter of the harmless birds is a real event, not a dream, and in that it is the observer himself who extracts the lesson of the omen.

2.2.4. Reluctance to accept lesson of omen

Penelope rejects the lesson of her dream, claiming that it comes from the 'gate of ivory', the source of dreams that deceive; and she continues to doubt, even after the reassurance given by Odysseus.

Having decided to attack the camp during the night, Aśvatthāman wakes his two companions and tells them his project (it is not clear whether he tells them about the birds). Initially, the companions disagree with him, and Kṛpa (maternal uncle to Aśvatthāman) tries to dissuade him. But after a long debate, they follow Aśvatthāman as he sets off (10,5.36).

2.2.5. Irritating noise made by enemy

While Odysseus tosses and turns on his skins, the [servants who are] lovers of the suitors leave the hall, laughing happily (20.6–8). In his first speech to Kṛpa, Aśvatthāman comments on the sounds of laughter and triumph coming from the Pāñcālas (10,1.59–62).

2.2.6. When to punish?

Hearing the servants, Odysseus wonders whether to punish them at once or to let them spend one more night with the suitors. He thinks angrily of their culpable behaviour (*kaka erga* 20.16), but defers the punishment.

In India, the debate, far from taking place within the mind of the leader, opposes Aśvatthāman to the brahmin Kṛpa, who favours the more honourable option of putting off the attack until the morrow and carrying it out in daylight, after a night's rest. But Aśvatthāman recalls the numerous offences committed by the Pāṇḍavas against the rules of war, and his plan of inflicting immediate punishment prevails.

2.2.7 Exit blocked by two subordinates

While the suitors are attempting to string the bow, Eumaeus and Philoetius leave the Great Hall. Odysseus follows them and assures himself of their loyalty: among his slaves, they are the only ones eager for the return of their master. Taking care not to attract the attention of his enemies towards what is happening (21.228–231), he finally gives his instructions. Eumaeus is to block the exits from the Hall, and Philoetius is to seal the courtyard (234–242) – tasks which they carry out (386–389).

Followed by Kṛpa and Kṛtavarman, Aśvatthāman reaches the gate of the camp (10,6.1f.), where he confronts Śiva. Then, whispering to his companions, he entrusts them with guarding the gate (8.6–8), while he himself penetrates the camp elsewhere. Those who attempt to escape the camp are killed by the two companions (8.100).

2.2.8. Aid received from deity

As she has promised [13.393], Athena helps her protégés in the massacre, and not only in the form of Mentor; she diverts the spears thrown by the suitors (22.256, 273) and causes them to panic by shaking her aegis (22.297–298).

At the gate of the camp there arises a monstrous figure (perhaps an emanation of Śiva), who absorbs without any harm all the weapons thrown at him by Aśvatthāman. The latter hesitates for an instant, recalling the warnings of Kṛpa. He invokes Śiva and prepares to enter a fire and sacrifice himself to the god. Śiva appears in person (10,7.59), gives him a sword, and possesses the body of his devotee (who, by birth, is already in part an incarnation of the god).

2.2.9. Victims' leader is first to die

Having strung his bow, Odysseus shoots Antinous, the leader of the suitors. Aśvatthāman's first victim will be Dhṛṣṭadyumna, the Pāṇḍava marshal who, in addition, has killed Aśvatthāman's father, Droṇa. Various details are shared by the two massacres: the cries and groans of the fighters, men running in all directions, the agonies of the wounded, blood and corpses all around. Such phenomena are to be expected at a massacre, so I skip them.

2.2.10. Bard who survives

The last to die in the Great Hall is Leiodes, the diviner. Then the bard Phemius, who sang for the suitors, seizes the knees of Odysseus and begs to be spared. Telemachus immediately addresses his father: 'Stop: don't strike this innocent man [with your sword]!' (22.356).

The Sanskrit parallel comes at the end of the battlefield massacre of Kauravas at Kurukṣetra. Except for the dying king Duryodhana and the three nocturnal attackers, the sole survivor of the great army is the bard Saṃjaya, the *sūta* who was granted by Vyāsa the ability to see everywhere and could thus report to the Kaurava capital the events of the Great War. Sātyaki, a Pāṇḍava ally, raises his sword to kill the bard, but at that very moment Vyāsa arrives and says, 'Let Saṃjaya stay safe and sound; he must not be struck!'

Thus the rapprochement compares three roles: the would-be killer (Odysseus ~ Sātyaki), the rescuer (Telemachus ~ Vyāsa), and the bard who survives, despite having served the Baddies (Phemius ~ Saṃjaya). One can add that both bards sang of subjects bearing on what is currently happening in the epic: the difficult *nostoi* of the Greeks after the Trojan War (1.326–327) ~ the progress and end of the Kurukṣetra war. Finally, the intervention of both rescuers consists of a verse falling into two parts: starting with a verb in the imperative issuing a positive command, it ends with a command in a negative form.[17]

This rapprochement suggests a theoretical observation. Many rapprochements can be expressed in the form agent A ~ agent B, for example Phemius ~ Saṃjaya, but the analytical weight to be given to such formulae is not a constant. Some of them recur in numerous contexts: when one finds A, he or she is often like B; A and B are comparable characters. At the other end of the scale some rapprochements are limited to a single context: is there any other instance of Telemachus ~ Vyāsa? Their characters are absolutely heterogeneous. In fact, the rapprochement links two *actions* – saving a bard by uttering words – rather than linking two *agents*. In the same way, the rapprochement 2.2.8 is not intended to suggest any systematic correspondence between Athena and Śiva (on the contrary, I envisage Athena ~ Kṛṣṇa and Poseidon/Apollo ~ Śiva).

2.3. Laertes' farm ~ Vyāsa's hermitage

One might expect the massacre in the enclosure to conclude the Great War, but this is not the case, in either tradition. The day after the massacre, Odysseus and his team leave the palace to visit the home of the hero's father Laertes, who lives on his farm in retirement from the world. At the same time, Eupeithes, father of Antinous, addresses the Ithacan assembly and gathers friends and relatives of the suitors. Bent on taking revenge for the massacre, they advance on the farm. Odysseus and his supporters await them, and Laertes kills Eupeithes. The gods impose peace and the epic ends.

We know that the Pāṇḍava brothers, with two friends, did not sleep in the camp, and thus they escape the massacre. In the second half of Book 10, they discuss the disaster, and Bhīma sets off to take revenge on Aśvatthāman. Followed by the others, he finds his enemy beside the Ganges at the *āśrama* of Vyāsa (11,10.21, cited by Scheuer 1982: 321). Though not killed, Aśvatthāman is defeated and exiled. This is the end of the Great War.

One notes first a global rapprochement between these two 'appendices' to the massacres: in both epics, the passage from an enclosed location to an open one immediately precedes the resolution of the conflict. One can write:

Great Hall, then Laertes' farm ~ camp of Pāṇḍava [allies], then Vyāsa's hermitage

But at the same time, one must not forget the major difference relating to comparison 2.2. In the *Odyssey*, the Goodies, the victors in the enclosed space, confirm their victory in the second episode, while in India, the passage from one location to the other exhibits an inversion: Aśvatthāman, the Baddy, victor in the first episode, is defeated by the Goodies in the second. We shall come back to this difference. Meanwhile, moving to similarities of detail, I consider the disputes generated by the massacre.

2.3.1. Reaction of defeated party

Eupeithes expresses the sorrow and anger of the suitors' relatives. If he cannot have his revenge, he would rather die (24.435–436). In India, it is Yudhiṣṭhira who laments (10,10.7), while it is Draupadī who expresses her anger. If Aśvatthāman is not punished, she will fast to death (11.14–15). In both cases, the protagonists ask themselves about the disaster and wonder if it was not caused by the faults of the victims or their associates. Halitherses talks of the shamelessness of the suitors and of the cowardice (*kakotēs* 24.455) shown by the Ithacans in allowing such abuses. Yudhiṣṭhira talks of the carelessness *(pramāda)* of his army (Biardeau 2002 II: 482), while the sarcasms of Draupadī (11.10–12) imply that Yudhiṣṭhira sacrificed his sons and nephews in order to win the throne.

Mobilization takes place at speed. Those who follow Eupeithes rush for their arms (24.466). First Bhīma and Nakula, then Kṛṣṇa with Arjuna and Yudhiṣṭhira, mount their rapid chariots to pursue Aśvatthāman.

2.3.2. The conflict

There are two sides, the one including the victors in the massacre (Odysseus and supporters ~ Aśvatthāman), the other consisting of their enemies (Eupeithes and supporters ~ Pāṇḍavas and Kṛṣṇa). The former are already installed in a peaceful location in the countryside, when the other side arrives to seek vengeance. The conflict is a short one, consisting only in the launching of two missiles.

The first missile, a killer, is launched by those who are already installed. After consulting Zeus, Athena again takes the form of Mentor and issues instructions to Laertes. She gives him strength, and the spear he throws penetrates the helmet of Eupeithes and fells him. The first missile in India is a *brahmaśiras*, a weapon of supernatural power, which threatens the destruction of the cosmos; it is assimilated to the fire of Yama (God of Death) at the end of a cycle of world-ages. Made from the stalk of a reed, it is launched by Aśvatthāman with the spell 'For the annihilation of the Pāṇḍavas' (10,13.18). But in the end, all it kills are the foetuses borne by the Pāṇḍava wives, and we learn of only one specific victim. Parikṣit (Arjuna's grandson) is still-born but will be resuscitated by Kṛṣṇa. One can write Eupeithes ~ Parikṣit, as well as Laertes ~ Aśvatthāman.

The latter pair resemble each other also as regards their get-up. During the conflict, Laertes wears armour, but when he first encountered his son, he was wearing clothes that were old, dirty, and ragged (24.227–228). A little later, expressing his grief, he drops dust onto his grey hairs (316–317). When Bhīma reaches the hermitage, he sees Aśvatthāman dressed in *kuśa* grass and bark, his head covered with dust (10,13.14). Surrounded by *ṛṣis*, the Baddy is wearing the dress of a Hindu ascetic.

After the death of Eupeithes, Mentor-Athena cries to the Ithacans to stop fighting. Odysseus wants to attack again, but Zeus sends down a burning thunderbolt – the second missile – which falls at the feet of his daughter. Mentor-Athena calms her protégé and establishes lasting peace between the two sides.

In India, the second missile, again a *brahmaśiras*, is launched by Arjuna to neutralize the one launched by his enemy. Thunder-claps are heard, and the seers Nārada and Vyāsa protest against the use of these supernatural weapons. Arjuna retracts his missile, but Aśvatthāman, being less competent, cannot do the same; all he can manage is to reduce its destructive force. He also agrees to yield to the Pāṇḍavas the jewel he has had on his forehead since he was born.

Thus the second missile, far from being fatal like the first, facilitates the establishment of peace. It is launched either by the Greek King of the Gods or by the incarnation of the Sanskrit equivalent, that is, by Arjuna, who has complete control of it. But although it marks the definitive end of the conflict, it cannot by itself establish the conditions for peace – a task that is not for warriors. The Greek mediator is Mentor-Athena, who corresponds to the seers and Kṛṣṇa (10,14.11–16.18).

The rapprochement between the mediators needs a little development: (a) For the benefit of all beings, the two seers interpose themselves between the two *brahmaśiras* weapons, wanting to neutralize their power to destroy the cosmos. According to the Vulgate they condemn both launchers of the weapon (10,63★). *(b)* After Arjuna's successful retraction and Aśvatthāman's admission of inability to follow Arjuna's lead, Vyāsa speaks again, praising Arjuna: Aśvatthāman ought to retract his missile and, to save his life, give up his jewel. (c) Once the jewel is handed over, Vyāsa demands a reduction in the effect of the missile. (d) Kṛṣṇa informs Aśvatthāman of the punishment he is to undergo and of the ultimate failure of his project (through the resuscitation of Parikṣit). (e) Vyāsa ratifies Kṛṣṇa's prediction.

Thus, in India, the mediation involves two types of being: Kṛṣṇa, active in (d), has taken on human form (he belongs to a family of *kṣatriyas* or warriors), but as Aśvatthāman himself is aware, he is really a god – the Supreme Being, the Puruṣottama (10,16.18). The *ṛṣis* (except in [a], only Vyāsa is mentioned) are brahmins, and as such represent the first function.[18] In Greece, the two categories are combined. Athena, a goddess, has taken the form of the mortal who (as we saw in §2.1) represents the first function in the massacre in the palace hall. The Athena ~ Kṛṣṇa parallel is not surprising: if the goddess is Odysseus' protector and friend par excellence, Kṛṣṇa occupies the same position relative to Arjuna.

3. Concluding discussion

In this essay, some sixty rapprochements can be found, though some of them have been presented only with great concision.[19] In the assessment of narrative similarities and differences, there will always be a certain margin of subjectivity, but is it possible to reject as a whole such a large number of rapprochements? Some may object that the Sanskrit epic is sufficiently long for it to be possible to find in it whatever one looks for, that this particular literary genre is characterized by certain widespread conventions, that the social worlds that produced the epics are similar (polytheist religions, military values, rural economies, etc.), and that the rapprochements result from chance and from the manipulations of analysts. However, this sort of scepticism can be countered by two important considerations. First, the detailed quality of the rapprochements (e.g. the dust on the head of the first launcher of a missile), and second their positioning within the plot. This detail is situated precisely within the epic: it occurs within the Farm ~ Hermitage comparison, which itself continues the Great Hall ~ Camp comparison. The explanation by historical common origin cannot be easily dismissed.

If one is thinking of written texts, east–west transmission is excluded: the Homeric texts probably existed in the seventh century BC, and writing existed in India only from the third century BC. West–east transmission, already envisaged by Dio Chrysostom (53.6–8), is almost as unlikely: the *Mahābhārata* is well anchored in the Vedic heritage (Feller 2004), not to mention Indo-Iranian. Naturally one can speculate on the east–west or west–east transmission of an oral version, but that approach raises many unanswered questions: when, by whom, in what language – let alone how the story was received and institutionalized. The simplest solution is to postulate a common origin. Theoretically, this origin could have been outside the IE world, for instance in the Middle East. However, given the [relative] rarity of cogent Greco-Mesopotamian rapprochements and the importance of the cultural heritage identified by Dumézil and his successors in almost all the branches of the IE language family, the natural hypothesis is that the rapprochements mentioned here also arise from an IE story.

Of the host of problems raised by this hypothesis, I shall discuss only two, which are interrelated. First, can one of the two traditions be identified as the more conservative, as closer to the 'proto-narrative'? Second, can useful hypotheses be formulated on the transformations (or other processes) intervening between the proto-narrative and the texts that we read? I do not expect to offer definitive answers but rather to propose some ideas for future research.

When one passes from synchronic rapprochements to diachronic questions, the margin of subjectivity increases. For the moment, I lack irrefutable evidence that the *Mahābhārata* is as a general rule more conservative than Homer, but when the question has arisen for me, this option has usually seemed the more likely. The four-functional ideology (or the trifunctional one) is more clearly demonstrable in the Sanskrit epic (cf. §2.1): often too the justification for the Sanskrit details is more direct, less convoluted – the five fictive self-presentations of the Pāṇḍavas are more clearly motivated than those of Odysseus (§1.5.2).[20]

Ideally, each one of our comparisons should be studied from this diachronic point of view, but for brevity I here accept the hypothesis that the Indian tradition is globally conservative. This procedure will help us envisage the major processes that fill the gap between the *Mahābhārata* and the second half of the *Odyssey*.

3.1. Doubling up and inversion

The *Mahābhārata* presents a central conflict: Pāṇḍavas (Goodies) versus Kauravas (Baddies). Homer presents us with two of them, one for each epic: Greeks (Goodies) versus Trojans (Baddies), and Odysseus plus team (Goodies) versus suitors (Baddies). The Indian conflict has here been compared with the *Odyssey*, while elsewhere it has been compared with the *Iliad* (Allen 2006a). The Trojan War and the Great Kurukṣetra War are both of them five-phase conflicts, the last phase being a nocturnal massacre. So the Greek tradition has two versions of a nocturnal massacre, the big one in the city of Troy and the small one in the Great Hall of the palace, but both of them resembling Aśvatthāman's attack. So they represent its doubling up. The situation is expressed in Table 17.1.

From a synchronic point of view, we stressed in §2.2 the difference between the Great Hall massacre, where the victims were Baddies, and the Pāṇḍava camp massacre, where the victims are Goodies. According to our hypothesis, the Greeks have inverted the configuration of the proto-narrative. It is the same at Troy: the victims are Baddies, and the Greeks have inverted the old configuration preserved in India. Theoretically, the two inversions could be independent processes, but a simpler solution is to envisage the inversion as preceding the doubling up of the massacre. Subsequently, the great battle and the great massacre would have constituted the Trojan War, while the small massacre, followed by the rural episode, would have contributed to the second half of the *Odyssey*.[21]

3.2. Demythification

In the *Mahābhārata*, myth colours everything. The Baddies as well as the Goodies incarnate supernaturals, and from this point of view, the conflict is just one episode in the ancient struggle between gods and demons, *devas* and *asuras*. The origin of the epic conflict is the complaint of the goddess Earth, addressed to the god Brahmā (1,58.35, etc.), and the eschatological resonances of the conflict are discussed by Dumézil, among others.

There is no point in minimizing the mythic aspect of the Greek tradition, on which there is considerable literature. Nevertheless, the Homeric heroes are not incarnations, and the suitors are not demons. In spite of the well-known fragment from the *Cypria* (fr. 1 Bernabé, see Vielle 1996: 40–46, 115–123), the explanation of

TABLE 17.1 Locations associated with the central or climactic conflicts of the *Mahābhārata* and the Homeric epics

Text	*Battlefield*	*Enclosed space*	*Rural environment*
Mbh.	Kurukṣetra	Pāṇḍava camp	Vyāsa's hermitage
Iliad	Trojan plain	city of Troy	– –
Odyssey	– –	Great Hall	Laertes' farm

the war by the overloading of the earth is scarcely detectable in the Homeric epics. The massacre of the suitors does not resemble an end of the world, and the lance of Laertes is not a cosmic weapon.

The reduction of the mythic aspect (correlating with an increase in the humanistic aspect) may contribute to the explanation of the inversion (§3.1). If in the proto-narrative, as in India, the massacre of the Goodies took its place in the process of relieving the earth of its burden, then perhaps with the decline of this mythic theme and the loss of the eschatological aspect of the final scene, the nocturnal massacre of the Goodies became unacceptable: preference was given to a story that was less paradoxical, more triumphant.

3.3. Weakening of the functional ideology

This is the phenomenon discussed in §2.1 (for other cases, see Allen 2006a). The trifunctional analysis of the *Mahābhārata* began with the Pāṇḍava brothers, who have been no less important in the four-functional analysis. In contrast, as we have seen, Odysseus' team manifests the functions but only up to a point: the situation of Mentor is ambiguous, and Telemachus does not represent the second function. Dumézil's remark (cited earlier) about the IE straitjacket (its *carcan* or *corset*) needs to be modified: Homer is *in the process* of escaping it.

3.4. Amalgam

Our hypothesis proposes that, for each of our eight global comparisons, the proto-narrative contained an episode more or less similar to what we read in the *Mahābhārata*. The following is a list of the Sanskrit episodes in the order they were treated earlier. For each episode, I give the location in which it takes place, its position in the text and, as a reminder, an indication of the theme or themes at the heart of the comparison:

§1.1 Kāmpilya (1,174): archery competition at *svayaṃvara*
§1.2 Vidarbha (3,50): prudence of the wife organizing the return of her husband
§1.3 Indraprastha (1,205): husband returns from journey characterized by sexual liaisons
§1.4 Gandhamādana (3,146): hero encounters aged animal
§1.5 Matsya (4): fictive self-presentations, massacre of a suitor and his followers
§2.1–2.3 'the block' (6–10): Great War proper, massacre in enclosure, and final scene

Except in §1.2 (an autonomous story, standing outside the main plot), the order turns out to be that of the Sanskrit text, even though the episodes are scattered and do not form an uninterrupted series. The parallel Greek passages form a sequence that is less spaced out; they are more entangled one with another. Thus, the archery competition forms the opening of the massacre, and the fictive self-presentations, far from being concentrated in a single episode (as in *Mbh.* 4), form a recurrent motif between Books

13 and 24. To suggest an explanation, one must envisage for the Greek tradition a process of synthesis. But the word 'synthesis' implies an action that is more or less conscious and deliberate, while a more plausible scenario, in this oral context, is a gradual process, perhaps extending over centuries. Hence my preference for 'amalgam'.

How should one model this process? At the present stage of research, the undertaking may appear artificial and rather arbitrary, but I shall later try to justify it. Let us start with the only comparison we made (§1.3) that links the two halves of the *Odyssey*. The hero (Arjuna) returns home (to his palace) after a long journey and is reunited with his wife. This provides a preliminary parallel with Odysseus – but the returning Arjuna is accompanied by an additional wife and is not in disguise. So let us imagine amalgamating this story with the return of Nala to Vidarbha (§1.2): the hero, in disguise and alone, returns to the home of his wife, who hesitates to recognize him. The amalgam has moved closer to the *Odyssey*, but it still lacks the motif of competing with other suitors, the hero's rivals. Following the same method, let us introduce into the amalgam Germain's comparison (§1.1): the hero (Arjuna), in disguise, wins his wife in an archery competition against other suitors.[22] This is better, but we still lack a massacre. So we recall the Matsya episode (§1.5): the hero (Bhīma), by himself, kills one suitor, then massacres the followers; and the same episode introduces into the amalgam many other motifs familiar from the *Odyssey* (fictive self-presentations, etc.). But we have studied here another episode centring on Bhīma (§1.4) – one which, among other things, introduces the motif of awaiting the return of the hero (Arjuna). Finally, the amalgam can be given 'the block', that is, aspects or episodes of the central conflict.

Clearly, this model is only one possibility among many others; perhaps it represents the simplest type from a formal point of view. There is no need to accept either the order in which episodes were introduced, or the unilineal series, or the inclusion, on the same level as the others, of the Vidarbha story (§1.2), which does not belong in the central plot. But the exercise may be worthwhile as an illustration of method. If the rapprochements are objective facts, as I believe, they demand explanation, and a notion as vague as 'mixture' or 'amalgam' is inadequate. The model exemplifies the style of explanation that would be needed. At present it is not clear what rules should govern the formulation of such models or what degree of elaboration they could reach. The example of IE linguistic comparison can provide inspiration, even if it is perhaps too optimistic to hope to attain the rigour or (relative!) degree of consensus found within that discipline.

So let us continue to read Homer in light of the *Mahābhārata*, deepening, extending, and bringing together the comparisons already made, and integrating them with the insights of Homerists. However, we must not forget that Indo-Greek comparativism will one day have to take its place in a much fuller IE comparativism.[23]

Notes

1 First published in 2009, as 'L'Odyssée comme amalgame : Ulysse en Ithaque et comparaisons sanskrites'.

2 They are mostly Francophone. Most of their names can be found by skimming through the journal *Ollodagos* (published in Belgium), but see also (e.g.) Garbutt (2006), West (2006), [De Martino 2017].

3 For a more detailed outline, see Dumézil (1968: 34–42); for a very substantial summary enriched with interpretations, see Biardeau (2002); for a recent translation of selections, see Schauffelberger and Vincent (2004–5).

4 I omit Baldick (1994), who presents a number of Greco-Sanskrit comparisons, some of which can be accepted, but they are too cursory and insufficiently interconnected. I am not persuaded that the story of Odysseus' *nostos* is built on the trifunctional schema name-arms-female, as is argued by Meulder (2002).

5 *Mahābhārata* references are to the CE. Biardeau prefers the Vulgate but gives CE chapter numbers in brackets.

6 Even if, in one of the explanations given by the text (1,189), all are equally incarnations of Indra.

7 Since Arjuna's departure the other Pāṇḍavas have been miserable (3,161.14–15).

8 The passage, called the *Durgāstava*, is relegated to a CE Appx since it is absent from many manuscripts; it is translated by Biardeau (2002 I: 768).

9 According to the southern manuscripts, it is Dharma who, on the request of Yudhiṣṭhira, gives their disguises to the Pāṇḍavas (4, Appx 1.5: 29 ff.).

10 A methodological comment, no doubt obvious: the rapprochement links not two isolated wrestling matches but episodes within two consistent and coherent stories (events at Matsya ~ events at Ithaca).

11 Two among the suitors, the herald and the bard, escape the massacre, but since they are not included in the total given by Telemachus, their relevance remains uncertain.

12 No methodological difficulty is raised by an element in one text having multiple comparanda in the other. Here is another case. The noise made by Nala as he approaches his wife's palace causes the animals he left behind – his horses – to become excited (3,71.3 = rappr. 7 in Gresseth 1979). The Argos ~ horses rapprochement in no way damages the Argos ~ Hanumān rapprochement.

13 Because of his relative age, he himself does not become king, but he sometimes represents the totality of the Pāṇḍavas.

14 He is the third of the five marshals who follow each other as leaders of the Kauravas – cf. the third place of Arjuna in the Pāṇḍava birth order.

15 Further evidence for this interpretation will be given in §2.3.2.

16 Is it the camp that the Pāṇḍavas have occupied since the beginning of the War, or the abandoned camp of the Kauravas, now taken over by the victors? Are most of the Pāṇḍavas (the victims of the Book 10 massacre) in their own camp or that of their enemies? The unclarity of the text is noted by Johnson (1998: 104).

17 Greek: *iskheo, mēde ti touton anaition ontae khalkōi*. Sanskrit: *mucyatāṃ saṃjayo jīvan, na hantavyaḥ kathaṃcana*. Note the indefinite forms *(ti ~ kathaṃcana)*.

18 The two *ṛṣis* address both parties, speaking together. Mentor-Athena first addresses the Ithacans, then Odysseus, but her words are similar on both occasions: *iskhesthe ptolemon* (24.53), *iskheo . . . polemoio* (24.543) – 'you lot, stop fighting', 'you (singular) stop fighting'. The rapprochement links what is said by a single individual who talks twice, with what is said by two individuals talking simultaneously.

19 The figure does not include those that can be added by consulting the publications cited or the englobing ones that have been used as subtitles (Ithaca ~ Kāmpilya, etc.).

20 Naturally, this is a hypothesis about the general character of the Indian tradition, not an absolute rule. For instance, I doubt that the animal in §1.4 was originally a monkey. The *Mahābhārata* and the proto-narrative are not the same thing. Moreover, even if one rejects the hypothesis of Sanskrit conservatism, the following methodological explorations are not necessarily valueless.

21 In the Greek, the victims of the great massacre are at home, while the victims of the small one have occupied the palace of their enemy. The same duality recurs in the hesitations of the *Mahābhārata* noted by Johnson. Moreover, the two Greek massacres both involve Apollo: the god is protector *par excellence* of the Trojans, and the day of the smaller massacre is his festival (20.267–268). Compare Śiva, God of Destruction – see §2.2.8.

22 At each stage in the model-building, we retain what brings the amalgam closer to the *Odyssey* and eliminate what has the opposite effect. For instance, we retain the fact that the hero comes to the *svayaṃvara* accompanied by his brothers, who are also in disguise.

23 [For instance, consider the fact (*Od.* 16.122–224, 247–253) that the suitors come from four locations – fifty-two of them from Dulichium, twenty-four from Same, twenty from wooded Zacynthus (totalling eight dozen), plus one dozen from Ithaca. By itself, our Greece–India comparison has nothing to contribute here: the Kauravas are not said to come from four locations. But we need to enlarge our framework and bring in an Ireland–India comparison (cf. Allen 2000b).

In the *Táin Bo Cuailnge* ('*The Cattle Raid of Cooley*'), Ulster is raided by outsiders from Connaught, whose army consists of eighteen divisions. Connaught's royal couple Medb and Ailill, plus their seven sons, contribute nine divisions, while the exiled Ulsterman Fergus controls the others – one consisting of his fellow Ulster exiles, one from Leinster, seven from Munster (Ó Cathasaigh 2014: 195, 219; Connaught, Ulster, Leinster, and Munster are the four peripheral provinces of the island). Compare the *Go-grahaṇa-parvan*, 'The Cattle-seizing-section' (Upaparvan 47), which occurs towards the end of *Mbh.* 4. The two-pronged attack is launched against the Matsyas by the Kauravas and their Trigarta allies. So in both cattle raids, the attackers are divided into two more or less equal halves. In addition, in both raids the defence exhibits two contrasting modalities. Fighting alone, Cú Chulainn resists the enemy until the other defenders are ready to fight *en masse*; fighting alone, Arjuna defeats the Kauravas, while the other defenders, fighting *en masse* elsewhere, defeat the Trigartas. Such similarities suggest that early PIE tradition narrated, from the point of view of the defenders, at least one failed cattle raid. Presumably, this body of tradition also contained a fourfold division of the aggressors; however, the quadripartition, which survived in the *Odyssey* and in the *Táin*, was not retained in *Mbh.* 4.

This mini-comparison, which clearly calls for both expansion and theorization, is included to emphasize the limitations intrinsic to a comparative approach that deals with only two branches of the IE tradition. Rich and exciting though it is, the India–Greece comparison is only one subfield within the even richer and no less exciting field of IE comparison.]

18

HANGING OVER ABYSS

> Than he loked downwardis into þe pyttes grounde, and þere he sawe an horrible dragoun . . . He had his mowthe euer open and euer was redy to have deuowred hym.
>
> – *Barlam and Iosaphat*

The present chapter arose from a fascinating article by Yaroslav Vassilkov (1994–5) entitled 'Parable of a man hanging in a tree and its archaic background'.[1,2] I shall focus on the parable itself, ignoring the many other themes in a wide-ranging article (it refers, for instance, to Tolstoy's autobiography, archetypes, hook-swinging rituals, and the inverted cosmic tree). The parable is known in many versions from varied sources, including the *Mahābhārata* and the Middle English text excerpted earlier (from Hirsch 1986: 55–57). Briefly surveying the literature, Vassilkov claims (1994–5: 41) that there are ample grounds to define the peculiar imagery of the parable as 'specific to the Indo-European mythology', and I shall try to support his view by comparing the Sanskrit passage with a passage from the *Odyssey*, which he does not mention. Having considered their implications, I end with a brief attempt to relate these comparisons to others bearing on the same Greek passage.

The comparanda

Mahābhārata materials

After his crushing defeat in the Great War, Dhṛtarāṣṭra asks Vidura for philosophical and lifestyle advice and is answered with an account of 'how the supreme sages speak of the wilderness of life *(saṃsāra-gahanam)*'.[3] Here is a summary of the whole passage (*Mbh.* 11,5–6):

> A brahmin finds himself in a huge impenetrable forest, full of dangerous wild beasts. The forest is surrounded by a net and encircled by the outstretched arms of a fierce woman. It also contains five-headed snakes, tall as cliffs, and vast trees. The panic-stricken brahmin runs this way and that, seeking shelter. In the middle of the forest stands a well-shaft or pit, hidden amid creepers and vegetation, into which he falls; but he is entangled in the densely woven creepers and finds himself hanging upside down like a jackfruit. He now becomes aware of other dangers: a snake at the bottom of the well, and a pied elephant with six heads and twelve feet steadily approaching its mouth. In a tree growing at the mouth is a hive of fierce bees. Honey falls from the hive, and the man eagerly drinks it; though his thirst remains unsatisfied, he does not abandon hope of survival. However, white and black rats (or mice) are nibbling at the tree, which will eventually fall. In spite of the six threats – from wild beasts, fierce woman, snake, elephant, rodents and falling tree, and bees – the man continues to hope.

Dhṛtarāṣṭra is moved by the story and would like to help the brahmin, but he is told that it is only a parable *(upamānam)* used by specialists in *mokṣa* to expound their doctrine. Vidura then explains the meaning of each element in the story. Essentially the brahmin represents the ordinary man in this world surrounded by dangers: the beasts represent illnesses, the giant female Old Age, the snake at the bottom of the well Time or Death, and so on. The honey represents our foolish pleasures, which keep us attached to this life.

The central image of the parable, the one Vassilkov chooses for his title, recurs elsewhere in the epic in a story that might be called *Hanging Ancestors* or *Childless Ascetic* (cf. Schneider 1959). It is told twice of the seer Jaratkāru, father of Āstīka (in 1,13.9 ff. and, more fully, in 1,41 ff.), and once of the seer Agastya (3,94 ff.). Relative to Vidura's parable, *Hanging Ancestors* presents the image without situating it within the fearsome forest but as part of a larger story. The following paragraph presents the common pattern of the three texts, ignoring their minor differences:

> A sage finds his ancestors suspended head downward in a cave, hanging from a strand of grass, which is being gnawed by a rat. He learns from them that they are about to fall into hell because their sole descendant (that is, himself) is failing to continue the family line. In spite of difficulties (to some extent self-imposed), the sage obtains a wife and begets a son. Then he leaves her and returns to *tapas*.
>
> Jaratkāru's wife, also named Jaratkāru, is a serpent, sister of Vāsuki; she is abandoned in early pregnancy when she breaks an agreement and wakes her irascible husband, who is sleeping with his head in her lap. Agastya's wife Lopāmudrā is synthesized by her husband so as to constitute female

> perfection. She is brought up by the king of Vidarbha and, after marrying Agastya, sends him on a successful search for wealth.[4] Thereafter she too produces the son demanded by the sage's ancestors, though only after a seven-year pregnancy.

The soteriological message of *Hanging Ancestors* clearly differs from that of *Hanging Man*, being almost the reverse. While the parable tries to instil a desire for *mokṣa*, the ancestors condemn any such desire, insofar as it interferes with ensuring continuity of the patriline. As to narratological status, all three versions are different. The parable is used by one character in the main plot to console and advise another. Jaratkāru's story (the version encountered first by the audience of the epic) is told by the bard Ugraśravas, as part of the outer frame story. Finally, Agastya's story is told by the seer Lomaśa to the Pāṇḍava party near the start of their pilgrimage. This version falls in the category of subtales or 'ancillary stories' – those told to characters who belong in the main story.

The global differences are accompanied by many differences of detail. Examples are cave versus well, plurality of hanging ancestors versus lone brahmin, visit from seer versus complete isolation, single threat of falling to death and hell versus multiple dangers from all sides, a descendant who can bring help versus no prospect of rescue, and no current pleasures versus the dripping honey. Vidura's story tells how the brahmin's predicament arises (running man falls into unseen hole), while the process leading up to the ancestors' plight is left to our imagination.

Nevertheless, there is a common denominator, a shared basic schema. In both cases, brahmins are hanging upside down from a thin suspending line of vegetable matter. The latter is being nibbled by rodents, and when it breaks the humans must expect utter disaster.[5] In both cases, their pitiful plight arouses sympathy, whether from the blind Dhṛtarāṣṭra who hears the story (11,6.1–3) or from Jaratkāru on witnessing the situation (1,41.6–11). Both of these characters enquire about those they pity *(sa deśaḥ kva nu; ke bhavanto)*, both mention their own vicarious distress (*kṛpā me mahatī jātā* 11,6.3; *me duḥkham utpannaṃ* 1,41.6), and both offer practical assistance. Dhṛtarāṣṭra will exert himself *(sādhu ceṣṭāmahe)*, and Agastya will donate some or even all of his *tapas*, that is, the merit earned by it. But both offers are based on misunderstanding. The king does not realize that the story is a parable; the sage does not realize that his *tapas* is the cause of the ancestors' plight rather than a solution to it. These misunderstandings are promptly corrected by the respondents, though the ancestors too are under a misconception: failing to recognize their descendant, they suggest that he carry a message to Jaratkāru.

This second level of misunderstanding has as a result that the explanation the ancestors give of their own plight is inserted in a speech that covers several other matters (enquiry as to the sage's identity, criticism of their childless descendant, the message to be delivered to the latter by their visitor), whereas Vidura can concentrate simply on expounding his parable. However, it is worth comparing the two passages devoted to explanation (11,6.5–11 and 1,41.22–25b). When Vidura explains thirteen features present in his parable, each explanation is presented by means of an identical grammatical structure. A relative clause containing the feature in question is followed by the main clause with a demonstrative giving the interpretation. For instance (6), *ye ca te kathitā vyālā vyādhayas te prakīrtitāḥ* ('those wild beasts that were mentioned in the parable – they (second *te*) are proclaimed to be illnesses'). The ancestors use just the same grammatical pattern for the four items of which they offer an explanation: thus, 'The roots which you see, brahmin, of this plant here – they *(ete)* are our threads, consumed by time'.[6] The interpretations themselves are not identical and will not be closely studied here. My point, to which I return at the end of the chapter, concerns only the form in which they are expressed.

In view of these similarities between *Hanging Ancestors* and Vidura's parable, we can provisionally treat them together, as constituting one limb of the comparison with the Greek (*Od.* 12.37–450).

Greek material

Having reached Scheria (the land of the Phaeacians), Odysseus is recounting to them the second half of his adventurous return voyage from Troy to Ithaca. I summarize[7]:

> Leaving Circe's island, Odysseus comes to an area which we can call the Straits. It contains three sources of danger – the Sirens, Scylla, and Charybdis. Following the advice of Circe, he escapes the fatal charms of the Sirens and enters the Straits proper, which lie between the two cliffs. He passes close to the cliff of Scylla, who eats six of his crew, and after a visit to Thrinacia, he loses the remaining crew in a storm that wrecks his boat. Drifting on the wreckage, he is blown back to the Straits, close to the cliff that adjoins the whirlpool Charybdis. He avoids the vortex by leaping up to a lofty fig-tree that overhangs the whirlpool. '(I) clung close against it like a bat, because there was no firm foothold there, and no chance of climbing either; the roots were far below, and the big long branches hung out of reach overhead' (*Od.* 12.433–436, tr. Shewring). When the wreckage emerges from Charybdis, Odysseus drops back into the sea, regaining his 'vessel'. Escaping Scylla's notice, he continues his journey and reaches the island of Calypso nine days later.

India–Greece comparison

In comparing the two traditions, I rely in the first instance on Vidura's parable but turn to *Hanging Ancestors* from time to time and occasionally introduce some non-*Mbh.* eastern texts.[8] The order of the comparisons is not crucial.

1 *Lone male.* The brahmin is anonymous, while Odysseus is among the best known of Greek heroes, but in both cases, the protagonist is a lone male. In

Hanging Ancestors, the protagonist is the named sage, who goes on to produce a son, not the anonymous ancestors.

2 *Perils, focal and adjacent.* The focal predicament is that of a man hanging perilously over an abyss, but this central image is set in an environment filled with other perils. Even before falling into the well, the brahmin is threatened by wild beasts, ogress, and snakes. The environment of Charybdis includes Sirens, Scylla, and Clashing Rocks.[9]

3 *Abyss.* The shaft into which the brahmin falls is usually called a *kūpa*, which Ganguli mostly translates as 'pit'. However, the first two references to the shaft have *udapāna* and *salilāśaya*, and Paranjpe's note translates *(kūpa)vīnāha* as 'circular masonry on the top of a well'. Such watery associations make one prefer Fitzgerald's translation 'well', which also offers a better parallel to Homer's whirlpool. The Tibetan version actually has a whirlpool (representing *saṃsāra*) situated below a precipice, in place of the usual snake at the bottom of a shaft.

While the brahmin hangs *in* the well, Odysseus hangs *above* the whirlpool, but the difference is bridged by Moule's version, where the protagonist hangs *above* a well. In any case, the man risks falling to his death in an abyss. The great snake at the bottom of the well (representing Time, the destroyer of all creatures) parallels the black sand of the sea bed, visible when Charybdis sucks down the sea water (12.242–243).

4 *Concentric structure.* The well is in the centre of the forest (*vana-madhye* 11,5.10) and is itself circular – Paranjpe glosses *velā* in shloka 13 as 'the circular edge' (sc. of the well). A whirlpool is a circular and concentric phenomenon, and when Odysseus plunges back into the sea, he lands 'in the middle' (*messōi* 12.443) – presumably in the middle of the area occupied by the whirlpool when it is active.

5 *Spaces within spaces.* Whatever the best readings and translations, it is only after leaving a wider sphere of existence that the brahmin arrives within the impenetrable forest (*vanaṃ durgam anuprāpto* 11,5.3); so the forest is a space within a space. Similarly, the Straits constitute a small area relative to that covered by Odysseus' return journey from Troy. But by the end of the episode, the protagonist finds himself in an even smaller space – the well, or the domain of Charybdis.

6 *Tree beside abyss.* The botanical picture in the Sanskrit is not wholly clear. The shaft is hidden or blocked by hard, grass-covered creepers *(vallī)* which are interwoven, or it is tangled with creepers and trees. The man hangs from a cluster of creepers, but it is the tree that is being nibbled and will fall. Logically – if one insists on logic – the creepers must be hanging from the tree.[10]

The fig tree grows in or on the cliff that stands over Charybdis (12.103). Odysseus cannot reach the large branches that overshadow the whirlpool, but even so, when he finally lets go with hands and feet, he falls well away from the base of the cliff. The copious foliage of the fig tree (*phulloisi tethēlōs* 12.103) perhaps parallels the branches or twigs (*praśākhāsu* 11,5.15), where the bees swarm around their hive.

7 *Fruit tree.* Since Homer provides no obvious reason why Odysseus' tree should be a fig, it is intriguing that the Sanskrit refers to a *panasa*, a jackfruit tree or the closely related breadfruit tree (Yule and Burnell 1986 s.v. Jack).[11] The shloka in question (11,5.12) describes the posture of the hanging man: he hangs like a large fruit borne from that tree and connected to it by a stalk. The epic does not equate the breadfruit tree in the simile with the tree being nibbled by rats, but both Jain versions have the man hanging from a banyan *(vaṭa)*, the Indian fig tree. Possibly then, in some versions of the eastern story, the hanging man enjoyed *fruit* falling from the tree rather than honey. The alternation honey ~ fruit ~ *amṛta* is noted by Vassilkov (1994–5: 41).

8 *Hanging posture.* The brahmin explicitly hangs with his feet up and head down (*ūrdhva-pādo hy-adhaḥ-śiraḥ* 12), and all three accounts of the ancestors mention the head-down posture (*adho-mukhān*, as well as *pādair ūrdhvair* in 1,13.11). All we know about Odysseus' posture is that he clings to the tree 'like a bat' (*hōs nukteris* 12.433). The simile strongly suggests that the hero is upside down and can be compared not only with the breadfruit simile (7) but also with Jaratkāru's ancestors, who hang *śakuntān iva* (1,42.5): though Ganguli translates 'like birds', van Buitenen has 'like bats' (apparently being influenced more by the posture than by the dictionary). In both traditions, the simile is unelaborated, consisting simply of noun and comparative particle.

9 *Roots and branches.* Odysseus cannot reach either the roots or the branches of his tree (*rhizai . . . ozoi* 12.435). Vidura refers first to the smaller branches or twigs *(praśākhāsu)* of the tree in whose larger branches *(śākha)* the bees live, then to the nibbling by the rodents. According to Ganguli, they are attacking its roots, and this makes good sense, even though Vidura does not refer explicitly to roots. In any case, in Jaratkāru's story, it is the root or roots of the tuft of grass that is being attacked (1,41.6–7). In addition, his ancestors (by way of anticipation) say that their own roots have been cut (*chinnamūlān* 1,41.26).

10 *Tall objects.* In the forest, there are great trees that touch the heavens (*nabhaḥ-spṛśair mahā-vṛkṣaiḥ* 9), and there are five-headed snakes as tall as mountains or cliffs *(śailair-iva samunnataiḥ)*.[12] One can think of a nexus of tall objects – trees, snakes, and (inside the simile) cliffs. In Greece, the fig tree itself, with great long branches (435), is large and tall (*megas* 103, *makros* 432), as is Scylla's cliff. Higher than that of Charybdis, its sharp peak reaches the spreading heaven (*ouranon eurun hikanei* 12.73, 101). So let us look to Scylla for the third item in our nexus, namely the snakes.

11 *Snaky monsters.* Scylla is not explicitly snake-like, but her six necks are extremely long (*perimēkees* 12.90), and since she uses them to search around for sea beasts or passing sailors, they are certainly flexible. This makes them snake-like, as I have noted elsewhere [Ch. 13].

12 *Six heads, twelve legs.* Scylla has twelve feet, all dangling down, and a grisly head on each of her six necks (12.89–91). The elephant has six faces or mouths and walks on two sextets of legs (*ṣaḍ-vaktraṃ . . . dvīṣaṭkā-pada-cāriṇam* 11,5.14). Thus, both Scylla and elephant have the normal human ratio of heads to feet rather than the normal animal ratio. In Scylla's case, this may relate to the tradition in post-Homeric sources (e.g. Ovid *Met.* 13.734) that she was originally a human female; the elephant becomes more fantastic and frightening (though, as we shall see, there is more to it). While the elephant is gradually approaching the tree (11,5.14; 6.9ab), Scylla seems to be fixed to her cliff, which is located a bowshot away from Charybdis and the tree.

13 *Female monster.* Scylla is not only living in a tall cliff, but she herself is a vast female. Up to her middle she is hidden in a cave situated more than a bowshot above sea level (12.93, 80–84), yet her necks reach the sea in which she fishes. Similarly, the fearsome woman who embraces the forest in her arms (11,5.8) is gigantic (*nārī bṛhat-kāyā* 11,6.6). The last few comparisons can be brought together: one can envisage Scylla either as conflating (synchronically) the three types of being distinguished in the Sanskrit (snakes, elephant, ogress), or as being fragmented into them.[13]

14 *Killers and carnivores.* The forest is teeming with carnivores or carrion-eaters *(mahat-kravyāda)* and crowded with voracious and terrifying forms of lions, tigers, and elephants (11,5.3–4). The parable itself, while listing the terrifying female among the dangers, does not state that she kills or eats people, but Vidura says she is Decrepitude (Jarā), who ruins one's complexion and beauty (6.6ef). Charybdis herself is of course a swallower of humans, and her environment includes not only the explicitly man-eating Scylla but also the Sirens – surrounded as they are by mouldering corpses (12.45–46).

15 *Noise.* The Vulgate text says that the wild beasts are emitting loud roars (reading *mahāsvanaiḥ* for CE *mahāśanaiḥ*). Certainly, when Charybdis sucks down the water, the rock roars terribly (*deinon ebebrukhei* 12.242), Scylla yelps terribly (*deinon lelakuia* 85), and the booming in the Straits (*doupon* 202) is audible even from a distance. Being alluring and not frightening, the Sirens' singing should probably be ignored here.

16 *Fear.* The terrors of the forest are noted repeatedly within the parable, and when he first finds himself in it, the brahmin's hair stands on end (11,5.5). Though he once admits to fear (12.244), Odysseus seems to avoid showing it, but both before entering the Straits and on seeing Charybdis his crew are terrified (203, 243).

17 *Look everywhere.* In his search for safety, the brahmin runs to and fro looking in all directions (*vīkṣamāno diśaḥ sarvāḥ* 11,5.6). As the boat approaches Scylla, Odysseus tires his eyes as he gazes everywhere towards the misty cliff (*pantēi paptainonti* 12.233). Both texts have the present participle and the everyday word for 'all'.

18 *Inaccessibility.* The forest is *durga*, 'hard to reach or pass through'. In Homer, the whole area of the Straits is difficult to pass through, as is clear from the

corpses on the Sirens' island and from Circe's remark that ships never pass Scylla unscathed (12.98–99). Moreover, Scylla's smooth cliff is unscalable; even if a man had twenty hands and feet,[14] he could not reach its top (77–78).

19 *Even a god* . . . The forest would be frightening *even to Mṛtyu* (death personified – *mṛtyor api bhaya-pradam* 11,5.4); in the Vulgate text, this phrase is replaced by a clause with a conditional verb: 'On seeing which (sc. the forest) surely Yama would tremble' *(yat sma dṛṣṭvā trased yamaḥ)*. Scylla is such that *even a god*, if he met her, would not enjoy the sight (12.87–88), and as for Charybdis, when she sucks down the water *not even the earth-shaker* [Poseidon] could save her victim (12.107). The Sanskrit expresses the point positively (the forest would frighten . . .), the Greek negatively (not even a god could. . .), but both traditions here bring in a named god (i.e. Mṛtyu, Yama, or Poseidon) who is only in the background of the story, ostensibly to emphasize the fearsome nature of what is being described.

20 *Honey and beeswax*. The frightening bees swarming around their hive in the tall tree may parallel the permanent black cloud surrounding the peak of Scylla's cliff (12.74–75). More cogently perhaps, the hive from which the honey drops recalls the wax, described by Circe as 'honeysweet' (*meliēdea* 12.48), which is moulded by Odysseus and used by him to stop the ears of his crew, so that they cannot hear the Sirens' song.

21 *Honey versus horrors*. The Greek passage contains just one further reference to honey: the Sirens describe their own singing as honey-sweet (*meligērun* 12.187). That both references to honey come in the Sirens sub-episode makes sense within the Homeric context since, like honey, the Sirens appear attractive – in contrast to the obviously horrifying Straits monsters who threaten the boat from either side. Similarly, in the Sanskrit, the honey, representing the apparent pleasures of this life, contrasts with the obvious dangers that threaten the brahmin on all sides. In both epics, the apparent attractions are seen through and rejected by the wise – by Odysseus acting on Circe's advice, and by the Indian religious renouncer. In other words, the honey/horrors contrast in the Sanskrit appears in the Greek as Sirens sub-episode versus other sub-episodes.

So far most of the rapprochements have taken their *Mahābhārata* limb from the parable only, though a few important ones have drawn on the *Hanging Ancestors* in addition (§1: Lone male, §8: Hanging posture, §9: Roots and branches). The following draw only or mainly on the *Ancestors*.

22 *Cave*. The ancestors hang in a *garta*, 'a hollow, hole, cave, grave', or in a *mahāgarta*, or in a *bila* 'cave, hole, pit, opening'. Scylla too lives in a cave (*speos* 80, 84, 93).

23 *Pity for associates*.[15] We saw earlier how both Dhṛtarāṣṭra and Jaratkāru felt pity for the hanging victims. Thinking about the former, the auditor of Vidura, one asks whether the audience for Odysseus' account of hanging in the tree were moved to pity. A few lines after the sub-episode, the start of Book 13 describes the Phaeacian audience as silent and spellbound but makes no reference to

pity. On the other hand, Jaratkāru's pity for his ancestors has a parallel in the Scylla sub-episode. As his boat passes the monster, Odysseus looks back from the prow, only to see the six crewmen already in the air, writhing in the jaws of the monster and vainly imploring his help. The victims are stretching out their arms to him (*kheiras . . . oregontas* 257) in their awful death struggle; this was the most pitiful (*oiktiston* 258) of all the sights Odysseus saw on his wanderings. The ancestors are starving and emaciated, miserable and desirous of rescue (*trāṇam icchataḥ* – a present participle, as in the Greek), but even though the description is less vivid than Homer's, their impact on the sage is such that, even without knowing their identity, he is willing to donate to them all the ascetic merit he has accumulated. When he does learn who they are, he is utterly miserable and his speech is affected by sobbing (1,42.1).

As the crewmen are being lifted up to Scylla's cave they call on Odysseus *exonomaklēdēn*, by name (12.250). Agastya's ancestors address him by name, albeit without having been told it (3,94.14).

24 *Suspended by thread.* The pitiful ancestors hang in the cave from a single thread (*tantu* 1,41.4): compare the crewmen, each writhing in the jaws at the end of one of Scylla's long flexible necks. But a better comparison is with the relevant Homeric simile. 'As when a fisherman on a promontory takes a long rod to snare little fishes with his bait and casts his ox-hair line down into the sea below, then seizes the creatures one by one and throws them ashore still writhing; so Scylla...'[16] In comparing the crewmen to fish caught by rod and line, the text in fact leaves the 'line' implicit (despite Shewring's translation); however, a *linon* is mentioned in another Homeric version of the same simile (*Il.* 16.408), which describes Patroclus' treatment of an enemy. While the ancestors' thread (like the brahmin's creeper) are in the main story, the fishing line, like the stalk of the breadfruit (its *vṛnta*), is in a simile.

25 *Two modes of hanging.* The last two rapprochements show that, despite the similarities between *Hanging Man* and *Hanging Ancestors* (brahmins, abyss, head down, rodents, interpretations), they are two separate themes, and that they parallel respectively Odysseus (alone) hanging from his fig tree and the crewmen (six of them) hanging in the jaws of Scylla.

26 *Teeth and eating.* Scylla's heads each contain three rows of teeth, crowded and close-set (12.91–92), which must have been used to grip the writhing crewmen and to consume them *(katēsthie)*, once they were lifted up to the cave. The rat gnawing the thread of Jaratkāru's ancestors uses its sharp teeth (1,41.7d) and is interpreted as Time gradually killing off the foolish ascetic (25ab and *paribhakṣ-* in 23d).

27 *Pitier is wanderer.* In the first two lines of the *Odyssey* (1.1–2), we learn that its hero is a wanderer *(hos mala polla | plagkhthē)*, but so is Jaratkāru: he is introduced, not only as the equal of Prajāpati, but also as meeting his ancestors in the course of his wandering (*aṭamānaḥ* 1,13.11). Indeed, he wanders the whole earth (1,36.7c, 1,41.1).[17] Moreover, neither wanderer is wholly alone. Athena is keeping a friendly eye on Odysseus, and Zeus tells us that the hero is destined

to return to Ithaca (5.41–42). Jaratkāru is constantly watched by the snakes (1,35.12, 1,42.16), since they know Brahmā's prediction that Jaratkāru's son, Āstīka, will prevent complete destruction of their kind (1,34.12–13).[18]

I come finally to three points that relate less to the substance of the stories than to their style and, in the Sanskrit, primarily to the parable.

28 *Obscurities*. Both texts contain obscurities or incoherencies. For instance, what is the precise threat posed by the ogress or the elephant, and how exactly is the tree related to the creepers? What exactly is the posture of Odysseus on his tree, why should he hang from it like a bat when he has leaped upward to grasp it, and what is to be made of the Clashing Rocks?

29 *Binary oppositions*. There are enough examples to merit comment, notably:

snake at bottom of well, elephant at top;
white rats and black, representing days and nights (light and dark halves of the month in the Jain versions, or sun and moon in Moule's Chinese version);
hope for continued life *(āśā)* versus indifference to life (*nirveda* 11,5.22).
tall figure on periphery of forest, pit extending downward in its centre.

In the Greek:

Scylla versus Charybdis, that is larger cliff versus smaller, hollow cave versus protruding tree, one who reaches out and snatches upward versus one who sucks in and down;
attractive paired Sirens versus repellent paired Cliff Monsters (§21);[19]
Charybdis sucks down the sea, then belches it forth (i.e. downward motion versus upward).

30 *Use of numbers*. In the Sanskrit, apart from the number two implicit in §29 and the beings with six heads and twelve legs (§12), we can add the five-headed snakes, and in the summary of the perils (11,2.21) the numerical adjectives applied to the fifth and sixth items. In Greece, Scylla has three rows of teeth per head, and her hypothetical climber has twenty arms and legs. Charybdis repeats thrice daily her routine of sucking down and belching forth. These numbers are explicit, but implicitly there are four threatening animate beings in Homer or five in the sources with three Sirens, but only three different types of monster. If the Clashing Rocks are included, there are four types of hazard.

Wider considerations

The rapprochements presented earlier are heterogeneous. As we noted, they may relate to the parable alone, to *Hanging Ancestors* alone, or to both, and they may bear either on subject matter or on style. Their importance also varies widely: some (such as §15: Noise) bear on such minor details that one might prefer to omit them, while others are deep or structural (e.g. §21: Honey versus horrors). Four of them bear on similes: in §7 and §10, the simile is in the Sanskrit (hanging man like breadfruit; snakes like cliffs), while in §8 (hanging man like bat) the simile is in both epics. The most interesting case is §23 (crewmen like caught fish), where the fairly elaborate Homeric simile parallels the main story about the ancestors. In a somewhat similar case [Ch. 3], the Sanskrit comparandum comes in the main plot rather than, as here, in a frame story or subtale.

Since in both cases we are dealing with quite limited stretches of text, the number and detail of the rapprochements implies a historical connection between the two traditions. However, direct influence of one written text on the other (in either direction) or even of slightly earlier oral forms of one tradition on the other, is implausible, for many reasons. Among them is the enormous difference that separates the *Mahābhārata* and Homeric traditions. The situation is quite different from the parable of *Barlam and Iosaphat*, where (say) the Middle English version and Chavanne's Chinese version are immediately recognizable as being the same story as Vidura's. Homer uses the same elements as the Sanskrit, but he does not tell the same story. Thus, the historical connection must lie in remote common origin. Unless really good evidence can be found to situate it in Mesopotamia (followed by spread both east and west), the likeliest common origin is in early IE oral tradition. In other words, we must think in terms of a proto-narrative, which developed differently as the bearers of the tradition spread east and west.

To try and envisage such a prehistoric narrative, to reconstruct an outline of it, would not necessarily be a waste of time, but the material is too rich and the task too complicated for the present essay. Even a diachronic linkage between the *Hanging Ancestors* (closer to the Scylla sub-episode) and the *Hanging Man* (closer to the Charybdis sub-episode) raises difficult questions. Perhaps, as in the Greek, the two stories originally concerned a single male protagonist who saw some of his associates hanging in a desperate plight and later found himself hanging over an abyss – but perhaps not. So let us focus less on the content of the proto-narrative than on its orientation or genre.

My first question, prompted by Vassilkov's reference to IE mythology and its cosmic trees,[20] is whether the six perils in the *Hanging Man* hint at a cosmology. Certainly a vertical axis is suggested by the brahmin's situation in the middle of the well (*kūpa-madhye*, 11,6.8) between bees above and snake below. Horizontally, the well, with the brahmin in it, is again in the centre (§4, *vana-madhye*), and there are four remaining perils – from centre outwards the rats, elephant, wild beasts, and ogress. Not being linked with cardinal points, the quartet does not fit the standard cosmological schema of zenith, nadir, and four cardinal points surrounding a centre. Nevertheless, that schema is suggested by those versions that have four malevolent snakes on the four sides of the shaft, well, or tree (e.g. the Chinese Buddhist ones). The snakes are said to represent the four elements or (Hemacandra) the four passions but, as Georg von Simson has suggested to me, the Diṅnāgas, ordinarily understood as elephants of the cardinal points, were no doubt originally snakes (the interpretation as elements would be secondary).

The Greek picture can now be viewed as a transformation of the cosmological scheme in which the vertical axis has, as it were, been laid out flat, so that the perils can be encountered sequentially in the course of a journey. Odysseus, the focus of attention – like the brahmin – meets first the honey-voiced Sirens, corresponding to the zenith (§21); then the multi-headed Scylla, corresponding to the forest perils on the horizontal plane; and finally Charybdis, corresponding to the nadir. It becomes clearer why Homer's hero meets exactly three types of monster, and in this particular order. Homer's black sea bed parallels the explicitly black snake in the Jain abyss, which itself perhaps contrasts with the implicitly golden honey above.

I now turn from the spatial aspect of the cosmology to its temporal aspect (cf. Vassilkov 1999). According to Vidura, the elephant represents the year, its six heads the seasons, and its twelve legs the months.[21] In view of §12, the same interpretation may originally have applied to Scylla or to some differently named oral-tradition predecessor of hers. In addition, Vidura links the black and white rodents with diurnal time (night and day), and the ancestors are preoccupied with generational time (the time of genealogies). It is not clear that the diurnal alternation underlies any of the Greek dualisms (§29), but it is interesting that Charybdis is active three times a day (12.105: dawn, noon, dusk?). One other sort of time is probably alluded to: when the Sirens claim to know everything that happens, and in particular what happened during the Trojan War, they are talking about 'historical' time (12.189–191). More adventurously, one might try to recognize in the story the temporality of the life cycle. In the Sanskrit, the hive and its honey are linked (a little awkwardly perhaps) with childhood (11,5.16, tr. Ganguli 1993 III Book 11:8), while the snake at the bottom of the well relates to death; so should the Greek females be associated with stages of life (Siren songs ~ lullabies)? More soberly, the numerical associations of Scylla and elephant are enough to connect the proto-narrative with considerations of time. Nor is this surprising: cosmogonies (certainly Indian ones) tend to narrate the origins both of space and time, and cosmogonies stand close to cosmologies.[22]

Another question is prompted by the highly didactic character of the eastern texts. The parable is told to promote the doctrine of *mokṣa*; *Hanging Ancestors* inculcates a classical doctrine of this-worldly Hinduism, namely that the ancestors are owed a debt payable only by producing a son to continue the family line; and the Buddhist allegories are attributed to the Buddha's own teaching. The Greek story has a very different atmosphere. Despite the importance of Homer in Greek education, and the possibility of deriving moral lessons from the behaviour of Odysseus, the Straits episode is not openly homiletic and can be read simply as an adventure story. So has didacticism been lost by the Greek or gained by the Sanskrit? Or perhaps both processes have operated, so that the proto-narrative *was* didactic, but less so than the Sanskrit is now.

In favour of this latter view is the generalization that myths are usually believed to be true in some fundamental sense. So if the multiple dangers faced by the protagonist of the proto-narrative were linked to the mythic articulation of space and time, the story was surely told as more than entertainment. I envisage a story that was already to some degree ideological or philosophical, that is, a reflection on the human condition, and hence not without didactic content. More specifically, although the Greek lacks interpretations such as are advanced by Vidura and the ancestors, in both traditions, the elements of this particular story receive two treatments. Vidura first tells the story and then interprets its elements, while Odysseus first recounts Circe's warnings about the perils of the Straits, then recounts his experience of them. An intra-narrative warning about future dangers is not the same sort of speech act as an interpretation of a previously narrated story, but in both cases, the same events are covered twice. Moreover, since [like Yudhiṣṭhira] Vidura the interpreter incarnates the god Dharma and Circe is a minor goddess, probably in the proto-narrative a story of experiences on the human level was accompanied by a more authoritative account of them, given by someone in a position to be didactic.

The comparative picture presented so far – already complicated – is further enriched by two other India–Greece comparisons bearing on the same Homeric passage. Since both of them imply their own proto-narratives, the question arises how the various stories interrelate. At this point, it may be worth glancing ahead to Figure 18.1. The proto-narrative postulated in this chapter is there labelled **Hang over abyss*, the asterisk indicating that it is hypothetical, like the starred forms reconstructed by linguists.

The first comparison to strike me [Ch. 2, Allen 2006a] was between the Straits area and the lakes near the Southern Ocean visited by Arjuna during his Penance (1,208–209), or more precisely, between the inhabitants of these locations. In both epics, this location belongs in a sequence of four peripheral or remote locations, at each of which the hero encounters different females, before returning to his wife at home. Thus, at the Southern Ocean, Arjuna encounters five *grāha* or crocodiles – in reality *apsarases* under a curse – who correspond to the Greek Straits Monsters.

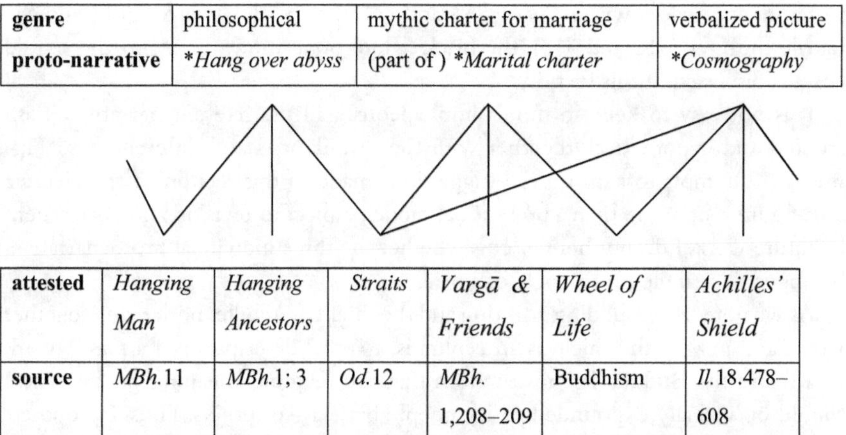

FIGURE 18.1 Links between selected extant texts, in light of the theory that they descend by oral transmission from hypothetical Indo-European proto-narratives

Note: The incomplete diagonals are to be read as joining up, so that *Hanging Man* derives not only from **Hang over abyss* but also from **Cosmography*.

I argued that the crocodiles/monsters were one element in a five-element proto-narrative that served as charter for the modes of marital union recognized by the early Indo-Europeans. Let us call this story the **Marital Charter*. One now asks whether the crocodiles/monsters in **Marital Charter* had any input to the *Hanging Man/Ancestors* story. But although the crocodiles' efforts to drag the hero to a watery death in the lake may vaguely recall §3: Abyss, the resemblances are too unspecific to be of use.

The more recent comparison [Ch. 13] is also the more instructive. One of the comparanda here is the Buddhist painting called the *bhava-cakra* or Wheel of Existence, together with the narrative that describes its origin in the travels of Maudgalyāyana and in the words of the Buddha himself. This painting shows a number of similarities with the Iliadic account of the shield of Achilles (concentric layout, vignettes of everyday life, macrocosmic scope, combination of words and image) – enough to suggest that both go back to a proto-narrative that might be called **Cosmography*.

However, the Buddhist picture also shows a number of similarities with the episode of the Straits. At its centre or hub are three animals, the cock, the snake, and the pig – compare the three types of Greek monster.[23] Outside this, souls are being carried up and down between heaven and hell (white half going up, black half going down) in a rotating waterwheel – compare the whirlpool. Outside this again are the six divisions of the cosmos, and at the outer rim of the wheel the twelve links in the chain of causation – compare the six plus twelve body parts of Scylla. The wheel is in the grip of a large demonic figure, sometimes female, typically with prominent canines – compare Scylla herself. These details already suggest that **Cosmography* influenced not only the Buddhist painting and Homer's Straits episode but also *Hanging Man*. The more obvious similarities are the concentric structure and spaces within spaces (§4 and §5), the six plus twelve motif and the female monster (§12 and §13), the black–white opposition (§29), and the sixfold cosmos discussed in this section.

It is not easy to keep in mind simultaneously all the relevant narratives, both attested and hypothetical, together with their similarities and differences, so Figure 18.1 attempts to sum up the suggestions made in this section of the chapter. The figure is no more than a provisional model, subject to revision and enrichment by future work. I do not here discuss whether the three individual proto-narratives belonged to a single proto-cycle of stories.

As we noted, the Buddhist painting and the shield of Achilles both bring together words and images: the shield is an ecphrasis, a verbal description of a plastic work of art, and the Buddha left instructions that the religious meaning of the Wheel should be verbally expounded to lay people by learned monks. Thus, I proposed, **Cosmography* probably belonged to that widespread genre of performance art in which a bard relies not only on his words but also on a picture. Perhaps the same was true of **Hang over abyss*. The idea finds support in the impact of our stories on the visual imagination (cf. Moule's woodblock, also Vogel 1937), as well as in the interpretations of *Hanging Man/Ancestors* offered by Vidura and by the ancestors.

The ancestors not only use demonstrative adjectives to make their points but also regularly use the verb *paśyasi* 'you see', plus the vocative 'O brahmin'. Such language accords well with the context of the story but would accord at least as well with a bard using a picture.

If any doubt remains about the cosmological aspect of *Hanging Man*, we can leave the last word to Vidura, when he brings his interpretation to a close (11,6.12):

> *evaṃ saṃsāra-cakrasya parivṛttiṃ sma ye viduḥ* |
> *te vai saṃsāra-cakrasya pāśāṃś chindanti vai budhāḥ* | |
> Those wise men who in this way understand the turning of the wheel of life cut through its snares or fetters.

The *saṃsāracakra* is just another name for the *bhavacakra*, but its reference to *saṃsāra* covers both the spatial and temporal wanderings of the transmigrating soul.

Notes

1 First published in 2009 as 'The hanging man and Indo-European mythology'.

2 I thank the author for sending me a copy of this not easily accessible paper (a slightly different version – *non vidi* – appeared as Vassilkov 1995). I also thank Georg von Simson and Mislav Ježić for very helpful critical comments on an earlier draft of this paper, and Ulrike Roesler for references. For further bibliography, see the classic Kuhn (1888); also Shokhin (1988: 129–139), and Grey (2000: 254–255).

3 For translations, see Ganguli 1993 III: Book 11: 7–9 and Fitzgerald 2004: 37–38.

4 In his search for treasure, Agastya visits three kings in succession and puts his polite request to each of them. Each time he receives a polite refusal but is accompanied by the king as he moves on. Finally, the party, now consisting of four members, visits Ilvala, a demonic brahmin-killing Asura. Agastya overcomes Ilvala and obtains wealth both for the three royal seers and (even more) for himself (that is, for Lopāmudrā). Whether or not the triad can be associated with the classical functions, the story presents the typically Indo-European 1+3+1 pattern (noted in many of my previous papers).

5 The line and rodents are absent from Agastya's story, which treats the central image only briefly. The significance, if any, of the story attaching to brahmins rather than anyone else, is not clear. Trifunctionalists have sometimes associated hanging with the Dumézilian first function, which is also represented by that varṇa (Sergent 1995: 375).

6 *yāni paśyasi vai brahman mūlānīhāsya vīrudhaḥ* | *ete nas tantavas tāta kālena paribhakṣitāḥ* (1,41.23).

7 12.39–127, 165–259, 426–50.

8 The Jain versions are from Haribhadra (seventh century) and Hemacandra (twelfth) – see de Bary et al. (1951: 57); Fynes (1998: 53). The Chinese Buddhist versions are from Julien (1860 I: 131–134, 190–193), Chavannes (1962 II: 83–84) (no. 205, which retranslates Julien's second version), and Moule (1885). A Tibetan version, ultimately from Po-to-ba's *Dpe-chos* (Chapter 3, sixth example), is summarized by Shokhin (1988: 132–133). Two further somewhat divergent versions are Chavannes (1962 III: 257–258) (no. 469) and Dubois (1978: 433–434).

9 Thrinacia seems to be an insertion within an episode that is otherwise located at or near the Straits. I treat this episode as having three sub-episodes, centring respectively on Sirens, Scylla, and Charybdis.

10 Jaratkāru's ancestors hang from a *vīraṇa-stamba(ka)*, a tuft of a particular type of fragrant grass, whose root is being nibbled. In the ancestors' explanation the reference is to the

roots of a *vīrudh* 'plant, herb, esp. creeping plant or low herb'. Elsewhere the vegetation surrounding the shaft is quite variable.

11 The two species of Artocarpus belong, as does the fig (Ficus), in the family of Moraceae. [On the significance of fig trees in connection with Indra (the *aśvattha*), Dionysus, and Demeter, see Janda 2000: 276.]

12 Some manuscripts here omit reference to the trees and make the snakes touch the heavens.

13 Since the female is huge and fearsome, I refer to her as an ogress, but she is a human *(strī, nārī)* and not (for instance) a *rākṣasī*. If *aōros* means 'dangling', Scylla's legs would parallel the hanging root of the banyan in Hemacandra, which resembles a coiling serpent. In that case, Scylla would relate to the tree as well as to the other entities.

14 If this number of limbs implies five heads, it offers a parallel with the five-headed snakes.

15 'Associates' is not ideal but is meant to cover ancestors and fellow sailors, as distinct from strangers.

16 *Od.* 12.251–5, tr. Shewring. The reference to oxen in 253 is obscure and disputed. [Cf. Allen 2017.]

17 The former is the only non-*anuṣṭubh* reference in this chapter. The comparativist approach offers no support for the theory that such passages are particularly old.

18 The parallel extends to the wives of the wanderers (Penelope and the female snake Jaratkāru) insofar as both have a single son whom they bring up alone. Moreover, when a great massacre takes place, Telemachus saves the bard and the herald (22.356–357), while his mother's suitors all perish (108 of them, from four geographical locations), and Āstīka saves the good snakes, his mother's relatives, while very many bad snakes perish – eighty-seven names are listed from five families (1,1.52), though there were many others. But this is taking us too far from the *Hanging Man*.

19 Perhaps it is to achieve this balance that Homer has only two Sirens rather than the three which I take to be older [Ch. 6].

20 He cites a comparison made long ago by the Grimm brothers (1813: 80) between a thirteenth-century German version of *Barlam und Iosaphat* and the Norse god Odin hanging in the cosmic ash tree, Yggdrasil.

21 For the six seasons in India, see *Mbh.* 1,3.172–173, 12,237.32; also Smith (1994: 173).

22 Since the large elephant and the small rodents represent larger and smaller temporalities, the remaining perils may also constitute a meaningful pair. According to Vidura, the wild beasts and ogress represent respectively illnesses and Decrepitude (so prominently conjoined in Buddhism), but perhaps in earlier versions they represented animals and humans, or nature and culture. A link between the ogress and human material culture is implied: the brahmin sees, more or less at once, that the wood is surrounded by the hunting net *(vāgurā)* and by the arms of the ogress (11,5.8).

23 Not to mention the three dragons in the well (Moule 1885), which recall Charybdis' triple daily rhythm.

19

GODS DESCEND TO BATTLEFIELD

Introduction

If Homer is a foundational text for Greek culture and hence for the entire European literary tradition, the Sanskrit *Mahābhārata* (which includes a compressed version of the *Rāmāyaṇa* story) is of comparable status within the Hindu tradition.[1] Both grew from oral traditions, Homer reaching written form around 700 BC, while the Sanskrit epic emerged around the turn of the eras. The Sanskrit epic is about seven times as long as the two Greek epics combined. Greek and Sanskrit are of course cognate languages within the Indo-European (IE) family, so the hypothesis of a common origin for the two epic traditions (in a 'proto-narrative') is an obvious one. However, surprisingly few people have presented detailed comparisons of the two traditions, and I shall spend most of this chapter simply doing that. At the end, I shall try to assess the methodology, asking how convincing are such comparisons and what conclusions can be drawn from them.

Both traditions are so extensive that exact holistic comparisons at a useful level of detail are impossible, so how does one choose what to compare with what? I will not provide a general answer to this question here, but merely explain how the present essay originated. Having become interested in the similarities between Greek and Sanskrit theories about the elements, I was reading an article on the conflict between the fire god and the river god in *Iliad* Book 21 (Wathelet 2004) when I was reminded of the final section in Book 1 of the *Mahābhārata*. I soon recognized that both texts combine the following four themes:

God of fire fights god associated with water.
Gods *en masse* participate in the conflict.
Central hero of each epic is allied with god of fire.
Fire prevails.

The fire–water conflict remains at the heart of this chapter, but the comparison becomes more convincing if its scope is extended. We shall focus centrally on *Iliad* Books 18–22 (only glancing at 23–24) and on the subparvan called 'The Burning of the Khāṇḍava Forest' (*Mbh.* 1,214–225).[2]

In view of the genesis of the chapter, I have so far referred to Greece before India, but for various reasons I shall now reverse the order and consistently put India first. A long précis of the two texts is unnecessary since the important points will emerge in the course of the comparison. However, brief summaries are indispensable.

Mbh. 214: Leaving their capital, Arjuna and Kṛṣṇa make a pleasure outing. A brahmin approaches. 215: The brahmin is the god Agni and wants to burn the forest, but Indra (King of the Gods, and God of War) protects it with rain. Arjuna will help Agni but needs weapons. 216: Agni procures the weapons and starts his fire. 217: While the heroes prevent the inhabitants of the forest from escaping, the fire rages. Indra takes note, and rains, so fire and water are now opposed. 218: Arjuna counters Indra, who escalates the conflict. Kṛṣṇa kills demons, and other gods join in, but the heroes turn them back. 219: Indra and his troops return to heaven, and the fire goes on burning. In all, only six beings escape the fire, including the four Śārṅgaka birds. 225: After six days, Agni is satisfied. Indra rewards the heroes.

Il. 18: Achilles learns of Patroclus' death. His mother Thetis visits and will help him take revenge: she will get him new armour, made by Hephaestus. Helped by Athena, Achilles frightens the Trojans, showing them that he is rejoining the fray. 19: Thetis brings the armour, and the reunited Greek army mobilizes. 20: Calling a divine assembly, Zeus tells the gods to join in the fighting, though they do not yet fight each other. Achilles kills various Trojans, but two major foes are saved by divine intervention. 21: Many Trojans flee into the Scamander.[3] Becoming angry at the bloodshed and corpses, the river attacks Achilles, whose life is at risk. Hera summons Hephaestus to attack the river, who yields. The other gods fight each other, or contemplate doing so. Achilles goes on fighting on the plain. 22: He kills his arch-enemy Hector.

Let us start with an overview of the parties involved in the conflict (see Table 19.1).

TABLE 19.1 Participants in the battles we are comparing

	Protagonists	*Side F(ire)*	*Side W(ater)*
Sanskrit	gods	Agni	Indra (and his troop of gods)
	humans	Arjuna (and Kṛṣṇa)	Khāṇḍava forest and its inhabitants
Greek	gods	Hephaestus	Scamander (and Simoïs)
	humans	Greeks, esp. Achilles	Troy and Trojans

Note: Agni (Sanskrit *agni* is cognate with Latin *ignis*) is god of Fire. Indra is king of the gods (like Zeus in Greece). Arjuna, son of Indra, is the central hero of the Mahābhārata and friend of the incarnate god Kṛṣṇa. Khāṇḍava is north of Delhi. Following the abduction of Helen, the Greeks attack Troy. Hephaestus is a craftsman god and can also appear as fire. Achilles is the central hero of the Iliad. Scamander is a river near Troy, as is Simoïs.

The two stories differ greatly, but let us explore the similarities before the differences. To do this in an orderly way, I divide each story into five successive phases (A–E), with the main fire–water conflict emerging in phase D. Each phase is introduced with a summary of the Sanskrit and Greek and an italicized statement of what the two phases have in common. We can now work through the phases, collecting rapprochements. For brevity, I minimize intra-tradition or intra-epic comparisons (i.e. Sanskrit–Sanskrit or Greek–Greek) – even though they are sometimes very interesting.

Rapprochements

Phase A: background conflict

Sanskrit: Having developed a passionate desire to consume the forest, Agni has repeatedly been prevented by Indra from doing so.

Greek: The Greeks have long been fighting the Trojans. Achilles withdraws. When he loses Patroclus, he develops a passionate desire to kill Trojans, particularly Hector.

Shared: *A long-standing background conflict precedes our episode. Someone on side F conceives a craving to destroy a component of side W.*

A1 *Arrogant king causes disaffection.* A certain King Śvetaki indulges excessively in sacrificing. He shows a lack of consideration and judgement by overworking his brahmins, who eventually refuse to serve him, and he also overworks Agni (the sacrificial fire), who falls ill, losing colour and appetite (Appx 1.118).

The leader of the Greeks, King Agamemnon, shows arrogance and lack of consideration for his followers. Achilles therefore refuses to serve him, withdraws his troops (the Myrmidons), and temporarily loses his own appetite for fighting.

A2 *Intense desire.* Agni learns from the supreme god Brahmā that the remedy for his depression is to consume Khāṇḍava forest and the fat of its inhabitants. Seven attempts fail because the fire is doused by water (either rain sent by Indra or water brought by the forest's inhabitants). Brahmā now advises Agni to call on Arjuna and Kṛṣṇa to help him satisfy his intense hunger.

Deprived of their best warrior, the Greeks fail in their attempts to defeat the Trojans. However, when Patroclus is killed by Hector, Achilles' profound grief leads on to fury and, more precisely, to a determination to kill Hector.

A3 *Absent male friend.* One or other side is strongly influenced by a personal friendship. Indra (side W) wants to protect Khāṇḍava forest because it is the home of his friend, the snake Takṣaka (215.7). Achilles (side F) wants to kill Trojans to avenge his dear friend Patroclus. Neither friend is physically involved in our conflict: Takṣaka is elsewhere (in fact at Kurukṣetra), and Patroclus is already dead.

A4 *Divine helper to central hero.* Although the Sanskrit has two heroes and the Greek only one, the difference is misleading. Kṛṣṇa is not only less prominent than Arjuna in this episode, but he is also far more of a god – as is clear in the *Bhagavad Gītā* (part of *Mbh.* 6). In fact, Kṛṣṇa often relates to Arjuna as Athena relates to Achilles or Odysseus (a huge topic!). Kṛṣṇa helping Arjuna here parallels Athena helping Achilles, as (e.g.) at 21.304.

Phase B: preparation

Sanskrit: Arjuna and Kṛṣṇa help Agni prepare to consume the forest and its inhabitants.

Greek: Achilles prepares to resume helping the Greeks against the Trojans.

Shared: *To join or rejoin the background conflict, the heroes prepare for battle.*

B1 *Deity visits hero.* Agni visits the heroes in the form of a red, blazing brahmin (214.29f), and Thetis with her sea nymphs visits Achilles (18.65–72). This visit marks the transition from the background to our episode proper and is one of many cases where the rapprochement is based on the action, not the agent. The similarity between Agni and Thetis is limited to this context and accordingly can be referred to as 'fleeting' when compared with more consistent and lasting resemblances.

B2 *Heroes need military equipment.* When Agni explains his situation and desires, Arjuna is happy to help him, but he needs equipment (bow, arrows, chariot, horses) – as does Kṛṣṇa. Agni agrees to provide it.

Thetis hears from her son of the death of Patroclus and of the loss of the armour he had borrowed from Achilles. Thetis promises to obtain what is needed (18.73–144).

B3 *Deity obtains equipment, which is welcomed.* Agni thinks of Varuṇa, who at once appears and supplies Arjuna's needs. Agni himself gives Kṛṣṇa a disk (used as a weapon) and a club. Thetis goes to Mount Olympus and visits Hephaestus, who promptly makes the panoply, including the famous shield.

When the equipment arrives, a dialogue takes place between the supplier and the hero. Agni and Thetis both praise the equipment, and the respective heroes are enthusiastic. Arjuna expresses his gratitude (216.26–29), as does Achilles (19.18–19).[4]

B4 *Craftsman god.* The divine arms given to Arjuna and Kṛṣṇa are described, but the only origin mentioned is that of the chariot, which was created by Prajāpati Viśvakarman. Viśvakarman is a craftsman god like Hephaestus.[5] Moreover, Varuṇa, Guardian of the Western Quarter, lives in the water as its lord (*jaleśvara* 216.1), and Hephaestus recalls spending nine years working amid the Ocean, when Hera threw him from heaven (18.394–403). So in both cases a deity who supplies arms lives or has lived in the sea.

B5 *Missile returns to thrower* (so that it can be reused). This motif applies to Kṛṣṇa's discus (216.24, 219.7) and to three missiles in the Greek (20.324, 20.441, 22.277).

B6 *Chariot and horses.* Arjuna's divine chariot and horses are described when he receives them but they fairly soon disappear from the text. Nothing is said about the heroes dismounting, but by the last line of the book (225.17) they are sitting on a river bank.

Similarly, Achilles' chariot and divine horses are mentioned early in the episode, but the hero soon seems to be on foot and has certainly abandoned his chariot by phase D. The chariot and horses simply fade out.

B7 *Fearsome noise helps side F.* On the flagpole of Arjuna's chariot there perches 'a divine monkey . . . which seemed to roar out', and on the flag itself large creatures are portrayed whose roars make enemies swoon (216.13–14). When Arjuna strings his bow, its twang causes fear (216.19), while Kṛṣṇa's club roars like a thunderbolt (216.25).

While the Trojans are trying to take the corpse of Patroclus, Achilles utters furious shouts, his voice reinforced by Athena's. The sound causes consternation among the Trojans, who abandon Patroclus' body (18.215–33).[6]

B8 *Happy scenes in town and country.* The subparvan opens by describing the peaceful and orderly life in the Pāṇḍava capital (214.1–13). Arjuna and Kṛṣṇa then leave the town with a crowd of women to enjoy a luxurious picnic in the countryside, after which they meet Agni. Achilles' shield is ornamented by Hephaestus with scenes, first of city life, then of rural life.

At the Indian picnic, the women wear garlands, receive fine clothes, and dance rapturously (214.22–23). On the shield, the country scenes end in a dance, involving garlanded maidens clad in fine linen (18.595–597, [see Ch. 13, 14]).

Phase C: conflict begins

Sanskrit: Arjuna and Kṛṣṇa start helping Agni by killing the creatures that try to escape.

Greek: Achilles starts fighting. His duels with Aeneas and Hector are abortive, but he kills other Trojans.

Shared: *Side F starts destroying side W, but the watery component of W is not yet actively involved.*

C1 *Victims thrown to destruction.* When animals try to jump out of the forest, Arjuna laughingly kills them and throws them back in the fire. In phase D,[7] Lycaon tries to leave the river and escape; when he begs for mercy, Achilles mockingly kills him and flings him back in the water (21.95–121).

C2 *Flames reach sky.* Agni's flames rise to the sky and worry the gods, who then involve Indra. When Achilles frightens the Trojans (B7), Athena makes him blaze, and the gleam goes towards heaven. It is as when a city is under siege and at sunset the beleaguered citizens light beacon fires and the glare shoots upward; the citizens hope that neighbouring islanders may sail to help them

(18.202–227, phase B). The islanders who potentially respond to the flames parallel the Sanskrit gods who actually respond.[8]

C3 *Fire burns forest.* Agni's activity finds another parallel within a Greek simile. Achilles (on side F), as he continues his slaughter, is compared to a fire raging through deep forests, driven on by the wind (20.490–494). In the main story too, Hephaestus, instructed by Hera, burns the trees on the banks of the river (21.337–338, 350–352).

C4 *Aquatic being.* In Khāṇḍava forest, the watery places (streams, marshes, ponds?) come to the boil, and turtles and fishes die in their thousands (217.9). In the Greek phase D, fishes are mentioned several times (21.121–127, 203–204), but the closest comparison is when Hephaestus, acting as Fire, torments the eels and fishes in Scamander's eddies (21.353).

C5 *Hither and thither.* Just before the reference to the turtles and fishes the creatures of the forest are described as darting 'hither and thither' (*tatra tatra* 217.7). Tormented by Hephaestus, the eels and fishes plunge 'this way and that' (*entha kai entha* 21.354).

Phase D: conflict of elements

Sanskrit: Indra now tries to protect the forest, using rain, thunderbolts, and rocks, but the heroes prove invincible.

Greek: After some Trojans flee into the Scamander – mostly in vain, the river attacks and threatens to overwhelm Achilles, Hera calls on her son Hephaestus to help the hero, who survives.

Shared: *Conflict rages, involving multiple participants.*

D1 *Element-linked new participants.* The new figures who now join the battle add to its scale and give it cosmic resonance. The most important among them are individuals closely linked with elements. As already implied, Indra's rain represents water, being opposed to Agni (Fire), who is already involved. In Greece, the new participant is Hephaestus (here in the role of fire, not as an anthropomorphic craftsman); his opponent is Scamander, who is already involved.

In both epics, the new participant is assisted by wind (the mobile and macroscopic form of the element air). Vāyu, the wind god, assists Indra in raising the rainstorm, and to help Hephaestus, Hera rouses the West and South winds (21.334). So the winds help side W in India, side F in Greece. However, the wind also helps Agni, by serving as his charioteer (*agniḥ . . . vāta-sārathiḥ* 219.36). We shall come back to the inconsistency. The point here is simply the involvement of beings linked with the three mobile elements.

D2 *Other divine participants are listed.* There is also a less important class of new participants. When Arjuna has countered Indra's thunderbolt, he is attacked by several types of supernatural entities, including snakes, demons, and gods (218.23). In fact, some fifteen gods are listed as accompanying Indra, each with his own name and weapon (218.31–35). One final verse (36) lists groups of gods, such as Rudras, Vasus, and Maruts.

In Greece, Zeus calls a divine assembly, attended by individual gods and by two groups, namely rivers and nymphs [20.5–9]. He tells the gods to choose one or other side to support on the battlefield, and the text gives us five pairs of names, one pro-Greek god paired with one pro-Trojan. Hephaestus and Scamander come last in the list [at 20.73–74], though they actually fight first.

D3 *Side W birds.* During this phase, birds *(garuḍas)*, resembling thunderbolts, fly down from the sky to attack the heroes (218.20) but are killed by Arjuna. In the next book, just before Achilles kills him, Hector darts down like an eagle swooping through the clouds to seize a lamb or hare (22.306–311).

D4 *Side W's anger and aggression.* The new participants contribute to an escalation of the conflict. In Sanskrit Phase C side F encounters no opposition, and the only emotions mentioned are the terror of victims and the happiness of Agni. We now meet anger. When Indra's rain shafts are evaporated by Agni, and his initial attacks are countered by Arjuna, Indra is enraged and charges furiously on his elephant, wielding thunderbolt, rocks, and a mountain peak.

In Greek Phase C, Achilles meets little resistance. But after the hero kills Lycaon and Asteropaeus, Scamander loses patience and, with Apollo's encouragement, starts to attack him. He pursues Achilles across the plain, beats down on his shoulders and, still furious, calls on his brother river Simoïs to help.

D5 *Hero almost killed.* When Indra charges, he announces to the gods that the two heroes are dead (215.29). We must understand 'as good as dead' – it is a threat, heightening the tension, not an erroneous statement of fact.

Achilles thinks he is about to drown, and Hera recognizes this danger (21.281–283, 326–329).

D6 *Rescued or spared.* Six beings escape from the forest fire. Indra rescues the son of the snake Takṣaka (see A3), Arjuna spares the palace-building demon Maya, and Agni spares the four Śārṅgaka birds.

The comparable cases in the Greek are Aeneas, saved by Poseidon (20.75–350); Hector, temporarily saved by Apollo (20.419–454); and Agenor, also saved by Apollo (21.544–611). In both epics, the three instances of rescue are dispersed across the episode.

When saving the snake, Indra uses his *māyā*, his power of deception, and dazes Arjuna with wind and rain (218.9–10). When saving Aeneas, Poseidon sheds a temporary mist over the eyes of Achilles (20.321, 341), and when Apollo saves Agenor, he too uses trickery (*dolos*, 599, 604).[9]

D7 *King of Gods is happy.* Both our traditions share a curious air of light-heartedness, of being not quite serious. Indra may be a friend of Takṣaka, but he is the divine father of Arjuna, and their relations are normally excellent. His anger (noted in D4) can only be simulated (or perhaps a minor component in a mixture of emotions). As the text makes clear, what the god is really doing is testing his son. When the heroes successfully resist the gods, Indra is delighted (*paramāprīto*, 218.43), and he sends a rain of stones as a further test of Arjuna's bravery (*vīryaṃ jijñāsuḥ*, 'desiring to know' it, 44). When he sees the gods retreating, Indra's good mood is confirmed *(avastithaḥ prītaḥ)*, and he praises the two heroes (219.11). At the end of our episode, Indra offers the hero boons, mentioning his satisfaction at their achievement (*tuṣṭo 'smi*, 225.8).

When Zeus tells the assembled gods to join in the fighting, he tells Poseidon that he himself will stay on Olympus and enjoy the spectacle (*phrena terpsomai*, 20.23). He also explains that the gods are to fight in case the Trojans yield too easily to Achilles, but this seems a flimsy excuse, comparable to Indra's alleged friendship with Takṣaka. In any case, when the gods do begin to fight, Zeus' heart within him 'laughs for joy' (*egelasse . . . gēthosunēi*, 21.389–390). Here then, Indra resembles not Scamander, but Zeus.

Phase E: conflict contracts and ends

Sanskrit: Side W gods retreat. Voice tells them to return to heaven. Agni is finally satisfied.

Greek: Scamander yields to Hephaestus and Hera. After half-hearted fighting, most gods return to heaven. Achilles continues killing Trojans and finally kills Hector.

Shared: *Reinforcements to side W accept defeat and withdraw. Side F fulfils original desire.*

E1 *Combatants obey higher power.* Having enjoyed his son's success, Indra might have departed spontaneously, but in fact a disembodied Voice (*vāg a-śarīriṇī*, 219.12) instructs him to do so, mentioning that the forest is destined for destruction. Indra accepts the authority of the Voice, and Agni is implicitly allowed to continue.

Having failed to conciliate Hephaestus, Scamander prays to Hera, who stops the two gods from fighting. In prompting the de-escalation of violence, Hera's authority parallels that of the Voice. Possibly this Voice–Hera correspondence finds extra support in the sex of Vāc ('Voice'); this goddess is sometimes said to be the consort of Brahmā, as Hera is the consort (wife as well as sister) of Zeus.

E2 *Undefeatable, so calm down.* The Voice states that the heroes 'cannot be vanquished in any world' (219.16), and after hearing it, Indra 'sheds his wrath and indignation' (*kopāmarṣau*, 19). In conceding defeat, Scamander remarks that Hephaestus cannot be matched (*antipherizein*, 21.357) by any of the gods, and on Hera's instructions, the river's 'fury is quelled' (*damē menos*, 21.383).

E3 *Hero like lion.* When the gods depart, the Indian heroes emit a lion's roar. Although no roar is mentioned, Achilles is compared twice to a lion. The comparison is made once by the poet in a lengthy simile during the fight with Aeneas and again by Achilles himself in his final dialogue with Hector [20.164, 22.262].

Lions tend to kill deer, and deer appear on side W. A list of the forest inhabitants includes *mṛgās* (219.2), and the twelve Trojan princes captured by Achilles are compared to frightened fawns (*nebrous* 21.29).

E4 *King of Gods watches.* The Voice tells Indra to watch the forest fire, and no doubt he does. As he has planned (D7), Zeus enjoys the sight of the gods bickering on the plain of Troy, and he also watches the final Achilles–Hector duel (22.166–167).

E5 *Shelter under banks.* Desperate to escape, the forest inhabitants seek shelter behind banks (*rodhaḥsu*, 219.28). The Trojans who jumped into Scamander cower beneath its steep banks (21.25).

E6 *Hot fat.* Although Agni sometimes says he wants to consume the forest as such (e.g. 215.10), what he most desires is its inhabitants – their flesh and blood, and above all their fat. According to Brahmā (A2), it is the fat that will restore Agni to normality (Appx 1.118, line 108). Fat becomes liquid when heated, and references are made (29.2–4) to 'floods of fat' (*medaughair*, 219.32), to melted fat *(vasā)*, and to the elixir or nectar *(sudhā)*, procured for Agni by the heroes, to rivers (*kulyās*, 225.6) of fat and marrow, to eating flesh and drinking fat and blood (225.16).[10]

When Scamander gives in to Hephaestus, his fair streams are seething – as when a cauldron is heated and the lard of a fatted pig melts and bubbles [21.361–5].

E7 *Satisfaction of initial desire.* Our episode began in an atmosphere of contentment (B8), and it ends similarly. Agni is completely satisfied, and Indra returns to congratulate and reward the heroes. At the very end of the book, Arjuna and Kṛṣṇa are sitting on 'the lovely river bank' and chatting constructively with Maya, one of those spared from the fire (D6).

Like Agni, Achilles achieves in Book 22 – by killing Hector – the vengeance that he so passionately desired at the start of the episode (A2). However, he only achieves peace of mind in Book 24 when he hands over Hector's corpse to Priam. Though the war will continue, for the moment the mood is one of reconciliation.

E8 *Closure.* In the Sanskrit, our episode forms a demarcated textual unit (*Upaparvan* 19). Introducing his commentary, Kirk (1985: 45f) proposes that the most natural division of the *Iliad* may be into three 'movements'. The second would end with the death of Patroclus, and the third would open with Achilles' return to battle. The *upaparvan* corresponds to the third movement.

This comparison can be reinforced in three ways. First, in both epics, the distinct or distinguishable episodes we have been studying are situated just before a major break in the narrative. In other words, looked at simply in terms of form, the end of *Mbh.* 1 corresponds to the end of the *Iliad.*

Second, within this short section of the narrative, but towards its end, we encounter subordinate parts that are distinct in character and introduce new individuals and themes. The Śārṅgaka sub-episode narrates the response of Agni (see D6) to the plight of four birds. A sage who wants children becomes a bird, mates accordingly with a wife in Khāṇḍava forest, and produces four fledglings. He leaves his nest for a new partner (Lapitā), but when Agni spares his offspring, he returns (for a fuller summary and discussion, see Hiltebeitel 2007: 118–123). The story is still about Agni's forest fire, but it concentrates on the family relationships between seven newly introduced characters, all of whom are named.

Even though the war remains in the background, *Iliad* Books 23 and 24 are not about fighting but about the fate of two corpses. Patroclus, killed by Hector in Book 17, is now cremated, and his death is marked by the funeral games; Hector, who was killed by Achilles in Book 22, is now ransomed by his father Priam and cremated by the Trojans. The new characters (new relative to our episode) include competitors at the games and the women who mourn Hector.[11]

Third, both epics display a similar ring composition. In phase A, Agni and Achilles conceive their desire. After the preparation phase B, they start consuming and killing in phase C. In phase D, the climax, they meet and overcome 'watery' opposition. Phase E starts by de-escalating the conflict so that the participants are as in phase C, then moves towards a degree of closure, both emotional and narratological.

Differences

It is useless to aim for a 'complete' comparison, since similarities need to be weighed against differences, and the differences are so many and so large that a long list would be of questionable use. A certain number of differences have already been implied, and I shall now list a few more, ignoring (among much else) the different languages, metres, names, and geographical/cultural settings.

> The two episodes are differently situated within the story line of the whole epic (whether one takes the Greek whole to be 'Homer' or 'The Cycle'). In India, the forest fire is a minor event occurring long before the Great War (which occupies Books 6–10 out of the 18), while our Greek episode is a major event *within* the corresponding Greek war.[12] This bears on the motif of testing the hero (D7). Arjuna is tested by Indra *in advance of* the Great War; Achilles is already fighting that war.

Agni and Hephaestus contrast in many ways. Agni is a major figure in the cult, while Hephaestus is not; Agni is scarcely a craftsman, and differs from Hephaestus in his motives. He is active throughout, and he consumes living beings, while Hephaestus, as Fire, is active only in phase D and consumes only corpses and vegetation. One of the greatest differences between the two epic traditions is the timing of the fire god's intervention. It contributes a good deal to the difficulty, at first reading, of appreciating how similar the two stories really are.

However, fire is much more pervasive in the Greek than the Agni–Hephaestus comparison suggests. Achilles himself is 'fiery'. During the entire episode, he is assimilated to fire no fewer than twelve times (Richardson 1993: 138, commenting on the last such passage, 22.317–321). In general, the mortal Achilles resembles the mortal Arjuna (both are active throughout the episode). However, Achilles' fiery quality makes him resemble a fire god, while Arjuna is not particularly close to Agni. The quality shared by Achilles and Hephaestus reinforces the validity of 'side F' as an analytic concept, but it also hints at the great complexity of Achilles' persona.

The great Indra of side W, the atmospheric god of storms, clouds, and rain, contrasts markedly with the minor figure of Scamander. Although he attends Zeus' assembly, Scamander is normally tied down to the plain of Troy and to the physical form of a river. Moreover, one reason for his fighting is obedience to Zeus' orders. However, Indra corresponds not only to Scamander (D4, E1, etc.). As king of the gods, who enjoys himself, and watches the end of the conflict from afar (D7, E4), he also corresponds to Zeus.

Apart from Agni, the mass of the Indian gods are on side W. The Greek gods distribute themselves in mutually hostile pairs between the two sides (recalling the chief human warriors in the *Mahābhārata* Great War, and the gods in Norse and Iranian eschatological wars).

The forest and its inhabitants contrast with Troy and the Trojans (despite, for example, E5). The contrast might be thought of as nature versus culture, except that the forest contains supernatural beings who are neither plants nor animals.

A different type of contrast concerns the emotions of the audience. Sympathy is scarcely elicited for the victims of Agni, as it is for the Trojans and their downfall. This must relate partly to the first difference we noted. The Sanskrit episode is only a rehearsal: in the Great War itself Arjuna's victims do sometimes attract sympathy.

Cosmic overtones are implicit in the Sanskrit. The forest fire foreshadows the Great War, which itself is but one episode in the ever-renewed cosmic battle of gods and demons. Moreover, the Great War represents a break in cosmic time – it is debated whether the break separates *yugas* ('ages') or *kalpas* (sequences of yugas). Greece knows of cosmic battles, such as the

Titanomachy, and of cosmic sequences or cycles (Hesiod's five ages or five races), but within our episode demons are ignored, and the end of the heroic race seems far off.

A difference that would merit fuller treatment concerns theories of IE ideology. Dumézil's trifunctionalism is by now well known, but it can be argued that the ideology in fact exhibited a more inclusive pentadic structure, of which the five elements are one expression [Ch. 12]. Fire, air, and water would represent the traditional functions in the standard order – F1, F2, F3, while ether and earth (both essentially immobile) would represent respectively F4+ and F4−. The Sanskrit story conforms reasonably to the pentadic schema. Agni, appearing as a brahmin, represents F1 and opposes water, which Dumézil already linked with F3 (fertility, etc.). F2 is represented by air or, as here, by wind or its god, whose position seems intermediate or ambiguous: Vāyu assists Indra's brief storm, but he is also, and more enduringly, Agni's charioteer. A comparable ambiguity affects Indra, traditionally understood by Dumézilians as representing F2 (though there is more to be said [see Allen 2012a]). Publicly he joins side W and fights using water, but his true feeling is delight at the success of his son in championing side F. In other words, both Vāyu and Indra are in some sense allied with Agni – giving us the classic Dumézilian structure F1 + F2 versus F3.

However, the Sanskrit contains other important figures, even if we ignore Indra's troops. Above the fray, yet behind the action – uninvolved yet highly relevant, there stands Brahmā the Creator, representing F4+. It is he who sets in motion the whole epic, by agreeing to lighten the load of beings who oppress the earth, and it is he who sets in motion this particular episode by advising Agni to consume the forest and to call on Arjuna's help (A2).[13] At the other end of the hierarchy are the demonic inhabitants of the forest, representing F4−.

A similar analysis of the Greek would at best be partial. One can argue for Zeus F4+, winds F2, 'twinned' rivers (recalling Simoïs) F3, Trojans F4−, but without calling on the hypothetical element-function linkage (which would be circular), I see no reason to interpret Hephaestus or the 'fiery' Achilles as representing F1.[14] Here, as often, it seems that Sanskrit epic has retained more of the old IE functional ideology than the Greek.

As I say, it is easy to think of further differences, but these are not an obstacle to the common origin theory. They are exactly what one expects when oral traditions are passed on independently over long periods (the common linguistic ancestor of Greek and Sanskrit was perhaps spoken around 2500 BC).

Broader issues

Let us assume that the similarities we have listed are genuine, that is, that the texts say what I have alleged and that the 'shared features' have been accurately identified.

Could such a degree of similarity be explained other than by common origin? Independent invention, even in societies of comparable socioeconomic type, is surely impossible, and direct influence of one epic on the other (as if the *Mahābhārata* derived from Alexander taking Homer to India) is at least as unlikely. The natural explanation is that the similarities derive from a common origin in a proto-epic or proto-narrative, and the most economic hypothesis is that this was told in an early unwritten IE language.

In work of this sort, everything turns on whether the rapprochements are convincing. I shall comment first on their variety. One dimension of this can be called scope. The most global similarities are the *Two sides*, which form a framework dominating the whole episode, and the *Sequence of five phases*. Each phase in itself is a rapprochement applying to substantial parts of the narrative; one can also recall the twelve dispersed passages that link Achilles with fire and thus relate him to the fire gods. All these are broad-scope similarities. At the other end of the scale are tiny details such as C5, *Hither and thither*, which turns on the repetition of a single adverb and may perhaps be coincidental.

A common type of rapprochement links the Sanskrit main story with something in a Greek simile, for instance C3, *Fire burns forest*. My favourite example is E6, *Hot fat*, which reads oddly in Homer but makes perfect sense in the Sanskrit. The same phenomenon has been noted elsewhere [Ch. 3] and shows that narrow-scope comparisons can sometimes carry considerable weight. Rapprochements can also be formal, in that they concern the organization of the text rather than its content (E8).

The most important consideration is no doubt the number of rapprochements. Precise figures mean little, since the analyst can often bisect a single rapprochement or combine two or more separate ones. Nevertheless, we have assembled well over thirty. This number should be sufficient for it not to matter if a few (like C5) are rejected. Moreover, this particular chapter does not stand alone. The larger the number of acceptable rapprochements between the Sanskrit and Greek epics (some papers are already published, others will be), the more likely it becomes that the epics are cognate and the less sceptical one needs to feel a priori towards each new proposal. Moreover if, as I believe, a great deal of IE common heritage still remains to be recognized in other parts of the IE-speaking world, it is not only Sanskrit–Greek comparisons that are relevant to judgements of what is plausible.

What is the future for this sort of work? The implication is that the great majority of the similarities we have identified represent features that were already present in a proto-narrative. Theoretically, one can reasonably envisage the reconstruction of abstract schemes of proto-narratives, together with hypothetical accounts of the steps leading from there to the texts we read now. However, this can wait. A vast amount of basic intricate work is needed first. It is not only a matter of extending to other parts of the epic narratives the style of comparison attempted here and integrating the results, while giving due attention to the other branches of IE tradition, since we also need to incorporate intra-tradition comparisons. A hint of the complexities to be expected is given by some of the more stable rapprochements we have met; while Indra corresponds to Scamander and Zeus, Zeus corresponds to Indra and Brahmā. Significant and stable one-to-one correspondences may prove rare.

It would facilitate reconstruction if, given a particular rapprochement, we could say which attested version was the more conservative – the closer to the proto-narrative. My view, or hypothesis, is that the Sanskrit is usually the more conservative, the Greek more innovatory. For instance, one can plausibly derive Homeric similes, which are – speaking comparatively – a rare phenomenon, from ordinary stories such as the Sanskrit preserves, but not vice versa; and the Indian separation of the fire god and the craftsman god is probably older than their fusion in Hephaestus. But one cannot assume that the Greek is never the more conservative.

Notes

1 First published in 2010 as 'Hephaestus and Agni: gods and men on the battlefield in Greek and Sanskrit epics'.

2 Within the subparvan, 'The Śārṅgakas' (1,220–25.4) forms a distinct sub-story, labelled as such in some of the manuscript colophons; it is of only limited use here. I use the CE, which is translated by van Buitenen (1973: 412–431, including the sub-story). This edition relegates a good deal of text to its footnotes or to Appx 1. Such text, normally omitted by van Buitenen, can usually be found in Ganguli (1993 I Book 1: 432–455). Unless specially mentioned, all references are to *Mbh.* 1.

3 I use this name (its 'human name') throughout, though the gods call the river Xanthus [20.74].

4 Arjuna then urges Agni to burn vigorously (216.30), and the fire starts straight after this. Just before the start of the fire–water battle in the Greek, Hephaestus receives similar encouragement from his mother (21.333).

5 Another supernatural craftsman appears at the end of the episode, namely the *asura* Maya, who is allowed to escape the fire. He describes himself as the Viśvakarman of the demons (2,1.5).

6 Achilles also utters a fearful cry when he calls the Greeks to the assembly (19.41). Loud noises are frequent in both texts and might reward a more systematic study.

7 Comparisons that straddle phases are presented according to their position in the Sanskrit.

8 Cf. also a later comparison: the suffering Achilles inflicts on the Trojans is as when the smoke rising from a burning city 'reaches broad heaven' and the anger of the gods drives it on (21.522, phase E).

9 Arjuna tells Maya not to be afraid (*mā bhair* 219.38), and Poseidon says much the same to Achilles (21.288).

10 Also to rivers *(kulyās)* of fat and marrow, and to Agni eating flesh and drinking fat and blood (225.6, 16). If Agni consumes meat, Achilles wishes he could carve up Hector and eat him raw (22.347); cf. also the Greek hero's assimilation to a lion (E3).

11 The two sub-episodes are not closely related, though a few points can be noted: the emphasis on pity (for the helpless Śārṅgakas, for the two fallen warriors), a female (Hera, Lapitā) reproaches a male (Apollo, the sage), and a father (the sage, Priam), who yearns for his son(s), alive or dead.

12 One of the arguments for the correspondence is the five-phase structure of the wars. Four leaders of the Kauravas and four leaders of the Trojans succeed each other before a final nocturnal massacre in an enclosed area (Allen 2011).
13 If the disembodied Voice is his, or expresses his views, he also directly steers events.
14 The approach in terms of functions could be enriched by bringing in eschatological battles from Scandinavia, where the fiery Surtr fights and kills third-functional Freyr, and from Iran, where the fiery Aša Vahišta fights Indra (here demonic).

20

HEROES AND SUPERCATEGORIES

That the Greek epic tradition draws on the linguistic, poetic and cultural traditions of early Indo-European (IE) speakers is not controversial,[1] but how far the same prehistory applies to the narrative substance of the tradition – the major personalities, divine and human, and the events in which they participate – is another matter. In practice, most Homerists, even those who refer to folklore, the Bible, *Gilgamesh*, and/or other West Asian sources, give little attention to IE cultural comparativism and its potential contribution to their field. The present chapter, following up essay (Allen 2011), argues that the major Homeric heroes tend to conform to a pattern that is characteristically IE. Along with comparisons presented elsewhere, this chapter is part of a larger argument claiming that Greek epic tradition goes back to an early IE proto-narrative, aspects of which can be reconstructed by comparison with the Sanskrit epic tradition, especially the *Mahābhārata*.

Paradoxically, the slow and halting progress in appreciation of the IE dimension of Greek epic has been due in good part to the dominant IE cultural comparativist of the last century. In his mature work, Georges Dumézil said relatively little about early Greece, explaining that in his early work (pre-1938) Greek evidence had often led him astray, so that he subsequently became excessively prudent (Dumézil 1987: 125, 163). He did not think that Greek tradition totally lacked the 'trifunctional' patterns so characteristic of the rest of the early IE world but rather that it marginalized and de-emphasized them.

Dumézil's attitude is expressed particularly clearly in his massive *Mythe et épopée* (1968–1973). The first volume, subtitled *L'idéologie des trois fonctions dans les épopées des peuples indo-européens*, consists of four parts, of decreasing length, devoted respectively to the *Mahābhārata*, to Rome, to the Nart traditions of the Caucasus, and to 'Epica Minora'. Since the Nart traditions come originally from the Ossetes, whose language belongs to the Indo-Iranian taxon of IE, Parts I–III between them cover the Indo-Iranian East and the Roman West, both of which are relatively conservative in other linguistic and cultural respects. Discussion of Greek epic is limited to the 'Judgement of Paris' and occupies a mere six pages in Part IV (580–586).

Dumézil's volume ends by contrasting the extremities of Indo-Europaea with its centre, and with Greece in particular. It is the extremities that make most use of trifunctional patterns in their epics – so much so that the individual characters, entirely defined by their functions, scarcely present any psychological interest; the main figures examined in his Parts I–III conform so consistently with the types they represent that their reactions become predictable. Greece is different. Though Homer knew the trifunctional story of the three goddesses, he did little more than allude to it, and as regards mortals, the Greek bards avoided imprisoning them in the corset of the functions: Achilles is a figure as complex as the historical Alexander or Julius Caesar. In other words, Greece broke free from the traditional ideological schema, with its pre-established relationships, and 'looked at man, society and the world with fresh eyes' (Dumézil 1968: 633). Because of this 'Greek miracle', the style of exegesis called for by the *Mahābhārata* and provided in his Part I casts no light on the genesis of the world's most famous epic (*ibid*: 580–581).

This view seems to me exaggerated. One objection lies in something that Dumézil recognized elsewhere, on the basis of Sanskrit–Norse comparisons, namely that early IE-speakers possessed an oral epic literature (*ibid*: 257, and Dumézil 1971: 132). If so, it is unlikely that the Greek epic tradition diverged from the proto-narrative so radically that comparativism has *nothing* useful to say about its narrative content. Indeed, various comparisons have been proposed, and if I do not attempt a review it is largely because of a second weakness in Dumézil's case. To compare Sanskrit and Homeric heroes – as for many other purposes – trifunctional theory is insufficient. For twenty years, arguments have been accumulating that it needs to be subsumed within a pentadic theory of IE ideology. Since this theory has been stated many times (e.g. Allen 2000a: 39–60, 2011: 344f), the following introduction gives only the bare minimum required for this essay.

Let us construct a model ideology for a society consisting of five social units – say clans. In rituals, the clans show a hierarchical division of labour, specializing respectively in the functions of master of ceremony, priest, warrior, producer, and scapegoat. Let each clan have its own appropriately specialized deity, and let each clan or deity be linked with a region of space (centre and four quarters), with an element, and with a colour. If we write each domain as a row and one row beneath another, entries sharing a column will be ideologically linked. Each column now represents one of five supercategories – 'super-' in that it cross-cuts the rows or domains, which themselves may consist of categories in the normal sense (categories of activity, of space, etc.). Clearly, the society can use the same pattern for an indefinite number of other domains, for instance when narrating a myth or epic. If so, one will find contexts having delimited sets of five agents (or events, episodes, locations, stages in a life cycle, etc.), such that each entry falls convincingly into one and only one column. Whether the natives label each supercategory or are simply aware of vertical associations within columns and of horizontal oppositions between them hardly matters, but supercategory labels are indispensable for the analyst.

The model, though anthropologically not implausible, is presented here only as a short cut to understanding the sort of phenomenon we shall look for in Homer. Since I am building on Dumézil and not starting from scratch, I label the IE supercategories using F for 'function' and the well-established numerals that he attached to the three functions he recognized, but we need to add F4+ and F4− respectively at the top and bottom of his hierarchy, as in row 1 of Table 20.1. As to the content of the supercategories, a single English word cannot be expected to provide a full definition, but row 2 of Table 20.1 makes an attempt in that direction: each entry suggests a focus for the bundle of ideas applying to its column:

TABLE 20.1 Overview of the argument

1, label	*F4+*	*F1*	*F2*	*F3*	*F4−*
2, focus	*transcendence*	*wisdom*	*force*	*abundance*	*devaluation*
3, *Mbh.*	Arjuna	Yudhiṣṭhira	Bhīma	Nakula+Sahadeva	Duryo./Karṇa
4, *Od.* 22	Odysseus	Mentor	(Telem.)	Eumaeus+Phil.	Antinous
5, *Il.* 3	Odysseus	Agamem.	Ajax	Castor+Pollux	Priam
6, *Il.* 9	Odysseus	Phoenix	Ajax	Odius+Eurybates	Achilles
7, *Od.* 1	Odysseus	Agamem.	Ajax	Achilles(+Patro.)	(Persephone)
8, *Od.* 24	Hermes/Odysseus	Agamem.	(Ajax)	Achilles(+Patro.)	Amphimedon
9, death	Odysseus	Agamem.	Ajax	Achilles, Patro.	Palam./Iphig.

Note: Row 1: labels used for the supercategories or functions recognized by pentadic theory. Row 2: 'focal' concepts in the definitions of the functions. Rows 3–8: manifestations of the ideology in particular epic contexts; bracketed entries are problematic in various ways, as discussed in the text. Row 9: the sequence of deaths, to be read right to left.

Within the Dumézilian tradition the interpretation of kingship has been a longstanding problem, but I do not think it is solved by including 'sovereignty' in the definition of F1. The idea of abundance (under F3) is to be understood as extending to cover its conditions and consequences, for example fertility and good health. The valued and devalued F4 supercategories contain entries that belong to the pentads laid out horizontally but are in some sense heterogeneous relative to the remaining triad of entries (the 'core' of the ideology).

Taken together, rows 1 and 2 indicate the structure or pattern of early IE ideology according to pentadic theory. My aim is to show that this pattern can be recognized, albeit with some blurring, among the personnel of Homeric tradition; Table 20.1 indicates the course we shall be taking. But before turning to Homer, it will be helpful to glance at the Sanskrit tradition, where the pattern is particularly clear and prominent (Allen 1999a).

Pāṇḍavas and Kauravas

The *Mahābhārata (Mbh.)* centres on an eighteen-day Great War, and when used in a broad sense, 'Pāṇḍavas' refers to the coalition that defeats the Kauravas. Used more narrowly, the term refers to the central figures among the victors, namely the five sons ascribed to King Pāṇḍu. Owing to a curse, Pāṇḍu cannot beget them himself, but his senior wife Kuntī summons, one after another, three gods to act on his behalf. A single use of Kuntī's spell is allowed to her junior co-wife Mādrī, who cannily summons the Sanskrit Divine Twins and thus gives birth to twin heroes. The births take place at yearly intervals, the gods and heroes being matched as follows:

Divine begetters:	Dharma	Vāyu	Indra	Aśvins (twins)
Pāṇḍava heroes:	Yudhiṣṭhira	Bhīma	Arjuna	Nakula+Sahadeva

After the Pāṇḍava victory, it is the eldest brother, Yudhiṣṭhira, who becomes king. The twins, being youngest and born from the junior wife, rank lowest (their mutual birth order being little emphasized). When the text presents the Pāṇḍavas as individuals, it typically does so by birth order, eldest first.

Trifunctional analysis uses several types of argument. The divine begetters manifest the functions by virtue of their intrinsic attributes and relationships. The heroes fall under the same functions as their genitors by virtue of their birth stories, their characteristic attitudes and behaviour, and the disguises they choose when they spend a year incognito. The arguments for seeing Yudhiṣṭhira, Bhīma, and the twins as representing respectively F1, F2, and F3 are mutually reinforcing and extremely strong.

However, the third son is special. Rather than reflecting his position as her youngest, Arjuna's birth forms the climax of Kuntī's child-bearing: it needs exceptional preparation and receives exceptional welcome from celestials. It is Arjuna who wins Draupadī, the wife shared by the brothers in polyandrous union, and it is he who accompanies the royal horse in the great Horse Sacrifice. He enjoys a unique relationship with the god-man Kṛṣṇa, and his marriage to Kṛṣṇa's sister enables the long-term survival of the dynasty. Moreover, unlike Dharma, Arjuna's father Indra is often and emphatically King of the Gods. In one passage (*Mbh.* 1.189, summarized by Smith 2009: 74), all five Pāṇḍavas are presented as Indras – they are never presented as five Dharmas, Vāyus, or Aśvins.

To accommodate the very different figures of Bhīma and Arjuna, trifunctional theory distinguishes two aspects of F2, respectively the brutal and the chivalrous. But the comparative evidence for such a split is limited, and pentadic theory argues instead that Arjuna, like his divine father, is in certain ways transcendent. We must distinguish two ways of ranking him. In terms of birth order or seniority, he occupies the central position within the pentad, and the F2 interpretation makes sense. But fundamentally he belongs at the top of the hierarchy, under F4+.

Although there are *five* Pāṇḍava brothers, the twins are so closely interlinked that the set of brothers covers only *four* of the supercategories, leaving vacant the F4− slot at the bottom of the hierarchy. As is not uncommon, more than one candidate is available for this position, each being satisfactory in different contexts or from different points of view. In the global context of the Great War, the enemy *par excellence* is the Kaurava leader Duryodhana, the Pāṇḍavas' cousin, an incarnation of the demon Kali (who presides over the fourth, last, and worst of the cyclical eras or *yugas*). This interpretation fits the pattern of journeys in Book 3, where Arjuna (F4+) ascends to Indra's heaven, the other Pāṇḍavas (F1–3) travel on earth, and Duryodhana (F4−) descends overnight to the underworld (Allen 2000a: 122–135).

However, in the narrower familial context, the devalued outsider is Kuntī's bastard son Karṇa. Born before Kuntī married Pāṇḍu, and cast adrift on a river, Karṇa is rescued by a low-caste couple and becomes a loyal ally of Duryodhana. One need not choose between Duryodhana and Karṇa as fillers of the F4− position; the need is rather to develop a sense of structure flexible enough to accommodate such alternatives. So we can write:

3, *Mbh.*	Arjuna	Yudhiṣṭhira	Bhīma	Nakula+Sahadeva	Duryodhana/Karṇa

Since all the legitimate Pāṇḍavas belong to the F2 social estate of Warriors, their classification according to supercategory (Table 20.1, row 3) is involuted within the superordinate classification of society into the four estates *(varṇas)*.

Massacre of the suitors (*Od.* 22)

While the *Mahābhārata* centres on a single great conflict, Homer gives us one for each epic. Pāṇḍavas-versus-Kauravas corresponds not only to Achaeans-versus-Trojans but also to Odysseus+team-versus-suitors – all three cases representing Goodies versus Baddies [Ch. 17]. Odysseus' team consists of himself, his son Telemachus, and the two stockmen, but during the battle they are for a while reinforced by a fifth figure who looks and sounds like Mentor, and is addressed and referred to as such (22.205–240, 249; 24.445–446). Mentor is in fact the human disguise repeatedly adopted by Athena, as is known or suspected by some who see her, but if we emphasize the human form rather than the divine essence, the victorious team consists of five mortals.

Within this team the top and bottom of the hierarchy are clear. Odysseus the king is leader, while Eumaeus and Philoetius, respectively swine-herd and neatherd, are servants who, for present purposes, can be treated as of equal rank. Of the other two, Mentor the Ithacan, more or less the same age as Odysseus, is his old friend; it was to him that the king entrusted his household when he left for Troy (2.224–227, 22.208–209). Although Telemachus is of royal blood, his youth and inexperience make it seem natural that in practice he subordinates himself to Mentor the *gerōn* [elder].

Hierarchy alone does not demonstrate that a set manifests the pentadic ideology: the members of the set also need to fit the definitions of the supercategories. A king often transcends the society he rules and, as the only king in the context, Odysseus qualifies as F4+. Mentor is closely associated with the diviner Halitherses, an aged hero (*gerōn* again), who surpasses his contemporaries in augury and prophecy (2.157–159, 24.451–456). The two of them speak insightfully in the Ithacan assembly in Book 2 – the only context in which the veritable mortal Mentor enters the story. The canny Odysseus would hardly befriend and entrust his family to a dimwit, and it is equally unlikely that a goddess would choose one for her disguise – especially a goddess who is the daughter of Metis ('Cunning Intelligence'), and claims a reputation for that attribute.[2] Even Mentor's name, from IE **men* 'think', implies his good sense. So Mentor fits well under F1.

The next figure in the hierarchy is more problematic. As Homer presents him, Telemachus is neither outstandingly strong in physique nor particularly strong in character: the portrait is rather that of an adolescent, still finding his feet in the adult world. Admittedly, Telemachus aspires to strength and martial prowess (e.g. 21.369–373, 24.506–515), and he would probably have strung Odysseus' great bow if his father had not discouraged him (21.125–129). But the best argument for associating him with F2 is the phrase *hierē īs Tēlemachoio*, which occurs seven times in the *Odyssey* (Russo 1992: 49–51). It belongs to a curious but much-discussed class of formulae in which the nominative of a proper name is replaced by a reference to the quality *(menos, īs)* of the individual, whose proper name is in the genitive (West 2007: 89). The adjective *hieros* is cognate with Sanskrit *iṣirá* 'strong, impetuous', and the noun, meaning 'force, strength', is cognate with Latin *vis*. So although Telemachus does not qualify synchronically as F2, the formula implies that he derives from one or more figures of whom at least one was notably strong.

Within Odysseus' team, the final pair presents no such complication. Responsible for livestock, Eumaeus and Philoetius produce what is both a major form of wealth and a major component in the copious nourishment enjoyed by the suitors at their feasts. They qualify excellently as F3. As for the F4− supercategory, from the viewpoint of Odysseus' team, the suitors in general are the devalued outsiders, and they are epitomized in their leader (S. West 1988: 121–122). Antinous, the 'contrary-minded', is the first to die in the massacre, and he alone dies without knowing the identity of his killer. Hence row 4:

4, *Od.* 22	Odysseus	Mentor	(Telemachus)	Eumaeus+Philoetius	Antinous

Telemachus is in brackets because, regarded synchronically, he earns his place in the F2 column by his presence in the team and his place in the hierarchy rather than by fitting the definition of F2. Possibly Mentor too could be bracketed since his divine nature sets him apart from the rest of his row – moreover, Athena's attributes overflow F1. However, I treat him as a mortal and leave him unbracketed.

Some brief comparisons with row 3 reinforce the analysis. Arjuna corresponds well to Odysseus in certain contexts [e.g. Ch. 5]. Yudhiṣṭhira is an indifferent warrior, and Mentor, while he encourages and defends Odysseus, and frightens the suitors with the aegis (22.256, 297–298), apparently kills no one. The pairing of Mādrī's twins and of the two stockmen is a phenomenon typical of F3 figures, probably reflecting the notion of abundance.[3] Among the Kauravas, the F4− Duryodhana is often addressed as 'king', though the title really belongs to his blind father; Antinous is once referred to by the phrase *hieron menos Antinooio* (18.34), which may suggest royal rank since the formula usually applies to King Alcinous. But in addition to individuals we can compare relationships. Among the Pāṇḍavas, before the Great War, Arjuna's ascent to heaven contrasts with his brothers' terrestrial pilgrimage much as, among the Goodies, Odysseus' journey to other-worldly Scheria contrasts with the stories of his helpers, who have either remained powerless in Ithaca or made the earthly journey to Pylos and Sparta. And just as Arjuna will recover the capital city that Duryodhana has occupied, so Odysseus is recovering the palace Antinous has occupied.

My next three sections examine selected passages that focus on a small number of Achaean leaders. I treat them in the Homeric order.

Teichoscopia (*Il.* 3.161–244)

Iliad 3 focuses on the duel between Menelaus and Paris, but after the initial arrangements the story is interrupted by the curious episode of the 'Viewing from the Wall'. Helen is told to go to the walls of Troy, where Priam and other elders are watching events on the plain. She is called over by Priam, who points out individual Achaean warriors, and asks her to identify them. Having quarrelled with Agamemnon in Book 1, Achilles is of course absent.

Priam asks first (166) about a tall figure who looks to him royal and proves to be Agamemnon. Having reacted, Priam now asks about a second figure (*deuteron* 191). This is Odysseus, as is confirmed by the Trojan Antenor, who has met him earlier. The third question (*to triton* 225) concerns Telamonian Ajax, who is identified in a single line (229). Without further questioning, Helen continues talking: near Ajax is standing Idomeneus, a frequent guest in her original home in Sparta, and she claims that she can recognize and name all the others. However (236), she cannot see her brothers Castor and Pollux. She wonders whether they failed to take part in the expedition, or have merely absented themselves today. The scene ends with a wry couplet from the 'omniscient' narrator: the brothers are in fact dead and buried in Sparta.

The Achaeans named in the passage are therefore Agamemnon, Odysseus, Ajax, Idomeneus, Castor, Pollux. Menelaus' name is mentioned by Antenor, and by Helen when she recalls Idomeneus' visits, but he is not pointed out. Among the other six, the first three are parallel in that each is the subject of a separate question by Priam and each is named by Helen in a line beginning *houtos* (followed by *ge* or *de*); the remaining three are introduced and treated differently.

Within the initial triad, no doubt Agamemnon comes first because he is the Greek leader, and Ajax last because he is the least significant. Some such hierarchy is suggested by the length of the questions and answers regarding each hero: Agamemnon has five and four lines respectively, Odysseus seven and three, Ajax two and one. However, this criterion leaves unclear the relative rank of the first two, and the issue is not resolved by the reactions to the names. Hearing about Agamemnon, Priam responds in a nine-line speech mainly concerned with the size of armies. Hearing about Odysseus, Antenor responds with twenty-one lines comparing him with Menelaus, recalling a visit to Troy made by the pair when they tried to negotiate the return of Helen. No response is given to the identification of Ajax.

The matter is not resolved either by the appearance of the two men. Agamemnon is large and tall *(pelōrios, megas)*, handsome *(kalos)*, and looks like a *basileus* [king]. Odysseus, though shorter, has broader shoulders and looks to Priam like a ram among ewes. To interpret the two heroes, we must look outside the immediate context.

Although Agamemnon is the recognized Achaean leader, and the Achaeans win the war, it can hardly be said that Agamemnon wins the war. During its fifth and final phase, he is far less prominent than Odysseus *ptoliporthos*, the sacker of the city. Moreover, the whole expedition is possible only because, when the suitors gathered to woo Helen, Odysseus proposed the oath obliging them all to help the successful suitor should his matrimonial rights be challenged. Again, in Book 2, when the army seems about to abandon the campaign, it is Odysseus, encouraged by Athena, who stems the defeatism and single-handed, as it seems, ensures that the war continues. So, while Agamemnon is the figurehead, Odysseus is the mastermind or *éminence grise* behind the Greeks. Being responsible for the genesis, continuation and successful conclusion of the campaign, he transcends and in that sense outranks the other Greeks.

Thus, hints can be found in the Iliadic tradition that Odysseus might represent F4+, as shown in row 4, but it is not clear that Agamemnon qualifies as F1. He is not presented as particularly knowledgeable, pious, or wise (anything but!), and although in the oath-taking that follows the *Teichoscopia* he takes on roles that other traditions might regard as priestly (killing the victims, praying), such actions can be read as a natural part of his duties as commander-in-chief. So let us turn to the Sanskrit.

The Pāṇḍava brothers present a very similar problem. Yudhiṣṭhira is the eldest and as a result becomes king, thereby in a sense outranking Arjuna. But Arjuna, son of the king of the gods and central in the birth order, represents F4+, while the pious Yudhiṣṭhira, son of Dharma, is among the clearest representatives one can find of F1. The Yudhiṣṭhira–Agamemnon homology can be approached from many points of view, for instance via the comparison between the brief quarrel of the former with Arjuna and the far more salient quarrel between the latter and Achilles; similarly, the Arjuna–Achilles homology is clear in the parallel episodes during which the heroes take on deities associated with water [Chs 16, 19].

If acceptable candidates are available for the top two functions, could Ajax represent F2? Physically, he is the largest of the Achaeans, and Helen sums him up as their defence *(herkos)*. Relatively little characterizes him apart from his warrior prowess, in which he is second only to Achilles. Like Bhīma, the F2 Pāṇḍava who is physically the largest of the brothers, Ajax is a good candidate for F2. Thus the triad Agamemnon+Odysseus+Ajax covers the same range of supercategories as the triad Yudhiṣṭhira+Bhīma+Arjuna – the three legitimate sons of Kuntī.

Of the remaining three names in the *Teichoscopia* list, Idomeneus is mentioned by Helen (she says) because he is standing close to Ajax, and indeed the two are often juxtaposed, spatially and in other ways (West 2011: 87). Possibly Homer includes him to explain why Helen starts thinking of her home and hence of her brothers

(Kirk 1985: 298), but whatever the reason for his presence, he is of less interest here than Castor and Pollux. Greek evidence connecting the pair to the definition of F3 is scanty, but the view that these 'Divine Twins' are cognate with the Aśvins enjoys 'a rare consensus among comparativists' (West 2007: 187), and the Aśvins, like their Pāṇḍava offspring, certainly represent F3.[4]

Helen's mention of the Aśvins prompts a slight digression to the interesting non-Dumézilian comparativist paper by Jamison (1994). Here the *Teichoscopia* is linked to an episode in *Mbh.* 3, during which Draupadī is forcibly abducted by King Jayadratha, only to be rescued a few hours later by the Pāṇḍavas. As the rescuers approach, the king tells his abductee to identify each husband, and she describes and names them in birth order. Jamison not only shows that the Greek and Sanskrit passages are cognate but also argues persuasively that the similarities are rooted in IE marital law. Her second objective tends to overshadow the first so that, for instance, nothing is made of the fact that the first figure described by each abductee is both the official leader and a relatively undistinguished warrior. Similarly, she notes that Helen ends the scene by referring to her twin brothers (who are absent) and that Draupadī ends her list by referring to her twin brothers (who are present), but she comments that 'it is probably wiser not to make too much of this' (Jamison 1994: 14). On the contrary!

Within the *Teichoscopia*, an obvious filler of the F4− position is Priam, the father of the abductor Paris, but also the king who represents the Trojans in general (including Antenor). Priam finds one of his parallels in Jayadratha, who is among the eleven Kaurava generals and eventually is blamed for the death of Arjuna's beloved son Abhimanyu. Very possibly Priam shares the F4− position with Helen, but I cannot here discuss such a fundamental question.

Let us simply sum up thus:

5, *Il.* 3	Odysseus	(Agamemnon)	Ajax	Castor+Pollux	Priam

Agamemnon is bracketed since he owes his position to his rank within the row and to comparative arguments, not to conformity to the definition of the column. Possibly the twins should be bracketed similarly. Comparisons can be made with row 4 but would distract us from the main purpose of the paper.

Embassy to Achilles (*Il.* 9)

In the absence of Achilles, the Trojans dominate the battlefield. When Nestor proposes an attempt at reconciliation, Agamemnon makes a generous offer. The terms will have to be put to Achilles by a deputation, and Nestor suggests its members: first Phoenix *(prōtista)*, who is to lead the way *(hēgēsasthō)*, then *(epeita)* Ajax and Odysseus, with two heralds in attendance – Odius and Eurybates. Nestor urges Odysseus in particular to speak persuasively. After a prayer and libation, the five-strong embassy sets off for Achilles' hut.

The envoys are received hospitably by Achilles and Patroclus. When Odysseus presents the agreed offer, Achilles forcefully rejects it. In tears, Phoenix speaks at length, but he too is rejected. Achilles invites him to spend the night, with a view to deciding the next day whether they should both sail back to Greece. Making the final and rather desperate appeal, Ajax gains the concession that Achilles *may* rejoin the fray when Hector starts burning boats and huts. Phoenix stays behind while the other four return. Odysseus reports the failure of the embassy.

Despite the priority that Nestor explicitly attributes to Phoenix when selecting the members, Odysseus is clearly the leader of the deputation and can again be interpreted as representing F4+. At the other end of the hierarchy, the heralds, who do not speak, occupy the lowest rank within the embassy, and their pairing suggests F3. There is no reason to change the interpretation of Ajax as F2, so the interesting question concerns F1 and Phoenix, who (as it were) replaces the Agamemnon of the *Teichoscopia*. When he speaks, Phoenix is introduced as an old man (*gerōn* 9.432), and he is addressed as one by Achilles (*atta geraye* 9.607). His age suggests long experience and corresponding wisdom, and his lengthy speech includes both theological moralizing and ancient lore. But the strongest internal argument is that, as he recalls, Phoenix was sent by Peleus to accompany the young and inexperienced Achilles as he set off for the Trojan War. In other words, Phoenix came to the Troad as a teacher (*didaskemenai* 442). He does for Achilles what Mentor (also a *gerōn*) did for Telemachus – indeed West very naturally refers to Phoenix as the young man's 'mentor' (2011: 13, 218). Moreover, just as at the Ithaca massacre Athena chose the form of Mentor to encourage Odysseus, so in the battle for Patroclus' corpse she chooses the form of Phoenix to encourage Menelaus (*Il.* 17.555).

From the point of view of the embassy, Achilles is the outsider. As a warrior he is of course not devalued – far from it, but his behaviour is deplored, and Ajax describes his attitude *(thumon)* as obdurate and evil (*kakon* 636). In effect, Achilles is now helping the Trojan enemy, and in this context (but certainly not in all others), he should be read as F4−. So:

6, *Il.* 9	Odysseus	Phoenix	Ajax	Odius+Eurybates	Achilles

It is interesting that the order in which the envoys are listed at their first mention – Phoenix+Ajax+Odysseus – is the birth order of their Sanskrit homologues, the three Pāṇḍavas born to Kuntī (row 3). Moreover, in *Mbh.* 5, which narrates the exchanges of embassies just before the outbreak of the Great War, the first ambassador sent by the Pāṇḍava coalition is the unnamed house-priest of King Drupada (e.g. Smith 2009: 293–294). In the standard classification of Hindu society into four estates, Brahmins represent F1, so in both epics, an F1 figure opens or leads the set of negotiators.[5] Finally, Achilles' adamant rejection of peace overtures parallels that of F4− Duryodhana and Karṇa.

Achaean heroes in the *Nekuia* (*Od.* 11.385–565)

During his *nostos*, Odysseus is sent by Circe to consult Tiresias in Hades, but while he is there he finds himself talking with or viewing many other figures. His encounters fall into four sets, separated into pairs by an 'intermezzo' [set in Phaeacia] after the first pair (Heubeck 1989: 77). The third set consists of the spirits of certain comrades from the Trojan War, and we need to consider both the identities of the comrades and what is said.

The first to approach Odysseus is Agamemnon, accompanied by those who were murdered alongside him when he returned home. Next comes Achilles, who is accompanied by Patroclus, Antilochus, and Ajax. Odysseus dialogues with Agamemnon and Achilles before being questioned by 'others' (*Od* 11.541–2), but we hear neither the wording of these latter questions nor whether or how Odysseus replied to them. Finally, he addresses Ajax, but receives no answer. If we ignore the unnamed 'others', the sub-episode contains four significant figures – the living Odysseus and the spirits of Agamemnon, Achilles, and Ajax.

As Heubeck (1989: 77) notes, this triad of spirits, which opens the post-intermezzo half of the *Nekuia*, balances the triad of figures that opens the first half of the story. Odysseus transcends this post-intermezzo triad in two senses. Being alive, he enjoys freedoms and possibilities totally beyond the reach of the inhabitants of Hades, with their restricted, dark, and miserable existence. Moreover, he unifies the whole scene, by interacting with each member of this triad (as he did with the initial triad), while each member has to take his turn. Thus, he is given six speeches (out of the ten), while Agamemnon and Achilles have only two each. Even if attention is confined to the *Nekuia*, Odysseus, the fortunate outsider to Hades, is an excellent candidate for F4+.

Three lines of intra-*Nekuia* argument can be used to analyze the triad of Achaean spirits. The first exploits the gap between Agamemnon and the other two heroes. If Agamemnon comes first, Achilles and Ajax come later (as members of the quartet). Agamemnon's priority, plus the fact that he has an escort, suggests that he still enjoys the higher rank that he had in the Troad, where we construed him as F1. No doubt another explanation for the priority is possible. As is well recognized, the *Odyssey* emphasizes the contrast between Odysseus returning to Penelope and Agamemnon returning to Clytemnestra – a contrast expressed in the juxtaposition. However, the two explanations are entirely compatible.

A stronger line of argument builds on Agamemnon's response to Odysseus' opening question about mode of death. Did Agamemnon die at sea in a storm? Or in armed conflict, either during a cattle raid in the country, or during a 'slave and plunder' raid on a city? Picking up these suggestions, Agamemnon uses them in a priamel.[6] His death was neither at sea, nor was it in armed conflict on land. Instead, Aegisthus invited him to a feast and then, with the help of Clytemnestra, killed him as one kills an ox at a stall. and his companions were slaughtered around him like pigs at a wedding feast or banquet.

Thus, the text presents in parallel three modes of death, all of which contrast with natural death from illness or old age: drowning, warfare, and the mode suffered by Agamemnon. Comparable triads have often been discussed by folklorists and trifunctionalists. Sometimes the different modes are inflicted on different victims, sometimes they are combined in the fate of just one; here they are alternatives envisaged for a single individual. Drowning is often linked with F3, and death from a weapon would fit F2; so the question arises whether Agamemnon's death could represent F1.

This is not the place to explore the point using later Greek texts.[7] Suffice it to say that, since F1 covers the wisdom embodied in law, insofar as Agamemnon's death is a punishment, it falls under the jural aspect of that function. What made the death so pitiful (*oiktistos* 412) is that, like an executed criminal, the victim was unable to defend himself. But a different view is suggested by the similes. The killing of defenceless domestic animals is central to most sacrifices, and although the similes present the event as secular rather than religious, other versions could have made it more like a sacrifice and closer to the religious aspect of F1. Perhaps this is hinted at by the emotional nature of the description – human sacrifice is often perceived as horrific and shocking. In any case, both points of view connect Agamemnon's death with F1.

This idea is strengthened by our third line of argument, which shifts the focus from Agamemnon to the triad of spirits. Ajax does not speak, but his attitude is clear from what Odysseus says, both to Alcinous (543–552) and to the spirit – as well as from the spirit's abrupt departure. In fact, Ajax is still furious at having lost to Odysseus in the contest for the arms of Achilles. The point is not how the loss occurred but the prize that was at stake – the arms themselves. Armour and weapons typically represent F2.

Achilles, like Agamemnon, ends his second speech by enquiring after close relatives (as do the unnamed spirits of 541–542), but he opens it by rejecting an attempt to comfort him. Odysseus has emphasized the respect that Achilles formerly enjoyed in the Troad and now enjoys among the dead, but the spirit claims that he would rather live as a hired labourer to a poor farmer than rule as king among the dead: 'Better *thēteuein* on earth than *anassein* in Hades', as Heubeck puts it. Agriculture – the production of food – is as closely linked with F3 as weapons are with F2. Can one imagine Ajax expressing this preference?

Agamemnon's preoccupation is different again. He is not a bad loser like Ajax, nor does he complain about being dead as such. His concern is rather with the moral issues and social relationships surrounding his death. He presumes to offer Odysseus misogynistic advice (such as has many parallels in the brahmanic *dharma* literature in India); he recalls his wife's failure to perform even such minimal rituals as closing his eyes and mouth as he lay dying (426); and he concludes that women are simply not to be trusted (*ouketi pistin gunaixin*, 11.456). Morality, teaching, ritual, and trust are all themes pointing to F1.[8]

The idea of Achilles as F3 may seem odd for two reasons. First, in row 6 he represented F4−, and second, as Odysseus recalls, Achilles surpassed Ajax in respect of his warrior deeds (his ἔργα 550; same wording as *Il.* 17.279) – which seems to give him an even stronger claim than Ajax to be entered under F2. But nothing about

Achilles is simple, and there are answers to both objections. On the most general level, even in the Sanskrit (where functional identities tend to be clearer and more consistent), an individual need not represent the same function in all contexts or in all respects (Allen 2012a). More specifically, Achilles represented F4− only during his mutiny, and his superiority to Ajax is to be interpreted by relating him to F4+ Arjuna, who is the supreme Pāṇḍava warrior. Arjuna's relationship to Bhīma was briefly compared with that of Achilles to Ajax by Vielle (1996: 140–141), and I have presented more detailed Arjuna–Achilles rapprochements elsewhere [Chs 16, 19].

The non-F3 aspects of Achilles are obvious and important, but his picture of himself as humble agricultural labourer (rather than, for instance, humble foot-soldier, craftsman, or slave), is only one among several pointers towards F3.

1 *Social rank.* Whatever the precise meaning of Agamemnon's claim to be more 'kingly' than Achilles (*basileuteros*, *Il.* 9.160), the latter clearly feels that the rank he is accorded is lower than it should be. Other respected warriors, notably Diomedes, sometimes complain of Agamemnon's leadership, but not for this reason. Commoners (the 'masses') generally rank as F3, and conflicts pitting F3 representatives against higher functions but ending in reconciliation are well recognized by comparativists (e.g. Dumézil 1968: 285–303).
2 *Property.* The third function covers all forms of wealth, including the nubile women who potentially produce offspring. Achilles resents Agamemnon's appropriation, not only of Briseis but also of the other wealth he himself won by plundering cities allied to Troy (*Il.* 1.167–168). Moreover, Achilles is a prominent collector of ransoms (for Lycaon 21.79; for Hector's body, esp. 24.594).
3 *Estrangement.* Achilles' estrangement from Agamemnon is comparable to three other Sanskrit stories in which a subordinate turns against a commander. Arjuna briefly quarrels with Yudhiṣṭhira; Karṇa refuses to serve under Bhīṣma; Madrī's brother Śalya, a very strong candidate for F3, transfers his loyalty from Pāṇḍavas to Kauravas because of his love of wealth [Ch. 16].
4 *Pairing.* F3 figures are often paired, as they have been in every row so far. Here too, Achilles forms a pair. In the *Nekuia*, he is accompanied by Antilochus as well as Patroclus, but it is to the latter that he is really close. Patroclus is his substitute or alter ego in *Il.* 16, and when they are both dead, their bones are mixed in a single golden urn. Antilochus is Achilles' *next* best friend, and his bones are buried separately.[9]
5 *Good looks.* F3 is recognized to extend to the physical beauty that facilitates sexual activity and fecundity and that characterizes the Pāṇḍava twins (Dumézil 1968: 56–57). Similarly, Achilles is the most handsome of the Achaeans (e.g. *Od.* 11.469, 550). This may be due in part to the golden locks that Athena seizes in *Il.* 1.197, though he is not the only hero whose hair is *xanthos*.
6 *Medical skill.* Good health also belongs under F3, as do the divine and human doctors who restore it. Among their other helpful skills, the Aśvins are divine doctors, and both Patroclus and Achilles can serve as human ones. The wounded

> Eurypylus is treated by Patroclus, who gained his knowledge from Achilles, himself a pupil of the Centaur Chiron. Achilles' best-known patient is Telephus (*Il.* 11.828–832; Apd. *Epit.* 3.20).

Further arguments will emerge in a later section (death sequence, cardinal points), but these six, taken together with Achilles' mention of agricultural labour, justify entering Achilles and Patroclus in the F3 column of row 7.[10] This leaves vacant only the F4− position in the row. Pentadic theory does not require that all five positions be filled in all contexts – trifunctional contexts manifesting only the core functions are common – so the *Nekuia* passage may simply lack an F4− representative. However, there exists one possible candidate.

The interaction with spirits cannot begin until Hades and Persephone have received a sacrifice (11.47), the Achaean heroes can approach Odysseus only when Persephone clears away the female spirits she had previously brought before him (226, 386), and the scene ends when Odysseus becomes afraid that the goddess may send against him the Gorgon's head (635). Homer sometimes describes Persephone as *epainē* 'dread', and in later sources, her abduction by Hades implies that she entered the underworld without dying – she is able to revisit her mother Demeter for part of the year. So, like Odysseus, she is present in the underworld but differs ontologically from its ordinary inhabitants, and she also differs from the Trojan heroes in her gender. Assuming she retains the devaluation or negativity that in most contexts hangs over everything connected with death, she qualifies as F4−. On the other hand, her involvement in the sub-episode is so marginal that I bracket her in row 7. Patroclus is bracketed since, although he could be among the 'other spirits' of line 541, he is not involved in any explicit dialogue.

7, *Od.* 11	Odysseus	Agamemnon	Ajax	Achilles(+Patroclus)	(Persephone)

Deuteronekuia (*Od.* 24.1–204)

Like the *Nekuia*, the *Deuteronekuia* involves a visit to Hades, but this time the visitor is not Odysseus, coming for a single night, but the dead suitors, who will stay indefinitely. For the purposes of this chapter, it is less helpful than the *Nekuia*.

Led down to the asphodel meadow by Hermes, the spirits first observe the quartet we met in the *Nekuia* – Achilles, Patroclus, Antilochus, and Ajax. When Agamemnon arrives, he is addressed by Achilles and responds with an account of what happened to Achilles' body after his death. When Hermes and his spirits approach the long-established residents, Agamemnon recognizes Amphimedon, with whom he stayed before the Trojan War on his recruiting visit to Ithaca. He questions the new arrival and hears about Penelope's tactics towards the suitors, Odysseus' return, and the massacre. Finally, Agamemnon contrasts the happy homecoming of Odysseus to Penelope with his own unhappy fate.

In one sense, Agamemnon has only two conversations – one with Achilles and one with Amphimedon. However, his final speech, although explicitly a response to Amphimedon (191), begins by addressing Odysseus: *olbie Laertao paï, polumēkhan' Odusseu*. It is as if Odysseus were present not only in Agamemnon's thoughts (as he was already in 116) but also in person. If this is accepted, we meet again three of the entries in row 7, and as for Ajax, he too (like Patroclus) is physically present. The fact that Ajax is ignored in the speeches does not much matter: he had the shortest treatment in the *Teichoscopia* and the shortest speech in the Embassy, and in the *Nekuia* he remained totally silent even when addressed.

This gives us four of the same entries as in row 7, and the similarity between the two *Nekuias* could make one wonder whether the second merits separate treatment. However, the F4 entries are more interesting. First, for the F4+ column, an additional or alternative entry is Hermes. Unlike Odysseus, the god is physically present; he outranks all the phantoms and, as psychopomp, transcends the life–death opposition that applies to mortals. Second, this context provides a really clear representative of F4−. As we saw at the start of the essay, the Suitors, corresponding to the Kauravas, globally fall under that supercategory, and they are here represented not by Antinous but, because of his link with Agamemnon, by Amphimedon.

8, *Od.* 24	Hermes/Odyss.	Agamemnon	(Ajax)	Achilles (+Patroclus)	Amphimedon

Times and places: Greek death order and cardinal points

So far we have studied sets of heroes who manifest the pentadic ideology within particular shortish stretches of text, but manifestations need not be limited in this way. The ideology is detectable in the five phases of the Trojan War, which themselves are demarcated by the deaths of Trojan leaders (Allen 2011: 348–350); so it might be worth considering the deaths of the Achaean leaders simply as a sequence, wherever the deaths are presented in the text. If we confine ourselves to figures who have already been mentioned and who are really prominent, we can ignore figures like Tlepolemus, son of Hercules, killed by Sarpedon in Book 5.

The first major Achaean casualty in the *Iliad* is Patroclus, who is followed by Achilles. The contest for the arms of Achilles leads to the suicide of Ajax, while Agamemnon, having survived the war, is assassinated on his return home. Odysseus outlives all of them and, says Teiresias (*Od.*11.134–136, will only die in old age. Thus, the deaths follow the hierarchy of functions in ascending order, starting from the lower ranking of the two F3 representatives. If we think of F3 Achilles as subsuming Patroclus, we can identify the quartet as the 'canonical' Achaean leaders. No doubt it is this special status that is reflected in the *Iliad*'s first list of Achaean heroes in 1.137–139: Agamemnon threatens to take the concubines of Achilles or Ajax, or even (the separation being expressed in the syntax) Odysseus.

In the Sanskrit, the death order is no less clear. All the Pāṇḍavas survive the Great War and enjoy the subsequent peace, but in the penultimate Book 17, the family walk north towards the Himalayas and the Other World. One by one, reversing the birth order, four of the brothers collapse and die, starting with the younger twin Sahadeva; only Yudhiṣṭhira reaches heaven without dying.

The next question is whether the sequence starts with a representative of F4−. In the Sanskrit, the first to die on the trek is Draupadī, her death being described in a manner exactly parallel to those of her husbands. The Greek presents two possible homologues. Though Homer does not mention it, later texts explain how the Greek fleet cannot leave Aulis unless Agamemnon sacrifices his daughter Iphigeneia. It is arguable that the victim of a Vedic sacrifice falls under F4− (Allen 2015b) and also that the same supercategory can cover a lone female in a set of males; this would make Iphigeneia a reasonable entry. The other candidate, equally ignored by Homer, is Palamedes. Apparently an important figure in the tradition, he is the subject of varied and discrepant stories, but the following facts are sufficient for our argument. His role was crucial in enabling the expedition to include the *ptoliporthos* Odysseus, without whom Troy might never have fallen. He thereby incurred the enmity of Odysseus, who engineered his death in the Greek camp – a death by stoning, sometimes at the bottom of a well (Gantz 1993: 603–606). Odysseus did this by persuading the Achaeans that Palamedes was a traitor, working on behalf of the Trojans – in other words that, like Achilles in row 6, he was an enemy such as we can put under F4−.

Both Iphigeneia and Palamedes die before Patroclus, so we can add a further row.

9, deaths	Odysseus	Agamemnon	Ajax	Achilles, Patroclus	Palamedes/Iphigeneia

Apart from illustrating again the variety shown by representatives of F4−, the row adds to the reasons for thinking that, in terms of functions, Odysseus outranks Agamemnon, and Ajax outranks Achilles.[11]

If the canonical Achaean heroes die in a temporal sequence reflecting the functions, one wonders if they show any comparable spatial patterning. The pentadic ideology fits well with the quincunx schema of transcendent centre plus four cardinal points – indeed the theory was initially suggested by the fivefold 'sacred geography' of early Ireland (Rees and Rees 1961: 121). The schema is prominent in Sanskrit epic, for instance in the various journeys during which travellers leave the centre and proceed clockwise around the four quarters of India (Allen 2007d). Similarly, during preparations for the inauguration of Yudhiṣṭhira in *Mbh.* 2, the latter stays in the centre and the other brothers conquer the quarters as follows: Arjuna, north; Bhīma, east; Sahadeva, south; Nakula, west. So are the Achaean heroes associated differentially with cardinal points?

At least by the early classical period, the Greeks located the centre of the world, its *omphalos*, at Delphi on Mount Parnassus. Odysseus comes from Ithaca, which lies west of Delphi, Agamemnon from Argos or Mycenae to its south, Ajax from Salamis more or less to its east, and Achilles from Phthia in Thessaly to the north. Although Patroclus was born to the north-east in Locris, he joined Achilles' household while still a boy. Of these figures, Agamemnon is said once to have consulted the oracle at Delphi (*Od.* 8.80), but only Odysseus has close family links with Mount Parnassus: he went there, for what is often regarded as his initiation, to visit his maternal grandfather Autolycus. Moreover, via his paternal grandfather Arcisius, his patriline can be traced upward to Hellen and Hellen's father Deucalion, who landed on Parnassus after the Flood.

The homes of the canonical heroes are not included in Table 20.1 since they do not manifest the pentadic ideology as such but correlate with a manifestation. If they were included, they would form a further row, associated with cardinal points:

(10, homes	Ithaca W	Argos etc. S	Salamis E	Phthia N[12]	– –)

If the dominant functional values are carried over from previous analyses, row 10 can be read either left to right/counterclockwise as a descending hierarchy starting in the west, or right to left/clockwise, as an ascending hierarchy starting in the north. The latter reading accords with the sequence of deaths in row 9.

Another way to present the facts (Table 20.2) is as a quincunx or mandala (I bracket Odysseus in the centre since it is not his normal home):

TABLE 20.2 Canonical Greek heroes arranged according to the cardinal points from which they come

	Achilles	
Odysseus	(Odysseus)	Ajax
	Agamemnon	

The major conflicts – Agamemnon versus Achilles and Odysseus versus Ajax – involve figures whose homes are diagonally opposite each other; relations between neighbouring figures tend to be better.

Though it is not necessary, it would be satisfying if a representative of F4– could be related to the schema. The best candidate is perhaps Thersites, who comes from Aetolia in the west, but I shall not pursue the idea or discuss his competitors. Instead, another spatial pattern merits attention. Ever since Aristarchus (second century BC), attempts have been made to establish the order in which the Greek leaders camped along the shore of the Troad, and the findings are summarized by commentators (Janko 1992: 131; Hainsworth 1993: 215). The positions of the canonical heroes are as follows:

West end	*Centre*		*East end*
Achilles (F3)	Odysseus (F4+)	Agamemnon (F1)	Ajax (F2)

In other words, Achilles (usually F3, but F4– when disaffected) is set apart from the group representing the higher functions; indeed, according to Nagy (2010: 162–163), Achilles' position was further from the 'centre' than Ajax's. But one can also arrive at the linear sequence of huts by starting from the circular model. Inserting a 'break-point' in the north-east, and moving clockwise from it, yields the same east–west sequence.[13]

Such consistency between the different sorts of phenomena – ideological, narratological, temporal, and spatial – could hardly arise by chance. It makes it unlikely that Greeks ever told versions of the Trojan War lacking F3 figures such as Achilles and Patroclus – as some have thought (West 2011: 42–45).

Concluding discussion

At this point, it will be useful to look back at Table 20.1.[14] After rows 1–2, which summarize the theoretical framework, row 3 reminds us that the question at issue is the relationship between epic traditions like the Sanskrit, where the functions dominate characterization of the heroes who represent them, and the Greek which, in Dumézil's view, has essentially broken free from the inherited ideology. If we were examining the Sanskrit for its own sake, row after row could be inserted presenting contexts in which the Pāṇḍavas and their enemies reflect the ideology – which is not to claim that every Sanskrit hero is always and only associated with one function.

Let us recall two other points. First, the left-to-right ordering of row 3, as of subsequent rows, is governed by the hierarchical order of the functions under which the entries are argued to fall, not by other principles, such as birth order or the sequence in which entries appear in a text. Second, the aim has been to use the central Sanskrit heroes as offering a reasonably clear manifestation of the pentadic ideology, useful in guiding and strengthening analyses of the Greek. A systematic comparison of the two narratives would be a different undertaking and would need to explore the contrasts between the two traditions. Obviously a set of brothers who die one after another in a single episode contrasts deeply with a set of unrelated heroes whose deaths are spread across numerous episodes. I believe that, in general, the Greek has moved further from the proto-narrative than the Sanskrit has but do not argue that case here.

The Greek rows 4–8 were selected with a view to showing that the pentadic ideology continued to pattern the narrative substance of some important Homeric figures, but many others of comparable importance have been left unstudied. However, the notion of an ideology patterning an oral narrative is ambiguous: it can be understood synchronically or diachronically. Theoretically, a poet who composes an oral text, or a bard who dictates it, may be more or less aware of the ideology expressed in it and may be able to explain it to an ethnographer, if questioned appropriately. But in the present context, a diachronic view is more plausible. However the written text originated, it drew on narrative material going back generations, even millennia, and the ideology it expressed could be one that was current long before writing. The hypothesis of a proto-narrative correlated with the language family tree provides a *terminus ante quem*, but the pentadic ideology and the narrative patterned by it could be older still.

The brackets in the Greek rows signal column entries whose justification is debatable. A critic might regard them as weaknesses in the argument and might propose other brackets, for instance around Odysseus in row 8. But, as we noted concerning Persephone, the influence of the pentadic ideology can be recognized even where one or two columns lack a perfect candidate. Moreover, the global history of the ideology in recent millennia has been one of decline, which implies processes of blurring and fragmentation – not to mention confusions and tensions between competing versions. What is surprising is not that the fit between texts and model is imperfect, but that so much pentadic patterning survives.

To look at Greek epic in an IE perspective is to adopt a paradigm with innumerable implications for topics that have long occupied Homerists and Hellenists. Instances that have been mentioned in passing are the interpretation of Phoenix in *Il.* 9 and the presence of an Achilles-like figure, no doubt paired, ever since the proto-narrative. But if indeed the proto-narrative contained a set of Goodies comparable to the Pāṇḍavas, the implications extend to most of what used to be called 'the Homeric question'. Systematic study of them lies in the future and calls for collaboration between Homerists and comparativists. The aim here has been to show that, with appropriate modifications, the approach taken in Dumézil (1968) does in fact, contrary to the author's own view, cast light on the genesis of the world's most famous epics. Indeed, it makes that genesis both more approachable and even more interesting.

Notes

1 First published in 2014 as 'Heroes and pentads; or how Indo-European is Greek epic?'
2 Metis: Hes. *Theog.* 886–896; Athena's claim: *Od.* 13.296–299.
3 Another instance is provided by Larcius and Herminius, the paired soldiers who help maintain food supplies during the siege of Rome by Porsenna (Briquel 2007, Ch. 3, esp. 103–104). For a proposed cognate pair in Buddhist tradition see, Allen (2002a).
4 Placed between Idomeneus and the twins, the many but unnamed 'others', the *allous pantas* of 234, may also be read as F3 – cf. the Viśve Devāḥ, the gods regarded either as a totality or as a mass distinct from their leaders (Dumézil 1968: 247–248; 1983: 25–27).
5 If the parallel is accepted, it should help with Homerists' long-standing difficulties in interpreting *Il.* 9.
6 This particular priamel is not discussed by Race (1982).
7 Cf. Evans (1979), which draws heavily on the *Oresteia*, but does not use any of our three lines of argument.
8 Regarding trust, see Dumézil on the Roman deity Fides (1968: 277, 1969a: 47–59).
9 *Od.* 24.76–79. I am not suggesting that Patroclus is *merely* a 'quasi-twin' to Achilles.
10 The processes (of amalgamation?) that have led from the proto-narrative to our current multi-aspectual Achilles are not studied here but might build on the 'closeness' between Arjuna and Karṇa, Kuntī's first- and last-born (fundamentally, I think, F4+ and F4−, respectively), also on the birth-order juxtaposition of Arjuna and F3 Nakula (the more military of the twins).
11 The modes of death *may* themselves reflect the functions [cf. now Allen 2018b]. Palamedes dies because of a malicious lie (F4−?); in later sources Achilles dies on a tryst (connoting F3 sexuality); Ajax dies by killing himself with a weapon; Agamemnon's death was linked earlier to F1; Odysseus' non-violent death falls outside the heroic norm.

12 Since Achilles and Patroclus have F3 medical skills, it is interesting that the two sons of Asclepius, the 'good doctors' Podalirius and Machaon (*Il.* 2.732), also come from the northern quarter (from Western Thessaly).
13 In India, the cardinal points associated with the gods called Lokapālas or 'World-Guardians' are usually north for F3 Kubera (god of wealth) and east for F2 Indra (god of war). During Arjuna's journey to heaven, Indra appears to him first as F2 Lokapāla and later as F4+ King of Heaven – cf. Odysseus' association with both west and centre.
14 The original paper here repeated that table.

21

CYAVANA AND PROMETHEUS

Though founded by linguists, the field of Indo-European (IE) studies has developed two offshoots or annexes – the archaeological and the socio-cultural.[1] The socio-cultural can be subdivided in various ways, for instance into domains (social structure, pantheon, myth/epic and ritual, legal systems, and so on), and/or by regions – which is to say, by branches of the language family. One tempting regional comparison is between India and Greece. This too can be subdivided, for instance on the basis of the texts used for the comparison. As regards India, much work has focused on the Vedas, especially the Rigveda, on the grounds that 'earlier' texts are more likely to contain IE heritage than 'later' ones.[2] However, contrary to this reasonable expectation, the allusive, elusive – even cryptic – Rigveda offers less narrative material suitable for comparison with Greece than does the copious epic tradition, especially the vast *Mahābhārata*.

A certain amount has been done on Homer–*Mahābhārata* comparison [e.g. Ch. 19], and another paper from the same point of view [Ch. 11] presented a Hesiod–*Mahābhārata* comparison. The present chapter continues the latter direction of study, though by no means exhausting its possibilities. The comparison concerns the myth of origin of a ritual. The Greek myth concerns animal sacrifice in general, while the Sanskrit is more specialized in that it concerns only *soma* sacrifices.

The first tasks are to introduce the figures who appear in my title and whom I call 'the protagonists,' and to contextualize the stories about them. Cyavana is a brahmin – a sage and ascetic. Of the various stories about him I discuss only the one best told in *Mbh.* 3.[3] At this point, Arjuna is visiting his divine father in heaven, and the other four Pāṇḍava brothers are starting their pilgrimage round India, guided by the brahmin Lomaśa. When the party reaches a sacred location, Lomaśa often tells a story associated with it – an 'encapsulated' story, that is, one that is not part of the main plot of the epic. At the location in question, in the course of a sacrifice,

Cyavana once helped the Aśvins, disputing with Indra and getting his own way. Part of the story is told again in Book 13, in a didactic passage about the superiority of brahmins to warriors.[4] This version ('Version II') is shorter than the other (Version I), and I make less use of it.

The story of Prometheus is told by Hesiod in the *Theogony* (West 1966). This poem contains genealogies of the gods (as its name suggests) but also the Succession Myth, which narrates the succession of Ouranos, Cronus, and Zeus as leaders among the gods. The Prometheus story (lines 507–616) comes between Zeus' rise to power and his war against the Titans. In the course of a sacrifice, Prometheus once helped humanity, disputing with Zeus and getting his own way. Part of the story is told again in *Works and Days* (*WD*, 42–105), Hesiod's other main poem, near the start. It is introduced as explaining why the life of mortals is so laborious and bears only slightly on the theme of sacrifice.[5]

The aim of the chapter is to compare two stories which, as far as I know, have not been compared before. We are studying not stories A and B in themselves, but in their mutual relationship, concentrating on similarities. For this purpose, it is not essential to explore at length secondary literature (either comparativist or specialist) that focuses on one of the stories without citing the other. Cyavana's story is in fact reasonably well known to IE cultural comparativists through the writings of Dumézil (esp. 1995). Dumézil compared it with the Norse story of Mímir and Kvasir, arguing that it illustrated a feature of IE doctrine. His point was that divine society, like human society, remained incomplete until [after a conflict] representatives of the third function (such as the Aśvins) were admitted to join with representatives of the first two functions. The interpretation seems to me persuasive but is only tangentially relevant here. As for the classicist literature on Prometheus, it is of course enormous.[6]

But what is the point of comparing the stories? My background assumption, like that of several IE comparativists, is that much of the narrative heritage of India and Greece goes back to shared ancestral narratives told in early IE times – to 'proto-narratives'. I have also [e.g. in Ch. 17] been exploring the hypothesis that the Greek tradition quite often fuses or amalgamates traditions that were separate in the proto-narrative and remain separate in the Sanskrit. I believe this applies to the present case. The similarities between the Cyavana and Prometheus stories go back to a proto-narrative, but I suspect that the Prometheus story draws on at least one other proto-narrative that is well preserved in the Sanskrit. In this short chapter, I do not discuss either this other Sanskrit comparandum or the other versions of Cyavana's story, – 'earlier' ones in the Jaiminīya and Śatapatha Brāhmaṇas, 'later' ones in the Purāṇas.[7]

Moreover, I narrow the focus even further by barely referring to the females involved in the stories – Sukanyā and Pandora – whom I hope to examine elsewhere. Sukanyā is central to the first part of the Sanskrit story (up to 3,123.19), while Pandora appears (unnamed) after the most relevant portion of the Greek story (namely 533–561), as well as (named) in *WD*. Because of this narrow focus, we shall much of the time be comparing only thirty-nine shlokas with twenty-nine hexameters. Here is a slightly fuller précis of the stories in question:

> The aged ascetic Cyavana is grateful to the twin Aśvin gods because they have rejuvenated him, thereby improving his marriage with Princess Sukanyā, daughter of King Śaryāti. Accordingly, he promises to secure them admission to *soma* sacrifices, whatever the attitude of Indra. He arranges for Śaryāti to lay on a suitable ritual and starts to officiate. Indra sees him preparing an offering to the Aśvins and objects: the Aśvins rank too low in divine society, they are too close to mortals. Sage and god argue, and Indra raises his thunderbolt. Cyavana uses his magic to paralyze Indra's arm and to conjure up a monster called Mada. Indra is terrified by Mada and agrees to admit the Aśvins to the ritual. Cyavana then releases Indra and disperses Mada.
>
> In Greece, gods and men have gathered and an ox is killed, presumably as a sacrifice. Prometheus arranges the meat in such a way as to induce Zeus to choose the less desirable portion – the bones and fat. Zeus is angry and withholds fire from mortals (so they cannot cook the meat), but Prometheus steals fire from heaven in the hollow of a fennel stalk. Thereafter Zeus punishes Prometheus and humanity, but this part of the story lies outside our main focus.

At first sight, the similarity consists in little more than a conflict between protagonist and god, leading to a change in sacrificial practice. However, on closer inspection, one can distinguish at least eighteen rapprochements.

Similarities

1 *Mythic precedent for humanity's offerings to gods*. Sacrifice is what ensures normal harmonious relations between humanity and gods, and both stories serve as myths of origin for significant features of the ritual. Vedic rituals fall into three main types, according to the type of offering. *Soma* rituals, the most elaborate and expensive type, enjoy the highest standing and, insofar as they continue to be performed, continue to include *soma* offerings to the Aśvins. Similarly, in most Greek sacrifices, gods continued to receive burnt bones. As Hesiod says, 'Ever since then [when Prometheus tricked Zeus], the peoples on earth have burned white bones for the immortals on their aromatic altars' (*Th*. 556–557).

2 *Brain versus brawn*. In both cases, the conflict is between a protagonist who relies successfully on his knowledge or ingenuity and a god who relies unsuccessfully on force. As Cyavana is a brahmin, his association with learning and knowledge is more or less guaranteed by the stereotype attached to that social category. More precisely, he owes his success on this occasion to knowledge of sacred formulae and magic (he operates *mantratas* and *kṛtyā*, 3,124.17). Prometheus is described repeatedly as crafty or subtle (511, etc.), being contrasted with his

stupid brother Epimetheus. In contrast, Indra is of course a warrior god, and Zeus certainly can be one, as he is for instance in the Titanomachy.

3 *Seniority of protagonist.* Version II of Cyavana's story is one of a set illustrating the superiority of brahmins over kṣatriyas, so in this context at least the god is implicitly aligned with human warriors, and brahmins were created before warriors (e.g. 12,329.5.6, in prose). Moreover, warriors are unlikely to be aged, while Cyavana, until his rejuvenation, is emphatically old; the Aśvins imply that he is too old to make love. In Greece, Titans are gods of the generation preceding Olympians, and Prometheus, son of the Titan Iapetus, must himself be a Titan. Moreover, Iapetus is older that Zeus' father Cronus (last-born of the Titans, *Th.* 132–138). So the Greek protagonist is the senior disputant in two senses.

4 *Named location.* Cyavana's contest with Indra took place near Mt Vaiḍūrya and the Narmadā River, at a lake (3.121.15, 125.11). Prometheus disputed with Zeus at Mecone (536), which is said to be the old name of Sicyon in the north-east Peloponnese. This rapprochement rests only on the fact that both places are named, while by no means all mythic events are given a geographical location. For instance, unlocalized myths include Indra's fight with Vṛtra and (in Hesiod) Zeus' with Typhoeus.

5 *Opening the dispute.* Both disputes are opened by the protagonist. Cyavana draws *soma* to offer to the Aśvins, while Prometheus cuts up the great ox and prepares portions for humans and for Zeus. Cyavana's action is explicitly part of a ritual, and the context suggests that the same applies to Prometheus' action.

6 *The protagonist's challenge.* As he implies in his initial promise to the Aśvins, Cyavana is aware of Indra's unwillingness to admit them as *soma*-drinkers (3,123.22); so in effect he is challenging the god, being confident that he can win. The crooked-schemer Prometheus, 'intent on deceit' (547), is doing just the same. The point is even clearer in the abrupt opening of Version II where, having made his promise to the Aśvins, Cyavana simply tells Indra to make them *soma*-drinkers: *somapāv aśvinau kuru* (second person singular imperative, 13,141.16).

7 *The god.* Indra and Zeus are not only typologically akin, both being kings within their respective pantheons, but also demonstrably cognate in some other stories. For instance, as I argued in [Ch. 19], Indra's role in the burning of the Khāṇḍava forest (1,214–15) parallels Zeus' role in *Iliad* 21, when the gods fight each other on the Trojan plain.

8 *Thunderbolt.* This weapon is wielded by both gods, not only in general but also in this particular story. Indra tries, but fails, to hurl it at Cyavana.[8] Zeus uses it to send Prometheus' brother Menoetius to the region of darkness (to *erebos*, 515).

9 *Words and deeds.* Both disputes combine verbal argument and physical action. As we saw in §6, the sage's initial challenge is an action: he draws a draft of *soma* for the Aśvins (presumably accompanying the act with invocations that make it clear to Indra who is to receive the offering). The god voices his objections and

starts the argument. Giving up the war of words, Cyavana resumes his activity. The god issues a final verbal threat and follows it up with his physical attack. In Greece, Prometheus makes his preparations. Zeus opens the dialogue, as did Indra. After one exchange of speeches, the god picks up the 'wrong' pile of meat, then reverts to words. Finally, he restrains or removes fire.

10 *The god's three speeches.* During the quarrel, Indra makes three speeches. The first two give reasons why the Aśvins should not be allowed to drink *soma*, and the third is a threat. In effect, he says, 'If you continue, I shall use my bolt'. In the *Theogony*, Zeus makes only two speeches. First he protests at the division of meat, then, after his 'wrong' choice, he blames the Titan for deceiving him. However, in *WD* (54–58), he makes a third speech, announcing his response to the theft of fire. In effect, he says to Prometheus, 'You may be pleased with yourself, but I shall punish humanity'. In both traditions, the first two speeches concern the past or present, while the third consists of two parts, of which the first concerns the behaviour of the protagonist (If you continue. . .; you may be pleased. . .), while the second concerns the god's intentions. Naturally it therefore contains verbs in the first person singular future: *prahariṣyāmi*, 'I shall throw [the bolt]' (3.124.15), and *dōsō*, 'I shall give [an affliction, i.e. Pandora]' (57).

The alignment of the third speech with the other two finds some support in the wording. All three of those by Zeus open with the vocative *Iapetionidē*, 'Son of Iapetus', which is then expanded with a phrase beginning *pantōn* ('all', genitive plural). The first expansion is *pantōn arideiket' anaktōn*, 'outstanding (or eminent) among all the lords', the second, identical with the third, is *pantōn peri mēdea eidōs*, 'clever above all others'.[9]

11 *Length of speeches.* All these speeches by the god are in *oratio recta* (in inverted commas, as it were), so they are clearly delimited, and each of Indra's speeches occupies just one standard shloka (124.9, 12, 15).[10] Since a standard shloka consists of two sixteen-syllable half-shlokas, it roughly corresponds in length to two Greek hexameters; a hexameter has a maximum of seventeen syllables, but on average somewhat fewer (average of 16.2). In the *Theogony*, each of Zeus' speeches, as well as the intervening one by Prometheus, are two hexameters long.

12 *Anger.* Since the story is about a quarrel, it is not surprising that the participants become angry, but it is worth noting how often the theme recurs. Right at the start Lomaśa mentions briefly the three things that happened at the sacred site (§18). The second thing is that this is where the great Bhārgava ascetic was angry with Indra (*cukopa* 121.21a) and paralyzed him. Yudhiṣṭhira picks up the point, asking why Cyavana became angry (*kopaṃ cakre* 22d). In the course of his dealings with Sukanyā, the sage waxes angry *(akrudhyat)*, being very irascible (*parama-manyuman* 122.13cd). Mada runs at Indra in fury (*saṃkruddhaḥ* 124.24a). Indra's submission ends the sage's anger (*manyur* 125.7c). In Version II, when his intervention is ignored by Cyavana, Indra

is *krodha-mūrchitaḥ* (13,141.21b), filled or pervaded with anger, while Cyavana is *amarṣākula-locanaḥ* – his eyes filled with anger (21f). The eight references to anger use four different roots.

In the Sanskrit, anger is attributed mainly to Cyavana or his creation Mada, and only in Version II to Indra, but in the Greek, Prometheus is never said to be angry, only Zeus. The theme occurs first in the introductory section in connection with the ending of Prometheus' punishment: irate though he was, Zeus ends the anger he had before. The 'anger vocabulary' here is *khōomenos* and *kholos* (533). Thereafter we find *khōsato* and *kholos* (554), *khōomenos* and *kholos* (561–562), *kholoō* (568), and one can add *daken d' ara neiothi thumon* 'it stung (Zeus) deep to the spirit' (567). *WD* has *kholōsamenos* in 47 and again in 53. So in all there are ten references to anger, using three roots.

13 *Protagonist smiles.* After Indra threatens him, Cyavana (despite his irascibility) looks at the god with a smile (*smayan* 124.16a), and when Zeus first objects, Prometheus responds with a soft or quiet smile (*ēk' epimeidēsas* 547). No doubt in both cases the smile expresses confidence that brain will outdo brawn (§2). The verbs *smi-* and *meidaō* are cognate (as is English 'smile'), and both forms are nominative singular masculine participles.

14 *Tit-for-tat.* After engaging in the dialogue, each god makes an aggressive move, which is immediately or promptly countered by the protagonist. Indra's attack is answered by Cyavana's two-pronged use of magic (to paralyze and to frighten). Zeus' removal of fire is answered by Prometheus' recovery of it. The similarity lies not in the actions themselves but in the sequence 'dialogue – god's act – protagonist's counter-act'.

15 *The god shows respect.* In Book 3, Indra is overcome by Cyavana's magic and makes his submission verbally: he admits the Aśvins to *soma* rituals, he recognizes the authority of what the sage says, and he asks for mercy. All this implies respect, but in Version II, the implication is also enacted non-verbally. The gods, with Indra, find themselves within the mouth of Mada, at the root of his tongue. Having conferred, they tell Indra to bow down or make obeisance to Cyavana, and he does so. The verb *praṇam-* 'bow' is thus used twice (13,141.26, 27).

Zeus certainly does not physically bow to Prometheus, but he does – rather surprisingly – show respect to someone who helps the Titan. As part of his punishment, Prometheus is immobilized, and each day an eagle eats part of his liver, which grows again at night (so that the punishment can continue indefinitely). Zeus' son Heracles kills the eagle, saving Prometheus from that affliction and setting him free from distress. Zeus accepts this (for a reason discussed in §16); thus, the god does reverence and honour to his eminent son (*taut' ara hazomenos tima arideiketon huion*, 532).[11]

So in both stories, the king of the gods shows respect to a mortal. But the rapprochement can be pushed further, if we focus on a third agent in the picture. The Aśvins help the sage by freeing him from his senility, while Heracles helps Prometheus by freeing him from his distress, and each helper receives respect from the relevant god. In other words, in submitting to Cyavana's demands, Indra is agreeing to respect not only the sage, but also the Aśvins, so the possibility arises of comparing the Aśvins with Heracles. In the Rigveda, the Aśvins are often the sons of Dyaus (West 2007: 187); Heracles is the son of Zeus; and the two high gods are etymologically cognate. Moreover, just as the Aśvins are emphatically twinned, so Heracles too has a twin brother: Iphicles is begotten by the mortal Amphitryon a few hours after Zeus begets Heracles, and the pair share the womb of Alcmene. The Aśvins, initially regarded by Zeus as excessively close to mortals, are promoted to the rank of *soma*-drinking gods, and at his death, Heracles is promoted from hero to god. [One might expect the muscular Heracles to represent F2, but his interpretation can hardly be that simple.]

16 *'Spin'*. At first sight, both our warrior gods suffer humiliation, indeed Zeus suffers it several times. Indra is paralyzed, frightened, and forced to do what he initially says he does not intend to do. Zeus is tricked at the sacrifice; his first attempt at punishment fails when the fire is recovered, and his second attempt is terminated by Heracles, apparently sooner than expected. Both gods remind one of politicians who suffer what is potentially a blow to their prestige. Employing spin, they try 'put a brave face on it', to 'make the best of things', offering explanations that may or may not convince their audience. Similarly, the gods imply that appearances were deceptive. Indra claims that the promotion of the Aśvins was what he himself all along intended – with a view to glorifying the sage. After Prometheus replies to Zeus' first speech, Hesiod comments that Zeus recognized the trick and did not fall for it (*gnō r'oud' ēgnoiēse dolon*, 551). When Heracles terminates the sufferings of the Titan, Hesiod comments that Zeus was not unwilling for this to happen (*ouk aekēti Zēnos*, 529), so that his son should become more famous.

17 *Phraseology*. Though one hardly believes them, the gods' explanations merit close attention. Actually, three instances of divine spin need consideration, since Indra offers two of them (the duality is emphasized more in Ganguli's translation than in van Buitenen's):

125.5cd *bhūya eva tu te vīryaṃ prakāśed iti bhārgava*
so that your power might once more shine forth, O Bhārgava,

125.6ab *sukanyāyāḥ pituścāsya loke kīrtiḥ prathed iti*
and so that the fame of Sukanyā and her father here might spread in the world.

530 *ophr' hēraklēos thēbageneos kleos eiē*
so that the fame of Heracles, born at Thebes, should be

531 *pleion et' ē to paroithen epi khthona pouluboteiran.*
greater still than before on the wide-pastured earth.

Syntax. The particle *iti*, whose function can roughly be described as 'close inverted commas', shows that the preceding clause presents the speaker's thinking. Despite the differing position, it corresponds to the purposive conjunction *ophra*.

Subject (in nominative). *Vīrya* 'power, heroic deed'; *kīrti* and *kleos* both meaning 'fame'. All three are abstract nouns.

Genitives. Each subject has a dependent genitive. The *te* 'of you' refers to Cyavana, as the vocative confirms. In the Sanskrit, where the second half-shloka refers to Cyavana's wife and father-in-law, the double genitive occupies a whole *pāda* (quarter of a shloka). In the Greek, the noun phrase consisting of Heracles and his birthplace occupies more than half the syllables of its hexameter. Both of these long genitival expressions precede the nominative word for 'fame', and a few Sanskrit manuscripts reverse the order of *loke* and *kīrti*, thereby juxtaposing the genitive and nominative as in the Greek. Anyway, it is obvious that the Greek is closer to Indra's second explanation than to his first.

Verbs. The verb *prakāś-* 'shine forth' (5d) is echoed in the noun that is the subject in 6d (*ato mayaitad vihitaṃ tava vīrya-prakāśanam*, 'Therefore that public manifestation of your powers was decreed (or destined) by me.' But let us leave this part of Indra's explanation for a moment and move to the next verb – *prath-* 'spread, extend', which is filled out by *bhūyas* 'more' – itself followed by the mildly emphatic particle *eva*. A similar meaning is conveyed in the Greek by the ordinary verb 'to be' associated with *pleion* 'more, greater', itself qualified by *eti* 'even, still' and the comparative phrase. Both *bhūyas* and *pleion* are placed emphatically at the start of the half-shloka or hexameter.

Spatial context. Situated towards the end, *loke* 'in the world' corresponds to *epi khthona* 'on/over the earth'.

Textual similarities of this kind are not uncommon if one looks for them (Allen 2017). Indra ends his speech with a plea for mercy and with a recognition of Cyavana's success ('Let it be as you want it,' 6f). The next shloka notes the prompt decline of Cyavana's anger – his *manyur vyagamat* (7c). Zeus' approval of his son (532, discussed in §15) is immediately followed by his calming down ('irate though he was, he ended the wrath *(pauthē kholou)* he had before', 533). West reads the genitive of *kholos* 'anger', but a number of manuscripts have the nominative, that is, the same case as in the Sanskrit.

Here is one final textual similarity, a little less obvious. Indra claims that he ordained (*vidhā-* 6c) Cyavana's demonstration of power. As for Zeus, just before introducing Prometheus' punishment, Hesiod mentions the task given to Prometheus' brother Atlas, namely to hold up the sky, 'for Zeus the resourceful assigned to him this lot' (*tautēn gar hoi moiran edassato mētieta Zeus*, 520). Atlas is not Prometheus, but in both passages, the god's will is referred to, and in both, the vocabulary relates specifically to dividing up or sharing out. Thus, *vidhā-* means 'distribute, apportion, dispose' (the prefix *vi-* implying division); *moira* 'portion, fate' is from *meiromai* 'receive as one's share'; *dateomai* means 'divide, share out'. Given the proximity of the other verbal parallels, coincidence seems to me unlikely.

18 *Sequencing.* This final rapprochement concerns the order in which events are narrated or mentioned. When the Pāṇḍavas reach the sacred site, Lomaśa introduces it by mentioning three events (3,121.20–21). (a) This is the site of Śaryāti's sacrifice, where Indra drank *soma* with the Aśvins in person. (b) It is where Cyavana was angry with Indra and paralyzed him. (c) It is where Cyavana obtained Sukanyā as his wife. Curiously, these events are mentioned in the reverse order to that in which they occur. In the story proper, the sage's marriage precedes his dispute with Indra, which itself precedes the Aśvins' *soma*-drinking. Yudhiṣṭhira, asking for a fuller account, ignores Lomaśa's (c) but picks up his (a) and (b), putting them in the 'right' order.

Hesiod starts his account with Iapetus, father of Prometheus, and with Iapetus' four sons. He has something to say on each of them, on Epimetheus, Menoetius, Atlas, and finally Prometheus. He refers first to Prometheus' punishment and Heracles' intervention, then backtracks to the dispute at Mecone. In moving from later events to earlier ones, Hesiod's introduction to the sacrifice story follows the same course as Lomaśa's introduction.

Differences

The differences between the two stories are innumerable: for instance, different sorts of protagonist (brahmin and Titan), different offerings (*soma* and meat), different recipients for them (Aśvins and gods in general), and many more; moreover, the Sanskrit ending is more or less happy, while the Greek ends with an emphasis on punishment – both of Prometheus and of mortals. However, I hope to have presented enough evidence that the two stories are related, and there is more evidence to be found. The comparison can certainly be taken further by including the females and going beyond Hesiod to later Greek sources, and as I said, further Sanskrit stories need to be brought into the picture – not to mention the Norse. My argument here has only been that the proto-narrative lying behind Cyavana's story is *one* component of the Prometheus story.

Notes

1 First published in 2015 as 'Cyavana helps Aśvins, Prometheus helps humans: a myth about sacrifice'.
2 The inverted commas serve to emphasize that the date at which a story is first written down may or may not correlate with the date when the story was first told orally.
3 In the CE (which I use), the whole story runs from 3,121.15 to 125.11, but the section relating to the sacrifice starts at 123.20. For a translation, see van Buitenen (1975: 457–462).
4 13,141.15–30. Translation by Ganguli (1993) IV Book 13 (pt. II): 364–365. Brief allusions to the story can be found elsewhere: 1.22.117–118; 3,288.9; 4,20.7; 12,329.14.3 [in prose].
5 Text of *WD* in West (1978). Translations of both poems in West (1988a), from which I usually quote.

6 See, for example Dougherty (2006). For comparison with the Caucasus, see Charachidze (1986).
7 I thanked Emily West for showing me her [then] unpublished article [2017] on the story of Cyavana. Cf. also Witzel (1987).
8 In Version II, Indra supplements the thunderbolt with a huge mountain, which he seizes (13,141.21).
9 A second vocative *ō pepōn*, 'my good sir' occurs in speeches I and II, but is irrelevant here.
10 Cyavana's response to the first occupies two shlokas.
11 The same word for 'eminent' is applied (sarcastically) by Zeus to Prometheus (cf. §10). [Cf. also the promotion of the twin Dioscuri (Apd. *Bibl.* 3.11.2).]

22

TELEMACHY

[I omit a one-page foreword which was added to the paper so as to link it to the theme of that particular number of the journal. My main point was that, if the Telemachy is indeed cognate with the Pāṇḍavas' pilgrimage as narrated in Mbh. 3, we can probably infer that the proto-narrative presupposed the ritual of pilgrimage; and perhaps other journeys in that book originally presupposed rituals of shamanism and necromancy.]

★ ★ ★

Named after its major hero, the *Odyssey* is mainly about that hero's long-drawn-out return from Troy to Ithaca and his post-return adventures.[1] So why are the first four books mostly about the journey of his son Telemachus? Why does the epic of Odysseus contain this secondary and subordinate journey? Explanations can be sought within the text and filled out by relating them to the rest of the Greek epic tradition, supplemented perhaps by 'folklore'. However, while not rejecting such approaches, I do not here engage with them, partly for reasons of space, but mainly because I come at Homer from the viewpoint of Indo-European (IE) cultural comparison.

Considerable published evidence now suggests that Homeric epic is cognate with Sanskrit epic. In other words, it seems that these two narrative traditions go back to a common ancestor, versions of which diverged and were transmitted separately from at least the Greco-Aryan period onward (and perhaps from earlier still). So the central question here is whether the related and overlapping journeys of the major Greek hero and his less important son correspond to cognate journeys in the *Mahābhārata*. Vyāsa is the reputed composer of this Sanskrit epic, and I used his name in my original title as if he were the Indian equivalent of Homer.

The *Mahābhārata* reached its current form only in the early centuries CE, while the written *Odyssey* is most often dated to the seventh century BCE. But the common origin hypothesis assumes that the written versions of both epics were preceded by very long periods of oral transmission. During the transmission, the language and narrative content were of course changing, but I scarcely consider the sequence of changes, let alone their dating. My central aim is to explore the similarities that survived the changes and that were presumably already present in the proto-narrative or proto-epic. Theoretically such similarities could derive, not from common origin, but from chance, independent invention or borrowing (whether east-west or west-east). I regard such rival interpretations as implausible but do not discuss them here. My minimal claim is that the similarities demand *some* explanation.

Reduced to essentials, the *Mahābhārata* recounts the quarrel between two branches of a royal family. The Pāṇḍavas, five brothers married polyandrously to Draupadī, have a legitimate claim to rule but are denied their rights by the Kauravas. Each side assembles a vast coalition and fights the other in a great eighteen-day battle (Books 6–10). After enormous losses on both sides, the Pāṇḍavas win and regain the throne. Books 11–18 cover the aftermath of the battle while Books 1–5 cover the lead-up to it. The journeys in question occur in Book 3.

Following a disastrous game of dice [in Book 2], the Pāṇḍavas leave the capital (Hāstinapura) for a humiliating twelve-year exile in the forest, not returning until Book 12. During this exile, certain journeys of shorter duration can be distinguished. First, after the first year of exile, Arjuna (third-born of the Pāṇḍavas) leaves his brothers to visit his divine begetter Indra, King of the Gods, who lives in heaven. I refer to this journey as Arjuna's Visit to Heaven. Second, soon afterwards, the remaining brothers, led by Yudhiṣṭhira (the eldest), undertake a pilgrimage around the four quarters of India.[2] Third, after the pilgrimage proper, Bhīma (the second Pāṇḍava by birth order), undertakes two one-day excursions in the Himalayas, being followed by the rest of his party. These paired journeys are so similar that some scholars regard them as doublets, and I refer to them as Flower Journeys A and B. Eagerly awaited, Arjuna now returns from heaven and is reunited with his family. [Together, for Year 13, they all travel to the court of King Virāṭa.]

Rapprochements

Let us start the search for rapprochements with the most abstract ones, for which the main facts have already been given.

1 *A journey within a journey.* As we saw, the Pāṇḍavas leave Hāstinapura as exiles and return as victors after the Great War. Situated within this eventful journey, which lasts more than thirteen years, Arjuna's Visit to Heaven is only one episode, lasting five years. It is a subordinate component of a larger whole.

Odysseus leaves his palace in Ithaca for the Trojan War and returns to it twenty years later. His return journey (his *nostos*) can be subdivided in various ways, but for our purposes the most relevant distinction is between the part of the journey that Homer describes through the words of Odysseus – from Troy to Ogygia, and the part that he describes in (as it were) his own words [as narrator] – from Ogygia to Ithaca. Both parts are subordinate components of the twenty-year journey, but the second has the more important role: Odysseus is in Ogygia at the very start of the whole epic, and his return from there would round off the superordinate twenty-year journey even if the first part of the *nostos* (the flashback) were omitted.

Without similarities, comparison is pointless, so they have to take priority over differences, which can always be found. We shall not have much space for differences, but here is a major one. Within the Sanskrit superordinate journey, the Visit to Heaven comes fairly early on and the Great War comes close to the end, while in the Greek superordinate journey, the Trojan War precedes what we can call the Visit to Scheria. But the contrast is less straightforward than it appears, for two reasons. Many considerations demonstrate that the Kurukṣetra Great War is cognate with the Trojan War, but it can also be argued that the fifth phase of the former – that is, the nocturnal massacre in Book 10 – corresponds to the nocturnal massacre not only of Trojans but also of the Suitors. Second, although the Visit to Heaven is followed eventually by the Great War in Books 6–10, it is followed much sooner by the Pāṇḍavas' defeat of a Kaurava raid during the thirteenth year (end of Book 4); and this too shows notable similarities to the massacre of the suitors. I have tackled these complex comparisons elsewhere [Ch. 17], and I raise them here in passing only as back-up to the present similarity. My point is that rapprochement 1 is not invalidated by the differences between the two superordinate journeys.

2 *Overlapping journeys.* The Visit to Heaven starts before the Pilgrimage and continues after it. So the period during which Arjuna is away from his brothers overlaps with and includes the period during which the pilgrims are travelling. In the Greek, the boundaries of the Visit to Scheria are less clear-cut. The story might or might not be said to start with the prolonged imprisonment on Ogygia and to end with the early morning arrival on the Ithacan beach, but the present rapprochement does not need such precision. Whatever delimitations one posits, a substantial overlap exists between the Visit to Scheria and the Telemachy, as it does between the Visit to Heaven and the Pilgrimage.

3 *Objectives and significance.* When the Visit to Heaven is first mooted, its aim is for Arjuna to obtain divine arms (3,37.28, 30), and he emphatically succeeds (3,41–42, 171.2). Arjuna is the central Pāṇḍava warrior and will need these weapons for the Great War. He also receives, from a divine musician (a *gandharva*), the knowledge of music and dance that he will need for his disguise in Year 13, which the Pāṇḍavas have to spend incognito.

When Arjuna departs, his family feel bereft and depressed (e.g. 3,161.14–15). The Pilgrimage distracts them from grieving, exposes them to much mythic lore, and earns them religious merit. But it provides them with nothing as practical as what Arjuna acquires.

The Visit to Scheria is mooted at the very start of the *Odyssey*, in the first Divine Assembly on Olympus. In Athena's first speech, she laments that the hero is becalmed on Ogygia, and in her second, she proposes that he be helped to complete his *nostos*, and that his son's journey be set in motion. Her first proposal is fundamental to the overall story of a deeply missed hero who, after long absence and many difficulties, regains his wife and home, but whether the Telemachy contributes significantly is debatable. The young man returns from Sparta with greater confidence and maturity, having acquired scraps of information about the Trojan War and its aftermath, and bearing some non-military gifts from Menelaus. Thereafter he helps his father in the fighting, but he could surely have done the same if he had stayed at home throughout, like Eumaeus and Philoetius. We can enjoy the presence of the Telemachy and the Pilgrimage in our epics even while recognizing that their contribution to the plot falls far short of that made by the Visits to Scheria and Heaven.

4 *The travellers*. In comparativism, it is often useful to devise a single label to cover entities that are taken as cognate. Analogous to the starred forms used by linguists, such labels can be read diachronically as referring to something that was present in the common origin. Let us accordingly refer to the more important pair of cognate journeys as Journey I, in contrast to the less important Journey II.

Journey I is made by a solo traveller, Journey II by a group. On Yudhiṣṭhira's pilgrimage, the group includes not only the three remaining Pāṇḍava brothers and Draupadī but also, as pilgrim guide and protector, the seer Lomaśa – not to mention the Pāṇḍavas' chaplain Dhaumya, other brahmins, a head charioteer, cooks, and other servants (3,91.25–28). Telemachus sets off accompanied not only by Athena in the form of Mentor but also by the oarsmen that the goddess recruits (twenty of them, as planned in 1.280). Within Journey II, Lomaśa parallels the guide and protector Athena/Mentor, and the drivers of the fourteen chariots parallel the Ithacan oarsmen.

The Journey I solo traveller is a very close male relative of the central traveller in Journey II: Arjuna is the younger brother of Yudhiṣṭhira, and Odysseus is the father of Telemachus. Rapprochements between the two solo travellers have been presented elsewhere [Ch. 5, Allen 2005d], but the apparent parallel between Yudhiṣṭhira and Telemachus cannot be regarded as significant. To explore the point properly would require introducing and applying the pentadic theory of IE ideology and cannot be attempted here. One can recognize that the *Pilgrimage* and the *Telemachy* are cognate journeys while remaining agnostic as to the identity of the chief traveller in the proto-narrative.

5 *Journey II: the group splits and reunites*. The *Pilgrimage* follows a common pattern in proceeding clockwise from the east. When the pilgrims have reached the northern quarter and are entering the Himalayas, Lomaśa warns of the dangers that lie ahead. Yudhiṣṭhira notes that such anxiety represents something new (3,140.15) and proposes that the party split up. Eventually the charioteers, servants, overseers, cooks, and Draupadī's entourage are left behind to stay with King Subāhu, from whom they will be recovered in 3,174.14. Without their

chariots, the Pāṇḍavas and brahmins proceed on foot or, when necessary, are carried by *rākṣasa* spirits. The party are now aiming primarily for the expected meeting with Arjuna. The area is inhabited by seers and supernaturals, and the party cultivate scrupulous purity and find accommodation at hermitages, but they no longer seem like pilgrims.

Telemachus' party is much smaller, but it too splits up. After the visit to Nestor at Pylos, Athena/Mentor departs (as a bird, 3.372), and the next day the crew are left behind with the boat at Pylos, to be recovered on the return journey (15.217–219). Telemachus proceeds overland to Sparta in a chariot, borrowed from Nestor and driven by Nestor's youngest son, Peisitratus.

6 *Journey II: before and after the split.* Yudhiṣṭhira's journey is preceded by two substantial accounts of pilgrimages made by earlier travellers; one is spoken by the seer Nārada, whom we shall meet again, the other by Dhaumya. During the Pilgrimage proper, Lomaśa (or others) comment on the numerous *tīrthas* that they visit, often narrating stories associated with them. A *tīrtha*, originally meaning 'ford', is a sacred site, close to water and usually on the banks of a river, where a pilgrim bathes or performs oblations. Thus, the first chapter to describe the itinerary of the pilgrims (3,93) refers explicitly to at least six rivers where they bathe, and they also perform several other ritual acts – donations to brahmins, offerings of forest produce, and sacrifices. The same chapter ends with the party reaching the Lake of Brahmā, whence all rivers spring and where Śiva is always present. The brahmin Śamaṭha tells them about an extraordinarily large-scale sacrifice once performed here by the royal ascetic Gaya: there were 'mountains of rice by the hundreds and thousands', and twenty-five such mountains were left over.

When Telemachus and his party reach Pylos, they find its inhabitants gathered on the sea shore performing a large-scale sacrifice to Poseidon. Nestor's people are seated in nine groups, each consisting of 500 members and each having nine black bulls as victims (3.4–8).

Let us pause here to compare this initial Greek sacrifice to Gaya's. Both events are on a vast scale, as is emphasized by the use of numerals – eighty-one victims and 4,500 participants at Pylos.[3] Each ritual is held beside water: Poseidon is of course god of the sea while Śiva is not, but as Lomaśa explains (3,108.9, 16), the god played a crucial role in the descent of the Ganges from heaven to earth, and it was the Ganges that filled the sea with water. Moreover, both gods wield a trident, and both offer temporary but serious opposition to the progress of the hero in Journey I [Ch. 5 §1.11–17].

Whatever is made of the Gaya–Nestor comparison, the *Telemachy* certainly emphasizes Nestor's piety (not particularly in evidence in the *Iliad*). The initial seaside ritual is terminated in the evening (3.341), and after Athena departs, Nestor recognizes her divinity and promises her a sacrifice. Thus, the next morning, she receives a heifer whose horns are overlaid with gold, the ritual being described in some detail. The pairing of Poseidon and Athena is interesting, but my point here is that, during his one-night visit to Pylos, Telemachus participates in two sacrifices.

After the Split, the Pāṇḍava party, as we noted, cease to behave like pilgrims following a recognized circuit. Their aim is now to rendezvous with their brother they have missed so deeply (3,142). As they traverse the mountainous terrain, the scenery, landmarks, and inhabitants (mostly supernatural) are described, but no reference is made to sacrifices. Indeed, the next salient event, Flower Journey A, has little to do with piety or religion.

> A north-east wind brings a fragrant lotus, and Draupadī asks Bhīma to fetch more of them. Forcing his way uphill through rocks, forest, and creepers, the hero encounters and interacts with Hanumān, King of the Monkeys and, like Bhīma, a son of the god Vāyu (Wind). The elder brother promises to help Bhīma and Arjuna on the battlefield, and the younger continues to the lotus-filled pond. It lies close to the palace of Kubera, god of wealth, and its guards *(rākṣasas)* challenge him. After killing a hundred of them, he picks the flowers, but when Kubera is informed, he takes the news cheerfully. Back at base, Draupadī explains Bhīma's mission. The party is transported to the pond and rejoins Bhīma. Yudhiṣṭhira rebukes his brother for recourse to violence.

After a night at Pherae, Telemachus and Peisander reach Sparta, where a double wedding is in progress. The wedding quickly fades from view, and most of the text consists of speeches by the two visitors and their royal hosts. On the first evening, we hear about Odysseus' resourcefulness in the later stages of the Trojan War: Helen recalls meeting him when he entered Troy in disguise, and Menelaus recalls Helen visiting the Wooden Horse in which he and Odysseus were hiding. The next day (4.333–592), Menelaus gives his lengthy account of the post-War returns of himself, Agamemnon, the lesser Ajax, and (as far as he knows it) Odysseus. In Book 15, on the urging of Athena, Telemachus departs with his gifts. At the departure, Menelaus brings wine for farewell libations (15.148–149), but in Sparta, this is the closest Telemachus comes to personal involvement in religious activities. The hecatombs Menelaus had to perform to leave distant Egypt (4.582) are irrelevant to the young man.

The present rapprochement is between two contrasts. The *Pilgrimage* proper contrasts with the Himalayan journey that climaxes with *Flower Journey A* as Telemachus' visit to Pylos contrasts with his visit to Sparta. Within each tradition the first item is oriented to religion, the second (after the Split) is not.[4] But the rapprochement would gain in cogency if, rather than merely contrasting in this way with the two pre-Split stories, the two post-Split stories had something positive in common; and they do.

Despite the help he promises and provides to the Pāṇḍava champions, Hanumān's role is a minor one in the *Mahābhārata*, a major one in the *Rāmāyaṇa*. The latter Sanskrit epic, far shorter, is set in an earlier era of epic pseudo-history, and its theme is the abduction and recovery of Rāma's wife Sītā. The demonic

Rāvaṇa has transported her across the sea to Laṅkā, and Hanumān, in the service of Rāma, is the first to communicate with the captive. He enters his father (the Wind), leaps across a hundred leagues of sea, and finds Sītā in the women's quarters of Rāvaṇa's palace. The two establish each other's *bona fides*, and Hanumān fires the city before returning. Hanumān's role is alluded to by both interlocutors during Flower Journey A (3,147.10–12, 34–35) and is presented at greater length in the summary of the *Rāmāyaṇa* that is narrated later in the twelve-year exile (see esp. 3,266.57–68).

We cannot here discuss the oft-noted parallel between the abduction and rescue of Sītā in the Indian epic tradition and that of Helen in the Greek. My point is simply that both post-Split episodes of Journey II emphasize a visit made in the past by a male hero to someone else's abducted wife who is living in an enemy city. In other words, Hanumān entering Laṅkā in a previous era parallels Odysseus entering Troy ten years before Telemachus hears the story.

The parallel is reinforced by the absence of comparable stories in the pre-Split narratives. The *Pilgrimage* proper includes numerous stories from the past – nine are set apart under separate *upaparvan* titles, but it lacks references to the hero of the *Rāmāyaṇa*. Nārada's account of Pulastya's pilgrimage refers in passing to the *tīrtha* from which Rāma and his associates went to heaven and to another where Rāma crossed the Ganges (3,82.63; 83.62), but these fleeting references do not recur in the itinerary of the Pāṇḍavas. Nestor has something to say about the wisdom and wiliness of Odysseus at Troy and recounts one detail from the very start of that hero's *nostos* (3.162–164), but although he presumably knew the stories told by Helen and Menelaus, he does not pass them on.[5]

7 *Journey II: intervention of an enemy. Flower Journey A* is immediately followed by a single-chapter *upaparvan* called the Slaying of Jaṭāsura (3,154). Presenting himself as a brahmin, this demon has been living with the Pāṇḍavas, enjoying their hospitality, but scheming to acquire both their weapons and their wife. One day when Bhīma is away hunting, Jaṭāsura makes off with Draupadī and the remaining brothers. Bhīma catches up with them and kills the demon.

In Book 15, Telemachus is summoned back to Ithaca by Athena. He leaves promptly and, nearing Pylos, separates from Peisander to rejoin his crew. As Athena has warned him, a party of Suitors is waiting to ambush and assassinate him during his return voyage, but with divine help, he eludes them.

The event and its outcome are very different in the two traditions: Jaṭāsura dies, while the twenty suitors under Antinous are merely disappointed. However, the rapprochement is based partly on the unsuccessful intervention of an enemy at just this point in Journey II and partly on the behaviour and intentions of the enemy before the moment of aggression. Like the Suitors, Jaṭāsura has been abusing the hospitality of a royal family whose most potent member (Arjuna, Odysseus) is absent, and he wants to seduce their queen.

8 *Prelude to the reunion.* The Slaying of Jaṭāsura is followed by the *upaparvan* called *War of the Yakṣas* – a reference to *Flower Journey B* (3,157–159). Much as previously, flowers are blown to the Pāṇḍavas, and Draupadī challenges Bhīma to clear the top of the mountain from which they came. Storming uphill by a narrow and rugged path, the hero massacres the mountain's guardian spirits *(yakṣas)*, including Kubera's friend Maṇimat. The Pāṇḍava males follow him and are welcomed by Kubera. The god is grateful since he has been freed from a curse by Bhīma's deed; he will now ensure that the party are fed and protected while they await their brother Arjuna. A month later, Arjuna descends from heaven in Indra's chariot (3,161.16–19).

Arriving from Ithaca, Telemachus is put ashore before his boat enters the harbour and walks to the home of Eumaeus (15.555), where the reunion at once occurs (16.11–12). At first sight, the preludes to the reunion have little in common, but the rapprochement can be justified on four grounds. First, Telemachus' journey on foot from the shore of Ithaca to Eumaeus' home echoes the journey made by Odysseus three days earlier, as the second Flower Journey echoes the first. This parallel is distinctly abstract, since in Greece the two travellers, father and son, are completing separate journeys, while in India a single individual, Bhīma, is completing Journey II, but it is not negligible. Second, the rough foot-path to Eumaeus' home goes uphill through woods (14.1–2, cf. 17.204), much as does Bhīma's route. Third, Eumaeus proves highly welcoming and hospitable, as does Kubera. Finally, both the God of Wealth and the humble food-producer can be interpreted as representing the third function. Like so many F3 figures, they are paired – respectively with Maṇimat and with Philoetius – and they are members of sets that contain representatives of the other functions, namely the Lokapālas and the participants in the massacre of the suitors.[6]

9 *Narratology.* A narrator describing two simultaneous journeys, I and II, has various options: he can recount the whole of I first and then move on to II; he can start with I, interrupt it with II, and then complete I; or he can zigzag back and forth in more complex ways. Vaiśaṃpāyana combines the second and third options. Arjuna's journey starts in 3,37–38, and by 3,45 the hero is ensconced in heaven. The next three chapters treat first the Kauravas, then Yudhiṣṭhira's party, then the Kauravas again (3,46–48). After this interlude, the focus fixes on the future pilgrims, who are told the story of Nala (3,50–78). This is followed by the Pilgrimage *upaparvan* (3,80–153), [which includes Flower Journey A]; there remain Flower Journey B and finally (3,161) the Reunion. Vaiśaṃpāyana now reverts to Journey I. [On his return] Arjuna picks up the story from the day he left the Pāṇḍavas (so duplicates a little) but now rounds it off, reaching the Reunion again in 3,171.

In Greece, the idea of overlapping journeys is proposed at the first Divine Assembly (1.80–95), where Athena mentions the Visit to Scheria before the *Telemachy*; however, the subsequent narrative reverses this order. Journey II is recounted up to the point when Telemachus is settled in Sparta, and Journey

I starts only after the second Divine Assembly in Book 5. Odysseus' Visit to Scheria is followed all the way to Eumaeus' home, and the account of Telemachus' return from Sparta is deferred until Book 15. Now comes a zigzag. The scene shifts abruptly back to Odysseus *chez* Eumaeus in 15.301, then back again to Telemachus in 15.497.

If we ignore the 'interlude' (3,46–48) in the Sanskrit and the concluding zigzag in the Greek, we can formulate as follows. Having opened with Journey I, Vaiśaṃpāyana breaks off when Arjuna has reached his intended destination, he then narrates the whole of Journey II, and finally he rounds off Journey I. Having opened with Journey II, Homer breaks off when Telemachus has reached the furthest point of the trip that Athena planned; he then narrates the whole of Journey I before rounding off Journey II. The difference is between I–II–I and II–I–II, but the similarity is that one journey is sandwiched between two parts of the other.

A narratological rapprochement that might merit a separate title concerns the hero of Journey I and his first-person account of his adventures. When he returns – so, after the Reunion – Arjuna tells his family about his trip, from the moment he left them. When Odysseus is fully at home, after the massacre, he gives his wife an account of his *nostos* from Troy onward (23.310–341), but this account is in Homer's words and is only a brief summary of the first-person narrative in the Phaeacian palace (Books 9–12). Let us, for once, think diachronically. If Journey I took the proto-narrative hero to heaven (as I suppose), he would hardly have needed to tell his story to the supernaturals. This suggests that the Greek tradition has innovated by situating the first-person narrative before the Reunion. In any case – returning to synchrony – both traditions allow their central hero to give a substantial account of Journey I in his own words.

10 *Mobilization for Journey I.* Now that the content and ordering of the overlapping journeys have been explored, we are in a better position to consider their genesis.

The Pāṇḍavas have started their twelve-year exile and are discussing their situation. When Vyāsa arrives (3,37.20 – he is a prominent seer within the epic, as well as its composer), he privately gives Yudhiṣṭhira encouraging prophecies and instructions. To obtain weapons, Arjuna is in due course to be dispatched to meet certain gods; for this, he will need a magic spell *(brahman)* that Vyāsa entrusts to Yudhiṣṭhira. In addition, the Pāṇḍava leader is to leave Dvaita forest and take his party elsewhere (he will choose Kāmyaka). One reason is that after a long stay in a single place, the deer are consumed and the plants and herbs dwindle – for the Pāṇḍavas are supporting many brahmins (37.31–33, 36). Vyāsa vanishes, and in the next chapter, after the move, Arjuna receives the spell from his eldest brother, together with (somewhat amplified) instructions.

At the first Divine Assembly, Athena proposes that Hermes be sent to Calypso to tell her to release Odysseus, and at the second, Zeus duly despatches his messenger, adding some particulars of the hero's future journey (5.28–42). Hermes delivers Zeus' message and departs.[7]

Although Vyāsa does not claim to be a messenger from Indra, he can hardly be acting on his own initiative; it is clear enough that Indra expects and wants the visit from his son. But the rapprochement rests on a better argument than the inference that Vyasa is transmitting the god's desire. It is striking that neither Vyāsa nor Hermes speaks directly to the hero he mobilizes: both leave their instructions with an intermediary. In that role, Yudhiṣṭhira fleetingly parallels Calypso.

11 *Mobilization for Journey II.*

The Pāṇḍavas are lamenting their absent brother when the seer Nārada arrives (3,80). Asked by Yudhiṣṭhira about the benefits of pilgrimage, he responds at some length and urges the Pāṇḍava party to set out; they are to travel with Lomaśa (83.106). After Dhaumya's account of the pilgrimage route, Lomaśa arrives. His wanderings have taken him to the world of Indra, where he saw Arjuna. After reporting the hero's achievements, the seer details Indra's instructions. Lomaśa (about to embark on his third pilgrimage) is to teach and protect the travellers, ensuring their purity. Vyāsa and two other seers visit and re-emphasize the need for purity (91.17).

Immediately after the first Divine Assembly, Athena herself, taking the form of Mentes the Taphian, comes to the Ithacan palace and is greeted hospitably by Telemachus, who explains his plight. Suggesting that Odysseus is still alive and will return, Athena/Mentes offers her advice, including the idea of an expedition to seek news of the absent father (1.280–285, following up 1.93–94). The next day, Telemachus announces his expedition in the Ithacan assembly (2.212), and afterwards Athena, this time in the form of the Ithacan Mentor, offers him her vigorous help (2.287).

Thus, in India, although the idea of a pilgrimage is Yudhiṣṭhira's, it is promoted in succession by two seers. In Greece, the corresponding idea is Athena's, but she promotes it by adopting in succession two different human forms. More cogently, it is the second seer and the goddess in her second human form that set off with the Journey II travellers.

12 *Mobilization for both journeys.* In all, each tradition has three mobilizers, one for Journey I and two for Journey II. Comparison of the triads is not facilitated by the difference in order of presentation, but it is interesting that of the six mobilizers, three are said to come to the travellers directly from a divine world, namely Lomaśa, Athena/Mentes, and Hermes. In promoting Journey II, Lomaśa parallels Athena/Mentes, and Lomaśa's report on Arjuna parallels

> Athena's cautiously worded report on Odysseus (1.196–199; the caution is expressed in the particle *pou* 'I think', though the goddess actually knows the facts). But Lomaśa also parallels Hermes as mobilizer of the 'sandwiched' journey, that is, the one that interrupts whichever journey started first.

A more straightforward rapprochement concerns Vyāsa, who left instructions not only for the Visit to Heaven but also for the move away from Dvaita. The move involves all the Pāṇḍava exiles, including Arjuna, and is not part of the Pilgrimage, but its justification depends on ecology, or more precisely on the food supply. Vyāsa thus parallels Athena in the first Divine Assembly in two respects. Both figures envisage two journeys and mention first that of the solo hero (the future Journey I), and then, abruptly, as if it were an afterthought, a second journey, focusing respectively on Yudhiṣṭhira and Telemachus, who will be central to Journey II. In addition, this second journey is partly motivated by over-exploitation of the available livestock. Vyāsa's reference to the *mṛga* (forest animals, especially deer) killed for the Pāṇḍavas and accompanying brahmins parallels Athena's reference to the domestic animals (sheep and goats), being killed specially for the Suitors (1.91–92).

Concluding discussion

This chapter has been deliberately restricted to comparing the pair of journeys in the *Odyssey* with the pair in *Mahābhārata* Book 3. But the Visit to Scheria can also be compared to Arjuna's previous solo journey in Book 1 [Chs 2, 6], and in a fuller study, the two comparisons would need to be integrated. In both Sanskrit passages, Arjuna returns to Draupadī as Odysseus returns to Penelope, but in Book 1 he brings back, not supernatural weapons, but the additional wife who (unlike Draupadī) will ensure the continuity of the dynasty. Of course nothing guarantees that these two are the only Sanskrit or IE narrative comparisons that can cast light on Homer. The field is so enormous that many still regard the whole undertaking as hopeless, and I should like to express my gratitude to our honorand, who has so openly recognized its legitimacy.[8]

Whatever is understood by 'Homer' – an individual bard (literate or not), an editor or *Bearbeiter*, a bardic tradition, or some combination of these, a student of the *Odyssey* is likely to wonder why the epic combines the *Telemachy* with the last part of the main hero's *nostos*. Part of the answer is that, in some form or other, the two overlapping journeys were already present in the proto-epic from which both the Greek and Sanskrit traditions descend.

Afterword on anti-comparativism

This chapter, written to a strict word limit, was originally intended as a contribution to a festschrift for a distinguished Homerist, but in due course I received a polite rejection note together with the referee's reports on which the rejection was based. Anti-comparativists usually simply ignore the work of comparativists, so I thought it would be useful to publish these explicit criticisms – to which there are answers. Here was a rare and valuable opportunity not to be missed! However, as the reports were (very properly) anonymous, I could not ask their writers for permission to reprint the reports in full, so I extract and translate what seem to me their main points.

One report, in German, was clearly by an Indologist, while the other, in French, was clearly by a classicist. The Indologist opines that I have created a system whose components may fit together internally, but are sealed off as regards everything external. In particular, I have ignored essentially all the secondary literature except my own previous publications. This alone would justify rejection of the essay, quite part from the 'wholly implausible and absolutely undemonstrable thesis that the Mahābhārata *and* Odyssey *both go back to an Indo-European proto-epic which dealt with two interrelated journeys'. Should there after all be pressures to include the paper in the projected volume, the Indologist strongly recommended that at least some mention be made of the secondary literature offering explanations that arise out of the* Mahābhārata*. He or she then supplies six references bearing on the two journeys in the Sanskrit and on their relationship.*

Having (correctly) located the paper within the comparative field of study examined magisterially by Georges Dumézil in his Mythe et épopée *(1968), the classicist states at once that he or she is not convinced. The impression given is that I extract from the texts what suits my case and disdain what does not. For instance, regarding the Journey II travellers (in rapprochement 4), I 'see no difference' between someone's father and someone's brother. When a marked difference arises between the two epics, a rather vague similarity is called on to justify the claimed parallel. The more everything is made to resemble everything else, the less plausible the rapprochements become. Moreover, against my apparent view that the epics are linked by a stemma, as are the languages, one need only recall that the name 'Odysseus' has consonantal variants that point to a non-Greek (and hence probably non–Indo-European) source. Similarly, Mycenaean Linear B texts show the co-existence of Mediterranean substrate deities alongside the future Olympian ones. Thus Greek tradition may well include elements completely alien to Sanskrit tradition. All this is apparently ignored, says the critic, before ending on what is admitted to be a personal note: to explain the presence of the* Telemachy *in the* Odyssey *in terms of descent from a proto-epic appears to devalue a poet who merits better treatment.*

Thus, reacting from within their respective disciplines, both reviewers criticize the failure to cite secondary literature from those disciplines. But as its [original] title was intended to suggest, the paper is fundamentally comparative, and if I cite previous publications by myself it is because they are what is most relevant to this particular comparative study. To evaluate the rapprochements presented here, it does help to be aware of the very considerable number of rapprochements that have been presented elsewhere. Naturally, the vast non-comparative literature on each epic is often interesting to a comparativist, but the questions it addresses, and the assumptions it embodies, are so different from mine that I doubt whether references to it here would really help the reader.

Regarding more specific points, failure to cite does not necessarily prove ignorance. All three of the German scholars recommended by the Indologist have received mention somewhere in my previous publications; one of the recommended articles [is mentioned in Ch. 7]. In any case, all the recommendations concern the order in which parts of the Mahābhārata *were written down, which is a different issue from whether or not the oral tradition lying behind the epic is or is not cognate with that lying behind Homer.*

Nowhere do I claim that Homer drew solely on the tradition descending from the IE proto-epic; nor do I exclude the possibility of input from substrate cultures (or from loans, either in Greece or India). The aim, here as previously, has been to look for similarities between the two traditions – detailed similarities, hitherto unrecognized. I unapologetically put the emphasis on similarities since, provided they convince, they are more interesting than differences. I think similarities tend towards being finite in number, while one can always find innumerable differences – in language, geography, names, events, relationships. . . . It is not the difference between the names Odysseus and Arjuna that is interesting but the similarities between the journeys they make. It is not true that I see no difference between the fraternal link of Yudhisṭḥira and Arjuna and the filial link of Odysseus and Telemachus; on the contrary, I call attention to this puzzling difference. However, I am grateful to the critic for stimulating me to think further about it and can now offer a brief addendum on the problem.

In general, the Sanskrit seems to me more conservative than the Greek, so let us take it as starting point and rephrase the question. Does the Sanskrit contain a story about the youthful son of a major character who is sent on a journey to seek knowledge but returns having learned rather little but presumably having gained confidence? It does indeed.

Vyāsa the seer is both the composer of the epic as recited by Vaiśaṃpāyana and the biological grandfather of Duryodhana and Arjuna. Intervening quite often in the action of the epic, he certainly qualifies as a major character. Apart from his well-known role as begetter (on behalf of a king who died childless) of Dhṛtarāṣṭra, Pāṇḍu, and Vidura (1,99.21–100.30), he has a less prominent son called Śuka. Śuka belongs to the inner frame story rather than to the main story: he was the first of the five pupils to whom Vyāsa taught the epic (1,1.63, 57.74). However, his career is not recounted until Yudhiṣṭhira asks about it in 12,309.1. Born miraculously via a boon from Śiva, the youth devotes himself to the religious studies that will lead him to mokṣa. *When he is twenty-five (309.62), he is sent by his father to put any further questions he may have to King Janaka of Mithila (312.6), for whom Vyāsa officiates as priest. Making the long solo journey overland to the capital, he questions the king. Janaka offers fairly conventional replies before admitting that his teaching is already known to Śuka (313.41). The youth returns happily to his father and fellow pupils. Later he makes the journey he longs for to reach Brahmā and find release from the round of births and deaths.*

It would be easy to list differences from the Greek, but if the proto-narrative contained earlier versions of Śuka's knowledge-seeking journey as well as of Yudhiṣṭhira's pilgrimage, the Telemachy *could have conflated those two journeys, drawing elements from each.*[9] *This proposal clearly does not amount to a complete comparativist account of Telemachus, but it exemplifies the method by which the critic's objection can be countered.*

To end on a personal note, I agree with the French scholar that the whole comparative enterprise becomes pointless if everything can be made to resemble everything else, but I leave it to the reader to decide whether I succumb to being tendentious or vague (dangers of which I am very conscious). However I do not think that the paper somehow disparages Homer. If Homer was an individual (a controversial view), to show the debt of a poet to his predecessors is not to disparage him (one might think of Vergil, Dante, Milton, etc.). As for the German scholar, I am somewhat surprised at the confident dismissal of my thesis as völlig unwahrscheinlichen und absolut unbeweisbaren; *I would rather describe it as 'unexpected', and especially so for those unfamiliar with previous comparativist publications. Does the judgement reflect a feeling that current disciplinary assumptions and boundaries are unchallengeable and immutable?*

Notes

1 First published in 2016 as 'Why the Telemachy? Vyāsa's answer'.

2 The Sanskrit title of this *upaparvan* (division of a book) is the *Tīrtha-yātra-parvan*. I use the CE, as do Smith (2009) and Schauffelberger and Vincent (2013). Biardeau (2002), while providing cross-references, prefers the Vulgate edition, [as does the Clay Sanskrit Series].

3 For other comparably lavish sacrifices by Gaya, see 3,121:3–12.

4 [Commenting on the Greek, Saïd (2011: 140–148) presents the contrast in terms of Nestor's piety versus Menelaus' wealth – displayed not only by his palace but also by the parting gifts he offers his visitor. Her emphasis on wealth supports my comparison: Kubera is God of Wealth.]

5 The Bhīma–Hanumān encounter as a whole is cognate not only with the second half of the *Telemachy* but also with the Odysseus–Argos encounter [Ch. 7]. Entities in one tradition often have more than one parallel in the other.

6 For more comparativism on Kubera and Eumaeus, see respectively Allen and Woodard (2013) (esp. 44–47), and Allen (2002a) [with Ch. 20].

7 Odysseus says later (12.374–390) that Hermes told Calypso more than is reported in the messenger god's 19 + 2 lines in Book 5.

8 The reference to an honorand is explained in the Afterword.

9 [Not the only frame-story to main-story similarity. Compare (but this is Sanskrit–Sanskrit!) Vyāsa father of Śuka with Pāṇḍu father of Arjuna. Both the seer and the warrior king (Allen 2007c) are responsible for three male births – respectively Dhṛtarāṣṭra–Pāṇḍu–Vidura and Yudhiṣṭhira–Bhīma–twins, as well as for this 'special', much-wanted son. The special births result from the father's *tapas* and from a boon granted by the relevant god (Śiva // Indra). Both are celebrated by vast celestial assemblies featuring dancing, drumming, and showers of flowers.]

23

DROṆA AND CHRYSES

Indo-European (IE) comparativists working on ancient Greece and India often relate the Greek material to the Vedas, and as regards language this obviously makes sense.[1] But if one's interest is primarily in culture, Sanskrit epic has much to offer. Despite the fact that the *Mahābhārata* began to reach written form only a millennium or more after the composition of the earliest hymns, its similarities to Greek epic are often so striking as to suggest a common origin – a 'proto-epic' or 'proto-narrative' – from which both traditions derive via oral transmission. For instance, my previous *Mahābhārata*–Homer papers have argued that both epics structure their Great War in more or less the same way: the conflict has four daylight battlefield phases differentiated by the four successive leaders of the losing side, but ends only after a nocturnal massacre within an enclosure (Allen 2011). I suppose that this five-phase structure was present in the proto-narrative.

Having worked on the topic over the last quarter century, I now believe that early IE speakers already possessed a substantial proto-epic, a view that the present chapter will support. I also think that Dumézil was working in the right direction when he proposed his trifunctional ideology – a triadic system of 'primitive classification' (to use an old expression – cf. Allen 2000a: 39–60). However, his hierarchical schema is too constricted: it needs expansion both at its top and bottom ends, so as to give a pentadic schema [cf. Ch. 20]. My main concern here is with narrative, but when working on narratives one often stumbles across pentadic structures, and since this will happen here, I cannot ignore the schema. To express it with maximal – even brutal – concision, if Dumézil posits F1 ('first function') as magico-religious sovereignty, F2 as force, F3 as fecundity and related ideas, pentadic theory posits F4+ as transcendent other, F1 as wisdom, F2 as force, F3 as fecundity and so forth, F4− as devalued other. When the ideology is manifested in the division of labour, it will take the form 'king, priest, warrior, producer, slave/enemy'.

My focus here is narrow. I consider only the Sanskrit and Greek, only the *Mahābhārata* and Homer, and only a single episode from each tradition. However, the episodes are important ones, and I compare not only narrative events but also context, roles, and modes of narrating, and also certain 'negative' phenomena (shared silences where descriptions might be expected).

By way of introduction, here is a précis that covers both versions of the episode in question:

> Early in the epic an arrogant king rebuffs a priest who has made a reasonable request arising from previous events. Following this confrontation, the priest mobilizes powerful helpers, who use force to gain recompense for the priest and to punish the king. However, the repercussions of the quarrel continue, and in the Great War that lies at the heart of both traditions, the king is a leading figure among the Winners or 'Goodies', while the priest himself in the Sanskrit, or his divine helper in the Greek, is aligned with the Losers or 'Baddies'.

Context, roles, narratology

In the Sanskrit, the central figures on the two sides are cousins – the children of two half-brothers. Usually referred to as the Pāṇḍavas and Kauravas, they are respectively Winners and Losers. But the same names are applied to the vast coalitions that form around the cousins, and among the closest and most important allies of the Pāṇḍavas are the Pāñcālas.[2] The alliance between these two groups is not only military. A few years after the king–priest quarrel, the Pāṇḍavas proper (the five sons of Pāṇḍu) take the Pāñcāla princess Draupadī (daughter of Drupada) as their common wife.

In Homer, the Achaeans are of course the Winners, the Trojans the Losers, but the two sides are scarcely related genealogically, and the Achaean leaders are not a set of brothers sharing a wife. On the other hand, in both traditions, the Great War is between two vast coalitions.

Before coming to the events of the quarrel, I need to introduce the major participants: the kings – Drupada and Agamemnon; the priests – Droṇa and Chryses; and the priest's helpers – Arjuna and Apollo. I emphasize that these one-to-one correspondences need not apply outside the episode we are considering; in other contexts, a figure will very likely correspond to someone else. For instance, in the Agamemnon–Achilles quarrel, Agamemnon corresponds to Yudhiṣṭhira [Ch. 16].

Drupada, king of the Pāñcālas, rules from Ahicchattrā (or Chattravatī). In the Great War, he leads one of the seven Pāṇḍava armies and is considered as a possible generalissimo for the entire Pāṇḍava host (5,149.4–17)[3]; however, the position eventually falls to his son Dhṛṣṭadyumna. Agamemnon, king of Argos, leads the whole Achaean coalition encamped on the shore of the Troad and is sometimes presented as its king.

Droṇa is a brahmin and the incarnation of Bṛhaspati, priest of the gods. Though often called *ācārya* ('teacher, esp. spiritual teacher'), he also specializes in martial arts and, as a child, he and Drupada together studied the Vedas and martial arts in hermitages (121.9, 122.25–26). He eventually becomes the second of the five Kaurava marshals and his death marks the end of the second phase of the Great War. We know far less of Chryses, who is not mentioned in the *Iliad* outside our episode. He is introduced in 1.11 as a priest *(arētēr)*, who arrives in the Achaean camp bearing, as an emblem of Apollo, a golden staff with the god's fillets attached to it.[4] Priest and god are on close terms, much closer than Droṇa is to Bṛhaspati.

> After his rebuff, the humiliated Droṇa seeks help. Leaving Drupada's realm he goes to Hāstinapura, the capital city of the Bhārata dynasty, which at this point is home to both Kauravas and Pāṇḍavas. Droṇa soon becomes weapons instructor to the young princes, his best pupil being Arjuna, the third Pāṇḍava brother. After their training, as part of his revenge and as payment for his teaching, Droṇa tells his students to capture Drupada.
>
> Chryses comes to the Achaean camp to ransom his daughter Chryseis (captured by the Achaeans and allotted as booty to Agamemnon). Rebuffed by the king, he seeks help from Apollo. The plague sent by the god causes so many deaths that Agamemnon finds himself obliged to propitiate both priest and god; he has to send back Chryseis and provide a hecatomb for Apollo. The rapprochement between Arjuna and Apollo (mortal and god) is based less on their intrinsic qualities than on their role in securing justice for the offended priest.

Two similarities concern how the story is told. First, our king–priest quarrel comes near the start of both epics. In the Sanskrit, it comes in first out of the eighteen books. Admittedly, within the Ādiparvan, it starts in Chapter 121 out of 225, but if we consider only the main story (ignoring introduction, frame stories, and accounts of remote ancestors), we can place it about quarter way through the book. In the Greek, the account of the quarrel starts in line 8 of Book 1 out of 24. This is misleading in the opposite direction, since of course the *Iliad* presupposes and often refers back to earlier events, many of them recounted in the oral tradition that lies behind the Epic Cycle. But despite these complications, the early positioning within both texts is a clear similarity.

Second, both traditions narrate the quarrel more than once. Vaiśaṃpāyana, the main narrator in the epic, tells the story, or parts of it, three times: in his own words, in those of Droṇa, and in those of an unnamed brahmin.[5] Homer first narrates the episode in his own words, then in those of Achilles talking to his mother Thetis (1.364–392).

We can now turn to the sequence of events.

The rebuff

It was as school children that Drupada and Droṇa became friends, and the prince swore to continue the friendship on becoming king (Telling II).[6] Although Homer does not refer to Chryseis' childhood, and although she was captured not at home but in Thebe (also in the southern Troad), it was presumably during family life in Chryse that her father came to love her.

The priest's journey to meet the king is described with the utmost brevity. In both traditions, he simply 'comes' or 'goes' (Sk *(ā)-gam-*, *ā-sad-*, *ā-vraj-*; Gk *ēlthe* in both tellings). In the Vulgate, Droṇa is accompanied by his wife Kṛpī and his young son Aśvatthāman (Appx I, 75.26–27, cf. also 1375*.3). Chryses is presumably alone but, apart from bringing the ransom, he holds his golden staff.

The two priests arrive with different purposes: Droṇa wants wealth (122.31), while Chryses wants his daughter and brings wealth in exchange. But no doubt both are confident. Droṇa is cheerful (*suprīta*, 121.23, 122.32), basing his attitude on the friendship and promises of his school friend. Chryses' feelings are not described, but ransoming a captive is a normal procedure, his ransom is generous (*apereisia* 'vast', literally 'boundless') and, as he says, his relation with Apollo should guarantee respectful attention. The army responds accordingly, greeting his proposal with applause (*epeuphēmēsan*, 1.22).

Both epics move straight from the priest's arrival to his request and present it in direct speech. Nothing is said about reactions to his arrival or about the physical location of the event. This concision applies also to the Sanskrit request, for in all three tellings it consists of just three words: 'Recognize me, your friend' (or 'me as your friend', *sakhāyaṃ viddhi mām*, with second person singular imperative). The king understands the implicit reference to his childhood promise.

Chryses' speech is longer than Droṇa's. Starting with plural vocatives, he addresses Agamemnon, Menelaus and the army in general (line 17). Lines 18–19 politely wish the Achaeans success, both in sacking Troy and in returning home. Then come the requests – return of his daughter and acceptance of the ransom. They should agree out of respect for Apollo (l.21). Although Chryses uses two verbs, *luō* 'release' and *dekhomai* 'receive', rather than one, he essentially makes a single request, namely that the Greeks agree to the exchange, and, again like Droṇa, he seeks restoration of an earlier state of affairs (childhood friendship, daughter living at home). Another similarity is negative. Both priests dispense with an introduction, assuming – rightly – that the king knows who they are and what lies behind their visit.

Between Droṇa's speech and Drupada's, Telling II in the CE comments on the king's reaction. 'He laughed at me [Droṇa] as if I were a person of no significance' (*nirākāram iva*, 122.34). However, most manuscripts fill out Telling I with a similar passage emphasizing anger rather than laughter (1348*, two shlokas). The king disliked or could not tolerate Droṇa's words. When he spoke, he was frowning with anger and impatience *(krodha-amārṣa-jihma-bhrū)*, his eyes were red with anger, and he was intoxicated with power *(aiśvarya-mada-saṃpanna)*.

After mentioning the army's approval, the Greek text too precedes the king's speech with a sort of anticipatory gloss: the proposal did not please Agamemnon, who dismissed the priest rudely and with threats. So both texts start their description of the king's feelings by using a negative verb *(na-amṛṣyata, ouk . . . hēndane)*, then shift to positive verbs to describe how he expresses the feelings.

The king's rejection speech is longer than the priest's. It is far longer in Sanskrit Telling I (eight shlokas compared with one-quarter shloka, i.e. one pāda), though the other tellings reduce it to just the start and finish (Telling II has three shlokas), or just the finish (Telling III, one shloka).[7] The Greek king, with seven lines, utters two lines more than the priest.

In their content, the kings' rejection speeches are rather different. Drupada talks cynically about friendship and how it decays over time and is only appropriate between people of similar nature or status; Droṇa is stupid to claim friendship with him.[8] In explicit imperatives, he urges the priest to give up a worn-out friendship and seek a new one (122.6). But an implicit imperative comes in his final remark (1375★.2): his visitor will be supplied with food for one night – that is, for *only* one night.

Agamemnon's speech is more overtly aggressive. It amounts to 'Don't hang around or come back; if you do, I'll ignore your religious status and use violence. I refuse to return your daughter, who will live with me in Argos. Be off, and stop annoying me.' So both kings are essentially saying 'Go away!'

A structural similarity may be less obvious. The Sanskrit contrasts the king's friendly promises when he was a child with his snobbish rebuff once he is in power. The Greek contrasts the army's friendly attitude towards Chryses with the harsh rejection by their commander. So the Sanskrit attributes the positive and negative attitudes to different stages in Drupada's life, while Homer gives them to different components of the Achaean force.

Priest's recourse to archers

If the king has any afterthoughts about his recklessly offensive remarks, we hear nothing of them – nor of any reactions by Drupada's courtiers or the Achaean army. The reactions we read of are the priest's and consist in thought and action. He offers no verbal riposte.

Droṇa is furious. He thinks for a moment, decides that he will oppose the Pāñcālas, and leaves Ahicchattrā for Hāstinapura (122.10–11). On arrival, he lodges for a while with his wife's twin brother Kṛpa, living in a manner described as *pracchannam* or *gūḍhātman* (1357★.2, 5). Ganguli (1993 I Book 1: 275–276) translates both terms as 'privately', but they can also mean 'secretly'. Either translation suggests that Droṇa avoids broadcasting his plans.

Droṇa knows that he needs talented students to carry out the revenge he promises himself (122.38, 1375★.4). Encountering the Bhārata princes while they are playing near a well, he impresses them with a feat of archery (Telling I) and asks them to report it to Bhīṣma (whom the Pāṇḍavas treat as a grandfather). After an interview (which includes Telling II), Bhīṣma takes on Droṇa as guru and military instructor to the princes and gives him presents, including food and a house (1379★.5).

Though Homer's Telling I presents Chryses as frightened (*eddeise*, 1.33), Achilles describes him as furious (*khōomenos*, 1.380), like Droṇa. He sets off along the beach/

shore silently (*akeōn*, 1.34). Presumably he goes home – the most natural place for him to pray to Apollo is in the god's temple at Chryse.

This brings us to the speeches by which the priest requests help. Droṇa makes two such speeches, one at the start of his teaching and one at the end, while Chryses makes only one. The difference is natural inasmuch as Droṇa's helpers are youthful mortals who need his teaching to become heroes, while Chryses' helper is a god. Had Droṇa sought the help of Bṛhaspati, the two stories would have been closer than they are.

Bhīṣma formally hands over the princes, and Droṇa accepts them. When they are alone together (*rahasi-ekaḥ*, 122.41), the teacher makes Request I: the students are to promise now that, when they are qualified, they will perform for him a service that he does not yet specify. Arjuna alone gives the promise (Telling II). The text then turns to sub-episodes from the training period including the final passing-out ceremony. Immediately after the ceremony, Droṇa makes Request II: his students are to capture Drupada and bring him before their teacher (128.2).

When alone, going apart *(apaneuthe kiōn)*, Chryses prays to Apollo (1.37–42). He praises the god, recalls his own pious acts, and asks the god to take revenge: 'Let the Achaeans pay for my tears with your arrows!' So in both traditions, the priest's request to his helpers takes place in private: in planning his revenge, he avoids publicity. Even the requests show a certain reserve in their wording: Droṇa does not tell his students his motivation or exact intentions, and when he addresses the god, Chryses does not mention his daughter.

Since we now have reasons to compare Droṇa's requests with Chryses' prayer, it is worth looking at some details of wording that would otherwise hardly attract attention:

> *kāryaṃ me kāṅkṣitaṃ kiṃcid dhṛdi saṃ-pari-vartate;*
> *kṛtāstrais tat pradeyaṃ me. tad ṛtam vadata-anaghāḥ* (122.42, cf. 154.19).

'Something that I desire and want to see done is turning over in my heart; when you have completed your weapons-training, it is to be granted to me. Make this promise, blameless (princes).'

> *Smintheu, ei pote toi* . . . (1.39)
> *ē ei dē pote toi* . . . (1.40)
> *tode moi krēēnon eeldōr* (1.41)

'O Sminthian, if ever for you I [did such and such], or if ever for you I [did such and such], accomplish for me this wish.'

So in making his request, each priest alludes to services that he either will perform or has performed. The compound adjective *kṛtāstrais* ('when perfected in weapons') refers to the future but corresponds in the Greek to Chryses' references to his acts of piety in the past. The etymologically linked pronouns or demonstratives *tat* (= *tad*) and *tode* connect respectively with *kāṅkṣitam* (from *kāṅkṣ-* 'wish, long for') and with *eeldōr* (from *eldomai* 'wish, long for'). The first person dative pronouns *me* and *moi* are also cognate. The gerundives *kāryam* 'to be done' (from *kṛ*-) and *pradeyam* 'to be granted' (from *pra-dā*-) correspond to the imperative *krēēnon* (from *krainō* 'accomplish, fulfil', which is remotely cognate with *kṛ*-).

For a parallel to Chryses' acts of piety, we must turn back to a detail that precedes the Sanskrit requests. When confirming Droṇa's position, Bhīṣma presents him not only with food (rice) but also with a house that is *suparicchanna*. The root *chad*- means 'cover' and (despite other possible translations) *su-paricchanna* probably just means 'well covered' – in other words, 'well roofed'. Chryses mentions just two of his cultic activities: he has roofed an attractive shrine for the god (1.39) and has made rich offerings to him (1.40 – naturally of sacrificial meat, not rice). The rapprochement links things given *to* Droṇa with things given *by* Chryses, but both texts refer in the same order to roofing and nourishment – as it were, to lodging and board.

As we saw, Request I in the Sanskrit was couched in general terms while Request II was more specific. The Greek compresses the same sequence into the single prayer: Chryses first asks in general terms for the accomplishment of his wish, then more specifically asks the god to use force to punish the Achaeans.

We must move on from the priest's requests for the use of violence to the actual use of it, whether in preparing for the revenge or in carrying it out. As we noted, the traditions differ here: Apollo needs no preparation. Furthermore, of the two agents who help the priest, the god outranks his protégé, while the hero is junior to his guru.

Use of violence

Having demonstrated his keenness by responding to Request I, Arjuna soon shows himself both Droṇa's most gifted pupil and his favourite (123.1), and the Vulgate (though not the CE) makes him the central agent in the revenge. The aim now is to look for rapprochements bearing on the relationship between the priest and his helper. I start with some points of detail.

1 *Tears*. Droṇa's response to Arjuna's promise is to embrace him repeatedly and weep tears of joy (*pra-ruroda mudā*, 122.44). In his prayer, Chryses too refers to tears – albeit tears not of joy but of sorrow, and/or of mortification at losing his daughter and being rebuffed so brutally when he tried to ransom her. But both priests weep, and do so in relation to a junior figure or dependent.
2 *Affection*. Droṇa's affection for Arjuna is explicit: 'Arjuna became dear to Droṇa' (*priyo droṇasya ca-abhavat*, 123.1). Similarly, in Achilles' view, Chryses was very dear to Apollo (*mala hoi philos ēen*, 1.381). Both texts characterize the relationship by using an everyday adjective and verse-end verb and attribute the affection to the senior figure.
3 *Respect*. Arjuna works hard to honour his guru (*guru-pūjane*, 123.1). Such an attitude is of course proper in a student – *pūjā* is the normal Hindu term for

cult or veneration directed to superiors, including deities.[9] Chryses' behaviour towards Apollo could be described with the same term. The priest receives the honour in the Sanskrit, gives it in the Greek, but in both cases the junior honours the senior.

4 *Helper as protector and ruler.* As we shall see, Arjuna once protects Droṇa from a crocodile. Chryses prays to Apollo as the god who protects *(amphibainō)* Chryse and holy Cilla. Moreover, although Arjuna's place in the birth order of the Pāṇḍava brothers means that he is never king, he is the son and incarnation of Indra, King of the Gods, so in that sense comparable to Apollo, to whom Chryses prays as lord or ruler *(anax, anassō).*

5 *Reciprocity.* The service Droṇa's students are to perform for him is repeatedly presented as the fee for his teaching (128.1–3).[10] When Chryses requests the god's help, it is in return for his work as a priest. Both priests are saying to their helpers: you should give to me, since I have given to you.

On a more general level, although each priest takes revenge on his king by employing violence, he does not inflict it in person. The unarmed Chryses clearly cannot use force against Agamemnon, surrounded as he is by his army, but Droṇa's case is different. He starts off by studying not only the Vedas with his father but also weapons with Agniveśya. Then he marries, has a son, and finds himself hard up. When he hears about another priest-warrior, Rāma Jāmadagnya, who is giving away his wealth before embarking on a life of asceticism, he sees a chance. But Rāma has already given away all his property to other brahmins, and Droṇa has to choose between accepting Rāma's weapons (with instructions for their use) and Rāma's body (Tellings I and III). He takes the weapons, including the supreme *brahmā* weapon (154.13).[11] We are not told why he does not himself use these weapons against Drupada but, whatever the reason, both priests employ violence by proxy.

Helpers' training and attack

The period between Droṇa's two requests is filled by five sub-episodes relating to military training. (a) Droṇa encourages Arjuna to practise archery at night, which he does. (b) Ekalavya is a tribal chief who, by shooting arrows into the mouth of the Pāṇḍavas' dog, shows that his skill as an archer rivals Arjuna's – until Droṇa demands and receives the rival's right thumb as *guru-dakṣinā.* (c) As an archery test, Droṇa fixes an artificial vulture high up a tree (*vṛkṣa-agre* 123.46) to serve as a target. All the pupils fail the test until Arjuna, who performs last. (d) When the group go to the Ganges to bathe, Droṇa is seized by a crocodile. The first to react appropriately is Arjuna, who shoots it, and is rewarded by Droṇa with a special weapon. (e) At the public passing-out ceremony, the nascent Kaurava–Pāṇḍava enmity is publicly manifested. The two most military Pāṇḍavas almost fight duels with their particular rivals – so Bhīma opposes Duryodhana and Arjuna opposes Karṇa, but both fights are aborted.

Are the five events in any way organized or structured? A hint is given by the three that have animal targets: Event (b) involves the dog, (c) the artificial bird,

(d) the crocodile. Dogs live on the surface of the earth, birds in the air, and crocodiles in water, which suggests that we should look for other cosmic levels. Unlike any of the others, Event (e) involves the heavens, where the deities Indra and Sūrya oppose each other, each supporting the hero he fathered, but Event (a) disappoints us in not relating to any lower level.[12] However, the subterranean level that we are looking for appears just a little earlier in the story – between Droṇa's arrival in Hāstinapura and his first request. The priest's archery feat consists in forming a 'chain' of reeds used as arrows and using this device to extract from a dry well a tipwood (a wooden ball, *vīṭā*), with which the princes were playing until it fell into the shaft. For good measure, Droṇa also throws into the well his own ring and extracts it similarly (1365*, 1368*). So these five events relate to the five cosmic levels, moving roughly but not precisely from below upward. The match would be precise if the crocodiles started the animal triad rather than finishing it.

As for the targets themselves, the sequence is as follows: first, inanimate objects (ball, ring), then three animals (dog, bird, crocodile). But the series continues, for in the passing-out ceremony the targets are *human*: Arjuna and Karṇa both raise their great bows with a view to a duel (126.30–31), and in heaven the opponents are *divine*. This amounts to an ontological classification, roughly correlated with the vertical spatial one.

A third organizing principle may also be relevant, since (as argued in Ch. 12) the five cosmic levels tend to correlate with the five elements: earth, water, air, fire, ether. Although fire is absent from the earlier events, the others seem to be implicit, and the whole set seems to be implied in the list of feats that Arjuna performs at the passing-out ceremony. With his Agni weapon *(āgneya)*, he creates fire; with his Varuṇa weapon, water; with his Vāyu weapon, wind; with his Pārjanya weapon, rain-clouds; with his Earth weapon, *(bhauma)* he enters (variant: creates) earth; with his Mountain weapon, he creates mountains. Finally, with his Invisibility weapon, he makes it all disappear again (125.19–20). Since clouds go with water and mountains with earth, the passage is built around the four ordinary elements, plus a final fifth entity that stands outside the others and can supersede them.

The set of training episodes in the Sanskrit usefully illustrates how close comparison of the two epics can bring to light what are arguably manifestations of the pentadic ideology or at least evidence of its earlier influence. It is tempting to speculate that the various pentads we have noted were once neatly correlated, but that over the generations the bards lost their awareness of the correlations, or lost interest in transmitting them. Be that as it may, the set of episodes has no global parallel in the Greek, but it will provide some of the material we need for detailed comparisons with Apollo's response to his priest's prayer. But first we need to summarize the response to Droṇa's second request.

The newly qualified young warriors set off on their chariots with Droṇa to attack the Pāñcāla capital. According to the Vulgate, although the city is entered, Arjuna doubts that Drupada will be captured in this way, so he and his brothers wait outside the town. Meanwhile, Drupada and the townsfolk resist stoutly, and the Kauravas flee. Led by Arjuna, the Pāṇḍavas now attack furiously. After a fierce archery duel with a Pāñcāla champion called Satyajit, Arjuna engages similarly with the king. Then he lays aside his bow, leaps onto Drupada's chariot, and captures him. He calls a halt to the violence, reminding Bhīma that their guru requested only that Drupada be captured (Appx I, 78).[13]

As for Homer, Apollo descends from Olympus, angered by the treatment of Chryses. The arrows rattle in his quiver and his coming is like the night. He sits at a distance from the ships and discharges an arrow with a frightening twang. He attacks mules and dogs first, then humans. The dead are cremated in large numbers.

Here are seven rapprochements:

1 *Archery.* When inflicting punishment, both helpers use bow and arrow. Moreover, in the Sanskrit, archery is involved in Droṇa's feat at the well, just as in all five of the events intervening between his two requests. Other weapons are not totally neglected. Duryodhana and Bhīma specialize in the use of the club, and the twins are swordsmen; Yudhiṣṭhira is best on chariots, while Arjuna excels with every weapon (123.40–41). Bhīma wields his club both in the passing-out ceremony and against the Pāñcālas, but otherwise the emphasis is firmly on the bow.

Apollo is equally emphatically linked with the bow. He is addressed by Chryses as '(god of) the silver bow' *(argurotoxe)*, and it is a silver bow that the god uses against the Achaeans (1.37, 49). Other epithets probably imply the same weapon, notably *hekēbolos*, often translated 'far-shooting', which qualifies the god when he is introduced in 1.14. Whereas Arjuna's arrows are not linked with infective illness, Apollo's are assimilated to a plague and spread death throughout the army for nine days.

2 *Twang of the bowstring.* In the first sub-episode of the training period, Arjuna practises by himself. When Droṇa hears the twang of his bowstring *(jyā-tala-nirghoṣam)*, he embraces his favourite pupil (123.5). Apollo's arrows rattle (*eklagxan*, 1.46) in the quiver on his shoulders as he descends angrily, and the same root is used (*deinē klaggē*, 1.49) for the terrible twang of the god's bow.[14]

3 *Night.* Arjuna practises at night (*rātrau* 123.4), and Apollo comes like the night. Moreover, in the passing-out ceremony, while Karṇa son of Sūrya stands in sunlight, Arjuna is almost hidden by the shadow of the clouds brought by his father, the storm-god Indra (126.25).

4 *Positioning of archer.* Having decided against joining the initial assault on Ahicchattrā, Arjuna and his brothers wait half a league outside the city (Appx I, 78.17–18).[15] Before shooting, Apollo seats himself at a distance from the ships (*apaneuthe neōn*, 1.48).

5 *Killing of animals.* As the Pāṇḍavas advance on Drupada, Bhīma is in the van (*ibid.* 44). He clubs down many elephants and drives forward the enemy's chariots, elephants, and horses, like a stockman in the forest who drives forward herds of cattle with his staff (56–59). However, he does not kill the soldiers (*na-avadhīt* – Ganguli translates the variant reading *nya-*). In general too, killing

of Pāñcālas is de-emphasized or avoided. Arjuna shoots the horses of Satyajit but does not kill the man, and at the end he prohibits sacking the city and tells Bhīma not to kill Pāñcālas (117). The comparison is with the initial phase of Apollo's attack: first *(prōton)* he kills mules and dogs, the Achaean soldiers come later *(epeita)*.[16] No victims are named either in Ahicchattrā or in the Achaean camp.

6 *Dogs.* If the mules correspond to the larger animals in the Sanskrit (elephants, horses, cattle), what about the Achaean dogs? Dogs go unmentioned in the attack on Ahicchattrā, but we have met the one who was shot in the Ekalavya episode. Ekalavya is king of the Niṣādas, but since this social group is regarded as impure, Droṇa refuses to accept him as a student. So the Niṣāda trains privately, using a clay image of the guru he had wanted. When Droṇa's pupils go hunting, their dog wanders off and comes upon Ekalavya. Irritated by its barking, Ekalavya shoots seven arrows into its mouth. The dog returns to the Pāṇḍavas, who are impressed by the feat of archery. Ekalavya is identified, and Droṇa gets him to self-amputate his thumb. In this context then, the Pāṇḍavas' dog parallels the Greek canine victims, and Ekalavya the dog-shooter parallels Apollo.[17]

7 *Fire.* The cremation of the victims of Apollo's plague-arrows is natural enough, but there could be more to it. When Arjuna begins to engage with Drupada, he blazes like the fire at the end of a yuga or cosmic age (*yuga-anta-agnir-iva jvalan*, Appx I, 78.63). However, this eschatological fire, which consumes the whole world, is not uncommon as a simile, so this particular rapprochement could be coincidental.

Continued punishment of king

The archery attacks by the priest's helpers do not exhaust the punishment of the king. Once he is captured, Drupada is brought before Droṇa who, after humiliating him, takes half of his kingdom. After ten days of plague, Achilles summons an assembly and proposes asking the priest Calchas why the god is punishing them. Agamemnon now plunges into a second priest–king quarrel, which leads on to the commander–subordinate quarrel with Achilles [Ch. 16]. By the end of Book 1, the king has been severely punished: he has had to return Chryseis, pacify the god with a hecatomb, and accept the loss of military support from Achilles. In addition to the general similarity (both kings are punished for their initial quarrel), a more interesting rapprochement is between the two halves of Drupada's kingdom and the two major captured concubines, Chryseis and Briseis, with their paired names. Initially, Agamemnon has rights over both of them, so that when he returns the former to the priest, he feels entitled to the latter. Taken together, the two women correspond to Drupada's realm before he is punished.

Strictly speaking, we are now breaching the limits set to this chapter, but a quick glance even further ahead may be allowed. During the Great War it is Droṇa who kills Drupada, and soon afterwards, he himself is beheaded by Drupada's son, who will in turn be killed by Droṇa's son. So the initial king–priest quarrel carries on into the next generation, and the priest's son, in a sense, has the last word. Similarly, in the *Iliad*, the chain of cause and effect leads on, via Achilles' withdrawal and the consequent military disasters, to Agamemnon giving Achilles enormous gifts, among them Briseis. Though I cannot argue the point at length, this part of Agamemnon's career may reflect the three traditional functions. His treatment of Chryses and Calchas relates to the sacred, F1. His multiple humiliating failures as a general fall under F2, and his vast transfer of property to Achilles falls under F3. Given a trifunctional set, one should look for representatives of F4, and one wonders whether, outside the Trojan War proper, his own death represents F4−, and whether an event representing F4+ occurs in the lead-up to the war. This paragraph is intended only as suggestive, but I include it as a further example of the type of question raised by the comparison.

Concluding note on values

I have tried to show that the Drupada–Droṇa quarrel early in the *Mahābhārata* and the Agamemnon–Chryses quarrel at the very start of the *Iliad* have enough in common to join the already substantial body of evidence that supports the proto-narrative theory. Since some comparisons carry far more weight than others, and separating one from another can involve subjective judgements, an exact count of rapprochements has little meaning. However, I estimate that the chapter has proposed well over thirty new ones (ignoring, for instance, the five phases of the Great War, which have been discussed elsewhere).

It is too soon to try to reconstruct the details of an 'original' king–priest quarrel, but I shall address briefly one question that has been implicit throughout and will constitute my last rapprochement. If each epic is regarded as a totality, then, despite certain complications, the Winners have to be seen as the Goodies, the Losers as the Baddies. *On the whole*, the Hindu gods incarnate in the Pāṇḍavas, the demons in the Kauravas, and *on the whole*, a Greek audience must have sympathized globally with the Achaeans, not the Trojans. Kings Drupada and Agamemnon fight for the Goodies while, of the priests, Droṇa fights for the Baddies, and Chryses, like the god he serves, is aligned with the Baddies. However, in the king–priest quarrel, the moral position is reversed: one disapproves of the king and sympathizes with the priest. Thus, both stories start with an anomalous episode: the king's arrogant behaviour makes him a temporary or virtual Baddy, so that his enemies, including the priest he alienates, become temporary Goodies. In the *Iliad*, owing to the two following quarrels, this anomalous phase lasts longer than in the Sanskrit, but eventually the king takes on or resumes his leadership role among the Goodies.

A similar reversal applies to other figures. During the quarrel, Arjuna champions the offended priest and captures Drupada, but not long afterwards Arjuna is the son-in-law that Drupada secretly wants (176.8), and the two are allies in the Great War. Though he retains proper respect for his guru, the Pāṇḍava effectively transfers loyalties. Apollo, helper of Chryses, does not fit this pattern: he supports the Trojans up to almost the last moment. But consider Achilles. The supporter of the Achaean priest Calchas and hence, in a sense, of the Trojan Chryses, Achilles is eventually reconciled to his king and dies fighting for the Goodies. So initially, as priest's helper, Arjuna corresponds to Apollo, but later, as the best Goody warrior, he corresponds to Achilles. It is typical of the complexity of *Mahābhārata*–Homer comparison that in other respects again Achilles corresponds to Karṇa [Ch. 16 Quarrel 3].[18]

Notes

1 First published in 2016 as 'The king-priest quarrel in the *Ādiparvan* and the *Iliad*'.
2 For the history of the paired ethnonym Kuru-Pāñcāla, see Witzel (2005).
3 Unless otherwise indicated, all Sanskrit references are to CE Book 1, the *Ādiparvan*. Passages marked with an asterisk are from the Vulgate; they are referenced by line number, not shloka.
4 An *arētēr* is a specialist in powerful words, that is, prayers and curses (Graf 2009: 22).
5 Telling I (121–128) includes Telling II (122.24–38); Telling III is in 154. I use whichever version best fits my argument.
6 He later claims to have had ulterior motives (unspecified) for befriending Droṇa (122.6).
7 So the final shloka recurs in each telling (and again in 122.9). Final pāda: 'An old friend – who needs him?' *(sakhipūrvaṃ kim īṣyate)*.
8 Friendship is appropriate between people of similar wealth (F3), similar education (F1), or similar warrior quality (F2), and between kings (F4+).
9 In the Ekalavya episode (see next section), when Arjuna makes a request of Droṇa, he does so *praṇayāt* 'with or from affection' (123.26), so in this context the student's respect is combined with affection.
10 Usually called *guru-dakṣinā*, the fee is here referred to four times with other expressions.
11 So Droṇa acquires first religious knowledge, then weapons from the two teachers [Agniveśya's gift is mentioned in 158.27c], and finally wealth from Bhīṣma – a trifunctional set of acquisitions?
12 The Vulgate (Appx I, 76) gives one further anecdote before Event (a): Arjuna shows intelligence and keenness in maximizing the amount of teaching he receives. But there is no shooting and nothing clearly subterranean.
13 The CE – much briefer – gives no prominence to Arjuna. The ex-pupils simply crush the city, capture Drupada, and bring him with his councillors to Droṇa (128.3–5). In Telling III, the request is to take Drupada's kingship or kingdom and give it to Droṇa. The five Pāṇḍavas defeat Drupada, fetter him and his ministers, and show him to the priest (154.20–22).
14 The rattle of Apollo's arrows probably finds a parallel during the attack on Ahicchattrā. Arjuna's advance is accompanied by the rattling or rumbling of his chariot, no doubt of its wheels (*ratha-ghoṣeṇa nādayan*, Appx I, 78.46).
15 *ardha-krośe tu nagarād atiṣṭhad bahir eva saḥ.*
16 Kirk (1985: 58), commenting that the animal victims are 'remarkable', wonders if they reflect some historical plague.
17 Ekalavya would have fought for the Kauravas if Kṛṣṇa had not killed him (7,156.2–3). The *seven* arrows might relate to 'the special role of the number seven in the Apollo cult', which Burkert (1985: 145) derives from Semitic tradition.
18 Do Droṇa's two attitudes (pre- and post rebuff) relate to the two priests in Homer? An answer should probably involve another Trojan priest, viz. Helenus.

24

AŚVATTHĀMAN AND THE WOODEN HORSE

Sanskrit epic tradition recognizes two Great Wars, but I shall here ignore the *Rāmāyaṇa*.[1] With that proviso, both the *Mahābhārata* and the Greek epic tradition recognize one Great War. This phrase is 'tradition-neutral' in that it covers both the Kurukṣetra and Trojan Wars. Comparativists need such tradition-neutral phrases and here are two others. I shall call the ultimate Winners of the Great War the Goodies, and the ultimate Losers the Baddies – despite the awkward fact that the Goodies are not always morally irreproachable and that Baddies sometimes behave honourably. So (imitating the usage of Dumézil 1968), I call Pāṇḍavas and Greeks Goodies, Kauravas and Trojans Baddies.

Five phases

One basic similarity between the Great Wars concerns the leadership of the Baddies. On the open battlefield both traditions give the Baddies four successive leaders, who are eliminated or killed one after another. The Sanskrit series is carefully structured. Bhīṣma is the first Kaurava marshal (Sanskrit *senāpati*) and continues in office for ten days; then come Droṇa for five days, Karṇa for two, and Śalya for a half-day. Each name provides the title of one among the eighteen books of the Sanskrit (Books 6–9). The Trojan series is spelled out more clearly in the Epic Cycle and later literature than in Homer, but the sequence is clear. In the *Iliad*, the Trojan forces actually consist of two components: the Trojans proper led by Hector, and their allies led by Sarpedon. Sarpedon is interesting partly because, being son of Zeus, he is neatly paralleled by Bhīṣma, who incarnates Dyu or Dyaus – Zeus' etymological cognate [Ch. 10]. Anyway, after the deaths of Hector and Sarpedon, the Trojans are led successively by Penthesilea, Memnon, and Eurypylus. Each of these receives a separate chapter or set of chapters in Quintus Smyrnaeus (QS) who, despite his late date (third century CE), turns out to be a very useful source for comparisons – he must have drawn heavily on earlier texts. The changes in Baddy leadership punctuate the course of the war and divide it into four phases.

However, the deaths of Śalya and Eurypylus are not the end of the Great War. In both traditions, the battlefield fighting is followed by a nocturnal massacre of victims who are sleeping within an enclosure. Thus, the tradition-neutral term 'phase 5' covers both the first part of *Mahābhārata* 10, which takes place on the night of Day 18, and the sack of Troy, described at length by Vergil as well as by Quintus. The Sanskrit victims, paralleling the Trojan victims, consist of two groups: first, the Pāṇḍava army (minus a small group including the Pāṇḍava brothers and Kṛṣṇa, who are removed to safety just in time), and second, the Pāñcālas, the Pāṇḍavas' allies.[2]

The second part of *Mbh.* 10 takes place on Day 19 and has a very different character (I think of it as the 'cosmic appendage'). On the one hand, it constitutes the true end of the Kurukṣetra War and has a parallel in the *Odyssey* [Ch. 17]. On the other hand, it is so different from the rest of the war that I avoid talking of a phase 6, and say no more about it here.

The five-phase structure of the war proper is fundamental to *Mahābhārata*–Greece comparison and suggests the articulation of the proto-narrative from which I think both traditions derive. However, phase 5 is very different in the two traditions. First, by this time, the active Kaurava force is reduced to three warriors – Aśvatthāman, the fifth Baddy marshal, and his two followers Kṛpa and Kṛtavarman; in contrast, the Trojans are still numerous. Second, whereas Aśvatthāman is formally appointed as a marshal, the Trojans have no obvious leader in phase 5.[3] But the issue is complicated by the third and most important difference. In Sanskrit phase 5, the attack and massacre are conducted by Baddies, while in the Greek, they are conducted by Goodies.

From this point of view, the Greek equivalent to Aśvatthāman is whoever leads the attack on Troy. Officially the Greek leader is still Agamemnon, but by now his role is quite muted and the effective leader is Odysseus (as is recognized in his epithet *ptoliporthos*, 'sacker of the city or cities'). Since Odysseus with his band of warriors is inside the Wooden Horse, can we link Aśvatthāman to the horse?

Horse and wood

The idea of such a comparison is not entirely new. Pizzagalli (1942) discusses the relation between the Trojan Horse and Vedic horse sacrifice (the *aśvamedha*), and the topic is explored in a wide-ranging article by Christian Rose (2006), but unlike these authors, I confine myself to narrative–narrative comparison, ignoring ritual. An obvious starting point is the name of the Kaurava leader: Sanskrit *aśva* is the ordinary word for 'horse', being cognate with both Greek *hippos* and Latin *equus*. But there is much more to be said.

Aśvatthāman, 'the Attacker', is an unusual figure. Most of the major *Mahābhārata* characters incarnate a single supernatural, but Aśvatthāman (uniquely) incarnates four gods – Śiva, Death, Anger, and Desire (1,61.66–67). As a human, he is a brahmin, son of the brahmin Droṇa, but Droṇa himself incarnates Bṛhaspati, priest of the gods. Droṇa too is ontologically curious, in that he lacks a human mother. Reacting to the sight of a partly naked *apsaras*, Droṇa's father (a great seer) ejaculated and placed the semen in a *droṇa*; this wooden ritual vessel, a sort of bucket, served as a womb [1,121.3–5]. So Aśvatthāman's father's mother is wooden, and the origin of his mother Kṛpī is not dissimilar. Reacting to a different *apsaras*, Kṛpī's father (another great seer) ejaculated onto a clump of reeds (*śara-stamba* 1,120.22–23); split in two, the semen forms the twins Kṛpa and Kṛpī. So the Attacker's maternal grandmother is also vegetable and more or less wooden.

The next step is to extend attention to the third syllable of Aśvatthāman's name. The *aśvattha* is a species of fig tree *(Ficus religiosa)*, whose wood is used in various ritual contexts, for instance in the apparatus for kindling a ritual fire. The third syllable is a prakritized form of the verb *sthā-* 'stand', and when making this point, the standard Sanskrit–English dictionary of Monier-Williams glosses the tree-name as 'under which horses stand'. The text of the *Mahābhārata* does not connect Aśvatthāman the hero with *aśvattha* the tree, and different views can be found on exactly how to interpret the last two syllables of Aśvatthāman's name and on how they relate to the first two (Scheuer 1982: 297). However, they hardly affect my case: the Attacker is somehow wooden.

Moreover, the horsy side to the hero is secure because, immediately at birth, Aśvatthāman neighed like Uccaiḥśravas, the mythical and prototypical horse born at the churning of the Primal Ocean; on hearing it, an anonymous celestial voice announced the infant's name and connected it with the neigh (1,121.13–14). A similar account is given later by Arjuna (7,167.29–30), who adds that the neigh caused an earthquake (or more precisely a cosmos-quake – it was the three worlds that shook). Quintus, emphasizing the realism of the newly constructed Wooden Horse, says that it seemed to be neighing (*khremethonti* 12.150).

Large quadruped

As well as being wooden and horsy, Aśvatthāman has an elephantine aspect. To see why, we have to go back to the start of the war. On Day 1, addressing Yudhiṣṭhira (the eldest Pāṇḍava), Droṇa says that he cannot be killed when fighting seriously; he becomes vulnerable only when he lays down his weapons. This he would do on hearing something very disagreeable from someone trustworthy (6,41.61). Despite being an eighty-five-year-old brahmin, Droṇa is still a great warrior, and under his marshalcy the Pāṇḍavas sustain great losses. By Day 15 (7,164, tr. Smith 2009: 471–480), they are seriously worried; their allies, the Pāñcālas, are perishing in great numbers, and they themselves may be wiped out next. Addressing Arjuna, Kṛṣṇa now recommends what to do. Droṇa is particularly fond of his only son, and if someone tells the old man that this son is dead, he will lay aside his weapons. The idea is taken up not by Arjuna but by Bhīma, who finds in the Pāṇḍava host a large war-elephant (a *mahā-gaja*, 'as fine as Indra's'), who is called Aśvatthāman. He kills it and shouts to Droṇa that Aśvatthāman is dead. At first Droṇa ignores the message, but later he turns to Yudhiṣṭhira, whom he trusts, to ask for confirmation. Despite the Pāṇḍava's deep embarrassment, Droṇa receives what sounds like confirmation. He lays aside his arms and is promptly beheaded by Dhṛṣṭadyumna (7,165.47). My point is that, though the fifth Kaurava marshal neighs like a horse, inside the lie he is replaced by a homonymous elephant.

In Greece, the horse contains well over thirty warriors (QS 12.314–30). Obviously, it is far larger than a naturalistic horse, and the poet uses half a dozen different adjectives to emphasize its size. Vergil says it is like a mountain (*instar montis* 2.15).

One final point concerns the sacred aspect of the phase 5 Attacker. As a brahmin, Aśvatthāman has a hereditary relationship to the world of the gods, in addition to incarnating no less than four of them. His father incarnated the priest of the gods and his maternal grandmother was a Vedic ritual object. If the *aśvattha* tree is relevant, the *Ficus* is called *religiosa* for good reason. Moreover, Aśvatthāman's neigh is not just loud and realistic; it resembles that of a mythic stallion who belongs in the world of the gods. But the Wooden Horse too is far more than a military artefact. It is presented to the Trojans as being a piacular offering to Athena (2.183–86), and it is because they ultimately accept this that they pull it into their city centre. We already see hints of the sacrificial dimension of phase 5, which will recur in various ways.

Deception

Moving on from the nature of the Attacker, let us focus in on the events of Day 15. We are still before the narrative Crossover: the Pāṇḍavas are attacking the Baddy Droṇa, just as the Greeks are attacking the Baddy Trojans. Kṛṣṇa recommends recourse to a trick or strategy (*yoga* 7,164.68), which is presented by the epic as an act of debatable morality. The statement about the death of the elephant is uttered in the expectation that it will be misinterpreted by Droṇa as referring to his son, and eventually it is. Essentially, as Kṛṣṇa himself admits, it is a lie, an *anṛta* (164.99), albeit one necessitated and justified by the desperate circumstances. Globally, the Wooden Horse too is obviously a successful attempt at deception. Quintus provides plenty of detail.

Calchas the diviner sees that the war may continue indefinitely and assembles the Greeks. His proposal, backed up by an omen that we shall come to later, is that the Greeks abandon the use of force. Instead they should devise some plan or trick, *mētis kai dolos* (12.8–9), the same two words being repeated at the end of his speech (20, cf. also 48). According to Odysseus, Calchas is honoured by the heavenly gods, and in India, Kṛṣṇa, identified with Viṣṇu, enjoys a similar status. Both are non-combatants, and both urge replacing violence by some other method. So here the two speakers can be called (tradition-neutrally) the Proposers.[4]

In both epics, after raising the idea of a trick, the Proposer leaves it to someone else to flesh it out. In India, Bhīma takes the initiative and brings the elephant into the story. In Greece, it is Odysseus alone who responds to Calchas and proposes the whole plan of the Wooden Horse, including the lies to be told by Sinon. The initiatives of Bhīma and Odysseus (both of them warriors) are ratified by the

Proposers in a second speech. Kṛṣṇa's ratification takes the form of the advice he gives to Yudhiṣṭhira (98–99), when the Pāṇḍava is questioned by Droṇa some while after Bhīma's act of violence; whereas Calchas responds immediately to Odysseus' detailed plan. However, both Proposers warn of the threat posed by the enemy. If Droṇa fights for another half-day, the Pāṇḍavas face annihilation (164.98), and the Trojans are fighting with reckless bravery (12.60–65).

Scepticism

Although the Goodies' plan eventually succeeds, initially a note of scepticism is sounded: when Bhīma first announces the death of Aśvatthāman, Droṇa simply ignores him. Knowing that Bhīma could be lying *(mithyā)*, and also that his son cannot be overcome by enemies (*aviṣahyam arātibhih* 164.75–76), he runs off to attack Dhṛstadyumna with his arrows. A parallel at Troy appears in the episode of Laocoon. The priest does not believe Sinon's account (examined later), and rightly diagnosing a Greek trick (*dolos* 12.392), he urges the Trojans to burn the horse at once. According to Vergil (i.e. according to the story Aeneas tells to Dido), the Trojans are uncertain how to respond to the horse. Laocoon then runs down from the citadel, warns his compatriots against accepting Greek gifts, and throws a spear at the horse (*Aen.* 2.31–52). The two priests differ in that Droṇa's scepticism is internal – he does not discuss the 'lie' with the other Baddies, while Laocoon's is verbalized and addressed to the other Trojans. But in both traditions, the sceptical position is devalued by divine intervention.

In fact, divinities intervene not only against the sceptics but also in favour of the Deceivers. First a group of seers, led by the god Agni, comes to tell Droṇa that he is about to die. His morale shaken, Droṇa questions Yudhiṣṭhira, who is urged to lie by the divine Kṛṣṇa. According to Quintus, Laocoon is persecuted by Athena, who first blinds him, then, when he remains obdurate, sends the two snakes against his sons. But another factor that helps the Deceivers is the plausible story maintained by the Goody Sinon, in spite of the terrible tortures he suffers; his endurance is helped by the goddess Hera (QS 12.364–73).

In short, Droṇa is demoralized by Agni's group and blamed for violence that ill becomes a brahmin, while the Greek priest is punished by Athena for obstructing the progress of her protégé's plan (12.396), and/or for his hostility to the horse, which is an offering to herself. Yudhiṣṭhira is urged by Kṛṣṇa to support Bhīma's original lie, while Sinon is helped by Hera to stick to the story originally devised by Odysseus (12.32–40, 240–241). In a typical *Mahābhārata*–Greece comparison, Kṛṣṇa corresponds to Athena, but here, as supporter of the Goodies' lie, his parallel is Hera.

Both traditions allude to the death of the son or sons of the sceptical priest. The death of the human Aśvatthāman is of course the 'lie' that we have discussed, while Laocoon actually loses both his sons to Athena's monstrous snakes (or one of his two sons, according to the Cyclic *Sack of Ilium*).

An interesting rapprochement is conceivable at this point. After Yudhiṣṭhira's lie, fighting continues between Dhṛṣṭadyumna and Droṇa. Releasing a *brahmā* weapon, the brahmin causes the two teams of chariot horses to become entangled (*amiśrayat* 164.129); eventually Droṇa spears his enemy's horses and disentangles his own. The motif of entangled horses, which is not common, is introduced with the curious comment that it was a very beautiful sight *(bahv aśobhanta)*, apparently because of the mixture of the Goody's dove-coloured horses and the Baddy's red ones (7,164.130, 142–143).[5] This aesthetic note recalls the well-known Laocoon statue (first century BCE, already admired in antiquity), which shows the tangled mass of snakes and humans on the Troad. Intervening on the Goody side, the paired snakes match the two Baddy sons, but they also parallel Dhṛṣṭadyumna's horses, which must be harnessed in pairs; Laocoon as usual parallels Droṇa. However, there may be a hint of the Crossover: it is the Goody's horses who die at this point, and the Baddy's sons.

One final point about Day 15. In both traditions, one can find a three-phase structure: a preliminary attempt at deception is countered by scepticism, which itself is overcome by the definitive success of the Deceivers. Bhīma tells his quasi-lie; Droṇa doubts it; then the supposedly honest Yudhiṣṭhira confirms it. According to Apollodorus (*Epit.* 5.15), the Greeks inscribe the horse with a deceptive message saying that the object is a thank-offering to Athena, offered for the sake of their return. Cassandra, Laocoon, and others are suspicious. Then, though Laocoon sees the truth, the Trojans are again misled by the divine punishment he receives.[6]

Nocturnal massacre

Leaving Day 15 and the death of Droṇa, we now turn to Day 18 and the night attack on the Pāṇḍava camp carried out by Droṇa's son. At the very end of Book 9, the three Kaurava Attackers have spoken with the fatally wounded Duryodhana. Aśvatthāman, furious at the dishonest killing of both his father and his king, vows to avenge them with a massacre. Hiding for a while in a thicket near the enemy camp, the triad hear the triumphant shouting of the Goodies, whose revelry is described more fully in 10,1.59–62. Compare the Greek warriors, hidden in the horse, who hear the hubbub of the Trojan revelry (*homadon*, QS 12.577).

The triad move on and the two helpers fall asleep under a banyan tree.[7] Too angry to sleep, Aśvatthāman watches as a fearsome owl swoops down on crows sleeping in the tree and slaughters them; he will imitate the owl and attack the sleeping Pāṇḍavas. In Quintus, Calchas, in his initial speech, reinforces his advice by reporting what he had seen the previous day. A dove pursued by a falcon, escaped into a cleft; after a long and fruitless wait, the falcon hid in a bush; the dove now ventured out and was promptly killed. The Greeks should imitate this sign (this *sēma*) and use guile. So in both traditions, the phase 5 massacre is suggested by observation of a bird killing other birds. Fleetingly, Aśvatthāman parallels Calchas as observer, but the significant rapprochements are between the observations and the practical conclusions drawn from it. One could write 'owl vs crows // falcon vs dove', and Aśvatthāman // Odysseus (execution of project suggested by birds).

The plan of attack is not adopted without discussion. The brahmin Kṛpa objects on philosophical, practical, and moral grounds, making three substantial speeches. Though Odysseus' plan is welcomed by Calchas, it raises objections from Neoptolemus, who gives way only when Zeus shows his disapproval with an earthquake and thunderbolt. In both traditions, the Objectors, who want to continue fighting as usual, are paired – Kṛpa with Kṛtavarman, and Neoptolemus with Philoctetes (12.84–92), but no words are attributed to the second Objector.

Sinon is a complex figure who in different ways parallels no fewer than four figures in the Sanskrit. We met him earlier as confirmer of the lie, corresponding to Yudhiṣṭhira, but in his miserable decline he parallels Duryodhana. Duryodhana started the war as a rich and powerful king, but by the end of Book 9 he is lying on the ground, mortally wounded and writhing in agony. According to the account he gives to the Trojans (not necessarily true!), Sinon started the war in a reputable position as a follower of his relative Palamedes, but after incurring the enmity of Odysseus he ended up being chosen as a human sacrifice (*Aen.* 2.129). In any case, he was horribly tortured by the Trojans. But this is not all. After Śalya's death on Day 18, the Kauravas have been almost annihilated. Wounded and horseless, Duryodhana flees the battlefield on foot and takes refuge in a lake (9,28.24–25), hoping for an overnight rest (29.17). Sinon (in his lying story) is about to be sacrificed by the Greeks when he bursts his bonds and hides overnight in a muddy lake (*Aen.* 2.135).

Third, just as Aśvatthāman vowed revenge against Dhṛṣṭadyumna, who beheaded Droṇa, so Sinon vowed revenge against Odysseus, whose machinations caused the death of Palamedes. Moreover, just as Aśvatthāman offers himself to Śiva in a sacrificial fire on a golden altar outside the Pāṇḍava camp but remains unharmed (10,5.12–14, 50–59), so Sinon, sacrificing himself for the Greek cause, endures burning among other tortures (QS 12.364–373) but will not change his story.

The fourth parallel is with Śiva. The god is involved in phase 5 in many ways, but when he smilingly acknowledges Aśvatthāman's self-offering, he explains that despite his having previously protected the Pāñcālas, their time is now up. He gives Aśvatthāman a sword and possesses him, so that the hero moves towards the camp 'like Śiva himself'. Sinon too claims that he is now helping the Trojans (e.g. *Aen.* 2.157–161). This is of course a lie, while Śiva's words are true. But one can write 'Śiva // Sinon (change sides)'.

Let us focus on the composition of the Attacker groups. Within the Kaurava triad it is Aśvatthāman who enters the camp and carries out the massacre, while his two helpers are posted at the gate to stop victims escaping (10,8.5–8, 100–102); they also light three fires, which clearly represent the three fires at a Vedic sacrifice. The Greek has a comparable division of labour. It is the Wooden Horse that enters Troy, the warriors in it being led by Odysseus. Meanwhile, the rest of the Greek army burn their huts, leave the Troad for Tenedos, and will return to attack Troy during the night; they are led by Nestor and Agamemnon *as a pair* (QS 12.338–339). In both traditions, the Proposer of the plan enters the enclosed area, while the other two heroes stay outside, at least initially. Of them, the verbose brahmin Kṛpa corresponds to the verbose and wise Nestor, who makes two speeches bearing on the selection of warriors to enter the horse (QS 260–273, 287–296). In this context, the silent Kṛtavarman corresponds to the silent Agamemnon.

However, each tradition includes two further agents. Śiva too enters the camp, embodied in Aśvatthāman. A partial parallel is provided by Athena who, in so many ways, stands behind the attack, for instance by helping Epeius to build the horse and by blessing it (QS 12.154–156) – not to mention her special relationship with Odysseus. So much for the deities. But we must not forget Duryodhana. Though he remains at a distance from the camp, he is still the Kaurava king, and it is as such that he approves Aśvatthāman's vow of vengeance; he responds by appointing the Attacker as the fifth marshal (9,64.33–40), and he also receives the report of the triad after their massacre (10,10). In the Greek, we have already met Sinon as a partial parallel to Duryodhana. Whereas Duryodhana is in the process of dying, Sinon comes close to death in two senses: he genuinely risks being killed by the Trojans, and in his lying story he was almost sacrificed by the Greeks. That Sinon is a Goody and Duryodhana a Baddy is of course part of the Crossover.

Death of aged leaders

To compare the deception and death of Droṇa on Day 15 with the Sack of Troy is to compare an event from Sanskrit phase 2 with an event from Greek phase 5. Sanskrit phase 5 takes place on Day (or Night) 18, three days after Droṇa's death. This temporal gap provides an interesting rapprochement: after Odysseus proposes the construction of the horse (QS 12.28), the whole work is completed in three days (*tetelesto d'eni trisin ēmasi panta*, 12.147).[8] It is as if Greek tradition has compressed into phase 5 material that the Sanskrit separates by Books 8 and 9. This line of thought can be reinforced by a rapprochement between the deaths of two aged Baddy leaders. As we know, Droṇa the marshal (aged eighty-five) is killed by the much younger Dhṛṣṭadyumna on Day 15, which could parallel the killing of Priam, the Trojan king, by the much younger Neoptolemus in Greek phase 5.

Droṇa's death is described four times. Disheartened by the seers and by the reported death of his son, Droṇa, staying on his chariot seat, calmly devotes himself to yoga. This allows him to dispatch his soul to Brahmā's heaven – a feat invisible to most of those present. Ignoring reproaches from all sides, Dhṛṣṭadyumna begins to drag the bloody and by now soulless body; gripping its head, he lops it off with his sword (*parāmṛśat . . . mūrdhānam ālambya . . . vicikartāsinā śiraḥ* 165.46–47). Another account specifies that he grips Droṇa's hair with his left hand before beheading him (*keśān savyena gṛhītva pāṇinā . . . acchinac chiraḥ* 165.120). Both remaining accounts mention the gripping of the hair (*keśa-graha(ṇa)* 166.23, 167.40), which his son sees as particularly humiliating. Droṇa's grey hair extended to his ears (he was *ā-karṇa-palitaḥ* 165.49a).

As for the death of Priam (*Aen.* 2.506), it takes place by an altar in his palace courtyard. Despite his age, Priam has armed himself and watches, with horror, as the son of Achilles, Pyrrhus (aka Neoptolemus), spears Polites (one of Priam's sons). The king reproaches the Greek for his cruelty, contrasting him with Achilles and ineffectually throwing a spear at him. He is dragged to the altar, slipping in his son's blood. Pyrrhus winds his left hand in the old man's hair, then with his right hand raises his sword and plunges it deep into the king's side. But reference is also made to Priam's corpse as a head severed from its shoulders (*avolsumque umeris caput* 558). Indeed, Quintus gives only the latter mode of death: Neoptolemus lopped off the head of the hoary old man (*apekopse karēn polioio gerontos* 13.241) as easily as a harvester cuts an ear of corn. Priam is not afraid to see his killer approach since he wants to die amid his sons (13.222–224); compare Droṇa's yoga-induced tranquillity.

Skipping linguistic points,[9] I introduce one new fact: Droṇa killed Drupada (7,161.34). This opens up a complex rapprochement between what one might call two familial mini-feuds (Table 24.1).

Both epics tell of killings between two patrilines. If we label them A and B in the Sanskrit and A' and B' in the Greek, the story starts in row 1 with A killing B and A' killing B'. In row 2, revenge is taken by the relatives of B or B' – by the son in the Sanskrit, by the brother (with Apollo's help) in the Greek; so the original A and A' are now both dead. In row 3, the feud ends with the son of A killing the son of B and with the son of A' killing the father of B'. In both traditions the first two killings take place during the battlefield phases of the war, the third during phase 5.

Obviously, there are great differences. The symmetrical structure is clearer in the Sanskrit than the Greek. In the first two rows, the killings take place in the same order in both traditions, but not in the same phases of the war. Droṇa is a priest as well as a warrior, Achilles is not. In row 1, the killer's motivations differ: Droṇa is completing his revenge for Drupada's denial of friendship many decades earlier (see Ch. 23), while Achilles is taking revenge for the very recent death of Patroclus, his friend (some say his 'alter ego'). In row 3, it is primarily because he is king of the enemy that Priam is killed; unlike Dhṛṣṭadyumna, he has not in person killed anyone. Probably the most fundamental difference is that lineage A are Baddies, lineage A' are Goodies.

However, although there is surely scope for deeper study, I do not think the differences nullify the similarities. After all, each tradition presents two father–son pairs, and the Cyclic *Little Iliad* presents a third pair in the Greek: Achilles' son kills Hector's *son* – by flinging the child Astyanax from a tower (West 2003: 140–141; Gantz 1993: 654–657 mentions illustrations of the event). Furthermore, in most cases, the

TABLE 24.1 A family feud between leading figures on the opposed sides

Sanskrit	Greek
1. Droṇa kills Drupada (phase 2)	Achilles kills Hector (phase 1)
2. Drupada's son beheads Droṇa (phase 2)	Hector's brother Paris kills Achilles (phase 3)
3. Droṇa's son kills Drupada's son (phase 5)	Achilles' son beheads Hector's father (phase 5)

Note: Brackets indicate the phase of the Great War in which the killing occurs.

death scene includes allusions to the generation that is not directly involved. At Droṇa's death, we hear of the fictive death of Aśvatthāman. Priam alludes to Pyrrhus' father as well as reacting to the actual death of his son Polites. Despite the pleas of Dhṛṣṭadyumna, Aśvatthāman kills him in a particularly humiliating manner, explaining to his victim that he merits it for the sin of killing his teacher – that is, for killing Droṇa (10,8.19–20). At Hector's death, both parties refer to Priam and his potential ransom for the body (*Il.* 22.341, 352). Filial relationships run through all the events in Table 24.1.

Overview

The chapter started from the five-phase structure of the Great War and the final Crossover, the reversal of Goody and Baddy roles in phase 5. I have long supposed that the proto-narrative was more like the Sanskrit than the Greek, if only because the five Baddy marshals so neatly reflect the old PIE pentadic ideology. Moreover, since the Goodies have to win in the long run, it is clear why the climax to the Great War *should* be a Goody victory, and therefore why the tradition of a Baddy victory might be abandoned – while it is hard to see motives for a reverse change. I call this the *lectio difficilior* argument, borrowing the expression from editors, who assume that scribes were more likely to normalize a puzzling reading in a manuscript than to introduce one. But this argument bears only on the direction of the change, not on its motivation.

With this in mind, it is worth recalling one other massacre – the Khāṇḍava forest fire episode (Ch. 19). In the earlier study, the comparison was with *Iliad* 21, where individual gods supporting the Greek or Trojan side fight duels to amuse Zeus. However, the Khāṇḍava episode can also be compared with Quintus' description of the gods descending to the Troad to fight with each other, until Zeus and Themis stop them. This curious little 60-line *Theomachy* (12.157–218) comes between Epeius' completion of the horse and the selection of personnel for the two prongs of the attack on Troy. Since Quintus has already proved so useful here, perhaps his location of the story in phase 5 can cast light on the Crossover.

The Khāṇḍava episode tells how Arjuna and Kṛṣṇa are asked by Agni, God of Fire, to help him consume the forest with its inhabitants – animals and evil spirits. They accede, using archery to stop Agni's victims escaping. Indra brings a troop of gods, ostensibly to oppose them by force, but in reality to test his son's military mettle, as a sort of rehearsal for the Great War.[10] In the War proper, Dhṛṣṭadyumna, incarnation of Agni, is generalissimo of the Pāṇḍavas, so the incarnation parallels the hungry god in the rehearsal, and the Kauravas parallel the god's food. Aśvatthāman's two helpers, who guard the gate, parallel Arjuna and Kṛṣṇa, who block escape routes, and Aśvatthāman himself, rampaging in the camp, parallels Agni rampaging in the forest. The major difference is that Aśvatthāman and friends are Baddies, while Arjuna, Kṛṣṇa, and Agni are Goodies. But if the Khāṇḍava massacre was originally placed in phase 5 (and even if not), it could have helped to facilitate the reversal of moral polarity within the Greek tradition – especially since, in other contexts, Odysseus so often parallels Arjuna.

How persuasive is this explanation of the Crossover? I am glad to close with a question, for there is so much more work to be done before we can really grasp the relationship between these two great epic traditions. I hope to have shown conclusively that the prehistory of the traditions is a topic on which serious narratological evidence can be brought to bear, but we still know very little.

Notes

1 Unpublished seminar paper, presented since 2013 under various titles in various forums.
2 The leading Pāñcāla warrior is Dhṛṣṭadyumna, who is thus another parallel of Sarpedon; both these leaders of allies die at the start of a series. The Pāñcāla is Aśvatthāman's first victim in phase 5, and Sarpedon is the first major Trojan leader to die in the *Iliad* (phase 1). That Dhṛṣṭadyumna is a Goody, Sarpedon a Baddy, exemplifies the 'Crossover' phenomenon discussed later.
3 Could Aeneas be regarded as such? Certain similarities can be found between him and Aśvatthāman – both are Baddies who survive phase 5 and who show deep loyalty to their fathers – but I do not here pursue this idea.
4 I note the wording of the Proposers' speeches. Near the end, the words for deception appear in the nominative singular: *āsthīyatāṃ jaye yogo* (164.68a); *ei pou ti dolos kai mētis anussēi* (12.20).
5 In the same book, a different story (7,57, tr. Ganguli 1993 II: Book 7: 158–159) combines two fierce snakes – potentially killers, controlled by a deity (Śiva), who emerge from water – with the motif of paired colours (blue and red), but its relevance, if any, is unclear.
6 For the complexity of the evidence bearing on the Laocoon story, see Frazer (1921 II: 232–234).
7 The *nyagrodha* tree, *Ficus indica*, is grouped with the *Aśvattha* and two other species under the Sanskrit heading of *kṣīra-vṛkṣa* 'milk-tree'.
8 This *may* imply a proto-narrative with the duration of the phases of the Great War as in the Sanskrit. Is the ten-day duration of Sanskrit phase 1 reflected in the ten-year duration of the Trojan War?
9 Cognate vocabulary: *asi* ~ *ensis* 'sword'; *palita* ~ *polios* 'hoary'. Note the concise expressions for both Sanskrit beheadings.
10 The fire lasts six days (1,225.15; the Vulgate has fifteen days, 2138*); nothing is said of nights.

BIBLIOGRAPHY

The original versions of the papers presented in this book are indicated in **bold.** Abbreviations: *IJHS* = *International Journal of Hindu Studies. JASO* = *Journal of the Anthropological Society of Oxford. JIES* = *Journal of Indo-European Studies. RHR* = *Revue de l'histoire des religions.* UP = University Press.

Alden, M. 2011. The shield of Achilles. In Margalit Finkelberg (ed.), *The Homeric encyclopaedia.* Oxford: Wiley-Blackwell, 793–796.

Allen, N.J. 1974. The ritual journey: A pattern underlying certain Nepalese rituals. In C. von Fürer-Haimendorf (ed.), *Contributions to the anthropology of Nepal.* Warminster: Aris and Phillips, 6–22.

———. 1985. Hierarchical opposition and some other types of relation. In R.H. Barnes, D. de Coppet and R.J. Parkin (eds.), *Contexts and levels: Anthropological essays on hierarchy.* [JASO Occasional Papers]. Oxford: JASO, 21–32.

———. 1986. Tetradic theory: An approach to kinship. *JASO* 17/2: 87–109.

———. **1987 (= Ch. 1).** The ideology of the Indo-Europeans: Dumézil's theory and the idea of a fourth function. *International Journal of Moral and Social Studies* 2/1: 23–39.

———. 1991. Some gods of pre-Islamic Nuristan. *RHR* 208(2): 141–168.

———. 1993a. Arjuna and Odysseus: A comparative approach. *South Asia Librarians Group Newsletter* 40: 39–43.

———. 1993b. Debating Dumézil: Recent studies in comparative mythology. *JASO* 24/2: 119–131.

———. 1996a. Romulus and the fourth function. In E.C. Polomé (ed.), *Indo-European religion after Dumézil.* Washington: Institute for the Study of Man, 13–36.

———. **1996b (= Ch. 2).** The hero's five relationships: A Proto-Indo-European story. In Julia Leslie (ed.), *Myth and myth-making: Continuous evolution in Indian tradition.* London: Curzon, 1–20.

———. **1996c (= Ch. 3).** Homer's simile, Vyasa's story. *Journal of Mediterranean Studies* 6/2: 206–218.

———. **1997 (= Ch. 4).** Why did Odysseus become a horse? *JASO* 26/2 [for 1995]: 143–154.

———. 1998a. The category of substance: A Maussian theme revisited. In W. James and N.J. Allen (eds.), *Marcel Mauss: A centenary tribute.* Oxford: Berghahn, 175–191.

———. 1998b. Varṇas, colours and functions: Expanding Dumézil's schema. *Zeitschrift für Religionswissenschaft* 6: 163–177.

———. **1998c. (= Ch. 5).** The Indo-European prehistory of yoga. *IJHS* 2: 1–20.

———. 1998d. Cúchulainn in the light of the *Mahābhārata* and the *Odyssey*. *Cosmos* 14/1: 51–6.

———. 1999a. Arjuna and the second function: A Dumézilian crux. *Journal of the Royal Asiatic Society, Series* 3, 9/3: 403–418.

———. 1999b. Hinduism, structuralism and Dumézil. In E.C. Polomé ed., *Miscellanea Indo-Europea*, [JIES Monograph No. 33]. Washington: Institute for the Study of Man, 241–260.

———. **1999c (= Ch. 6).** Les crocodiles qui se transforment en nymphes. *Ollodagos* 13: 151–167.

———. 2000a. *Categories and classifications: Maussian reflections on the social.* Oxford: Berghahn.

———. 2000b. Cúchulainn's women and some Indo-European comparisons. *Emania* 18: 57–64.

———. 2000c. Scripture and epic: A comparativist looks at the biography of the Buddha. *Visvabharati Quarterly* 9: 51–62.

———. 2000d. Imra, pentads and catastrophes. *Ollodagos* 14: 278–308.

———. **2000e (= Ch. 7).** Argos and Hanuman: Odysseus' dog in the light of the *Mahābhārata*. *JIES* 28/1–2: 3–16.

———. 2002a. The stockmen and the disciples. *JIES* 30: 27–40.

———. 2002b. Mahābhārata and Iliad: A common origin? *Annals of the Bhandarkar Oriental Institute* 83: 165–177 (includes many misprints!).

———. **2002c (= Ch. 8).** Athena and Durgā: Warrior goddesses in Greek and Sanskrit epic. In S. Deacy and A. Villing (eds.), *Athena in the classical world.* Leiden: Brill, 367–382.

———. **2002d (= Ch. 9).** Pénélope et Draupadî: la validité de la comparaison. In A. Hurst and F. Létoublon (eds.), *La mythologie et l'Odyssée. Hommage à Gabriel Germain.* Geneva: Droz, 305–312.

———. 2003a. From mountains to mythologies. *Ethnos* 68/2: 271–284.

———. 2003b. The Indra-Tullus comparison. In B. Drinka and J. Salmons eds. *Indo-European language and culture: Essays in memory of Edgar C. Polomé, part I. General Linguistics* 40: 148–171.

———. 2004a. Tetradic theory: An approach to kinship. In R. Parkin and L. Stone (eds.), *Kinship and family: An anthropological reader.* Oxford: Blackwell, 221–235.

———. **2004b (= Ch. 10).** Dyaus and Bhīṣma, Zeus and Sarpedon: Towards a history of the Indo-European sky god. *Gaia: Revue interdisciplinaire sur la Grèce archaïque* 8: 29–36.

———. **2004c (= Ch. 11).** Bhīṣma and Hesiod's succession myth. *IJHS* 8/1–3: 57–79.

———. 2005a. The articulation of time: Some Indo-European comparisons. *Cosmos* 17 [for 2001]: 163–178.

———. 2005b. Romulus et Bhîshma: structures entrecroisées. *Anthropologie et Sociétés* 29/2: 21–44.

———. **2005c (= Ch. 12).** Thomas McEvilley: The missing dimension. *IJHS* 9/1–3: 59–75.

———. 2005d. Asceticism in some Indo-European traditions. *Studia Indo-Europaea* 2 [2002–5]: 37–51.

———. 2006a. Indo-European epics and comparative method: Pentadic structures in Homer and the *Mahābhārata*. In T. Osada (ed.), *Proceedings of the Pre-symposium of RIHN and the 7th ESCA Harvard-Kyoto Roundtable.* Kyoto: Research Institute for Humanity and Nature (RIHN), 243–252.

———. **2006b (= Ch. 13).** The Buddhist Wheel of Existence and two Greek comparisons. In M.V. García Quintela, F.J. González García and F. Criado Boado (eds.), *Anthropology of the Indo-European world and material culture: 5th International Colloquium of Anthropology of the Indo-European World and Comparative Mythology.* Budapest: Archaeolingua, 219–228.

———. 2007a. Bhīṣma as matchmaker. In S. Brodbeck and B. Black (eds.), *Gender and narrative in the* Mahābhārata. London: Routledge, 176–188.

———. **2007b (= Ch. 14).** The shield of Achilles and Indo-European tradition. *Cuadernos de filología clásica: estudios griegos e indoeuropeos* 17: 33–44. (French tr. 2014 in *Gaia* 17: 11–24.)

———. **2007c (= Ch. 15).** Dumont e Dumézil: una comparazione e una combinazione. *Quaderni di Teoria sociale* 7: 11–29.

———. 2007d. The Pāṇḍavas' five journeys and the structure of the *Mahābhārata*. *Religions of South Asia* 1/2: 165–181.

———. 2007e. Review of *Indo-European poetry and myth* by M. West. *Bryn Mawr Classical Review* 2007.10.53.

———. 2007f. The Heimdall-Dyu comparison revisited. *JIES* 35: 233–247.

———. 2007g. The close and the distant: A long-term perspective. In Georg Pfeffer (ed.), *Periphery and Centre: Studies in Orissan history, religion and anthropology*. Delhi: Manohar, 273–290.

———. 2009a (Ch. 16). The king-priest quarrel in the *Ādiparvan* and *Iliad* 1. In F. Delpech and M.V. García Quintela (eds.), *Vingt ans après Georges Dumézil (1898–1986): Mythologie comparée indo-européenne et idéologie trifonctionnelle: bilans, perspectives et nouveaux domaines* (VIe Colloque International d'Anthropologie du Monde Indo-européen et de Mythologie Comparée. Casa de Velázquez, Madrid, 27–8 novembre 2006). Budapest: Archaeolingua, 271–284.

———. 2009b (Ch. 17). L'*Odyssée* comme amalgame: Ulysse en Ithaque et comparaisons sanskrites. *Gaia* 12: 79–102.

———. 2009c (Ch. 18). The hanging man and Indo-European mythology. In P. Koskikallio (ed.), *Parallels and comparisons: Proceedings of the Fourth Dubrovnik International Conference on the Sanskrit Epics and Purāṇas*, September 2005. Zagreb: Croatian Academy of Sciences and Arts, 89–106.

———. 2009d. An interrupted embrace. *Romulus* (The Wolfson College Common Room Magazine), 11–12.

———. 2010 (Ch. 19). Hephaestus and Agni: Gods and men on the battlefield in Greek and Sanskrit epics. In W.M.J. van Binsbergen and E. Venbrux (eds.), *New perspectives on myth: Proceedings of the Second Annual Conference of the International Association for Comparative Mythology, Ravenstein (the Netherlands), 19–21 August, 2008*. [PIP-TraCS.] Haarlem: Shikanda, 357–372.

———. 2011. The Indo-European background to Greek mythology. In K. Dowden and N. Livingstone (eds.), *A companion to Greek mythology*. Oxford: Blackwell, 341–356.

———. 2012a. Idéologie indo-européenne et conflits des chefs dans le *Mahābhārata*. In H. Ménard, P. Sauzeau and J.-F. Thomas (eds.), *La pomme d'Éris, Le conflit et sa représentation dans l'Antiquité*. Montpellier: PULM, 187–200.

———. 2012b. Tetradic theory and omaha systems. In P. White and T. Trautmann (eds.), *Crow-Omaha: New light on a classic problem of kinship analysis*. Tucson: University of Arizona Press, 51–66.

———. 2014 (Ch. 20). Heroes and pentads; or how Indo-European is Greek epic? *Bulletin of the Institute of Classical Studies* 57/1: 1–19.

———. 2015a (Ch. 21). Cyavana helps Aśvins, Prometheus helps humans: A myth about sacrifice. *Comparative Mythology* 1/1: 13–22.

———. 2015b. Vedic sacrifice and pentadic theory. *Religions of South Asia* 9/1: 7–27.

———. 2015c. Review of *The Mahābhārata and Greek mythology* by F. Wulff Alonso. *Rivista degli Studi Orientali* 88: 241–247.

———. 2016a (Ch. 22). Why the Telemachy? Vyāsa's answer. *Nouvelle mythologie comparée* 3: 1–17.

———. 2016b. The common origin approach to comparing Indian and Greek philosophy. In R. Seaford (ed.), *Universe and inner self in early Indian and early Greek thought*. Edinburgh: Edinburgh university press, 12–27.

———. 2016c (Ch. 23). The king-priest quarrel in the *Ādiparvan* and the *Iliad*. *JIES* 44: 422–440.

———. 2017. Some verbal rapprochements between the *Mahābhārata* and the *Odyssey*. In A. Meurant (dir.), *Hommages à Bernard Sergent*. Paris: L'Harmattan, 69–87.

———. 2018a. Jupiter, Fortuna and Indo-Europaea: Reaction to a book by Marcello De Martino. In *The comparative mythology today. Müller, Frazer, Dumézil. Perspectives from the past to the future. Atti del convegno, Academia Belgica, Roma, 12 ottobre* 2017. Lugano: Agora.

———. 2018b. Khannās and Kaca: Threefold death and the elements. *Nouvelle mythologie comparée* 4: 1–13.

———. In press. Plato's *Republic* and the Indo-European pentadic ideology. To appear in *Classical Quarterly*.

———. and R.D. Woodard. 2013. Hermes and Gandharvas. *Nouvelle mythologie comparée* 1: 1–55.

Apollodorus, see Frazer 1976–9, and Hard 1997.

Baldick, J. 1994. *Homer and the Indo-Europeans: Comparing mythologies*. London: Tauris.

Balzani, M. 2003. *Modern Indian kingship: Tradition, legitimacy and power in Rajasthan*. Oxford/ Santa Fe: James Currey, School of American Research.

Barnett, L.D. 1907. *The antagaḍa-dasão and aṇuttarovavāiya-dasão*. London: Royal Asiatic Society.

de Bary, W.T., S.N. May, R. Weiler, and A. Yarrow (comp.) 1958. *Sources of Indian tradition*. New York: Columbia UP.

Becker, A.S. 1995. *The shield of Achilles and the poetics of ekphrasis*. Lanham, MD: Rowman and Littlefield.

Benveniste, E. 1969. *Le vocabulaire des institutions indo-européennes* (2 vols). Paris: Minuit.

Biardeau, M. 1981. *L'hindouisme: anthropologie d'une civilisation*. Paris: Flammarion.

———. 1985–86. See Péterfalvi.

———. 1989. *Histoires de poteaux: variations védiques autour de la Déesse hindoue*. Paris: Ecole française de l'extrême orient.

———. 2002. *Le Mahābhārata* (2 vols). Paris: Seuil.

Blaive, F. and C. Sterckx. 1988. Les trois péchés d'Agamemnon. *Antiquité classique* 57: 31–39.

Blaive, F. 1995. *Introduction à la mythologie comparée des peuples indo-européens*. Arras: Kom.

Bleichsteiner, R. 1937. *Die gelbe Kirche: Mysterien der buddhistischen Klöster in Indien, Tibet, Mongolei und China*. Vienna: Josef Belf.

Bodéüs, R. 1972. Société athénienne, sagesse grecque et idéal indo-européen. *Antiquité classique* 41: 455–486.

Boedeker, D.D. 1974. *Aphrodite's entry into Greek epic*. Leiden: Brill.

Bowles, A. 2006–8. (tr.). *Mahābhārata book eight: Karṇa*, (2 vols, CSL). New York University Press: JJC Foundation.

Boyce, M. 1975. *A history of Zoroastrianism, Vol. 1, the early period*. Leiden/Köln: Brill.

Briquel, D. 1978. 'Mahābhārata', crépuscule des dieux et mythe de Prométhée. *RHR* 194: 165–185.

———. 1980. La 'Théogonie' d'Hésiode: essai de comparaison indo-européenne. *RHR* 197/3: 243–276.

———. 1981. Jupiter, Saturne et le Capitole: essai de comparaison indo-européenne. *RHR* 198/2: 131–162.

———. 2007. *Mythe et révolution. La fabrication d'un récit: la naissance de la république à Rome*. Brussels: Latomus.

Brockington, J. 1998. *The Sanskrit epics*. Leiden: Brill.
van Buitenen, J.A.B. (tr., ed.) 1973. *The Mahābhārata: Book 1. The book of the beginning*. Chicago/London: Chicago UP.
———. 1975. *The Mahābhārata: Books 2 and 3*. Chicago: Chicago UP.
———. 1978. *The Mahābhārata: Book 4. The book of Virāṭa; Book 5. The book of the effort*. Chicago: Chicago UP.
———. 1981. *The* Bhagavadgītā *in the* Mahābhārata*: Text and translation*. Chicago: Chicago UP.
Burgess, J.S. 2001. *The tradition of the Trojan War in Homer and the Epic cycle*. Baltimore: Johns Hopkins UP.
Burkert, W. 1985, tr. J Raffan. *Greek religion*. Oxford: Blackwell.
Camps, W.A. 1980. *An introduction to Homer*. Oxford: Clarendon.
Carpenter, T.H. 1991. *Art and myth in ancient Greece: A handbook*. London: Thames and Hudson.
Celtel, A. 2005. *Categories of self: Louis Dumont's theory of the individual*. New York/Oxford: Berghahn.
Chandra, Lokesh. 2000. Bhava—cakra. In *Dictionary of Buddhist iconography* (vol. 2). New Delhi: International Academy of Indian Culture, 550–556.
Chantraine, P. 1968–80. *Dictionnaire étymologique de la langue grecque*. Paris: Klincksieck.
Charachidze, G. 1986. *Prométhée ou le Caucase*. Paris: Flammarion.
Chavannes, E. (tr.). 1962. *Cinq cents contes et apologues extraits du Tripiṭaka chinois* (3 vols). Paris: Maisonneuve.
Coomaraswamy, A. 1931. The Persian wheel. *Journal of the American Oriental Society* 51: 283–284.
Coutau-Bégarie, H. 1998. *L'Œuvre de Georges Dumézil: catalogue raisonné, suivi de textes de Georges Dumézil*. Paris: Economica.
Cowell, E. and R. Neil. 1886. *The Divyāvadāna: A collection of early Buddhist legends*. Amsterdam: Oriental.
Crudden, M. (tr., intro., notes). 2001. *The Homeric hymns*. Oxford: Oxford UP.
Dasgupta, S. 1992. *A history of Indian philosophy*, vol. 1 (of 7). Delhi: Motilal Banarsidass.
De Martino, M. 2015. *ARCANA VERBA:* Fortuna e Iuppiter *nel loro background indoeuropeo: Parte II, Il 'motivo della Sorte esteso'*. Bari: Edipuglia.
———. 2017. *The comparative mythology today. Müller, Frazer, Dumézil. Perspectives from the past to the future. Atti del convegno, Academia Belgica, Roma, 12 ottobre* 2017. Lugano: Agora.
Desbordes, F. 1981. Le comparatisme de Georges Dumézil. Une introduction. In *Georges Dumézil* 1981: 45–71.
Dougherty, C. 2006. *Prometheus*. London: Routledge.
Dubois, Abbé J.A. 1978[3], (tr. H.K. Beauchamp 1897, French original 1825). *Hindu manners, customs and ceremonies*. Delhi: Oxford UP.
Dubuisson, D. 1985. Matériaux pour une typologie des structures trifonctionnelles. *L'Homme* 25: 105–121.
———. 1991. Hélène et Sītā, ou le jeu des reines. *Ollodagos* 2: 219–230.
———. 1993. *Mythologies du XXe siècle (Dumézil, Lévi-Strauss, Eliade)*. Presses universitaires de Lille.
Dumézil, G. 1938. La préhistoire des flamines majeurs. *RHR* 118: 188–200.
———. 1939. *Mythes et dieux des Germains: essai d'interprétation comparative*. Paris: Leroux.
———. 1941. *Jupiter, Mars, Quirinus*. Paris: Gallimard.
———. 1948. *Mitra-Varuṇa: essai sur deux représentations indo-européennes de la souveraineté*. Paris: Gallimard. Tr. 1988 as *Mitra-Varuṇa: An essay on two Indo-European representations of Sovereignty*. New York: Urzone.

———. 1958. *L'idéologie tripartie des Indo-Européens.* (Collection Latomus 31). Brussels: Latomus.

———. 1959. Remarques comparatives sur le dieu scandinave Heimdallr. *Études celtiques* 8: 263–283 (tr. in Dumézil 1973.)

———. 1962. Les deux Palès (Déesses latines et mythes védiques 6). *Revue des études latines* 40: 109–117.

———. 1966. See Dumézil 1974.

———. 1968 (1981[4]). *Mythe et épopée, I: l'idéologie des trois fonctions dans les épopées des peuples indo-européens.* Paris: Gallimard.

———. 1969a. *Heur et malheur du guerrier.* Paris: Flammarion. Tr. 1970 as *The destiny of the warrior.* Chicago: University of Chicago Press.

———. 1969b. *Idées romaines.* Paris: Gallimard.

———. 1971. *Mythe et épopée, II: types épiques indo-européens: un héros, un sorcier, un roi.* Paris: Gallimard. Tr. of Part One 1983 as *The stakes of the warrior.* Chicago: University of Chicago Press. Tr. of Part Two as *The plight of a sorcerer.* Berkeley-Los Angeles: University of California Press. Tr. of Part Three 1973, 1988[2] as *The destiny of a king.* Chicago: University of Chicago Press.

———. 1973a. *Mythe et épopée, III: histoires romaines.* Paris: Gallimard.

———. 1973b (ed. E. Haugen). *Gods of the ancient Northmen.* Berkeley-Los Angeles: University of California Press.

———. 1974[2] [1966]. *La religion romaine archaïque.* Paris: Payot. Tr. 1971, 1996[3] as *Archaic Roman religion.* Chicago: University of Chicago Press. Tr. 1996[3], same title, Baltimore: Johns Hopkins University Press.

———. 1975. *Fêtes romaines d'été et d'automne,* suivi de *Dix questions romaines.* Paris: Gallimard.

———. 1977 (1980[2]). *Les dieux souverains des Indo-européens.* Paris: Gallimard.

———. 1979. *Mariages indo-européens,* suivi de *Quinze questions romaines.* Paris: Payot.

———. 1981a. See *Georges Dumézil.*

———. 1981b. Entretien de Georges Dumézil avec Jacques Bonnet et Didier Pralon. In *Georges Dumézil* 1981a: 15–44.

———. 1982. *Apollon sonore et autres essais. Vingt-cinq esquisses de mythologie.* Paris: Gallimard.

———. 1983. *La courtisane et les seigneurs colorés et autres essais, Esquisses de mythologie (26–50).* Paris: Gallimard.

———. 1985a. *L'oubli de l'homme el l'honneur des dieux, et autres essais: esquisses de mythologie (51–75).* Paris: Gallimard.

———. 1985b[2] (1966). *Heur et malheur du guerrier.* Paris: Flammarion.

———. 1986. Le messager des dieux, entretien avec François Ewald. *Le Magazine Littéraire,* avril, 16–21.

———. 1987. *Georges: entretiens avec Didier Eribon.* Paris: Gallimard.

———. 1992. *Mythes et dieux des Indo-Européens, textes réunis et présentés par Hervé Coutau-Bégarie.* Paris: Flammarion.

———. 1995 (ed. J.H. Grisward). *Le roman des jumeaux: esquisses de mythologie (76–100).* Paris: Gallimard.

———. 2000. *Mythes et dieux de la Scandinavie ancienne* (ed. François-Xavier Dillmann). Paris: Gallimard.

Dumont, L. 1977. *Homo Aequalis I. Genèse et épanouissement de l'idéologie économique.* Paris: Gallimard; tr. 1977 as *From Mandeville to Marx: The genesis and triumph of economic ideology.* Chicago, London: University of Chicago Press.

———. 1979[2] (1966). *Homo hierarchicus.* Paris: Gallimard; tr. 1980 as *Homo hierarchicus: the caste system and its implications* (complete revised English edition). Chicago, London: University of Chicago Press.

———. 1983. *Essais sur l'individualisme: une perspective anthropologique sur l'idéologie moderne.* Paris: Seuil; tr. 1986 as *Essays on individualism: Modern ideology in anthropological perspective.* Chicago, London: University of Chicago Press.

———. 1991. *Homo Aequalis II. L'idéologie allemande, France-Allemagne et retour.* Paris: Gallimard; tr.1994 as *German ideology: From France to Germany and back.*

Dumont, P.E. 1927. *L'Aśvamedha, description du sacrifice solennel du cheval dans le culte védique d'après les textes du Yajurveda blanc.* Paris: Geuthner.

Dundas, P. 1992. *The Jains.* London: Routledge.

Dundes, A. 1965. *The study of folklore.* Englewood Cliffs, NJ: Prentice-Hall.

Dunkel, G.E. 1988–90. Vater Himmels Gattin. *Die Sprache* 34, 1: 1–26.

Durkheim, E. and M. Mauss, 1903. De quelques formes primitives de classification. *Année sociologique* 6: 1–72 (reprinted in V. Karady (ed.) 1969. *Oeuvres de M. Mauss,* vol. 2. Paris: Ed. de Minuit.) Cf. Needham 1963.

Edwards, M.W. 1991. *The Iliad: A commentary, vol. V: Books 17–20.* Cambridge: Cambridge UP.

Eggeling, J. (tr.) 1882–1900. *Śatapatha Brāhmaṇa, according to the text of the Mādhyandina School* (5 vols). Oxford: Oxford UP.

Euler, W. 1987. Gab es eine indogermanische Götterfamilie? In W. Meid (ed.), *Studien zur indogermanischen Wortschatz.* Innsbruck: Innsbrucker Beiträge zur Sprachwissenschaft, 35–56.

Evans, D. 1979. Agamemnon and the Indo-European threefold death pattern. *History of Religions* 19/2: 153–166.

Evelyn-White, H.G. (tr.) 1982. *Hesiod, the Homeric hymns and Homerica.* Cambridge, MA: Harvard UP.

Farmer, S., J.B. Henderson, and M. Witzel 2000. Neurobiology, layered texts, and correlative cosmologies: A cross-cultural framework for premodern history. *Bulletin of the Museum of Far Eastern Antiquities* 72: 48–90.

Feller, D. 2004. *The Sanskrit epics' representation of Vedic myths.* Delhi: Motilal Banarsidass.

Feuerstein, G. 1980. *The philosophy of classical yoga.* Manchester: Manchester UP.

———. 1989. *The Yoga-sūtra of Patañjali: A new translation and commentary.* Folkestone: Dawson.

Filliozat, J. (tr. M. Shukla) 1991. *Religion, philosophy, yoga: A selection of articles.* Delhi: Motilal Banarsidass.

Fitzgerald, J.L. (tr., ed., notes) 2004. *The Mahābhārata: Book 11, The book of the women; Book 12, the book of peace, part one.* Chicago: Chicago UP.

Foley, C. 1894. Correspondence 4. *Journal of the Royal Asiatic Society,* 388–390.

Frauwallner, E. 1973. *History of Indian philosophy, vol. 1: The philosophy of the Veda and of the epic—the Buddha and the Jina—the Samkhya and the classical yoga-system* (tr. V.M. Bedekar). Delhi: Motilal Banarsidass.

Frazer, Sir J.G. 1976–9 (1921). *Apollodorus: The Library* (2 vols, Loeb). London: Heinemann.

Friedrich, P. 1978. *The meaning of Aphrodite.* Chicago: University of Chicago Press.

Fynes, R.C.C. (tr.) 1998. *Hemacandra: The lives of the Jain elders [Triśaṣṭiśalākā-puruṣa-carita].* Oxford: Oxford UP.

Galey, J-C. 1988. A conversation with Louis Dumont: Paris, 12 December 1979. In T.N. Madan (ed.), *Way of life: King, householder, renouncer: Essays in honour of Louis Dumont.* Delhi: Motilal Banarsidass, 13–22.

Ganguli, K.M. 1993 (1883–96). *The Mahabharata* (tr.). (1st paperback edn, 4 vols). New Delhi: Munshiram Manoharlal.

Gantz, T. 1993. *Early Greek myth: A guide to the literary and artistic sources* (2 vols). Baltimore & London: Johns Hopkins UP.

Garbutt, K. 2006. An Indo-European night raid? *JIES* 34: 183–200.

Geldner, K.F. 1951. *Der Rig-Veda aus dem Sanskrit ins Deutsche übersetzt* (4 vols). Boston: Harvard UP.

Georges Dumézil: cahiers pour un temps, ed. J. Bonnet. (A collection of essays by various hands, and an interview with the honorand). Paris: Centre Georges Pompidou/Ed. Pandora.

Germain, G. 1954. *Genèse de l'Odyssée*. Paris: PUF.

Giorgi, A.A. 1762. *Alphabetum Tibetanum: missionum apostolicarum commodo editum*. Rome: Sacra Congregatio de Propaganda Fide. [German tr. by Peter Lindegger, 2001. *Antonio Giorgi Alphabetum Tibetanum, Teil 1*. Zürich: Tibet-Institut.]

Gold, J. 1996. Plato in the light of yoga. *Philosophy East and West* 46: 17–32.

Gombrich, R. 1996. *How Buddhism began*. London: Athlone.

Gordon, A. 1963². *Tibetan religious art*. New York: Paragon.

Goudriaan, T. 1990. The Ātman as charioteer: Treatment of a Vedic allegory in the *Kulālikāmnāya*. In T. Goudriaan (ed.), *The Sanskrit tradition and Tantrism*, 43–55. Leiden: Brill.

Graf, F. 2009. *Apollo*. Abingdon: Routledge.

Gresseth, G.K. 1979. The *Odyssey* and the *Nalopākhyāna*. *Transactions of the American Philological Association* 109: 63–85.

Grey, L. 2000³. *A concordance of Buddhist birth stories*. Oxford: Pali Text Society.

Griffin, J. 1986. Greek myth and Hesiod. In J. Boardman, J. Griffin and O. Murray (eds.), *Oxford history of the classical world*. Oxford: Oxford UP, 78–98.

———. 1987. *Homer, the Odyssey*. Cambridge: Cambridge UP.

Grimal, P. 1982. *Dictionnaire de la mythologie grecque et romaine*. Paris: PUF (tr. Oxford: Blackwell, 1985).

Grimm brothers [J. & W.]. 1813. *Altdeutsche Wälder*, vol. I. Cassel: Thurneissen.

Grünendahl, R. 1993. Zu den beiden Gandhamādana-Episoden des Āraṇyaka-parvan. *Studien zur Indologie und Iranistik* 18: 103–138.

Guttal, V. 1994. *The* Iliad *and the* Rāmāyaṇa*: A comparative study*. Varanasi: Ganga Kaveri.

Hainsworth, J.B. 1993. *The Iliad: A commentary, vol. III (Books 9–12)*. Cambridge: Cambridge UP.

Hard, R. (tr., intro, notes). 1997. *Apollodorus, the Library of Greek mythology*. Oxford: Oxford UP.

Hartmann, A. 1917. *Untersuchungen über die Sage von Tod des Odysseus*. Munich: C.H. Beck.

Hauer, J.W. 1958. *Der Yoga: ein indische Weg zum Selbst*. Stuttgart: Kohlhammer.

Heffernan, J. 1993. *Museum of words: Poetics of ecphrasis from Homer to Ashbery*. Chicago/London: University of Chicago Press.

Hertz, R. 1909. La prééminence de la main droite: étude sur la polarité religieuse. *Revue philosophique* 68: 553–580, (tr. Needham 1973: 3–31).

Heubeck, A., S. West, and J.B. Hainsworth (eds.) 1988–92. *A commentary to Homer's* Odyssey (3 vols). Oxford: Clarendon.

———. 1989. Books IX – XII in Heubeck et al. (eds.) vol. II.

———. 1992. Books XXIII – XXIV, in Heubeck et al. (eds.) vol. III.

Heyne, C.G. 1802. *Homeri carmina cum brevi annotatione, vol. VII*. Leipzig.

Hiltebeitel, A. 1976. *The ritual of battle: Krishna in the Mahābhārata*. Ithaca: Cornell UP.

———. 1988. *The cult of Draupadī, I—mythologies: From Gingee to Kurukṣetra*. Princeton: Princeton UP.

———. 2001. Bhisma's sources. In K. Karttunen and P. Koskikallio (eds.), *Vidyarnavavandanam: Essays in honour of Asko Parpola*. Helsinki: Finnish Oriental Society, 261–276.

———. 2007. Among friends: Marriage, women, and some little birds. In S. Brodbeck and B. Black (eds.), *Gender and narrative in the Mahābhārata*. London/New York: Routledge, 110–143.

Hirsch, J.C. (ed.) 1986. *Barlam and Iosaphat: A Middle English life of the Buddha*. London: Oxford UP.

Hocart, A.M. 1970 [1936]. *Kings and councillors: An essay in the comparative anatomy of human society*. Chicago/London: University of Chicago Press.

Hopkins, E.W. 1901. Yoga-technique in the Great Epic. *Journal of the American Oriental Society* 22: 333–379.

Hornblower, S., A. Spawforth, and E. Eidinow. 2012. *Oxford Classical Dictionary*[4]. Oxford: Oxford UP.

Jamison, S.W. 1994. Draupadī on the walls of Troy: *Iliad* 3 from an Indic perspective. *Classical Antiquity* 13: 5–16.

———. 1999. Penelope and the pigs: Indic perspectives on the Odyssey. *Classical Antiquity* 18/2: 227–272.

Janda, M. 2000. *Eleusis: Das indogermanische Erbe der Mysterien*. Innsbruck: Institut für Sprachwissenschaft.

Janko, R. 1992. *The Iliad: A commentary. Vol. IV: Books 13–16*. Cambridge: Cambridge UP.

Johnson, W. 1998 (tr.). *The Sauptikaparvan of the Mahābhārata*. Oxford: Oxford UP.

de Jong, J.W. 1985. The over-burdened earth in India and Greece. *Journal of the American Oriental Society* 105: 397–400.

Julien, S.1860. *Contes et apologues indiens* (2 vols). Paris: Hachette.

Jurewicz, J. 2000. Playing with fire: The *pratītyasamutpāda* from the perspective of Vedic thought. *Journal of the Pali Text Society* 26: 77–103.

Kane, P.V. 1941. *History of Dharmaśāstra (ancient and mediaeval, religious and civil law)*, (5 vols, 1930–1962). Poona: Bhandarkar Oriental Research Institute.

Karanika, A. 2001. Memories of poetic discourse in Athena's cult practice. In Deacy and Villing eds., 277–291.

Katz, R. 1989. *Arjuna in the Mahābhārata*. Columbia, SC: University of South Carolina Press.

Kirk, G.S. 1974. *The nature of Greek myths*. Harmondsworth: Penguin.

———. 1985, *The Iliad: A commentary, vol. I: Books I – IV*. Cambridge: Cambridge UP.

Kortlandt, F. 2018. The expansion of the Indo-European languages. *JIES* 46: 219–231.

Koskikallio, P. (ed.) 2009. *Parallels and comparisons: Proceedings of the Fourth Dubrovnik International Conference on the Sanskrit epics and purāṇas*, September 2005. Zagreb: Croatian Academy of Sciences and Arts, 89–106.

Kozintsev, A. 2018. On certain aspects of distance-based models of language relationships, with reference to the position of Indo-European among other language families. *JIES* 46: 173–205.

Kuhn, E. 1888. Der Mann im Brunnen, Geschichte eines indischen Gleichnisses. In *Festgruss an Otto von Böhtlinck*. Stuttgart: Kohlhammer, 68–76.

Kvaerne, P. 1981. A bonpo version of the wheel of existence. In M. Strickmann (ed.) *Tantric and Taoist studies in honour of R.A. Stein*. Brussels: Institut Belge des Hautes Etudes Chinoises, 274–289.

Larrington, C. (tr., intro., notes). 1996. *The poetic Edda*. Oxford: UP.

Larson, G.J. 1979 [1969]. *Classical Sāṃkhya: An interpretation of its history and meaning*. Delhi: Motilal Banarsidass.

Leaf, W. (ed.) 1900–2. *The Iliad*[2] (2 vols). London: MacMillan.

Leslie, J. (ed.) 1996. *Myth and myth-making*. London: Curzon.

Lessing, G.E. 1990. *Laokoon: oder über die Grenzen der Malerei und Poesie*. In W. Barner (ed.), *Werke 1766–1769*. Frankfurt: Deutsche Klassike Verlag.

Lexicon iconographicum mythologiae classicae [LIMC], 1981–99. Zürich & München: Artemis Verlag.

Littleton, C.S. 1970. The 'Kingship in Heaven' theme. In J. Puhvel (ed.), *Myth and law among the Indo-Europeans*. Berkeley: University of California Press, 83–121.

———. 1980. The problem that was Greece: Some observations on the Greek tradition from the standpoint of the New Comparative Mythology. *Arethusa* 13: 141–159.

———. 1982[3] [1966, 1972]. *The new comparative mythology: An anthropological assessment of the theories of Georges Dumézil*. Berkeley: California California UP.

Lukinovich, A. 1998. Le cercle des douze étapes du voyage d'Ulysse aux confins du monde. *Gaia* 3: 9–26.

Macdonell, A.A. 1974 [1897, wrongly 1898 in Delhi edition]. *Vedic mythology*. Delhi: Motilal Banarsidass.

McClymond, K. 2003. Death be not proud: Re-evaluating the role of killing in sacrifice. *IJHS* 6/3: 221–242.

McEvilley, T. 1981. An archaeology of yoga. *Res* 1: 44–77.

———. 1981 [1898]. *Vedic mythology*. Delhi: Motilal Banarsidass.

———. 2002. *The shape of ancient thought: Comparative studies in Greek and Indian philosophies*. New York: Allworth.

McGrath, K. 2018. *Bhīṣma Devavrata: Authority in epic* Mahābhārata. Hyderabad: Orient Blackswan.

Maddock, K. 1973. *The Australian Aborigines: A portrait of their society*. London: Allen Lane.

Mahābhārata, 1933–60. Critical Edition (19 vols) by V.S. Sukthankar *et al.* Pune: Bhandarkar Oriental Institute.

Mair, V.H. 1988. *Painting and performance: Chinese picture recitation and its Indian genesis*. Honolulu: University of Hawaii Press.

Mallory, J.P. 1989. *In search of the Indo-Europeans: Language, archaeology and myth*. London: Thames & Hudson.

———. and D.Q. Adams (eds.) 1997. *Encyclopaedia of Indo-European culture*. London: Fitzroy Dearborn.

Marg, W. 1971. *Homer über die Dichtung*. Munster: Aschendorff.

Mattéi, J.-F. 1996 [1993]. *Pythagore et les pythagoriciens*. Paris: PUF.

Mauss, M. 1947, *Manuel d'ethnographie*. Paris: Payot. Tr. as *Manual of ethnography*. New York/Oxford: Berghahn/Durkheim Press.

———. 1969 [1927]. Rapports historiques entre la mystique hindoue et la mystique occidentale. In V. Karady (ed.) *Œuvres*, vol. 2, 556–560. Paris: Minuit.

Meulder, M. 2002. Séquences trifonctionnelles indo-européennes dans l'*Odyssée. Dialogues d'histoire ancienne* 28: 17–39.

Moule, G.E. 1885. A Buddhist sheet-tract, containing an apologue of human life. *Journal of the China Branch of the Royal Asiatic Society* 19/1: 94–102.

Moulton, C. 1977. *Similes in the Homeric poems*. Göttingen: Vandenhoeck and Ruprecht.

Murray, A.T. 1976–78. *Homer the Iliad: With an English translation* (2 vols). [Loeb]. Cambridge MA: Harvard UP, London: Heinemann.

Mus, P. 1939. *La Lumière sur les six voies*. Paris: Institut d'Ethnologie.

Nagy, G. 1979. *The best of the Achaeans: Concepts of the hero in archaic Greek poetry*. Baltimore: John Hopkins UP.

———. 2010. *Homer the preclassic*. Berkeley, Los Angeles, London: University of California Press.

Narten, J. 1982. *Die Aməṣ̌a Spəntas im Avesta*. Wiesbaden: Otto Harrassowitz.

Needham, Rodney (intro., tr., ed.) 1963. *Primitive classification*. London: Cohen and West.

———. (ed.) 1973. *Right and left: Essays on dual symbolic classification*. Chicago: Chicago UP.

Ó Cathasaigh, T. (ed. M. Boyd) 2014. Coire sois*: The cauldron of knowledge, a companion to early Irish saga*. Notre Dame: University of Notre Dame Press.

Oldenberg, H. 1988 [1916]. *The religion of the Veda* (tr. S.B. Shrotri). Delhi: Motilal Banarsidass.

O'Flaherty, W.D. 1975. *Hindu myths: a sourcebook*. Harmondsworth: Penguin.

———. 1980. *Sexual metaphors and animal symbols in Indian mythology*. Delhi: Motilal Banarsidass.

———. 1981. *The rig veda: An anthology*. Harmondsworth: Penguin.

———. 1987. Indra. In M. Eliade et al. eds. *Encyclopaedia of religion*. New York: Macmillan, 7: 214–215.

Pai, A. (ed.) 1989. *Mahābhārata – 14 (Arjuna's Twelve-year exile)*. Part 2 of Amar Citra Katha bumper issue 55. Bombay: India Book House.

Paranjpe, V.G. (ed.) 1956. *The Strīparvan* (CE). Poona: BORI.

Parkin, R. 2003. *Louis Dumont and hierarchical opposition*. New York/Oxford: Berghahn.

———. 2006. Louis Dumont: estructuralismo, jerarquia e individualismo. *Revista de Occidente* 300: 9–34.

Parpola, A. 2004–5. The Nāsatyas, the chariot and Proto-Aryan religion. *Journal of Indological Studies* 16–17: 5–67.

Parry, J. 1998, Mauss, Dumont and the distinction between status and power. In W. James and N.J. Allen (eds.), *Marcel Mauss: A centenary tribute*. New York/Oxford: Berghahn, 151–172.

Pauly, A. and G. Wissowa (eds.) 1894–1980. *Pauly's Real-Encyclopädie des classischen Altertumswissenschaft*. Stuttgart: Metzler.

Pauly, B. 1959. Fragments sanskrits de Haute Asie (Mission Pelliot). VII Prescriptions relatives au dessin de la roue de la transmigration (*saṃsāra-cakra*). *Journal asiatique* 247: 228–240.

Péterfalvi, J.-M. (tr.) and M. Biardeau (intro., comm.). 1985–86. *Le Mahābhārata* (2 vols). Paris: Flammarion.

Pizzagalli, A.M. 1942. Il cavallo di Troia e l'Aśvamedha. *Atene e Roma* 42: 110–116.

Pokorny, J. 1959. *Indogermanisches etymologisches Wörterbuch*. Tübingen: Francke.

Polomé, E.C. 1994a. Das Pferd in der Religion der eurasischen Völker. In B. Hänsel and S. Zimmer (eds.), *Die Indogermanen und das Pferd*. Budapest: Archaeolingua.

———. 1994b. L'Aśvamedha est-il un rituel de date indo-européenne? In *Nomina rerum: hommage à Jacqueline Manessy-Guitton*. Nice: Centre de Recherches Comparatives sur les Langues de la Méditerranée Ancienne [LAMA], 349–361.

———, D.Q. Adams, and J.P. Mallory. 1997. The Indo-European sky god. In J.P. Mallory and D.Q. Adams (eds.), *Encyclopaedia of Indo-European culture*. London-Chicago: Fitzroy Dearborn, 231.

Poucet, J. 1985. *Les origines de Rome: tradition et histoire*. Brussels: Facultés universitaires Saint-Louis.

Preciado-Solis, B. 1984. *The Kṛṣṇa cycle in the Purāṇas: Themes and motifs in a heroic saga*. Delhi: Motilal Banarsidass.

Prinsep, J. 1835. IV. Facsimiles of ancient inscriptions. *Journal of the Asiatic Society of Bengal*, 554–561.

Przyluski, J. 1920. La roue de la vie à Ajanta. *Journal asiatique* 16: 313–331.

Puhvel, J. 1987. *Comparative mythology*. Baltimore: Johns Hopkins UP.

Race, W.H. 1982. *The classical priamel from Homer to Boethius* (Mnemosyne Supplement 74). Leiden: Brill.

Raghu Vira 1936. See Vira, R.

Redfield, J.M. 1975. *Nature and culture in the Iliad: The tragedy of Hector*. Chicago: Chicago UP.

Rees, A. and B. Rees. 1961. *Celtic heritage: Ancient tradition in Ireland and Wales*. London: Thames and Hudson.

Renfrew, C. 1987. *Archaeology and language: The puzzle of Indo-European origins*. London: Cape.

Richardson, N. 1993. *The Iliad: A commentary, Volume VI: Books 21–24*. Cambridge: Cambridge UP.

Rose, C. 2006. Le cheval de Troie, l'*aśvamedha* et Asvatthāman (Esquisses indo-grecques IV). In M.V. García Quintela, F.J. González García and F. Criado Boado (eds.), *Anthropology of the Indo-European world and material culture: 5th International Colloquium of Anthropology of the Indo-European World and Comparative Mythology*. Budapest: Archaeolingua, 229–258.

Russo, J. 1992. In Heubeck et al. (eds.), *vol. III (Books XVII – XX)*.

Saïd, S. 2011 (French 1998). *Homer and the Odyssey*. Oxford: Oxford UP.

de Sales, A. 1991. *Je suis né de vos jeux de tambours: religion chamanique des Magars du Nord*. Nanterre: Société d'Ethologie.

Śatapatha Brāhmaṇa see Eggeling.

Sauzeau, P. and A. Sauzeau. 1995. Les chevaux colorés de l'Apocalypse, I. *RHR*, 259–298.

———. 2012. *La quatrième fonction. Altérité et marginalité dans l'idéologie des Indo-Européens*. Paris: Les Belles Lettres.

Schadewaldt, W. 1951[2]. Der Schild des Achilleus. In *Von Homers Welt und Werk*. Stuttgart: K.F. Koehler, 352–347.

Schauffelberger, G. and G. Vincent (tr., notes). 2004–5. *Le Mahābhārata* (3 vols, tr. of extracts). Presses de l'Université de Laval.

———. (tr.) 2013. Le *Mahābhārata* (2 vols, tr. of Books 1–3). ['Cardinales']. Paris: Orizons.

Scheuer, J. 1982. *Śiva dans le* Mahābhārata. Paris: PUF.

Schmidt, J. 1897–1909. Odysseus. In W.H. Roscher (ed.), *Ausführliches Lexicon der Griechischen und Römischen Mythologie*, vol. 3. Leipzig: Teubner, 602–681.

Schmitt, R. (ed.) 1968. *Indogermanische Dichtersprache*. Darmstadt: Wiss. Buchgesellschaft.

Schneider, U. 1959. Die Geschichte von den beiden Jaratkāru. *Wiener Zeitschrift für die Kunde Süd- und Ostasiens* 3: 1–11.

Schröder, F.R. 1927. Ein altirischer Krönungsritus und das indogermanische Rossopfer. *Zeitschrift für Celtische Philologie* 16: 310–312.

Sergent, B. 1995. *Les indo-européens: histoire, langues, mythes*. Paris: Payot.

———. 1997. *Genèse de l'Inde*. Paris: Payot.

———. 1998. *Les trois fonctions indo-européennes dans la Grèce ancienne, I*. Paris: Economica.

Severi, C. (2003). Warburg anthropologue ou le déchiffrement d'une utopie: de la biologie des images à l'anthropologie de la mémoire. *L'Homme* 165: 77–128.

Sharma, A. (ed.) 1991. *Essays on the Mahābhārata*. Leiden: Brill.

Shee, M. 1984. *Tapas und tapasvin in den erzählenden Partien des Mahābhārata*. Reinbek: Verlag für orientalistische Fachpublikationen.

Shewring, W. (tr.) 1980. *Homer: The Odyssey*. Oxford: Oxford UP.

Shokhin, V.K. 1988. *Drevnyaya Indiya v kul'ture Rusi (XI—seredina XV b.)*. Moscow: Nauka.

Skjærvo, P.O. 1998. Eastern Iranian epic traditions II: Rostam and Bhīṣma. *Acta orientalia Academiae Scientiarum Hungarica* 5/1–2: 159–170.

Smith, B.K. 1994. *Classifying the universe: The Ancient Indian* varṇa *System and the Origins of Caste*. New York: Oxford UP.

Smith, J.D. 2009. *The Mahābhārata: An abridged translation*. London: Penguin Classics.

Snellgrove, D. 1957. *Buddhist Himalaya: Travels and studies in quest of the origin and nature of Tibetan religion*. Oxford: Cassirer.

———. 1987. *Indo-Tibetan Buddhism: Indian Buddhists and their Tibetan successors*. London: Serindia.

Stanford, W.B. 1963[2]. *The Ulysses theme: A study in the adaptability of a traditional hero*. Ann Arbor: University of Michigan Press.

Stern, H. 1984. L'Occident vu d'en face. *Revue européenne des sciences sociales* 22: 57–66. (In G. Berthoud et G. Busino (eds.), *L'exploration de la modernité: la démarche de Louis Dumont*.)

Taplin, O. 1980. The shield of Achilles within the *Iliad*. *Greece and Rome* 27: 1–21.

Teffeteller, A. 2001. Greek Athena and the Hittite Sungoddess of Arinna. In Deacy and Villing eds., 349–365.

Thomas, E.J. 1949[3]. *The life of the Buddha as legend and history*. London: Routledge and Kegan Paul.

Thomas, N.W. 1901. On a pictorial representation of the Wheel of Life from Japan. *Man* 1: 1–4.

Tiryakian, E.A. 1981. Le mythologue et le sociologue. *Dumézil* 1981a: 83–100.

Trautmann, T.R. 1981. *Dravidian kinship*. Cambridge: Cambridge UP.

Vanderlinden, E. 1980. Le bouclier d'Achille. *Les études classiques* 48: 97–126.

Vassilkov, Y. 1994–5. Parable of a man hanging in a tree and its archaic background. *Jadavpur Journal of Comparative Literature* 32: 38–51. (Also 1995. In N.V. Gurov and Ya.V. Vasil'kov (eds.), *Sthāpakaśrāddham: Professor G.A. Zograph commemorative volume*. St Petersburg: Russian Academy of Sciences, 257–269.)

———. 1999. *Kālavāda* (the doctrine of cyclical time) in the *Mahābhārata* and the concept of heroic didactics. In M. Brockington and P. Schreiner (eds.), *Composing a Tradition*. Zagreb: Croatian Academy of Sciences and Arts, 17–33.

Varenne, J. (tr., comm.) 1975. *Célébration de la grande déesse (Devī-Māhātmya)*. Paris: Les Belles Lettres.

———. 1981. Iran préislamique. In Y. Bonnefoy (ed.), *Dictionnaire des mythologies et des religions des sociétés traditionnelles et du monde antique, A-J*. Paris: Flammarion, 574–586.

Vernant, J.-P. 1990 [1965]. *Mythe et pensée chez les grecs*. Paris: Découverte.

Vielle, C. 1996a. *Correspondances et transformations du mytho-cycle héroïque dans quelques traditions archaïques de l'aire indo-européenne: Helleno-Aryanica*. Doctoral thesis: Université catholique de Louvain.

———. 1996b. *Le mytho-cycle héroïque dans l'aire indo-européenne: correspondances et transformations helléno-aryennes*. Louvain-la-neuve: Institut orientaliste.

Vira, R. 1936. Introduction. In *Critical Edition of the Virāṭaparvan*. Poona: Bhandarkar Oriental Research Institute, i–xxvii.

Vogel, J.P. 1937. The man in the well and some other subjects illustrated at Nāgārjunikonda. *Revue des arts asiatiques* 11: 109–121.

von Simson, G. 1984. The mythic background of the *Mahābhārata*. *Indologica Taurinensia* 12: 191–223.

Wackernagel, J. 1925. Nochmals das Genus von *dies*. *Glotta* 14: 67–8.

Waddell, L.A. 1892. The Buddhist pictorial wheel of life. *Journal of the Asiatic Society of Bengal* 61: 133–155.

———. 1895. *The Buddhism of Tibet or Lamaism*. London: W.H. Allen.

Walcot, P. 1966. *Hesiod and the near east*. Cardiff: University of Wales Press.

Wathelet, P. 1995. Athéna chez Homère ou le triomphe de la déesse. *Kernos* 8: 167–185.

———. 2004. Le combat d'Héphaïstos contre le Scamandre et le Simoïs dans l'Iliade. In G. Capdeville (ed.), *L'eau et le feu dans les religions antiques*. Paris: de Boccard, 61–77.

Watkins, C. 1979. NAM.RA GUD UDU in Hittite: Indo-European poetic language and the folk taxonomy of wealth. In E. Neu and W. Meid (eds.), *Hethitisch und Indogermanisch*. Innsbruck: Inst. für Sprachwissenschaft, 269–287. (Reprinted in C. Watkins 1994, *Selected writings*. Innsbruck: Inst. für Sprachwissenschaft 593–601.)

———. 1995. *How to kill a dragon: Aspects of Indo-European poetics*. New York: Oxford UP.

West, E. 2006. An Indic reflex of the Homeric Cyclopeia. *Classical Journal* 101: 125–160.

———. 2014. Circe, Calypso, Hiḍimbā: The Odyssey and Graeco-Aryan Proto-Epic. *JIES* 42: 144–174.

———. 2017. The transformation of Cyavana: A case study in narrative evolution. *Oral tradition* 31/1: 77–122.

West, M.L. (ed., intro., comm.) 1966. *Hesiod*, Theogony. Oxford: Clarendon.

———. (ed., intro., comm.) 1978. *Hesiod,* Works and days. Oxford: Clarendon.

———. (tr., intro., notes) 1988a. *Hesiod,* Theogony *and* Works and Days. Oxford: Oxford UP.

———. 1988b. The rise of the Greek epic. *Journal of Hellenic Studies* 108: 151–172.

———. 1995. The date of the *Iliad*. *Museum helveticum* 52: 203–219.

———. 1997. *The east face of Helicon*. Oxford: Clarendon.

———. (tr., ed.) 2003. *Greek epic fragments from the 7th to the 5th century BC*. [Loeb]. Cambridge, MA: Harvard UP, London: Heinemann.

———. 2007. *Indo-European poetry and myth*. Oxford: Oxford UP.

———. 2011. *The making of the Iliad: Disquisition and analytical commentary*. Oxford: Oxford UP.

———. 2013. *The epic cycle: A commentary on the lost Troy epics*. Oxford: Oxford UP.

West, S. 1988. *Commentary to Homer's Odyssey, vol. I (Books 1–4)*. Oxford: Clarendon.

Wikander, S. 1952. Histoire des Ouranides. *Cahiers du Sud* 36: 9–17.

Willcock, M. 1997. Neoanalysis. In I. Morris and B. Powell (eds), *A new companion to Homer*. Leiden: Brill, 174–189.

Witzel, M. 1987. On the origin of the literary device of the 'frame story' in old Indian literature. In H. Falk (ed.), *Hinduismus und Buddhismus: Festschrift für Ulrich Schneider*. Freiburg: Hedwig Falk, 380–414.

———. 2005. The vedas and the epics: Some comparative notes on persons, lineages, geography, and grammar. In P. Koskikallio (ed.), *Epics, khilas, and purāṇas. Continuities and ruptures* [DICSEP 3]. Zagreb: Croatian Academy of Sciences and Arts, 21–80.

Woods, J.H. 1988 [1914]. *The yoga-system of Patañjali*. Delhi: Motilal Banarsidass.

Wulff Alonso, F. 2014 (tr. A. Morrow). *The* Mahābhārata *and Greek mythology*. Delhi: Motilal Banarsidass.

Wüst, E. 1937. Odysseus. In W. Kroll (ed.), *Paulys Real-Encyclopädie der classischen Alterthumswissenschaft*, vol.17. Stuttgart: Metzler, 1905–1996.

Yoshida, A. 1964. La structure de l'illustration du bouclier d'Achille. *Revue belge de philologie et d'histoire* 42: 5–15.

Yule, H. and A.C. Burnell 1986 [1886]. *Hobson-Jobson*. Calcutta: Rupa.

INDEX

Note: Italics indicate a table, bold indicates a Figure. A~B indicates a relation between A and B; sometimes this is a similarity, sometimes not. A+B indicates the emphatic pairing of A and B.